1939–1945

THE WORLD AT WAR

Grange
BOOKS

Published 2007 by Grange Books
an imprint of Grange Books Ltd
The Grange
Kingsnorth Industrial Estate
Hoo, Near Rochester
Kent ME3 9ND
www.Grangebooks.co.uk

The Brown Reference Group plc
(incorporating Andromeda Oxford Limited)
8 Chapel Place
Rivington Street
London
EC2A 3DQ
www.brownreference.com

ISBN 978-1-84013-915-0

Project Editor:	Selina Wood
Commissioning Editors:	Emily Hill, Selina Wood
Editors:	Sylvia and David Tombesi-Walton Rachel Bean, Jane Edmonds
General Editor:	Peter Darman
Designers:	Paul Griffin, Iain Stuart
Picture Researchers:	Andrew Webb, Becky Cox
Maps:	Mark Walker, Darren Awuah
Managing Editor:	Tim Cooke
Design Managers:	Sarah Williams, Lynne Ross
Production Director:	Alastair Gourlay
Editorial Director:	Lindsey Lowe

Consultant:	Professor Dennis Showalter, Department of History, Colorado College, Colorado Springs

CONTENTS

Europe in crisis: 1935–1939   6

Blitzkrieg   18

The fall of the Low Countries and France   30

Britain's isolation   40

The Battle of the Atlantic: 1939–1941   48

Africa: 1940–1941   58

The Balkans and Greece: 1941–1943   68

Operation Barbarossa   76

Germany's advance   88

Pearl Harbor   98

The defeat of the British and Dutch   110

The fall of the Philippines   124

North Africa: Allied victory in the desert   136

The invasion of Sicily and Italy   148

The Battle of the Atlantic: 1942–1945   158

The air war against Germany   170

Stalingrad   180

In the balance: Kharkov and Kursk   192

The Battle of the Coral Sea   204

The Battle of Midway   214

New Guinea, Guadalcanal,
  and the Solomons   224

On the offensive: 1943 in the Pacific   236

The U.S. submarine campaign   248

Burma and China   258

Italy: 1944–1945   268

The Soviet Union on the Offensive   280

Eastern Front: 1944   290

D-Day: Operation Overlord   302

Northern Europe: 1944   314

The fall of Germany   328

Island-hopping in the Pacific: 1944   342

The Battle of Leyte Gulf   354

Burma and China: 1944–1945   362

Retaking the Philippines: 1944–1945   374

Toward Japan: Iwo Jima and Okinawa   382

The surrender of Japan 392

The cost of the war 406

Postwar Europe 414

Europe divided 426

The war and memory 438

EUROPE IN CRISIS: 1935–1939

As Hitler's position grew more secure within Germany, he began a campaign of territorial expansion that was initially met with inaction by France and Britain but eventually drove the continent to war.

Adolf Hitler made no secret of his opposition to the 1919 Treaty of Versailles, which limited Germany's armed forces, and his intention to pursue an expansionist foreign policy.

Many Germans shared

his resentment at the treaty. They thought it was unjustifiably harsh. As early as February 1933, Hitler shared with his generals a plan to take back the Sudetenland—a German-speaking area of Czechoslovakia—and make a

union with Austria, before defeating France, Poland, and Russia. Few of his listeners took him seriously. Within a few years, however, it would become clear that Hitler was deadly serious.

International relations

In October 1933, Hitler took Germany out of the permanent disarmament talks in Geneva and the League of Nations, the body set up to solve international disputes. Hitler signed a nonaggression pact with his eastern neighbor, Poland, in January 1934, removing any danger of a preemptive Polish strike on Germany.

Hitler also sought to make alliances within Europe. The most obvious ally was Italy, governed by Benito Mussolini. There were parallels between Mussolini's fascism and Hitler's Nazism, and the Italians also resented Versailles, which they felt had failed to reward them for their part in the Allied victory. Mussolini also rejected the League of Nations. When he invaded Abyssinia (Ethiopia) in October 1935, he ignored its protests.

Suspicion

The alliance between Hitler and Mussolini started badly. Mussolini was not impressed by Hitler, and was suspicious of Hitler's plan to create a Greater Germany. Hitler envisaged an Anschluss, or union, with Austria, Italy's northern neighbor. Mussolini wanted to keep Austria independent as a buffer between Italy and Germany.

On July 25, 1934, Austrian Nazis, with Hitler's support, murdered the Austrian chancellor, Engelbert Dollfuss, a fierce opponent of the Anschluss, during a failed coup. Mussolini mobilized his army on the Austrian border, ready to support the government against Nazi aggression. Kurt von Schuschnigg, a pro-Italian fascist, became the new chancellor. To some observers in France and Britain, it seemed that Mussolini could be a useful block to Hitler's expansionism.

The Saarland and Stresa

In January 1935, the people of the Saarland, a southwestern region that had been removed from Germany by the Versailles treaty, voted to rejoin Germany. The result was celebrated as a victory for German nationalism.

In March 1935, Hitler announced that Germany would no longer accept the military limitations of Versailles. In fact rearmament had been going on for two years. By 1935, for example, the German army had increased from 100,000 to 300,00 men, while the air force—forbidden by Versailles—had about 18,000 personnel and hundreds of aircraft. Hitler had calculated that he could disregard Versailles with little danger of provoking the European powers into action.

The Stresa Front

Hitler's calculation proved correct. In response to German rearmament, Mussolini called a conference with France and Britain at the Italian city of Stresa in April 1935. The so-called Stresa Front agreed to use force to defend the Versailles Treaty. The agreement soon fell apart, however, when Hitler offered to make nonaggression pacts with his neighbors. Meanwhile Britain and Italy were suspicious of a French alliance with the Soviet Union, France was angered by an Anglo–German naval agreement, and both France and Britain condemned Italy's

◀ British prime minister Neville Chamberlain (center right) and German foreign minister Joachim von Ribbentrop (right) review a guard of honor at the Munich Conference in September 1938. French and British concessions at the conference failed to stop Europe's slide toward war.

▲ Adolf Hitler and Nazi naval chief Admiral Erich Raeder inspect the new warship *Scharnhorst* in October 1936. The Nazis ignored Versailles Treaty limitations on shipbuilding.

▶ Messerschmitt fighters are built in a German factory in 1938. When war began the next year, the Luftwaffe deployed more than 1,800 aircraft against Poland.

invasion of Abyssinia. The invasion effectively marked the end of both the Stresa Front and the League of Nations, which proved powerless to prevent Italy's aggression.

The Rhineland

With Germany openly rearming and its opposition fractured, Hitler made his next move. To protect France and the Low Countries, the Versailles Treaty had created a demilitarized zone in the Rhineland, German territory west and east of the Rhine River. The Rhineland's status had been reinforced by the Locarno Pact of 1925, under which the Allies evacuated their troops from the area in 1930. On the morning of March 7, 1936, Hitler sent 22,000 troops into the Rhineland.

Hitler's move was a gamble. He had promised his generals that he would withdraw if the French opposed him. The French did nothing, however, partly because they overestimated German strength and partly because they were waiting for support from Britain. The British, however, remained suspicious of France's alliance with the Soviet Union, and also underestimated the significance of the move.

Hitler and Mussolini

The failure of the democracies to prevent remilitarization of the Rhineland marked a great strategic victory for Hitler and for Europe's dictatorships. In July 1936, Mussolini acknowledged Hitler's claim to treat Austria as a German state. In October, Mussolini and Hitler formed the Rome–Berlin Axis, and in November, Germany and Japan signed an Anti-Comintern Pact directed against the Soviet Union.

Meanwhile Germany and Italy both supported Francisco Franco's Nationalists in the civil war that broke out in Spain in July 1936. The right-wing Nationalists were opposed by the Republicans, government forces, workers' militias, and brigades made up of volunteers from around the world. The war lasted three years before the Nationalist victory in March 1939.

Mussolini supplied some 70,000 troops, plus tanks, artillery, and aircraft, to aid the Nationalists. Hitler sent fewer men but some 100 aircraft; the pilots

▼ German troops cross the Rhine River during the reoccupation of the Rhineland on March 7, 1936. Hitler later said that waiting to see whether the Allies would call his bluff and move against him was one of the worst times of his life.

Britain and France, 1937–1939

A frequent question about the 1930s is why the French and British did not make a stronger stand against Hitler. Both had their own reasons for caution. France, on Germany's border, had a smaller population and economy than its neighbor, and would not be able to defeat Germany alone. The French tried to make alliances with other European states, but would still need British support to win a war against Germany. For its part, Britain faced different problems. The British empire was increasingly difficult to defend, particularly in East Asia, where Japan was growing in strength. However, a deeper reason for French and British reluctance to confront Hitler was that both countries had been traumatized by the losses of World War I, and were desperate to avoid another European conflict.

▲ The motorization of the Wehrmacht: This German army parade includes both horse-drawn 105mm howitzers and larger artillery pieces being pulled by half-track tractors.

used the conflict to perfect the techniques that would be vital in the blitzkrieg tactics Germany employed at the start of World War II.

Anschluss

The Rome–Berlin Axis opened the way for Hitler's next step after remilitarizing the Rhineland: the Anschluss. After the failed Nazi coup in Austria in 1934, Kurt von Schuschnigg had become chancellor with the support of Mussolini. Hitler made no secret of his determination to achieve the Anschluss, however, and the loss of Italian protection left Schuschnigg vulnerable.

In February 1938, Hitler gave Schuschnigg an ultimatum: If he refused to include Nazis in his government, Germany would invade. With no backing from the democracies, the Austrian initially agreed, but then announced a plebiscite to be held to reassert Austria's independence. As Hitler tried to force the Austrian president to replace Schuschnigg, Arthur

▲ The *fasces* and the imperial eagle, symbols of fascist Italy and Nazi Germany respectively, stand side by side in Berlin during a visit by Mussolini in 1937.

Seyss-Inquart, the leader of the Austrian Nazis, forced Schuschnigg to resign. At Hitler's insistence, Seyss-Inquart became chancellor. He then invited German troops into Austria.

On March 13, 1938, Hitler declared Austria a province of the German Reich, or empire. About a month later 99.7 percent of the Austrian people voted in favor of the Anschluss.

Czechoslovakia

The French and British had again failed to prevent German expansion. For many people in Britain, in particular, this policy of appeasement was a genuine attempt to resolve German grievances. They saw Hitler's aim to bring together all Germans under German government as an expression of the principle of self-determination, for example. They believed that Hitler would cease when he had achieved his aims. The French, meanwhile, were more suspicious of Hitler but were reluctant to act without British support.

The democracies' failure to resist his demands encouraged Hitler to further expansion. This time his target was the Sudetenland, a border area of Czechoslovakia that contained a large minority of Germans. Hitler used the Sudeten Germans as a pretext to claim the whole of Czechoslovakia.

In April 1938, under orders from Hitler, the leader of the Nazis in the Sudetenland, Konrad Henlein, began to demand more control for the Sudeten Germans. The Czech government of Eduard Benes reacted with alarm; it

▼ Austrian Nazis in the town of Graz celebrate the Anschluss in March 1938.

Appeasement

Appeasement was the policy adopted by Britain, and to a lesser degree by France, toward Hitler's demands. Many British regarded the Versailles Treaty as unfair toward Germany; they felt that some of Hitler's demands were just. By meeting his demands, they hoped to prevent him from making demands that risked another conflict. However, Hitler saw appeasement as weakness in his opponents. He followed each demand with another. After the occupation of Czechoslovakia, the policy lost much of its support in Britain and France. Leading politicians realized that they had to be prepared to go to war to stop Hitler.

called up its reservists and positioned troops along the German border. Hitler condemned what he called Czech provocation, and told his generals to prepare an invasion plan for October.

Again Britain and France chose not to resist Hitler's demands. British prime minister Neville Chamberlain had already told the French that he thought the Czechs should be prepared to give up territory. As the British and French convinced Benes to make concessions, however, so Hitler increased his demands. On September 12, he demanded self-determination for the Sudeten Germans and massed his troops on the border.

◀ Without French and British support, Czech president Eduard Benes had little choice but to give in to Hitler's demands.

Fearing war as imminent, Chamberlain called a conference at Munich on September 30, 1938, to discuss the crisis. The talks were attended by Britain, France, Italy, and Germany. The Czechs were not invited. Hitler got his way: The Czechs were told to evacuate the Sudetenland by October 10. If they did not, they would get no help to resist German aggression. Chamberlain claimed that the agreement promised "peace for our time." Within a year, however, Europe was at war.

The Munich agreement has become a notorious example of appeasement, a policy now widely discredited as naive and cowardly. Many historians believe that Hitler outwitted his opponents; Hitler himself came to the same

The Anti-Comintern Pact

In November 1936, Germany and Japan signed an agreement known as the Anti-Comintern Pact. It agreed that each country would help the other if either were attacked by the Soviet Union. The pact took its name from the Comintern, or Communist International. That was a Soviet committee set up in Moscow to coordinate the activities of Communist parties around the world in the attempt to create a global revolution. Italy, which had signed a treaty of friendship with Germany, joined the agreement in 1937. The effect of the pact was therefore to bring together the three chief aggressor countries that would be described as the Axis powers during World War II.

Neville Chamberlain (1869–1940)

Neville Chamberlain, Britain's prime minister in the approach to war, began a career in local politics in 1911. He joined the Conservative Party and was elected to Parliament in 1918. Chamberlain served as minister of health and chancellor of the exchequer (secretary of the treasury) before he became prime minister in 1937. In foreign policy Chamberlain followed a policy of appeasement, and has been widely criticized since for underestimating Hitler's territorial ambitions. Chamberlain himself had an intense dislike of criticism, and did not welcome advisers who advocated different policies from his own. After appeasement failed he acknowledged that war was inevitable, and reluctantly took Britain into the conflict.

▶ Neville Chamberlain has been widely portrayed as a naive politician who too easily believed Hitler's promises of peace.

conclusion. However, both Britain and France quickened their own re-armament. Hitler's assumption that they would not fight, based on what happened at Munich, would eventually lead him to overstep their patience.

After Munich

The Munich agreement marked the beginning of the end of Czech independence. Czechoslovakia's other minorities, such as Slovakians and Ruthenians, demanded independence. With Hitler's support, Hungary seized territory in the south of the country. On March 15, 1939, Germany occupied the rest of the country. That same month Hitler forced Lithuania, on the Baltic coast, to hand the city of Memel—formerly part of the German state of Prussia—to Germany.

Hitler's renewed expansion in Czechoslovakia forced the allies to recognize that his ambitions could not be appeased. Chamberlain warned that Britain's reluctance to fight did not mean that it would not fight. As war appeared increasingly inevitable, France and Britain made overtures to Germany and Italy, respectively, to buy time to rearm and to halt expansion, but such moves achieved little.

Mussolini in Albania

On April 7, 1939, Mussolini launched an invasion of Albania. The Italian dictator had expansionist ambitions of his own, and had declared an Italian empire after the invasion of Ethiopia in 1935. After World War I, Italy had

▼ Mussolini and Hitler, at left, face Chamberlain (right, next to a translator) in Munich in September 1938. The Italians, Germans, British, and French decided the fate of Czechoslovakia without inviting the Czechs to the talks.

Stalin and the European crisis _____

Wary of German expansion, Soviet leader Joseph Stalin was ready to use force to save Czechoslovakia in 1938. He would not intervene without support from France and Britain, however, and it was not forthcoming. The Western powers treated the Soviet Union as a threat rather than an ally, preferring to send diplomats rather than senior politicians to negotiate with Stalin.

Western suspicions of the Soviet Union seemed well founded. Under Stalin, Soviet military and industrial power had grown considerably. The state had taken control of the economy, forbidding some forms of economic activity and imposing a series of Five Year Plans (the first was from 1928 to 1933) to increase industrial output. Meanwhile Stalin had consolidated his control of the state and become effectively a dictator. In the late 1930s he launched a series of purges to eliminate many thousands of real and perceived opponents, including former Bolsheviks and experienced army officers. The loss of so many skilled military leaders would greatly weaken the Red Army.

expanded its territories along the Adriatic, the sea that separated it from the Balkans; now the Balkan state of Albania was a logical target.

Mussolini's territorial expansion was easily achieved. The invasion force of 100,000 troops and 400 aircraft soon overcame the Albanian army. The Albanian king, Zog, went into exile and Mussolini offered the crown to the Italian king, Victor Emmanuel III.

The question of Poland

Hitler, meanwhile, turned to what he termed "the Polish question." Modern Poland had been created by the peace treaties of 1919, and included two areas that between them were home to about a million Germans. The Baltic port of Danzig (Gdansk in Polish) was to be a Free City under League of Nations protection, while a narrow stretch of land known as the Polish Corridor linked Poland to Danzig and the sea, splitting Germany from its state of East Prussia.

▶ Sudeten Germans salute as German troops enter Friedland on October 3, 1938. Despite Czech concessions to the Sudeten Germans, Hitler pushed them to demand full self-determination.

When he had begun his policy of expansion, Hitler largely left Poland alone, signing a nonaggression pact with it in 1934. He reassured the Poles that he had no designs on their territory. After the events in Czechoslovakia, however, such promises did not seem worth very much. In October 1938, Hitler proposed building a German-controlled road across the Polish Corridor and passing Danzig back to Germany. He offered to guarantee Poland's borders in return. The Poles instead signed a pact with the Soviet Union, their eastern neighbor. The Poles also made warlike noises about fighting any loss of territory to Germany.

Protecting Poland

Poland's determination coincided with the acceptance in the western democracies that they had to make a stand against Nazi aggression. Britain and

▲ Italian Bersaglieri prepare to advance during the April 1939 occupation of Albania.

◀ Nazi banners decorate the main street of Danzig. Declared a Polish-administered Free City by the Versailles Treaty, Danzig was home to many Germans who embraced Hitler's promise to reclaim the city for Germany.

15

▲ German troops remove a barrier at a border crossing during the invasion of Poland on September 1, 1939.

France offered to guarantee Polish independence. In the event of German aggression, they were committed to military action on Poland's behalf. Some historians question whether the allies were really prepared to fight in March 1939, or whether they were trying to warn Hitler off. Whatever their intentions, Hitler's chief concern lay not in the west but in the east, where the Soviet Union could move troops into Poland far more easily than Britain or France.

Approaches to Stalin

Hitler wanted to avoid facing a possible alliance of the Soviet Union, Britain, and France. The Western democracies were equally aware of the Soviets' potential to deter German expansion, but their negotiations with Stalin did not lead to any agreement.

At the same time, however, Hitler had set aside his ideological differences with Stalin in the hopes of making an alliance. In August 1939 he offered Stalin a deal: If the Soviets allowed Germany to attack western Poland, they would receive eastern Poland, the Baltic states (Lithuania, Latvia, and Estonia), and Bessarabia in Romania.

The German-Soviet Pact

Munich had had an important effect on Stalin, who had been prepared to go to war to protect Czechoslovakia. The capitulation of France and Britain to Hitler's demands convinced Stalin that they would be unreliable allies. He decided that he had to cope with German expansion eastward on his own, without their help.

In late August 1939, German foreign secretary Joachim von Ribbentrop visited Moscow to sign a German–Soviet Nonaggression Pact, which included the deal over territory. The agreement between two nations at

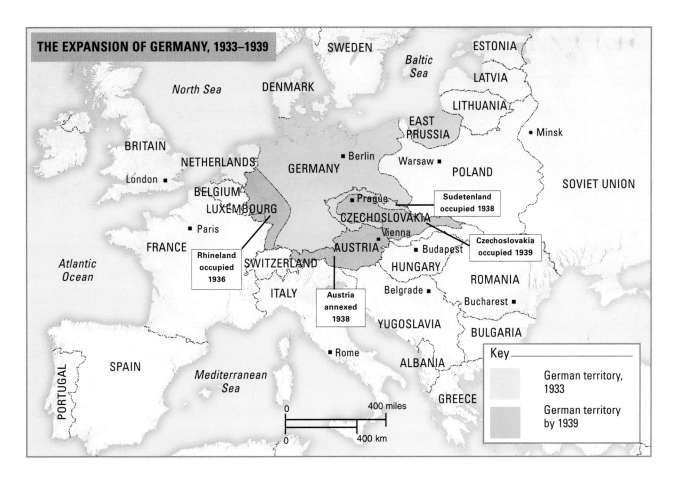

THE EXPANSION OF GERMANY, 1933–1939

SWEDEN

Baltic Sea

ESTONIA

LATVIA

LITHUANIA

North Sea

DENMARK

• Minsk

EAST PRUSSIA

BRITAIN

NETHERLANDS

GERMANY

■ Berlin

Warsaw ■

POLAND

London ■

BELGIUM

LUXEMBOURG

SOVIET UNION

Sudetenland occupied 1938

■ Prague

CZECHOSLOVAKIA

■ Paris

Vienna ■

Czechoslovakia occupied 1939

FRANCE

Rhineland occupied 1936

SWITZERLAND

AUSTRIA

■ Budapest

HUNGARY

Atlantic Ocean

ITALY

Austria annexed 1938

ROMANIA

Belgrade ■

Bucharest ■

■ Rome

YUGOSLAVIA

BULGARIA

SPAIN

Mediterranean Sea

ALBANIA

GREECE

PORTUGAL

0   400 miles

0   400 km

Key

German territory, 1933

German territory by 1939

▲ Motorized German troops advance into Poland. The invasion was an early triumph for the fast-moving blitzkrieg tactics the Germans used widely and to great effect.

opposite political extremes—fascism on one side, communism on the other—shocked the world. It also left Hitler with a free hand in Poland.

The war begins

Hitler now needed an excuse to invade Poland before the Poles and their allies could make more defensive preparations. On August 31, SS troops in Polish uniforms staged a mock raid on a radio station in the German border town of Gleiwitz. They left behind the bodies of 10 or so murdered concentration camp inmates in Polish uniforms.

Hitler used the apparent "Polish" raid as an excuse to invade Poland the following day, September 1, 1939. Two days later, on September 3, France and Britain declared war on Germany, as did Britain's dependencies. World War II had begun.

▲ From 1936 to August 1939, Hitler followed a policy of expansion that succeeded in creating a larger Germany without provoking war with Britain and France.

BLITZKRIEG

When German troops began streaming across the Polish border at 4:45 a.m. on the morning of September 1, 1939, they set off a chain of events that engulfed the world in a war that lasted for six years.

Between September 1939 and June 1940, Germany launched a series of spectacular military offensives. The first attack was against Poland and was code-named Operation White. The German invasion force deployed two army groups made up of 55 divisions, each containing about 15,000 men. Army Group North invaded southward from East Prussia and eastward from Pomerania (*see map, page 8*). The larger Army Group South attacked eastward from Silesia and Germany's ally, Slovakia. The German Air Force, or Luftwaffe, deployed over 1,800 aircraft.

Against the German forces were 30 Polish divisions of about 12,000 troops each. Not all of them were mobilized on September 1. Those that were mobilized were positioned along Poland's borders, rather than on natural defenses such as the wide rivers within the country, in order to protect Poland's important industrial centers. The Polish forces were very exposed, as some parts of Poland were surrounded on three sides by German territory. The Polish airforce had 1,900 aircraft, but of these 650 were trainers and 700 were outdated.

The German offensive

On September 1, 1939, the Germans began air, land, and sea attacks against Polish positions. Special forces teams were put ahead of the attack troops to sabotage telephone lines, blow up bridges, and spread confusion. During the first few days of the offensive the German forces inflicted heavy casualties on Polish

▶ A column of German armored vehicles advances into Poland, beginning the war in Europe in September 1939.

Lightning war tactics

During World War I (1914–1918) there were long periods of stalemate (deadlock), as soldiers took cover in lines of trenches. If they tried to leave the trenches to attack the enemy, they were shot down by enemy machine guns. During the 1930s German and British officers realized that using tanks offered a more effective way of waging war. Tanks had been invented during World War I, but by the 1930s had become much faster.

German officers, notably Heinz Guderian, believed that tanks could do more than break through a first line of defense. With their own support and supplies, tanks could penetrate deep into enemy territory, ruining enemy command and control, and ensuring final victory.

From this theory developed the idea that breaking through front-line defenses and creating confusion behind the enemy lines could be achieved in other ways, not just with tanks. Airborne troops, such as a paratroopers, could be deployed.

This method of waging war by concentrating on the attack was known in German as blitzkrieg, or "lightning war" in English. Against the other European armies, German blitzkrieg tactics were highly successful and allowed Hitler to dominate the continent.

Panzer divisions

The German armored or panzer division (*panzer* is short for *Panzerkampfwagen*, German for tank) was vital to Hitler's blitzkrieg campaigns. It was a revolutionary creation that used the tank's potential for mobility, protection, firepower, and shock.

In a panzer division, tanks were massed together in a large formation for maximum fighting effect. They were supported by motorized infantry and artillery.

It was only the Germans who set up armored divisions as war-winning formations. Other European armies were aware of the potential of the tank, but still used their tanks in small groups to support infantry actions.

Luftwaffe air support for the panzer divisions was crucial. It defended massed tank formations against enemy air attack, gave close air support, and protected exposed parts of the division.

German tanks in Poland in September 1939. The front tank is a Panzer I, while those behind are Panzer IIs.

front-line units and disrupted enemy supply and communication networks such as roads and railways.

Germany advances

The Luftwaffe took control of the skies within a few days. German Stuka dive bombers roamed deep behind Polish lines, machine-gunning and bombing columns of reserve troops heading for the front. German panzer divisions were sent into action against weak spots in the Polish line. Instead of fighting against the main defensive positions, they pushed behind enemy lines, aiming to capture key bridges over Poland's rivers. In the confusion, hundreds of thousands of refugees fled their homes, clogging up roads and making it difficult for the Polish to build up organized resistance.

The German and Polish infantry divisions fought dogged battles over the industrial regions of Krakow and Lodz.

The lack of Polish motor transport had an impact on the campaign, as the Poles could not retreat faster than the Germans were advancing. As the panzer divisions defeated them and pushed deeper inside Polish territory, the Poles were left open to encirclement. After six days the Polish high command ordered a withdrawal to the east but by then it was too late. The huge Polish armies from Posnan and Lodz were trapped around Kutno, to the west of Warsaw. The port of Danzig was surrounded and cut off. German troops driving south from East Prussia had almost linked up with panzers moving up from the south, trapping Polish troops around Modlin. Only in the south was Polish resistance holding. A determined force was driving off German troops attempting to cut off the Poles' route to Romania.

Romania was a potential ally and a possible entry point for Allied aid.

The trapped Polish troops at Kutno tried to make a dramatic breakout across the Bzura River to freedom. For two days the Polish kept attacking, only to be beaten back by German firepower, and by Luftwaffe attacks. The trapped troops resisted for three more weeks, when 170,000 Poles eventually emerged from the woods around Kutno to surrender.

By the second week of September, Warsaw was surrounded by German forces advancing from north, west, and south. It held out for another two weeks as, day and night, German bombers pounded the city.

The Soviets invade

Beaten back by the Germans, Polish forces were now attacked from the East.

▼ A German horse-drawn supply column crosses a river during the invasion of Poland. The German Army used horses throughout World War II to pull artillery pieces, transport food and ammunition, and evacuate the wounded.

▲ German troops remove a border marker on the Polish frontier in 1939, as Poland becomes part of the German Reich.

▶ In 1939, Poland had the huge disadvantage of having a long border with Germany and being surrounded by hostile countries.

THE GERMAN INVASION OF POLAND, 1939

Danzig •

EAST PRUSSIA

Pomerania

Narew River

POLAND

Vistula River

Modlin

Posnan •   Kutno •   ■ Warsaw

Bzura River

Lódz •

GERMANY

San River

Bug River

Silesia   • Kracow

• Lvov

0   100 miles

0   150 km   SLOVAKIA

HUNGARY

Key

→ German attacks

On September 17, the Soviet dictator Joseph Stalin, ordered his Red Army to cross into eastern Poland. He claimed that he wanted to prevent "anarchy" caused by the collapse of the Polish government. In fact, Germany and the Soviet Union had secretly agreed to divide up Poland between them in the German–Soviet Nonaggression Pact (*see Volume 1, Chapter 6*) signed in the previous month. Thousands of Soviet troops poured across the border and raced west to link up with German troops.

Organized Polish resistance to the invaders collapsed. In the last week of September Polish troops in Modlin and Warsaw surrendered to the Germans. A small garrison of 4,500 men held out on the Hel Peninsula near Danzig until October 2. Some 694,000 Polish troops were rounded up by the victorious Germans, and more than 217,000 Poles were seized by the Red Army. Both the Germans and Soviets treated the Poles with great brutality. Stalin ordered most of his prisoners deported to the gulag (a system of brutal labor camps) and later had thousands of Poles executed in secret (*see Volume 3, Chapter 6*).

Poland ceases to exist

Some 100,000 Poles managed to escape into Romania, from where they made their way to Britain and France. A Polish government-in-exile was set up in London, and many Poles joined the British armed forces. The Germans and Soviets divided up Poland, absorbing it between their countries. A new government was set up around Warsaw and run by Nazi party chiefs. They ordered the executions of Jews, intellectuals, and anyone who might rally resistance to German rule. As far as Hitler and Stalin were concerned, Poland had ceased to exist.

Britain and France

The British and French, who had declared war on Germany on September 3 (*see Volume 1, Chapter 6*), had expected the Poles to hold on long enough for them to organize a large-scale offensive against Germany. The first Allied attack against the Germans was the so-called Saar Offensive of September 8. Nine French divisions made a half-hearted attack into the Saarland, an area on the French-German border between the Rhine and Moselle rivers. The operation soon halted in the face of German defenses. The British Expeditionary Force (BEF) landed in France on September 9 in preparation for an offensive, but its armored division was not ready for action until spring 1940. The British and French were stunned by the speed of the German conquest of Poland. With no obvious way to influence the fighting in Poland, Paris and London ordered their armies to

remain on the defensive. In fact, after the occupation of Poland there was a seven-month lull in which very little fighting took place on land. The period was nicknamed the "Phoney War".

Eyewitness

❝ Very soon after that, menacing, dark bombers appeared in the blue sky over Chelm. My wife and I left the store and ran to the fields to hide. We wanted to hide in the tall wheat, but the wheat had just been harvested and we were exposed. We were terrified. German planes kept firing down at us with their machine guns, and they seemed to shriek like wild animals as they dived with their bombs and bullets. We decided to run home, and we made our way through the streets filled with panic-stricken people who were shrieking hysterically. When we arrived home, we found the old woman we had hired under the bed, holding our infant girl, Pesha, in her arms. She was so petrified that she was speechless. When the bombing ceased we went out, as did many others, on the street. ❞

Kalmen Wewryk
Chelm, Poland, 1939

◀ German forces with supplies march through the Polish capital, Warsaw, after the city has fallen.

No triumphalism

The mood at the opening of World War II was very different from that at the start of World War I in 1914. At the beginning of World War I Europeans had enthusiastically marched to war unaware of what was in store. The massive blood-letting of the Western Front during World War I had left deep scars on the European people. As a result, in the interwar years opposition to war, or pacifist, movements were strong. Visions of future wars with cities devastated by bombing and gas attack further fueled unease about what a new war would herald. When Britain and France finally resolved to fight Germany after the invasion of Poland, the mood among the Allies was gloomy.

British and French troops concentrated on building up the strength of their forces, in case they needed to come to the aid of neutral Belgium and the Netherlands, who were also under the threat of a Nazi attack. In the winter of 1939–1940 both the German and Allied sides also conducted reconnaissance flights on the enemy.

Preparations for war

Over the winter of 1939 and into 1940, the British and French began to convert their economies to a war footing. The governments of both countries introduced food rationing and began preparations in case of German bombing attacks on towns and cities. To protect the population of London, air-raid shelters were dug in gardens and underground subway stations were prepared for use as shelters during air raids. Gas masks were issued amid fears of terror attacks with chemical weapons.

Meanwhile Hitler saw no need to place the German economy on a war footing, since blitzkrieg was designed to bring victory in a short space of time, avoiding total war. Only 10,000 Germans had been killed in the invasion of Poland, which seemed very few for such a dramatic victory. Although conscription (a draft) had been in force in Germany since 1935, the removal of men from the work force into the forces had so far not affected the German economy.

There was little action on land during the Phoney War but events were occurring at sea. In October 1939, the

◀ Polish citizens read a directive from the occupying German forces in late 1939.

German submarine *U-47* made a daring raid into the anchorage of a British fleet at Scapa Flow in the Orkney Islands in the north of Scotland. It torpedoed the Royal Navy battleship, HMS *Royal Oak*, which sank with the loss of more than 800 sailors.

The German U-boat (submarine) fleet was still small at this stage and was prevented from striking out at Allied merchant ships in the Atlantic by British naval patrols in the Channel.

Focus on Norway

The Soviet attack on Finland in November 1939 (*see box below*) forced the Germans and Allies to focus on Scandinavia. There was great sympathy

The Winter War

After the German and Soviet occupation of Poland, Stalin took advantage of the free hand Hitler had given him in Eastern Europe. He demanded that Finland allow Soviet troops to occupy naval bases and a key border region.

The Finns refused and quickly mobilized their small forces; 120,000 Finnish soldiers were pitted against 600,000 Soviet troops. On October 30, 1939, the Soviets surged across the border. In response Finnish ski troops mounted hit and run attacks on Soviet troops as they moved through the forested landscape.

In a month of fighting, 27,500 Red Army troops were killed and 1,600 were taken prisoner; there were around 2,700 Finnish deaths. The Red Army troops had been poorly trained and equipped for the operation and many of its experienced officers had been lost in Stalin's purges of the 1930s.

A new Soviet offensive began on February 1, 1940. This time they used large-scale artillery barrages to destroy enemy strongpoints before launching a mass attack. The Finns were gradually worn down. They reluctantly signed a nonaggression pact with Stalin on March 12. The Soviets gained access to Baltic naval bases and were handed the border region near Leningrad.

Finnish ski-troops use reindeer as pack animals. The effectiveness and combat-readiness of the Finnish troops was crucial to their early successes against the Soviets.

▼ The German invasion of Norway 1940. German forces landed at several ports simultaneously, taking the Norwegians by surprise.

for the Finns in Britain and France, particularly as the Soviets had sided with Hitler during the invasion of Poland. Many leaders in London and Paris could also wanted to intervene in Scandinavia to damage Germany's war industry. Germany imported regular iron-ore shipments from neutral Sweden. In winter the ore had to pass through the Norwegian port of Narvik, from where it was shipped south, staying within Norwegian territorial waters. Hitler saw the supply of iron as a strategic priority.

Disagreements between the British and French meant that no Allied action took place in Scandinavia until early spring of 1940. The Allies began to plan to occupy several Norwegian ports, including Narvik, Bergen, Stavanger, and Trondheim, as a line of communications to aid Finland, and to open a new theater of war against Germany. The Germans realized they could no longer take Norwegian neutrality for granted. Hitler also believed it was necessary to conquer Norway to obtain naval and air bases in preparation for German operations against Britain and the USSR.

Hitler strikes north

In February, the British destroyer HMS *Cossack* breached Norwegian neutrality by seizing a German navy supply ship, the *Altmark*, in order to free 288 British merchant sailors being held captive on board. Convinced that the move was the start of an Allied operation to close Norwegian ports to German shipping, Hitler ordered his generals to strike north into Norway.

The German invasion of Norway, code-named Exercise Weser, began on the early morning of April 9. The German navy, air force, and recently formed airborne forces led the operation. Hitler wanted to avoid diverting large land forces from a future assault planned against France and the Low Countries. The German plan relied on surprise to avoid interception by the British Royal Navy and to prevent Norwegian forces from mobilizing. The sudden appearance of naval task forces took Norwegian

THE GERMAN INVASION OF NORWAY, 1940

Key
→ German attacks April–June

0 — 150 miles
0 — 200 km

North Sea

Narvik

Namsos

Trondheim
Alesund Andalsnes

SWEDEN

Glomma River

Bergen NORWAY

Oslo

Stavanger

Kristiansand

DENMARK

defenders by surprise and allowed airfields around Oslo, Trondheim, and Stavanger to be captured by the Germans intact.

At the same time German troops occupied airbases and ports in Denmark. Denmark was overrun within 24 hours. Soon the Luftwaffe had taken control of the skies over southern and central Norway.

Allied response

The German Navy suffered severe losses to British warships in the Norwegian waters. But despite this setback, much of southern Norway was under German control by April 16, 1940. The first British and French troops arrived on April 18, at Andalsnes and Namsos in central Norway. However, German ground

▲ Royal Navy aircraft attack the German naval invasion force in Bergen harbor on April 10.

▶ German infantry, wearing their standard field-gray greatcoats, march into the town of Aalborg, Denmark, in April 1940.

27

▲ German paratroopers land in Norway during the German invasion of 1940. The success of airborne forces in the German campaigns of 1940 led Britain and the United States to set up their own airborne divisions.

attacks and Luftwaffe bombing contained the British and French forces. By April 28, the Allies had decided to withdraw from central Norway. On April 30, German forces at Trondheim advanced and linked up with forces in Oslo. Norwegian forces in central and southern Norway began to surrender.

Fighting in Narvik

In northern Norway, the British and French deployed about 25,000 men to Narvik by mid-May, and made good gains against a small German force holding the port. Narvik fell to the Allies on May 27–28 but the Germans withdrew to the Swedish border, where they could accept internment in neutral Sweden rather than surrender to the Allies.

Allies withdraw

Meanwhile Germany had invaded France and the Low Countries on May 10 (*see Chapter 2*). Every British and French soldier was now needed in France. The Allies decided to pull out of Norway, evacuating forces from Narvik. Norwegian forces kept up assaults on the German troops to cover the Anglo-French withdrawal and tried to force the Germans into Sweden. By June 8, however, the Norwegian government had agreed to a ceasefire.

Norway's royal family and government fled to Britain. The last Allied

◁ German infantry crouch down behind a building to defend their position during the fighting in Norway in 1940.

They had shown themselves to be disorganized and ill equipped while the Germans were bold and efficient. Perhaps the most significant outcome was the damage it did to the British prime minister Neville Chamberlain. His government fell after a vote of no confidence in Parliament. A new leader was selected, who formed a government of national unity, drawing on support from all political parties. This new prime minister was Winston Churchill.

troops left on June 8, and the Germans occupied Narvik. Although the fighting in Norway was intense, it was nowhere near the scale of later battles of the war. Some 5,635 German troops were killed, as opposed to 1,335 Norwegians, and 2,400 Allied troops.

Disaster for Allies

In a dramatic finale to the Norwegian campaign, the British evacuation fleet was taken by surprise by the German battle cruisers *Scharnhorst* and *Gneisenau*. The British aircraft carrier HMS *Glorious* and two destroyers were sunk with the loss of 1,515 lives.

The Norwegian campaign was a disaster for the Allies.

▶ Vidkun Quisling gives a Nazi salute as he inspects troops on a visit to Germany.

Vidkun Quisling (1887–1945)

Vidkun Quisling was a Norwegian politician who rose to power during the German military conquest of Norway.

Before the invasion, Quisling, who was leader of the tiny Norwegian fascist party, made secret plans to "invite" the Nazis to occupy Norway to prevent British intervention. But Hitler did not trust Quisling and ordered German troops to launch a surprise attack instead. Quisling declared himself prime minister anyway, but his government soon collapsed. At first the Germans did not give Quisling any power, but in 1942 they allowed his party to become Norway's only legal political organization. He imposed strict measures to crush resistance to Nazi rule in Norway.

Hated by fellow Norwegians, Quisling's collaboration with the Nazis meant his name became a general term meaning "traitor."

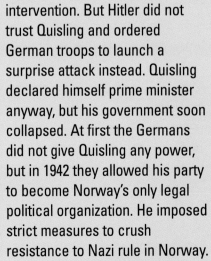

THE FALL OF THE LOW COUNTRIES AND FRANCE

In May 1940, Germany attacked westward, overrunning Belgium and the Netherlands in a matter of days. They then scored a stunning victory over the French and British armies, and occupied the French capital, Paris.

Germany had defeated Poland by early October 1939. Hitler now ordered the army to plan an offensive against the French and British armies in France. His commanders told him that they would be ready in spring 1940.

The army planners came up with a strategy similar to German strategy at the start of World War I in 1914: They would attack west from Germany into neutral Belgium, then swing south into northern France to take Paris. They extended the plan to include an invasion of neutral Holland, north of Belgium, but otherwise it was predictable. The Germans did not want to attack directly across the border with France itself because the French had built massive fortifications, the "Maginot Line," along the border.

A change in plan

The Germans knew the Allies would be prepared for an attack through Belgium, but believed that by also invading Holland they would make an advance to the Channel coast easier. In addition, blitzkrieg tactics using tanks and aircraft would aid a Wehrmacht (German army) victory.

In February 1940, however, Hitler learned of a plan devised by Major-General Erich von Manstein. Manstein knew the attack into Holland and Belgium would lure the French and British armies north. So he suggested another attack with large armored formations through the wooded hills of the Ardennes region, near Luxembourg. If these panzer divisions could cross the Meuse River near the town of Sedan, they could sweep behind the Allied forces advancing into Belgium, and destroy the Allied position.

Other senior officers were worried by Manstein's plan. If the panzer divisions did not cross the Meuse very soon after the offensive began, then they would be vulnerable to air attack in the narrow valleys of the Ardennes. Hitler liked the idea, however, and planning for it began late in February.

Equal numbers

By May 1940, 2.9 million German troops and 3,000 tanks had been massed along the border from the North Sea to Switzerland. They faced British and French forces totaling more than three million men with 3,600 tanks; there were also about 100,000 Belgian and Dutch troops. Many Allied vehicles were better armored and gun-

▼ French refugees flee the German advance on Paris in June 1940. The huge number of refugees on the roads of France severely hampered troops trying to move into position to face the Germans.

The Maginot Line and the Dyle Plan

After World War I the French built the Maginot Line, a string of fortifications along the border from Switzerland to Luxembourg, to deter any attack from Germany. The line consisted of huge forts linked by lines of bunkers.

The French believed that the Maginot Line would force any German attack to come through Belgium. In this event, Belgium and France would cooperate in a counteroffensive along the Dyle River in Belgium.

◀ A column of British troops marching into one of the huge semiburied forts built along the Maginot Line.

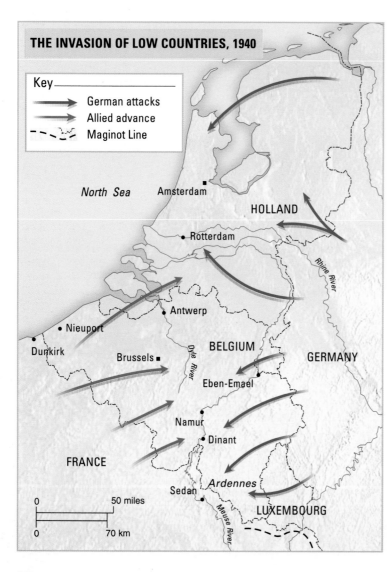

THE INVASION OF LOW COUNTRIES, 1940

Key
→ German attacks
→ Allied advance
╌╌ Maginot Line

North Sea
Amsterdam
HOLLAND
Rotterdam
Rhine River
Antwerp
• Nieuport
Dunkirk
Brussels ■
BELGIUM
GERMANY
Dyle River
Eben-Emael
Namur
• Dinant
FRANCE
Ardennes
Sedan
Meuse River
LUXEMBOURG

0 ___ 50 miles
0 ___ 70 km

ned than those of the Germans, but they were split up into small groups. In the air the Germans had a decisive advantage, with 3,200 aircraft against 1,200 French and 500 British planes.

Despite Germany's success in Poland, the Allies underestimated the enemy's leadership, morale, and battlefield skill. They also believed that the Maginot Line and defensive lines in Belgium would stall a German attack while an Allied counteroffensive could be launched.

Opening moves

Hitler's western offensive began at dawn on May 10, 1940. The Luftwaffe attacked Belgian and Dutch airfields, and paratroopers seized key bridges and airfields. The three army groups struck at different targets: Panzer and infantry divisions from Army Group B raced into the Netherlands while

◀ The German invasion of Holland and Belgium was made easier because of the flat terrain of the Low Countries.

◀ German armored vehicles stream through the countryside during the drive toward Sedan in May 1940. The town was a key objective in the invasion of France.

Army Group A, led by three panzer corps, advanced to the Ardennes; in the south, Army Group C advanced to the Maginot Line.

In a dramatic assault, airborne troops in gliders landed on top of the Belgian fortress of Eben-Emael and forced its surrender. The loss of the fort forced the Belgian Army to fall back to the Dyle River, to be reinforced by the British Expeditionary Force (BEF) and the French First Army. In a matter of hours German troops were heading deep into Belgium.

Farther north, paratroopers landed in the Netherlands to seize a string of canal bridges in order to breach Dutch defense lines. Dutch troops pinned the attackers into small pockets, and fighting raged as the Germans tried to relieve the trapped men. The Germans launched a huge bombing raid on Rotterdam to try to force the Dutch to surrender. Bombs flattened much of the city, making 77,000 people homeless. On May 14, the Dutch army surrendered. The Dutch government and navy

The Junkers Ju-87 dive bomber

With its screeching siren, the German Junkers Ju-87 dive bomber—known as the Stuka, a short version of its full name—spread terror across Europe during the blitzkrieg years. Stuka pilots dove down to only 3,000 feet (915m) to deliver their bombs accurately.

On the battlefield the Stukas closely supported panzer divisions by attacking enemy forces blocking any advance. The Stukas were known as the "flying artillery of the panzers."

▼ Although vulnerable to attack by enemy fighter planes, Stukas were a much-feared part of the German blitzkrieg.

Airborne forces

▲ German paratroops drop on Holland in 1940. They could operate behind enemy lines for days.

▼ German troops pass through the ruins of Nieuport, Belgium, in May 1940.

Hitler was an eager exponent of airborne forces. Sending troops into battle by parachute or glider appealed to his belief that new tactics were needed to avoid the stalemate of World War I.

The Luftwaffe set up an airborne force in the 1930s. The *Fallschirmjägers* (hunters from the sky) were trained to go straight into action on landing.

meanwhile fled to England.

By May 15, the Belgians, British, and French, making up some 35 divisions, had halted the German drive along the Dyle River. However, the Germans continued to battle to cross the river, and German forces were advancing from the Netherlands.

Ardennes offensive

The Allied command had fallen for Hitler's deception; the German advance had drawn the BEF and the French First Army into Belgium. The Germans now sprung their trap on the Belgian troops in the Ardennes. The Allies had assumed that tanks would be useless in the heavily forested region, so the Belgians had few antitank guns or heavy artillery.

On May 10, the three panzer corps advanced into the Ardennes, racing to reach the Meuse River on the border before the French could recover. By May 12, General Heinz Guderian's three panzer divisions reached Sedan on the

◄ Watched by their commander Erwin Rommel (on bank in peaked cap), panzer troops practice river crossing ahead of their invasion of France in 1940.

Meuse. The next day Guderian unleashed his artillery and tank fire on enemy defenses. On May 13, the infantry began to cross the river, supported by aircraft, artillery, and tank fire. The British Royal Air Force attacked the Germans, but suffered heavy losses. By May 15, six panzer divisions were across the Meuse and advancing west into France.

Race to the Channel

With the Luftwaffe in command of the air, Guderian ordered his tanks to move west at maximum speed. Although the tanks quickly outran their supply lines, he ordered his crews to refuel from French gas stations to keep moving.

The Allies were thrown into confusion. The advance into Belgium was called off, and Allied troops were ordered to counterattack against the German breakthrough into France. On May 21, British tanks struck south toward Arras, while the French launched a supporting operation. The British ground to a halt when they ran into a concentration of German tanks led by General Erwin Rommel. The attack shocked Hitler, however, who ordered the panzers not to press on to the lowlands near the English Channel. Hitler's "stop order" kept the panzers halted for two days, until May 26.

Trapped troops in northern France

Eyewitness

❝ Maneuvers had not prepared us for the refugees and empty houses. We did not go through big cities with our horses and artillery, but stayed in the countryside. The farms had been abandoned, and we often encountered the refugees from them. They had left their homes because they heard the sounds of battle coming toward them. Because they did not know what else to do, they had panicked and run away. It was sad to see them: women, children, and old men with bicycles and horse-drawn carts loaded with whatever they could carry, going they knew not where. ❞

Siegfried Knappe,
German soldier in France during May 1940

The German High Command now ordered the army to focus on the Allied troops trapped in northern France. They were retreating northward to the coast in the hopes of setting up a strong defensive line. In Paris politicians and military commanders sent every available man, tank, gun, and plane into action to try to stop the German advance. Four or five million refugees filled the roads in northern France, hampering troop movements. Stuka dive bombers machine-gunned and bombed vehicles and refugee columns. The morale of the French army and people was on the verge of collapse.

Order to retreat

▲ German forces such as these SS troops relied on motorcycles and other forms of motorized transport to advance rapidly through France.

▶ The German invasion of central France in June 1940. Having defeated the French and British armies in Belgium and northern France in late May, the Germans regrouped and swept south, forcing the French government to surrender.

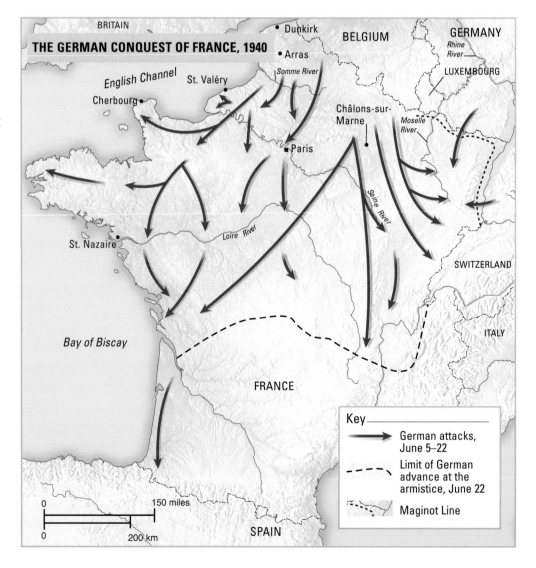

THE GERMAN CONQUEST OF FRANCE, 1940

BRITAIN

Dunkirk
Arras
Somme River
BELGIUM
GERMANY
Rhine River
LUXEMBOURG

English Channel
St. Valéry
Cherbourg

Châlons-sur-Marne
Moselle River

Paris

Seine River

SWITZERLAND

Loire River

St. Nazaire

ITALY

Bay of Biscay

FRANCE

Key
German attacks, June 5–22
Limit of German advance at the armistice, June 22
Maginot Line

0   150 miles
0   200 km

SPAIN

The "little ships" of Dunkirk

As the British Expeditionary Force retreated toward Dunkirk, the Royal Navy began an operation to bring the army home. Destroyers and merchant ships began to shuttle across the Channel, but soon the docks at Dunkirk could not take all of the Allied troops crammed into the shrinking bridgehead. Navy commanders turned to a fleet of so-called "little ships"—such as pleasure craft and fishing boats—to lift men off the beaches and carry them to larger ships offshore.

It had been intended to crew the little ships with Royal Navy sailors but in answer to appeals in Britain their owners volunteered to sail across the Channel. By May 26, some 30,000 men were being lifted off the beaches each day. German aircraft machine-gunned and bombed the evacuation day and night, sinking more than 200 ships. But the operation was a success. The bravery of the volunteer crews of the little ships entered British folklore as the miracle of Dunkirk.

The British government was equally confused, but the new prime minister, Winston Churchill, ordered the BEF to fall back to Dunkirk on the coast, where it was to be evacuated by the Royal Navy. He ordered the RAF to cut back its air support in France in order to preserve its precious fighters to defend Britain. Meanwhile, with his country all but overrun, the Belgian king surrendered on May 28.

The withdrawal to Dunkirk was a traumatic experience for the Allied troops. By the end of May they were penned into a small bridgehead and were being shelled and bombed around the clock. However, Hitler's order to halt his panzers outside Dunkirk gave most of the trapped Allied troops a chance to escape. A fleet of civilian ships helped the Royal Navy rescue more than 220,000 British and 113,000 French troops. The Germans rounded up some 1.2 million Allied prisoners in northern France and the Low Countries, however, along with 1,200 field guns, 11,000 machine guns, and 75,000 military vehicles.

Advance on Paris
The Germans now turned their attention south toward the capture of Paris, code-named Operation Red. They massed more than two million troops and almost all of their tanks against a demoralized and poorly equipped

▲ These Allied sailors and troops took to a lifeboat after their ship was bombed and sunk off the beaches of Dunkirk.

▲ These vehicles were abandoned on the beach at Dunkirk by retreating British troops.

French force of about a million men.

The advance began on June 5. The German panzers broke through resistance on the Aisne and Somme rivers. Army Group C, meanwhile, attacked the Maginot Line from the rear. French defense reached the breaking point: The government ordered a general retreat and declared Paris an open city to spare it from the effects of war. By June 14, German troops were march-ing past the Arc de Triomphe in Paris.

The French moved to end the war, despite some senior figures who argued that France should fight on. On June 16, the government resigned. Marshal Philippe Pétain, a World War I hero, was appointed president to open surrender negotiations with the Germans.

France was split in two. The north and west, including Paris, were placed under German occupation, while the

▶ Representatives of the French government sign the surrender on June 22, 1940. Hitler forced the French to surrender in the same railroad car in which the Germans had surrendered at the end of World War I in 1918.

southeast was handed to Pétain to govern from the spa town of Vichy. Pétain's government was largely influenced by Germany, however. A few French soldiers refused to accept the surrender. They included a tank commander, Charles de Gaulle, who went into exile in London, from where he organized French forces to fight for the Allies. They became known as the Free French.

French tragedy

The defeat was a tragedy for France. More than 92,000 French civilians and military personnel were killed and 250,000 wounded; about 1.4 million troops were taken prisoner. The battles in northern France had devastated towns and villages, leaving 15 percent of the country's population homeless. German losses were far fewer, with 45,000 troops killed and 111,000 wounded. In two months Norway, Denmark, the Netherlands, Belgium, and France had been conquered. Hitler was now the master of northern Europe.

Eyewitness

❝ Looking through the shutters we saw German soldiers gathering the French soldiers still around and taking them as prisoners, breaking their rifles. Very disheartening! Not long after, we saw with terror two Germans, fully armed and carrying a powerful torch, standing in the doorway of the dormitory. They were looking for two prisoners who had escaped and a house to house search was being conducted. We were petrified and hid under the bedclothes...❞

Suzanne Evans, née Garçon,
Bazouges-la-Pérouse, Brittany, 17th June 1940.

▼ German troops parade past the Arc de Triomphe in Paris to celebrate their victory over France in June 1940.

BRITAIN'S ISOLATION

Following the defeat of France and the Low Countries in 1940, Britain stood alone in Europe against the Nazi threat. It faced a formidable enemy that was poised to attack its shores.

By the summer of 1940, the future looked bleak for Britain in its war against Germany. British land forces had been crushed by the German army in France. And the German air force—the Luftwaffe—appeared to outclass and outnumber the British Royal Air Force (RAF). So it came as a surprise to Adolf Hitler when British prime minister Winston Churchill refused to consider peace terms.

On July 16, 1940, Hitler issued Führer Directive No. 16. It read: "Since England, in spite of her hopeless military situation, shows no signs of being ready to come to an understanding, I have decided to prepare a landing operation against England and, if necessary, to carry it out." The planned invasion of Britain was code-named Operation Sea Lion.

Preparing for invasion

Operation Sea Lion faced one major obstacle: the English Channel. This stretch of water, although narrow—only 21 miles (34km) separate Calais, France, from Dover, England—stood between German forces and the British mainland. German High Command estimated that Operation Sea Lion would require 260,000 men, 34,000 vehicles, and 62,000 horses. It would be a huge undertaking to land such a force on the south coast of England.

Firefighters silhouetted against flames in London in late 1940, after a bombing raid by the Luftwaffe.

Despite its retreat from France, Britain still had a powerful Royal Navy and a strong air force. High-ranking German officers knew that if these two forces were not defeated, Sea Lion's landing force would be destroyed in the Channel before it arrived on British shores. Hitler's Directive No. 16 called for the Luftwaffe under Hermann Göring to engage Royal Navy ships, destroy coastal defenses, and defeat the RAF. Once the RAF was neutralized, he believed, the Royal Navy would be unable to operate in the English Channel, clearing the way for the German invasion. The invasion date was set for August 15.

The opposing forces

The German and British air forces were finely balanced in June 1940. Both the German Luftwaffe and the RAF had lost many aircraft and crews during the fighting in France. The Luftwaffe took a few weeks to replace their losses while the British put as many new fighters and trained pilots into service as possible in preparation for the attack that they knew was imminent. Göring had around 1,260 long-range bombers, 320 Ju-87 dive bombers, and 1,080 fighters. The aircraft were allocated to three Luftflotten (Air Fleets) stretching from central France through to Scandinavia. The 1,000 bombers and 850 fighters of Luftflotten 2 and 3 based in France and Belgium would bear the brunt of the battle.

Ranged against the Luftwaffe was RAF Fighter Command, commanded by Air Chief Marshal Hugh Dowding. At the beginning of June 1940, the RAF had only 331 fighter planes. However, British factories were soon producing 500 Spitfire and Hurricane fighters a month, compared to the 140 fighters produced by the Germans. Soon the RAF had around 600 fighters available for combat every day.

The RAF also enjoyed other advantages. The short range of German fighters—about 400 miles (660km)—gave them limited time over British soil, whereas the RAF planes were on home territory. RAF pilots forced to bail out in action could parachute to safety over their homeland, whereas parachuting German pilots faced captivity—or drowning in the English Channel.

Most significantly, the RAF had the advantage of a revolutionary new

▲ British fighter pilots rush to their Hurricane planes in 1940. The RAF's use of radar to detect German planes enabled them to respond swiftly to the enemy threat.

technology. The Chain Home Radar System was a network of radar stations along the English coastline that could detect approaching enemy aircraft as they crossed the Channel. Details of the enemy's location and numbers could be quickly fed through to RAF squadrons ready to "scramble" (rush to their planes) to meet the enemy.

Eyewitness

❝ [My family was] sitting in the dining room, comfortable in front of a roaring fire…. Suddenly there was a roar like an express train, a hurtling, a tearing, all-powerful, overwhelming rush. Together we sprang to our feet. We got no farther. The earth seemed to split into a thousand fragments. A wrenching jar I thought signified the splitting of our outside wall. The subsiding rush of materials took, it seemed, all off the back… Outside there was a stifling, forbidding atmosphere… ❞

Colin Perry, office boy,
describing an air raid in London, October 18, 1940

The Battle of Britain

The opening phase of the Battle of Britain began even before Hitler announced plans to invade. From late June until August 12, 1940, the Luftwaffe fought the *Kanalkampf* (Channel Battle). The targets were British ships in the English Channel and British ports.

The aim of the *Kanalkampf* was to impose an aerial blockade on shipping and to draw the RAF out into open combat. Fighters fought desperate dogfights (air battles at close quarters) over the Channel while German bombers sank British ships below. However, Britain survived the shipping losses, and while the Germans destroyed some 150 RAF planes during the *Kanalkampf*, they lost nearly 300 aircraft themselves.

Hitler issues new orders

The British resistance led Hitler to push the schedule for Operation Sea Lion back to September. He ordered that the Luftwaffe should now focus on the destruction of the RAF, attacking its "flying units, their ground installations and their supply organizations." Göring decided to launch the attack on August 13, a day that he dubbed *Adlertag* (Eagle Day), the beginning of the *Adlerangriff* (Eagle Attack campaign).

Germany's Eagle Attack campaign

Eagle Day was not the glorious victory Göring had hoped for. Poor weather forced the Luftwaffe to commit itself piecemeal rather than to attack in one decisive wave. The British airfields were severely damaged, but not put out of action. The Luftwaffe lost 46 aircraft on Eagle Day; the RAF 13.

Two days later, German bombers launched an even bigger raid using planes from all three Luftflotten. Ninety German aircraft were lost in the August 15 raid. British losses included 42 fighter aircraft, as well as damage to the airfields at Manston, West Malling, Debden, and Biggin Hill. Biggin Hill was attacked six times in three days, losing 70 ground staff on just one day.

Change of tactics

The fighting went on day after day, with both sides reaching the point of exhaustion. British Fighter Command made efforts to relieve battle fatigue by rotating crews so that they had rest periods. But the stress of daily combat and the death of colleagues deeply affected the pilots. In the RAF, the loss of pilots was so great that 18-year-old pilots were rushed into battle with only 10 hours of training. Losses among these young men were appalling.

Göring again altered his tactics in mid-August. He increased the number of fighter escorts in ratio to bombers in order to accelerate British fighter losses.

▲ Barbed wire defenses were put up around the south coast of England in preparation for a German invasion.

Winston Churchill (1874–1965)

Winston Leonard Spencer Churchill was born on November 30, 1874, to an aristocratic family. As a young man Churchill became an army officer and a war journalist. He was known for his bravery, cheating death many times in wars in Africa and India.

Churchill later turned his attention to politics and first entered Parliament in 1900. In 1911 he became the First Lord of the Admiralty, but during World War I (1914–1918) he supported a disastrous campaign against Turkey and lost his post. His reputation as a reckless

▲ Churchill displays his "V for Victory" gesture, which became a symbol of hope and determination.

troublemaker won him few friends. During the 1930s, when many politicians supported appeasement, Churchill was a strong and often solitary voice attacking the expansion of Hitler's Nazi Germany.

Churchill again became First Lord of the Admiralty in 1939. After Chamberlain's resignation in May 1940 he became prime minister. His inspiring speeches sustained Britain through its "darkest hour," and he was vital in persuading the United States to support Britain and to prioritize the defeat of Germany before Japan.

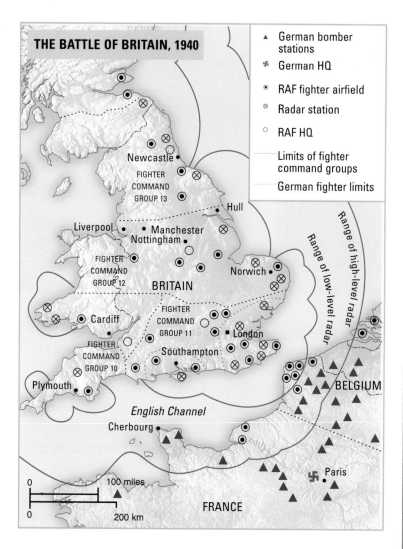

THE BATTLE OF BRITAIN, 1940

Legend:
- ▲ German bomber stations
- ⚡ German HQ
- ⊙ RAF fighter airfield
- ⊗ Radar station
- ○ RAF HQ
- ⋯⋯ Limits of fighter command groups
- ——— German fighter limits

Map labels: Newcastle, FIGHTER COMMAND GROUP 13, Hull, Liverpool, Manchester, Nottingham, FIGHTER COMMAND GROUP 12, Norwich, BRITAIN, Cardiff, FIGHTER COMMAND GROUP 11, London, FIGHTER COMMAND GROUP 10, Southampton, Plymouth, BELGIUM, English Channel, Cherbourg, Paris, FRANCE, Range of high-level radar, Range of low-level radar

0 ——— 100 miles
0 ——— 200 km

▲ This map shows the positions of British and German airbases during the Battle of Britain. The tight coordination between RAF Fighter Command groups helped Britain win the battle.

At the same time he continued the German assault on British airfields. Manston airfield was put out of action on August 24, and a total of 290 RAF fighters were destroyed between August 24 and September 7. The Luftwaffe lost 380 aircraft during the same period, but many of these were bombers, not the more tactically valuable fighters.

The bombing campaign

Despite the German successes, Britain still managed to keep 600 aircraft operational each day. Both sides were suffering, but neither was giving way. However, on August 24 a flight of German bombers accidentally dropped their bombs over London. City bombing had so far been avoided by both sides through fear of escalating the war against civilians.

The London attack drove Churchill to authorize a raid on Berlin by 81 bombers the following night. Hitler was enraged. With fall approaching fast, and the opportunity to launch Sea Lion slipping from his grasp, Hitler ordered that the Luftwaffe switch its focus to bombing London and Britain's other major cities.

The Germans believed that the British would have to throw every available fighter into the skies to protect their cities, and so open up

Eyewitness

❝ I was a student at the time, commuting between Coventry and Birmingham. They were the days of steam trains, and New Street Station was covered with a tremendous glass dome. The first air raid shattered all the glass; platforms were waist deep in glass...One night, when I was going home, there was only one other woman on the platform. The sirens went and the lady said to me, "We have to go down the luggage subway in the event of an air raid." So we went underground, to a dark musty passage. Suddenly, she grabbed me and shouted, "A rat! A rat!" I'd rather have an air raid than a rat. So we went back on the platform. ❞

Ivy Oates, student,
Birmingham and Coventry, 1940

Fighter Command to its final destruction. This did not happen, however. By taking the pressure off the airfields, the Luftwaffe allowed the RAF a breathing space to reorganize.

The bombing campaign against London began on September 7. During the next week the Luftwaffe dropped thousands of tons of bombs across the city. On September 7 alone, 2,000 Londoners were either killed or injured, and the London docks were an inferno. The new German strategy reached a climax on September 15, a day now remembered as Battle of Britain Day. About 500 German aircraft made a massive daylight attack on London. The RAF responded by sending every available aircraft into battle.

The RAF had developed new tactics. It sent up groups of 60 or 70 fighter planes together to destroy the large German formations. On September 15 British pilots shot down 57 German

aircraft for 26 losses, and threw the German planes off their bombing runs. The Luftwaffe had lost 175 aircraft in one week, losses it could not sustain.

The losses sent a clear signal to Hitler: The RAF was not beaten and was not likely to be in the foreseeable future. On

▲ St. Paul's Cathedral in central London survived the Blitz with only minor damage.

The Spitfire and the Hurricane

The Spitfire and the Hurricane were the RAF's main fighters in the Battle of Britain. The Spitfire is often credited with winning the battle, but the Hurricane actually shot down more enemy planes.

The Hurricane entered RAF service in 1937. The Mk IIA model had a top speed of around 336 mph (541km/h) and was armed with eight 0.303-in. (7.7mm) machine guns. The Hurricane was maneuverable and tough but was not as effective as the German Messerschmitt Bf 109.

Spitfires were equal and in some respects superior to the Bf 109. Spitfires were fast and agile, with a typical top speed of 374 mph (602km/h). They could climb to 20,000 feet (6095m) in 7.5 minutes.

▲ Two Spitfire fighters fly in tandem. Spitfires were known for their speed and maneuverability in battle.

▲ Bystanders look at a bomb crater in front of the Bank of England in London's financial district in January 1941.

September 17, Hitler announced that Operation Sea Lion was postponed indefinitely. Britain was saved from invasion. In Parliament on August 20, Winston Churchill delivered his now legendary words on the Battle of Britain: "Never in the field of human conflict has so much been owed by so many to so few."

The Blitz

Britain had been saved from invasion but the death and destruction continued. The raids over London in September 1940 were the start of the Blitz—a German bombing campaign directed against civilian and industrial targets during nighttime raids. Between mid-September and

mid-November 1940, London was bombed every night except one. The RAF had very limited night-fighting capability, and only 92 antiaircraft guns were available to London at the beginning of the Blitz. So the Luftwaffe suffered losses of less than 1 percent during the Blitz raids.

From mid-November other cities also suffered the devastation of the Blitz. Particularly hard hit were industrial centers such as Coventry, Sheffield, and Birmingham, and shipping centers such as Portsmouth and Swansea. Only in May 1941 did the Blitz slacken in pace as Germany pulled aircraft east to invade the Soviet Union (*see Volume 3, Chapter 2*). The Blitz had failed to

◄ Firefighters wade through water after extinguishing a major fire in London's docklands during the Blitz.

crush Britain industrially or destroy the morale of its people.

German air raids continued over Britain well into 1944 and cost the lives of about 60,000 civilians. Britain endured the air war in isolation, albeit with help from countries in its empire and commonwealth, and from expatriate pilots from occupied Europe. However, by the end of 1941 Britain was no longer in isolation—the United States had become its ally.

Air raids

Between 1940 and 1941, Londoners became used to regular nightly air raids. They prepared for a raid with the "blackout." During a blackout every window was shuttered and car headlights were reduced to a thin strip using black tape. The blackout was supposed to confuse German navigators trying to get their bearings from city lights, but it had little success: German crews tended to navigate by natural features, such as rivers. The blackout also led to a huge increase in road accidents.

As soon as raiding aircraft were detected, sirens sounded to warn civilians. They took cover in cellars, subway stations, or purpose-built air raid shelters.

▲ A family cooks an evening meal in a communal air raid shelter in London during the Blitz.

THE BATTLE OF THE ATLANTIC: 1939–1941

The Battle of the Atlantic began on September 3, 1939, the day Britain declared war on Nazi Germany, and did not end until May 7, 1945. The campaign was the longest and arguably the most important of the war.

British prime minister Winston Churchill once wrote "The only thing that ever really frightened me during the war was the U-boat peril." U-boats were German submarines (the German phrase was *Unterseeboote*, or "undersea-boat") that preyed on transatlantic shipping. If Germany gained control of the Atlantic, Britain could be starved into surrender, impacting the outcome of the whole war in Europe.

The longest battle begins

When Britain declared war on Germany, it planned to use the Royal Navy to stop ships entering German ports to starve German war industries of vital resources. The Royal Navy was the largest navy in the world, with 12 battleships, 58 submarines, 7 aircraft carriers, and more than 200 cruisers and destroyers. In 1939, the German navy, the Kriegsmarine, had just 3 battleships, 3 pocket battleships, 34 cruisers and destroyers, and 57 submarines. It could not hope to take on the British fleet in open battle.

Kriegsmarine commander Grand Admiral Erich Raeder instead planned to focus on sinking merchant vessels carrying supplies to Britain, many of which came from North America. Raeder intended to sever Britain's

▼ Two German U-boats undergo training in the Baltic Sea. German U-boats had a devastating effect on Allied shipping.

supply links by deploying warships far out in the Atlantic and U-boats around Britain's coast. To support the campaign, the Germans also laid mines in coastal waters and deployed long-range maritime aircraft to search for targets.

The convoy system

When the conflict broke out, Germany's planning soon paid off. The *U-30* sank the British passenger liner *Athenia* just 10 hours after Britain's declaration of war. More than 110 civilians and crew were lost, including 28 U.S. citizens. It was the first act of a long, bitter campaign.

Britain's response was to adopt a convoy system in which groups of merchant ships were escorted by warships. The system had been effective in World War I (1914–1918). Britain also formed patrol groups, based around large warships such as aircraft carriers, to hunt for U-boats.

The British did not have enough convoy escort ships, however, and large

> ## Eyewitness
>
> ❝ The mission seemed to be going well; boats were alongside and men were climbing up the rope ladders to safety. Suddenly, you could see the torpedo's trail as it knifed through the water towards the helpless *Patroclus*. We ducked behind the gun's shield to avoid shrapnel. A massive explosion rocked the ship when the torpedo struck ... and knocked us off our feet. Quickly getting back up, I looked down the side of the ship. What I saw can only be described as carnage, the men trying to reach safety having been exposed to the blast. The *Patroclus* began to list, but the U-boat continued to fire more torpedoes into the doomed ship. ❞
>
> George Clarke, a Canadian serving on HMS *Patroclus* in a convoy off the coast of Ireland, November 1940

vessels proved ineffective at hunting U-boats. On September 7, 1939, the aircraft carrier HMS *Courageous* was torpedoed while it was on patrol. Worse was to follow. On October 14, the Royal Navy was shaken when *U-47* sank HMS *Royal Oak*. It was not the loss of an old battleship that caused concern; rather it was the fact that the U-boat had penetrated Scapa Flow, the Royal Navy's main base in the Orkney Islands, north of Scotland.

Battle of the River Plate

Unlike the U-boats, the German surface ships were making few gains, although the pocket battleship *Admiral Graf Spee* sank 11 merchant ships in the South Atlantic and southern Indian Ocean between September and early December. The British marshaled large forces to hunt the pocket battleship down.

On December 13, the *Graf Spee* was engaged by three British cruisers in the Battle of the River Plate off Montevideo, in neutral Uruguay. They were outgunned and all three warships were damaged, but they hit the *Graf Spee* sufficiently hard to force it into Montevideo harbor.

Under international law, the ship had just 72 hours in the harbor to make repairs before it had to sail or be seized. Captain Hans Langsdorff knew he would be unable to complete repairs in time and was fooled into believing that he faced an over-whelming force of British warships. He scuttled (deliberately sank) the ship outside the harbor and then committed suicide.

Britain holds its own

Germany's other surface raiders were not faring much better. In the North Atlantic the pocket battleship *Deutschland* had to return home with engine trouble. The battle cruisers *Scharnhorst* and *Gneisenau* sank

▼ A crew member of a Royal Navy destroyer keeps watch for German aircraft in the North Atlantic in April 1940. The destroyer is escorting a convoy of British merchant ships loaded with supplies traveling from the United States to Britain.

Pocket battleships

Pocket battleships were designed as fast, heavily armed commerce raiders that could overtake and sink merchant ships, outgun enemy cruisers, and outrun enemy battleships. Known as *Panzerschiff* (armored ships) in German, they were called pocket battleships in English because they were a third of the size of full-size battleships. Germany planned to build six but only built three: *Deutschland*, later renamed *Lützow* (1931), *Admiral Scheer* (1933), and *Admiral Graf Spee* (1934).

The pocket battleships caused a sensation, but they were not as invincible as first thought. By 1939

other battleships had gotten quicker, and cruiser tactics had improved to deal with the new vessels. None of the pocket battleships had a particularly distinguished career.

▲ A painting of the *Admiral Graf Spee* during the Battle of the Plate River, off Uruguay, in December 1939.

several merchant ships, but then fled for home rather than engage British naval units.

At the end of 1939 the British were holding their own in the Atlantic. The first wave of German surface raiders had tied up large numbers of warships but had actually sunk few merchant vessels. About 80 Allied or neutral ships had been sunk by mines and 114 by the U-boats, but such losses were manageable. More than 5,500 vessels sailing in convoy had arrived safely, and nine enemy submarines had been sunk. By the end of 1940, however, Britain seemed to be close to losing the Battle of the Atlantic.

The Kreigsmarine makes progress

Germany gained a great advantage following the surrender of Norway and France in June 1940. The occu-

pation of these countries gave the Kriegsmarine bases on the Atlantic that increased the reach of the U-boats and made it easier for long-range aircraft to locate targets. U-boats began to operate in the eastern Atlantic, patrolling the

▼ Crewmen on a German cruiser watch a merchant ship sink after they have attacked it.

U-boat tactics

In the early part of the war the few German U-boats usually hunted alone, attacking targets in daylight when submerged. They only attacked on the surface with their deck guns against an unescorted merchant ship. As more U-boats were built, they continued to sail alone looking for prey. Once a convoy was sighted, however, the submarine tailed it while passing details of the location to other submarines. Once gathered in a "wolf pack" of around 15 to 20, the U-boats attacked together at night from all directions, surfacing to cruise up and down the columns of ships in the convoy.

Die Rudeltaktik (the wolf tactic), devised by Karl Dönitz, began in the fall of 1940 and was highly successful until 1943. Britain's initial lack of escorts made it a safe option, particularly as many escorts were slower than surfaced U-boats and lacked sonar to pinpoint U-boats underwater. Later in the war faster escorts, better sonar equipment, and naval air power doomed the wolf packs to defeat.

▼ A U-boat sails close to the English coast in 1940. Submarines would spend long periods of time on the surface, but would submerge when they wanted to attack targets during daylight.

shipping routes to West and South Africa, and entering the Mediterranean to assist Italian forces.

The British, meanwhile, faced a shortage of ships. They were given 50 old destroyers by the United States in September, but from June 1940 they were forced to take warships off escort duty to combat Hitler's planned invasion of England. Escorts now only accompanied convoys up to 200 miles (320km) west of Ireland. Although this had crept up to around 400 miles (640km) by the end of 1939, the newer longer-range U-boats usually hunted up to 700 miles (1,120km) out in the Atlantic. There, they could operate largely unopposed.

The U-boat "Happy Time"

Although probably no more than 16 U-boats were operating in the North Atlantic at any one time, they sank 3 million tons (2.7 million metric tons) of shipping in the second half of 1940. The German submariners called this

the "Happy Time." Successful commanders became Nazi heroes.

By December 1940, the British had lost 20 percent of their prewar merchant fleet and had no way of building replacements fast enough to offset the losses. Equally worrying was the Royal Navy's inability to sink U-boats. During the "Happy Time," just six U-boats were lost.

The Royal Navy's failure was partly due to old antisubmarine equipment. Its depth charges (underwater bombs) and Asdic, an early form of sonar, were ineffective. Successful tactics for finding and destroying submarines also had to be mastered. In addition, the Royal Navy's support aircraft had only a limited range.

The wolf packs

With 20 U-boats being built each month, the scale of their operations grew rapidly. In 1941, U-boat captains extended their operations in the central and western Atlantic, and

Admiral Karl Dönitz, commander of the submarine force, developed a new tactic. If a U-boat spotted a convoy, it radioed its position to other U-boats in the area. When a so-called "wolf

▲ A depth charge explodes as a British Royal Navy ship hunts for U-boats in the south Atlantic. In order to sink a submarine, a depth charge had to detonate within about 30 feet (10m) of its target.

◀ Technicians on a German U-boat ready torpedoes for firing, in 1941.

▶ This chart shows Allied shipping losses in the Battle of the Atlantic during 1939–1941.

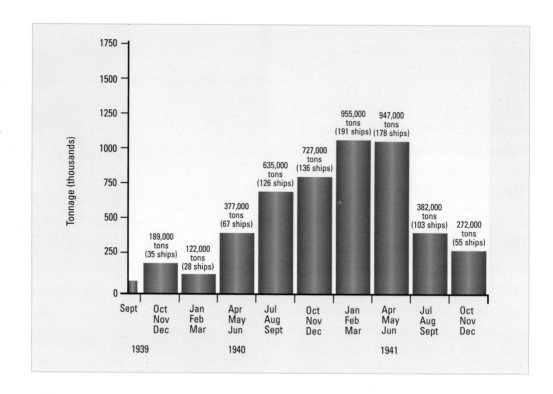

▼ The powerful German battleship *Bismarck* fires shells at the British battle cruiser HMS *Hood* during the Battle of the Denmark Strait in May 1941.

pack" of 15 to 20 U-boats had come together, they overwhelmed the escort vessels and attacked the convoy.

By the end of 1941, some 432 Allied ships had been sunk by submarines in the Atlantic and operational U-boat numbers had increased fourfold. The number of sinkings was below that of 1940, however, and some 35 U-boats had been lost, along with several of the top aces killed or captured.

The surface war

German surface raiders had mixed fortunes in 1940. In October, the pocket battleship *Admiral Scheer* slipped into the North Atlantic. On a four-month cruise in the South Atlantic and southern Indian Ocean, it destroyed 17 Allied vessels. However, the raid had not begun particularly well. On November 5, its captain spied a weakly escorted Allied convoy but

Enigma

In the late 1920s, the German military adopted a complex coding machine, a device that transformed a written message into rows of seemingly random numbers. The coded message was sent by radio and decoded by a similar machine at the receiving end. The British and French were given copies of the so-called Enigma machine by Polish decoders just before the war began. Code breaking remained extremely difficult, however, because the codes changed daily and there were several models of the machine.

British code breakers were able to build a basic decoding machine known as Colossus early in the war that could read the enemy's transmissions after a time delay. The major breakthrough came in the Atlantic in March 1941, when a boarding party recovered a naval Enigma machine from *U-110*. The intelligence the British gathered, named *Ultra*, was vital to the Allied victory. The Germans did not know that their codes had been so thoroughly broken until after the war.

Admiral Sheer's attack was met by HMAS *Jervis Bay*, an armed merchant cruiser. Although it was less well armed, the *Jervis Bay* kept the battleship at bay for an hour before being sunk: The delay allowed most of the convoy vessels to escape.

In 1941, Germany's surface raiders continued their efforts. On March 18, the *Scharnhorst* and *Gneisenau* met a convoy scattering from a U-boat attack. They sank 16 merchant ships in two days, before sailing to Brest on the French coast to escape British battleships. While at anchor both ships were bombed and put out of action for months. Meanwhile the heavy cruiser *Admiral Hipper* made successful raids into the North Atlantic in February before returning to Germany in April.

Sinking the *Bismarck*

Germany's most powerful battleship was the *Bismarck*, which in May sailed with the heavy cruiser *Prinz Eugen* from Norway. They aimed to destroy merchant shipping in the Atlantic. Two days later, in the Battle of the Denmark Strait, north of Iceland, *Bismarck* sank the British battle cruiser HMS *Hood* and badly damaged the battleship *Prince of Wales*. *Bismarck* had suffered a ruptured fuel tank, however, and headed for Brest while the *Prinz Eugen* sailed into the Atlantic.

The British sent all available ships to hunt down the *Bismarck*. By the evening of May 24, four battleships, two battle cruisers, two aircraft carriers, 12 cruisers, and several destroyers were in pursuit of the German ship. On May 26, torpedoes from aircraft based on the carrier HMS *Ark Royal* struck *Bismarck*, flooding the steering room and leaving the ship circling aimlessly. The next day the British battleships *Rodney* and *King George V* closed in

▲ The Enigma machine resembled a typewriter. When a key was tapped it set in motion a series of rotors and electrical circuits that turned the original message into code.

▲ The survivors of an Allied sinking merchant ship row to a U-boat to be taken prisoner.

and left *Bismarck* a burning wreck. It was finally sunk by torpedoes. Only 110 of *Bismarck*'s 2,200 crew survived.

Britain fights back

In the months following the loss of the *Bismarck*, British vessels sank or captured many of the supply vessels that supported Germany's warships. Meanwhile, the scale of Allied losses to submarines hid a deeper truth: The Allies were slowly discovering effective ways to defeat the German threat. The ever-present danger from mines was reduced, for example, as the Allies found more efficient ways to remove them. More significantly, the first convoy was escorted by warships all the way across the Atlantic thanks to the gradual expansion of the Royal and Canadian navies.

The British had also developed better equipment, including a radar to detect targets on the surface, and star-shells, which were artillery shells that released a shower of lights to illuminate targets at night. In September, they launched the first of a new type of small escort carrier, HMS *Audacity*, which was a merchant ship fitted with a flight deck to carry six fighter planes. The fighters could spot U-boats on the surface, and also fight off German long-range reconnaissance aircraft.

Audacity was sunk in December, but the concept of the small escort carrier was sound, and many more were built in 1942. Meanwhile long-range aircraft operating from Iceland, where Britain had had bases since May 1940, were also forcing U-boats to operate farther out in the Atlantic. Allied shipping losses fell dramatically in the final three months of 1941. This was partly because Hitler insisted that Dönitz send more than 25 U-boats into the Mediterranean, but was equally a result of growing skill of antisubmarine operations.

Help from the United States

Such improvements were important, but it was the involvement of the United States that really gave Britain renewed hope during 1941. In March the U.S. government introduced the Lend-Lease Act, which gave President Roosevelt the power to "lend" war equipment to countries whose defense was vital to U.S. interests. Britain soon placed orders for escorts and long-range patrol aircraft.

In April Roosevelt announced that Greenland, a distant part of Nazi-occupied Denmark, was to be made a U.S. protectorate to prevent it being

▲ A victorious U-boat crew celebrate as they return to port from the Atlantic.

U.S. sinkings

Even before the United States entered World War II in December 1941, its merchant and naval ships were active in the Battle of the Atlantic, either acting as convoy escorts or taking supplies to Britain. U.S. naval involvement increased in September 1941, when warships routinely began to protect convoys.

On October 17, the destroyer USS *Kearney* was torpedoed while attacking a U-boat, but managed to limp home. The destroyer *Reuben James* became the first U.S. ship to fall victim to enemy fire when it was torpedoed by *U-562* west of Ireland on October 31. The deaths of 125 seamen in these attacks hardened U.S. feelings against Nazi Germany.

used as an Axis base. In July the first U.S. troops arrived in Iceland to take over bases used by the British.

Roosevelt met Churchill in Newfoundland, Canada, in August and agreed that U.S. warships would escort convoys west of Greenland. The U.S. convoys began on September 16, allowing the British to intensify their antisubmarine operations with warships freed from escort duty.

A new phase

On December 11, four days after the Japanese attack on the U.S. base at Pearl Harbor, Germany declared war on the United States. On December 22, Churchill and Roosevelt met at the Arcadia conference in Washington and agreed that the Allies' priority was to defeat Germany and Italy. The Battle of the Atlantic was about to enter its decisive stage.

AFRICA: 1940–1941

In June 1940, World War II spread from Europe to the deserts of North Africa and the arid, mountainous terrain of East Africa, where the Italian dictator Benito Mussolini hoped to found a huge new empire.

Benito Mussolini's imperial ambitions in Africa changed the course of the war by extending hostilities between European nations to another continent. Warfare in Africa presented its own problems. Searing heat, sand, and rocky terrain put great strains on men and machinery. In addition, the huge distances meant that keeping troops supplied was a constant difficulty.

Mussolini declared war on Britain and France on June 10, 1940, at a time when Hitler was scoring victories in France. One of his first aims was the defeat of British forces in north and east Africa. Italy already had territorial interests in the region: It had colonies in Libya in the north and Ethiopia, Eritrea, and Somaliland in the east.

Mussolini hoped for an easy victory: In Libya Marshal Rodolfo Graziani led a force of 200,000 Italian and Libyan troops, and there were 290,000 Italian and native soldiers in Ethiopia. However, the army in Libya was not well supplied. Its 1,500 artillery pieces were old, and its tanks were obsolete compared to those of the British.

Weak opponents

Britain's African colonies, however, were militarily weak. In all there were only 19,000 British and African troops

▼ British forces advance toward the Libyan port of Tobruk during their successful campaign to capture the city from the Italians in January 1941. Tobruk changed hands three times during the war.

in Kenya, Sudan, Aden (now part of Yemen), and British Somaliland, with some 63,500 British soldiers in Egypt and Palestine. While the Italians had 1,700 aircraft based in Italy and in Africa, the British had fewer than 375 in the area.

The comparatively small number of British troops in Egypt was especially significant. They defended the Suez Canal, which links the Mediterranean Sea with the Red Sea. The waterway was of great strategic importance as the shortest shipping route between Europe and India and East Asia. Egypt was also close to the British-owned oilfields of the Middle East, which were a crucial source of fuel.

Italian victories

Fighting in Africa began in June 1940 on the Libya–Egypt border with skirmishes between Graziani's troops and soldiers of Britain's Western Desert Force. With Italian confidence growing, Graziani led a large invasion force into

Eyewitness

66 Our company found itself right in the thick of it, with Jerry [German] tanks and armoured cars everywhere. The only protection we had was our trucks. Having spent all our ammo, trying to shoot Jerry heads as they appeared from tank turrets, we found our shallow slit trenches were of no use, as the tanks and armoured cars rode over them... Some of our men held string attached to landmines and were pulling them across from truck to truck, trying to get the Jerry tanks and armoured cars to go over them. And, in all this, our Malay cook went about his business out in the open, making pancakes over a fire made by pouring petrol into the sand. The Jerries seemed to take no notice of him—and he brought around to each truck some of his cooking. At dusk an officer shouted, "Into your trucks, and join the convoy to the east." Most of our trucks had been destroyed, so we got on anything that moved and headed east. 99

South African Sapper Wesson,
The Battle of Sidi Rezegh, November 1941

▶ A British Mark VI light tank advances across the Western Desert in Egypt. The flat desert terrain was well suited to rapid tank advances—but also well suited to antitank guns.

▼ Members of the Bersaglieri, Italy's elite corps of motorized infantry, advance into Egypt in September 1940. The Bersaglieri underwent intensive physical training and were expert marksmen.

Egypt in September 1940. His troops reached the coastal town of Sidi Barrani, 60 miles (95km) inside British territory. The Italians were demoralized by British bombing and shelling, however, and short of food, clothing, fuel, tanks, and artillery pieces. Graziani decided to dig in in a line of fortified camps extending 50 miles (80km) inland. He then did nothing more for weeks.

Britain seizes the upper hand

The British commander in Africa, General Archibald Wavell, saw a chance to counterattack. On December 9, he launched Operation Compass to drive the Italians from Egypt. British-led forces began a stealthy advance toward the Italian line, in which they had identified a 15-mile (25km) gap. British troops cut through the gap and attacked the Italians. Another force moved to cut off Italian escape routes into Libya.

The Italians were routed. Their tanks were blasted at close range, and sleepy soldiers were shot down as they stumbled from their tents. One general was found dead in his pajamas, clutching a submachine gun.

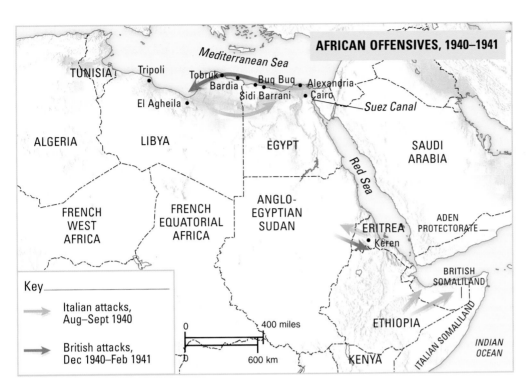

AFRICAN OFFENSIVES, 1940–1941

Key

→ Italian attacks, Aug–Sept 1940

→ British attacks, Dec 1940–Feb 1941

◀ Map showing Italian and British offensives in North and East Africa during 1940–1941.

▼ General Wavell, commander of British forces in North Africa and the Middle East until July 1941.

British troops retook Sidi Barrani on December 10. The next day another force captured Buq Buq, to the west. In three days of fighting, the British had pushed the Italians out of Egypt, capturing about 40,000 prisoners and some 70 tanks.

British advance through Libya

The British advanced rapidly into Libya. On January 6, 1941, they captured Bardia, a coastal town, and took a further 38,000 Italian prisoners. They captured the next big prize, the port of Tobruk, on January 22. On February 9, they reached El Agheila, some 600 miles (1,000km) from their starting point.

Wavell was forced to stop the advance. He faced what was to become a frequent problem of the war in North Africa: His supply lines were stretched to the breaking point. Wavell's position was further weakened by the decision of Prime Minister Winston Churchill to withdraw troops from Africa to fight the German advance in Greece.

Italian defeat in East Africa

Meanwhile, Mussolini had launched a series of raids in East Africa. In July 1940, Italian troops captured the

61

▼ Italian troops load a mortar during the desert war in early 1941.

and Indian troops invaded Eritrea and Ethiopia from Sudan. They faced some hard fighting. In Eritrea, for example, the Italians had built strong defensive positions amid towering rocky outcrops near the town of Keren. The British fought through these defenses for nearly two months. By the time they reached Keren, they had 1,500 dead and nearly 3,000 wounded. The Italians had suffered 3,500 dead.

Second prong of attack

By now the second prong of the British attack was underway. It involved an advance from Kenya east into Italian Somaliland and north through southern Ethiopia to the capital, Addis Ababa.

Nigerian, and Ghanaian troops led by General Alan Cunningham had invaded Italian Somaliland on February 11. In a remarkable campaign, Cunningham pushed his troops 1,700 miles (2,700km) north in two months. Meanwhile British troops captured

frontier towns of Kassala and Gallabat in Sudan and Moyale in Kenya. On August 3, Italian troops occupied British Somaliland, forcing the British garrison to withdraw. The British were reinforced by Indian and African troops, however, and planned a large-scale offensive.

Wavell decided to use a two-pronged attack. On January 19, 1941, British

▶ Italian naval prisoners leave the harbor of Tobruk after its capture by Allied forces on January 22, 1941. Possession of the port made it much easier for the British to keep their advancing forces supplied.

Erwin Rommel (1891–1944)

Remembered best for his victories in Africa, Erwin Rommel was a World War I veteran and expert tactician. In 1940, he brilliantly led a panzer division during the German advance into France before taking command of the Afrika Korps. In June 1942, he became Germany's youngest ever field marshal after capturing Tobruk. However, he was decisively defeated at El Alamein in Egypt in October 1942.

◄ Rommel was nicknamed the "Desert Fox" for his military skill.

Rommel commanded the defense of northern France following the Allied invasion in June 1944, when he was badly wounded. Implicated in a plot to kill Hitler, he was forced to kill himself to protect his family. He officially died of his wounds from the June invasion.

Addis Ababa on April 6. Fighting continued for six months along the mountainous Eritrean border, but by November 27, 1941, Ethiopia was entirely in Allied hands.

Germany enters the war in Africa

The British had gained significant victories, but they soon found themselves facing a new enemy. In February 1941, German troops landed in Libya. Although Adolf Hitler had not intended to get involved in Africa, he did not want to allow the British to crush his Axis ally and gain supremacy in North Africa. The region was of too much strategic importance, with its Mediterranean ports and the Suez Canal. Since the invasion of Britain had been postponed in September 1940,

▼ An Italian tank commander briefs his crews in North Africa. The Italian equipment was generally inferior to that of the British.

▲ A German tank passes a local man in sand dunes in Cyrenaica, the eastern province of Libya.

moreover, Hitler had been looking for another way to strike at the British.

Hitler chose one of his most highly regarded generals to lead the German campaign in Africa. Major General Erwin Rommel was an outstanding tactician who had distinguished himself in the battles for France in 1940. In Africa he commanded the newly created Afrika Korps, comprising a motorized division and a panzer (tank) division. Officially, he was under Italian command, but in reality he acted on his own behalf.

Rommel landed in the port of Tripoli in western Libya on February 12, 1941. The British held the eastern Libyan province of Cyrenaica, but Rommel sensed that the British were understrength—partly because troops had been sent to Greece—and quickly launched a major offensive.

The well equipped German troops sliced through British defenses, capturing a series of ports and threatening to encircle the retreating enemy.

Fighting in the desert

Desert combat presented unique challenges for both sides. In temperatures up to 122°F (50°C), vehicles overheated and men suffered from chronic sunburn, sun blindness, or heat exhaustion. The need for water was constant; troops needed to drink over 10 pints (5 liters) a day, although they often got less. At the same time sand clogged up engines and wore down mechanical parts.

By far the biggest problem was supply, with front-line units depending on routes back to often-distant ports. Rommel's eventual defeat was largely due to a collapse in his supply lines, which were cut when the Royal Air Force gained air superiority in 1942. Fighting was also complicated by desert conditions. The heat haze rising off the ground made it difficult for gunners to gain an accurate view of targets. Sand frequently stopped machine guns from functioning, while elsewhere rocky surfaces made it difficult to dig defensive positions.

► Under a searing sun, Allied forces keep up their attack on the Italians outside the coastal town of Derna in February 1941.

Meanwhile, the British reinforced the port of Tobruk with the 9th Australian Division.

Tobruk and the Halfaya Pass

Rommel began an assault on Tobruk on April 10–11, 1941, but could not pierce its defenses. The failure was a serious blow. Tobruk's port facilities would have reduced Rommel's reliance on supply lines that stretched back to Tripoli. Also, as Rommel continued his advance, the enemy-held city was a potential source of danger behind his lines.

Proceeding east, the Germans captured Halfaya Pass on April 27, a vital route through difficult terrain on the Libya–Egypt border. Rommel now halted and dug defensive positions. His advance had been tactically brilliant, but costly; some 38,000–40,000 German and Italian troops had been killed or wounded, and more than 300 Axis tanks had been destroyed.

Attempts to end the siege of Tobruk

Wavell took the offensive. Believing Rommel to be short of supplies, he launched a campaign to capture Halfaya Pass and other targets, and to end the siege of Tobruk. The attack began on May 15, 1941, and made good progress. Within a fortnight, however, German tanks had pushed the British back to their starting point.

Less than a month later Wavell attacked again. This time he seemed to

The Australians at Tobruk

The siege of Tobruk, from April 11 to December 10, 1941, confirmed the fighting reputation of Australian soldiers. Some 15,000 of the 23,000 men trapped by Rommel's forces in the port were Australians under the command of Major General Leslie Morshead. The Australians created formidable defenses, comprising lines of antitank ditches, minefields, strongpoints, and gun positions. Under constant artillery bombardment, they repelled numerous German and Italian armored assaults. They also took the war to the enemy, using Italian coastal guns to fire inland and sending out aggressive fighting patrols. One patrol took more than 800 prisoners from an elite Italian armored division. Rommel was forced to call off his costly attacks on Tobruk on May 4, and the action settled into a siege.

▼ The major campaigns fought between British troops and German and Italian armies in North Africa during 1941.

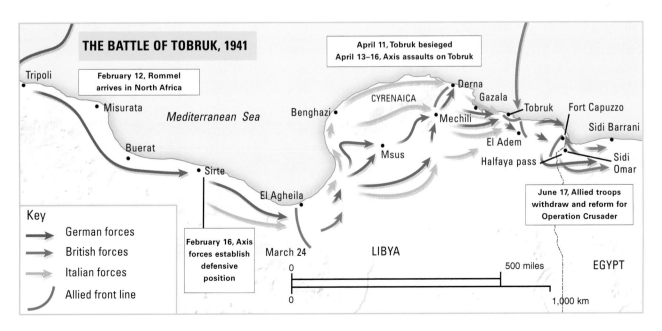

THE BATTLE OF TOBRUK, 1941

April 11, Tobruk besieged
April 13–16, Axis assaults on Tobruk

February 12, Rommel arrives in North Africa

Tripoli

Misurata

Mediterranean Sea

Buerat

Sirte

El Agheila

March 24

February 16, Axis forces establish defensive position

Benghazi

CYRENAICA

Msus

Mechili

Derna

Gazala

Tobruk

El Adem

Halfaya pass

Fort Capuzzo

Sidi Barrani

Sidi Omar

June 17, Allied troops withdraw and reform for Operation Crusader

LIBYA

EGYPT

Key
→ German forces
→ British forces
→ Italian forces
⌐ Allied front line

0   500 miles
0   1,000 km

▲ South African troops fighting for the Allies share their water with German prisoners at Sidi Rezegh in November 1941. Water was a precious resource: Both sides refrained from poisoning wells and water sources in the desert war.

be in a stronger position: He had planned the operation thoroughly and had received reinforcements, including 238 tanks. Operation Battleaxe began on June 15, 1941. British-led troops captured Fort Capuzzo and fought off a counterattack. Elsewhere, however, Wavell's forces suffered a huge blow.

Antitank measures

The Afrika Korps had defended Halfaya Pass with concealed 88mm antitank guns. With a maximum range of 6 miles (9km), the guns were highly effective in the flat, open desert. As British tanks rushed toward the pass, the German guns opened fire, destroying all but one of them. At Hafid Ridge, British tanks met a similar fate, or broke down—the new tanks had not been tested in the desert, and proved unreliable. By midday on June 16, Wavell had lost some 150 of the 200 tanks he had deployed.

Rommel now counterattacked. The 15th Panzer Division stormed Fort Capuzzo, and Wavell ordered an immediate retreat to avoid encirclement. Operation Battleaxe had been a disastrous and costly failure.

In July 1941, concerned by the defeats in North Africa, Winston Churchill replaced Wavell with General Sir Claude Auchinleck. Auchinleck consolidated British forces in North Africa into the Eighth Army—which included fresh troops from New Zealand and South Africa—and placed in command General Sir Alan Cunningham, who had defeated Italian forces in Ethiopia.

A lull in the fighting

Meanwhile the Germans also reorganized their forces. Rommel was promoted to the rank of full general and became the commander of Panzer Group Africa. The promotion gave him official control of both German and Italian forces in North Africa. Yet not everything was going Rommel's way. His supply lines were stretched and insecure, and Tobruk was still holding out, despite the efforts of the Luftwaffe to prevent it being supplied by sea.

There was a lull in fighting from July to October 1941, although German attempts to take Tobruk intensified in September and October. When British intelligence discovered that Rommel was preparing a final assault on the besieged port, Auchinleck—urged on by Churchill—aimed to act first.

Operation Crusader

On November 18, Auchinleck launched Operation Crusader to break the siege of Tobruk. A large British-led force swept west through the desert and then turned north to join up with a planned breakout by Allied forces from Tobruk. Within a few days, however, Rommel's troops had halted the British advance in a series of fierce battles, such as that fought at Sidi Rezegh on the outskirts of Tobruk. The Germans also prevented Allied attempts to break out of the besieged city. Heavy fighting followed, with both sides suffering heavy losses. On November 22, a second British-led force advanced westward along the Libyan coast road toward Tobruk.

The next day Rommel launched a fierce counterattack. On November 23, he ordered his forces to advance rapidly toward the Libyan–Egyptian border to divert Allied attention from Tobruk. Auchinleck remained focused on freeing the besieged port, however. British forces reached Tobruk on November 27, just as Rommel's advance on Egypt became bogged down due to lack of fuel. An Allied assault finally broke the German siege of the city on December 10.

Inconclusive victory

The Afrika Korps began a long retreat back into Libya. By January 6, 1942, they had withdrawn to El Agheila, the point to which Wavell's forces had pushed the defeated Italian army a year earlier. In two months of fighting Rommel's forces had suffered severely: 38,000 Axis soldiers had been killed or wounded and 340 tanks had been destroyed. The British-led forces had suffered 18,000 casualties and had lost 278 of their tanks.

Although it had been costly in terms of men and equipment, Operation Crusader was an important victory for the British. It was far from conclusive, however. Rommel immediately began rebuilding his strength for another campaign. The deserts of North Africa would remain key battlegrounds in World War II until well into 1943.

▼ A member of the Afrika Korps uses a periscope to look out for enemy forces.

THE BALKANS AND GREECE: 1940–1941

In 1940, with Germany's western and northern borders secure, Hitler turned to southeastern Europe. Unexpected military campaigns in Yugoslavia and Greece delayed his main ambition: an assault on the Soviet Union.

The victories of the German Army in Poland in 1939 and in north and west Europe in 1940 gave German leader Adolf Hitler a dominating position in Europe. In spite of the fact that he had signed a Nonaggression Pact with Soviet leader Joseph Stalin in 1939, Hitler had decided to invade the Soviet Union in spring 1941, and ordered his generals to start planing for an invasion in the Directive number 21 of mid-December 1940.

Southeastern Europe
Before invading the Soviet Union, Hitler planned to secure southeastern Europe: Hungary, the Balkans—including Romania, Bulgaria, Yugoslavia,

and Albania—and Greece. This would both safeguard his southern flank and get direct control of Romania's rich supplies of oil to support the German mechanized war effort.

The borders of southeastern Europe had been dramatically affected by the peace agreements of 1919, and in 1941 the region remained unstable. It was politically and ethnically fragmented: Almost every Balkan state had territorial claims against its neighbors and sizable ethnic minorities that resented the governing majority. The creation of Yugoslavia in 1918, for example—it was named the Kingdom of Serbs, Croats, and Slovenes until 1929—brought together ethnic groups with different cultures and religions and a history of mutual hostility.

Romania's oil fields

At the start of World War II, Romania was Europe's leading oil producer, extracting over eight million tons per year. By 1941, after Hitler had made an alliance with Romania, the oil wells near Ploesti were supplying 45 percent of Germany's requirements and were essential to Hitler's plans.

In 1943, U.S. Army Air Force bombers based in Italy attacked the oil fields to disrupt supplies. They were captured the following year by the Red Army.

▶ Oil wells in the hills north of Ploesti. Oil from the area fueled the German war effort until the summer of 1944.

◀ German soldiers keep up an attack on Yugoslav forces in April 1941 using a 37mm antitank gun. The shield on the gun protected the crew from enemy small-arms fire.

▶ On April 6, 1941, Hitler launched invasions of Yugoslavia and Greece. Within three weeks the Germans and their Axis allies had conquered both countries.

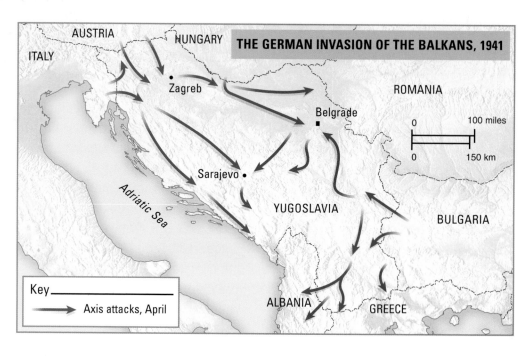

THE GERMAN INVASION OF THE BALKANS, 1941

Key —
→ Axis attacks, April

▼ King Boris of Bulgaria, in metal helmet, joins senior army commanders to watch the Bulgarian Army on maneuvers before the war. The Bulgarians joined the Axis, and would fight alongside German troops in the Balkans and on the Eastern Front.

Secret clauses in the 1939 German-Soviet Nonaggression Pact had provided for the division of eastern Europe into spheres of influence. The Soviet Union would control the Baltic states, Finland, and the Bessarabia area of Romania. Most of the Balkans would come under German influence, and both countries would divide Poland.

Hitler's first aim was to secure control of the Romanian oil wells: Germany had no oil reserves of its own. In May 1940, he signed an oil and arms pact with Romania and in August 1940 agreed to modernize the Romanian Army in order to protect German interests. German troops arrived in the Romanian capital of Bucharest on October 12, 1940. Meanwhile Soviet troops had occupied Bessarabia in June.

The British become involved

Hitler's next move was somewhat forced by events elsewhere. In April 1939, Italian troops had invaded Albania, northwest of Greece. On October 28, 1940, they invaded Greece. The attack was rapidly repulsed; by the middle of November Greek troops had expelled Italian forces from both their own country and much of Albania.

Mussolini's failed invasion disrupted Hitler's plans to bring Greece into the Axis. It had pushed the Greeks closer to their British allies, who had taken part in the military campaign. British troops landed on the Greek island of Crete, and British aircraft were sent to Greek bases from where they could

attack the oil fields in Romania. Hitler decided to occupy Greece in order to keep it out of Allied hands. The occupation needed to be completed in time to allow the invasion of the Soviet Union to begin in May 1941.

Hitler seeks Balkan allies

Throughout fall 1940 Hitler tried to form alliances with Hungary, Romania, Bulgaria, and Yugoslavia that would give his forces access to the Greek border. He was largely successful: An alliance with Germany promised economic and political advantages. In November 1940, Hungary and Romania signed the Tripartite Pact and joined the Axis powers. They allowed Hitler to move troops and supplies across their borders in preparation for an operation against Greece and ultimately the Soviet Union.

The Soviet Union, meanwhile, tried to increase its influence in the eastern Balkans; it asked Bulgaria to allow it to set up naval bases. Anxious to prevent this from happening, Bulgaria joined the Tripartite Pact on March 1, 1941; the next day Hitler moved troops into the country. In response, Britain sent 58,000 men to help defend Greece.

Yugoslavia resists pressure

Yugoslavia remained the only state in the region that had not signed the Tripartite Pact. As war grew closer, there was little agreement among its multiethnic population about whether to support the Axis or the Allies. Many Serbs, who dominated the government, were strongly nationalist: They opposed German domination. Other groups, such as the Croats, were more open to Hitler's advances. The division caused a bitter split whose effects lasted throughout the 20th century.

▲ Yugoslav infantry prepare to resist an Axis attack. The million-strong Yugoslav Army was poorly equipped and trained, and split by bitter ethnic divisions. Many troops deserted or refused to fight.

Balkan dilemmas

The weak and relatively new Balkan nations had to balance their independence and national interests with intervention from larger, more powerful countries. By 1940, with the balance of power in Europe changing, the Balkan nations were forced to rethink their allegiances. Hitler had overrun France, and Britain appeared to be on the verge of defeat. The Balkans were sandwiched between Germany and the Soviet Union, which vied for influence in the region. The Balkan countries were aware of their military limitations and knew they would not survive a German or Soviet attack. In the fall of 1940 Hitler used political and economic pressure to persuade the Balkan countries to become his allies. One by one they signed the Tripartite Pact. They hoped that siding with Germany, who at the time seemed the more likely victors in the war, might bring its own rewards.

▶ Captured Yugoslav artillery near Belgrade. The Yugoslav capital fell within a week of Axis forces crossing the borders, and the Germans split up the state of Yugoslavia.

▼ A German artillery crew man an 88-mm antiaircraft gun during the invasion of Yugoslavia. Artillery supported the rapid advance of the Wehrmacht's armored and infantry units.

With his country nearly surrounded by Axis powers, Prince Paul of Yugoslavia signed the Tripartite Pact on March 25. The deal enraged Serb nationalists, and two days later army officers overthrew Paul in a coup. They formed a new government, requested British military aid, and joined Britain and Greece in planning defensive operations against the Axis powers. They also signed a nonaggression pact with the Soviet Union.

The invasion of Yugoslavia

In response to the coup, Hitler ordered what

he called Operation Punishment, the immediate invasion of Yugoslavia. On April 6, 1941, German bombers attacked the capital, Belgrade, killing more than 17,000 people. Yugoslav troops in border regions were taken by surprise as German panzer (armored) units surged forward, supported by dive-bombers.

The attack came from four directions. In the northwest, the Germans struck from

Austria toward Zagreb. In the north and northeast they advanced on Belgrade from Hungary and Romania. In the east they advanced from Bulgaria to prevent any attacks from Greece.

Yugoslav forces, weakened by ethnic divisions, put up a poor defense. There were mass desertions by Croats and other non-Serbs, and tens of thousands of reservists refused to fight. Within days as many as 100 of 135 generals in the officer corps had surrendered.

German soldiers reached Belgrade on April 11, 1941. Six days later the occupation of Yugoslavia was complete. The Germans had lost around 150 men; they had captured more than 340,000 Yugoslav troops.

Hitler rewarded his Axis allies for their support by handing out Yugoslav territory. Serbia was placed under direct German rule; the Serbian province of Kosovo was given to the Italian colony of Albania; and Hungary, Romania, and Bulgaria all gained lands adjacent to their borders. Croatia was split between Germany and Italy, and Croatian fascists were rewarded with the creation of their own state, the Independent State of Croatia, which included parts of Dalmatia and Bosnia and Herzegovina.

The Germans took little notice of Yugoslav Army deserters who headed into the mountainous interior of the country. The refugees became the core of a powerful resistance movement.

Hitler invades Greece

On the same day that German forces attacked Yugoslavia, they also invaded Greece. On April 6, 1941, German forces attacked from Bulgaria. Despite Greek resistance that inflicted heavy casualties, a German column reached the Greek port of Salonika (now called Thessaloníki) on April 9, cutting off defenders in Thrace, the easternmost region of Greece.

In a further attack, a German panzer column raced through southern Yugoslavia and linked up with Italian

▼ German tanks rumble through the streets of the Greek port of Salonika (Thessaloníki) on April 9, 1941. German armor performed remarkably well in the difficult mountainous terrains of the Balkans and Greece.

The battle for Crete

British-led troops were evacuated to the island of Crete at the end of April 1941. They comprised some 32,000 men, including Australians and New Zealanders as well as 10,000 Greek soldiers. Hitler ordered a massive airborne assault on the island, involving 16,000 German paratroopers and air-landing troops. The invasion was the first major military operation in any war conducted solely from the air.

The assault began on May 20, 1941, but many paratroopers landed on top of Allied defensive positions, and some 2,000 were killed. On May 21, the Germans captured an airport, which enabled them to bring troops and equipment to the island.

The Germans launched an offensive to wipe out the British defenses on the northern coast. Backed by dive-bombers that attacked British armor, the ground troops soon gained momentum, although the British did defeat a German naval flotilla that attempted to land reinforcements from the sea.

As the German attack moved on, the British high command ordered an evacuation. The Allied forces retreated to the island's south coast and were evacuated by the Royal Navy between May 28 and June 2. Some 18,000 soldiers were evacuated; three cruisers and six destroyers were sunk in the process. Around 1,800 men had been killed and over 11,000 taken prisoner, along with all the Greek troops left on Crete. Despite the victory, however, Germany had suffered such serious losses—including 3,714 dead and 2,944 wounded—that Hitler never again agreed to a major airborne operation.

▲ Cretan civilians are rounded up by German paratroopers. They were to suffer at the hands of the German occupying forces for more than three years.

▶ Italian *alpini*, or mountain troops, march toward the front during the 1941 invasion of Greece. Hitler rewarded the Italians for their support by giving them control of Greek islands with which Italy had historical links.

troops in Albania before swinging south into Greece. They reached the main Greek and British defensive positions in a series of mountain passes before New Zealand and Australian units in the British forces managed to halt the advance.

The Germans sent patrols into the mountains to find routes behind the British and Greek troops. To avoid being surrounded, the British ordered a retreat, but 16 Greek divisions were trapped and surrendered. The rest of the Greek Army surrendered two days later, on April 22.

British withdrawal to Crete

As German panzer columns sped south toward Athens, British commanders ordered the withdrawal of their troops to the island of Crete. Between April 25 and 29, 1941, they evacuated around 42,000 troops, although they had to abandon heavy equipment and armor. The Greek royal family sailed on British vessels to exile in Egypt. Many Greek soldiers on the mainland,

meanwhile, simply took off their uniforms and went home.

Greece was placed under direct German rule, although Italy took control of several Greek islands. The Germans found few collaborators among the Greeks, however, and resistance fighters soon began to ambush isolated German garrisons. Hitler concentrated on defeating the British and Greek troops on Crete, which he accomplished in May.

A disastrous delay

The rapid victories in Yugoslavia and Greece had secured Hitler's southern flank. He could now focus on his invasion of the Soviet Union. However, having to make alliances in the Balkans and then defeat Yugoslavia and Greece had delayed the start of the invasion. Scheduled for May 14, it was put back to June 22. At the time five or so weeks did not seem a very significant delay: Ultimately, however, it would have a disastrous effect on the German advance through the Soviet Union.

▲ Greek prisoners walk into captivity past German armored vehicles. In the invasions of Yugoslavia and Greece, the Germans captured 90,000 Yugoslav, 270,000 Greek, and 13,000 British soldiers; they suffered only 5,000 casualties themselves.

OPERATION BARBAROSSA

The German Operation Barbarossa was the most ambitious campaign of World War II. In it Hitler hoped to conquer the Soviet Union to gain *lebensraum,* or "living space," for the German people.

The German High Command had begun planning Operation Barbarossa in the summer of 1940, despite the Nonaggression Pact signed with the Soviets the previous year. Hitler told his generals to plan to "crush Soviet Russia in one rapid campaign even before the conclusion of the war with England." Hitler originally set a date for the invasion of no later than May 15, 1941. After it took longer than expected to secure the Balkans and conquer Yugoslavia and Greece in April 1941, it was pushed back until late June. Nevertheless, Hitler and his generals still aimed to defeat the Red Army in five weeks.

Changing German–Soviet relations

Operation Barbarossa was directed against what was, in theory at least, a German ally. Under the Nonaggression Pact, Germany and the Soviet Union had agreed not to attack or support any act of aggression against the other. The pact had stunned Europe, as it brought together Hitler with his ideological opposite Joseph Stalin, the communist dictator of the Soviet Union. In practice, however, the pact was mutually beneficial: It let Hitler concentrate on fighting Poland (and then Britain and France) without worrying about a Soviet attack; and it allowed Stalin to build up the Red Army to face any eventual German invasion. The pact also included secret clauses dividing eastern Europe: Poland would be split, the Balkans would fall within the German sphere of influence, and the Baltic nations would be under Soviet control.

▼ German troops survey a burning village as they advance into the Soviet Union. The western parts of the Soviet Union suffered terribly during Operation Barbarossa and its aftermath.

▶ A German motorized column advances across the open terrain of the Soviet steppe. The invaders initially moved rapidly but were later slowed by dirt roads that turned to mud in heavy rains and became impassable.

With much of western Europe under Nazi control by June 1940, the pact had served Hitler well. He judged that a strike against Stalin was now feasible.

The timing of the decision was influenced by increasing tension with Stalin, who demanded more influence in the Balkans. Hitler justified his planned attack by claiming that Stalin was preparing to attack Germany. Stalin was indeed deploying large numbers of troops on his western borders. However, while some historians agree that he intended to attack Germany, most consider that his measures were precautions against a German invasion.

Planning the invasion

The German plan called for a rapid advance along a 1,000-mile (1,600km) front, from the Baltic Sea in the north to the Black Sea in the south. Fast-moving columns would encircle and destroy the Red Army in a series of *Kesselschlacten*, or "cauldron battles."

Master Plan East

Hitler and other senior Nazis finalized their *Generalplan Ost*, or Master Plan East, in 1941. The plan was a blueprint for the German resettlement of eastern Europe, shaped by the extreme nationalism, territorial ambitions, and racism that lay at the heart of Nazi ideology.

The plan had two parts: the Small Plan, which detailed action to be taken during the war, and the Large Plan, which covered a 30-year period after the war. It covered Poland, Czechoslovakia, the Baltic Republics (except Finland), and the western Soviet Union. People seen by the Nazis as ethnically inferior were to be moved to make room for Germans. Some 50 million Slavs were to be deported to

Siberia; others were to be enslaved. Peoples of whom the Nazis had a higher opinion were to be absorbed into the German race. All Jews were to be exterminated.

The aftermath of the conquest of Poland in 1939 was in many ways a precursor of the plan. The Germans deported thousands of Poles and seized their property, while squads known as *Einsatzgruppen* murdered many more. In the Soviet Union *Einsatzgruppen* executed communists and gypsies, but mainly Jews. On September 29 and 30, 1941, they carried out one of the worst massacres of the war: They killed 34,000 Jewish civilians from Kiev at a ravine near the city, named Babi Yar.

Dive-bombers from the German air force, the Luftwaffe, would destroy Soviet supply lines, supply dumps, and factories. *Einsatzgruppen*, or groups of commandos, would follow the army, rounding up and executing Jews, communists, and other "undesirables."

The operation was to be completed to a strict timetable. Any delay would leave the army fighting a winter war for which it was not prepared. The bitter Russian winter was a fearsome enemy. In 1812 it had destroyed the army of the French emperor Napoleon as it retreated from Moscow.

German forces and tactics

The Germans gathered one of the largest invasion forces ever assembled: more than three million soldiers, including motorized and panzer (armored) divisions. They were supported by 3,580 tanks, more than 7,000 artillery guns, and almost 2,000 aircraft.

▲ Jews in German-occupied Russia were forced by the Nazis to wear the Star of David.

Joseph Stalin (1879–1953)

The dictator Joseph Stalin was responsible for the deaths of millions of people during about 30 years in charge of the Soviet Union. Born into a poor family in the Caucasus, Stalin rose in the early 1900s through the ranks of the Russian Communist, or Bolshevik, Party, led by Vladimir Lenin (1870–1924). When the Bolsheviks came to power after the Russian Revolution (1917), Lenin made Stalin secretary general of the Central Committee of the Bolshevik Party. Lenin had increasing doubts about Stalin's character, but when Lenin died in 1924, Stalin outmaneuvered his rivals for the party leadership.

In the late 1920s Stalin imposed state control on the Soviet Union. He led a huge program of industrialization and collectivized farming that resulted in a famine

▲ Stalin appointed himself supreme commander of the Soviet Army in August 1941.

that killed millions. In the mid-1930s he initiated a series of purges: the persecution, torture, and execution of anyone he considered disloyal to his regime, including many of the nation's outstanding military officers.

Stalin refused to believe all warnings that the Germans would attack in June 1941, and this error, together with his slaughter of senior officers in the purges, make him directly responsible for the disasters that befell the Red Army in 1941. Stalin also made some serious strategic mistakes in 1942, such as ordering an offensive against Kharkov in May. However, at crucial times he listened to the advice of senior generals: In 1942 he allowed Zhokov to undertake Operation Uranus, which encircled the German forces at Stalingrad. This was in stark contrast to Hitler, who took on more and more low-level operational decisions and fired some of his best generals.

▲ Desperate Soviet civilians flee from advancing German troops. Following Hitler in his belief that the Slavs were an inferior race, the German Army on the Eastern Front often treated civilians with great savagery.

The offensive would comprise three massive thrusts. Army Group North, commanded by Field Marshal Wilhelm von Leeb, would advance toward Leningrad (now called St. Petersburg), while Army Group South, under Field Marshal Gerd von Rundstedt, would advance toward Kiev, capital of Ukraine. Between them Army Group Center, under Field Marshal Fedor von Bock, would push toward Smolensk, west of the Soviet capital Moscow.

German compromises over tactics

Many German commanders argued that most resources should be concentrated for the push on Smolensk, from where troops could advance on Moscow. The German High Command came up with a compromise. All three army groups were to advance simultaneously, but Army Group Center's thrust on Smolensk would be supported by two of the four available panzer groups, the cream of the Wehrmacht.

Stalin and the Soviet defense

Despite numerous warning signs, Stalin and his generals were taken by surprise when the invasion began. Most historians blame the Soviet lack of preparedness on Stalin's personality: Although he had seen many intelligence reports warning about German plans, he appears to have been unwilling to accept that Hitler would deceive him.

Yet Stalin was well aware of the potential threat that an expansionist Germany represented to the Soviet Union, and he had moved to strengthen his western borders. In the winter of 1939–1940 he had seized territories in Finland. In June 1940, he had taken over the Baltic republics—Estonia, Latvia, and Lithuania—and in August had incorporated them into the Soviet Union. At the same time he had taken Bessarabia from Romania. In winter 1940–1941, as German troops moved into the eastern Balkans, Stalin massed troops to face them. Even if Stalin was

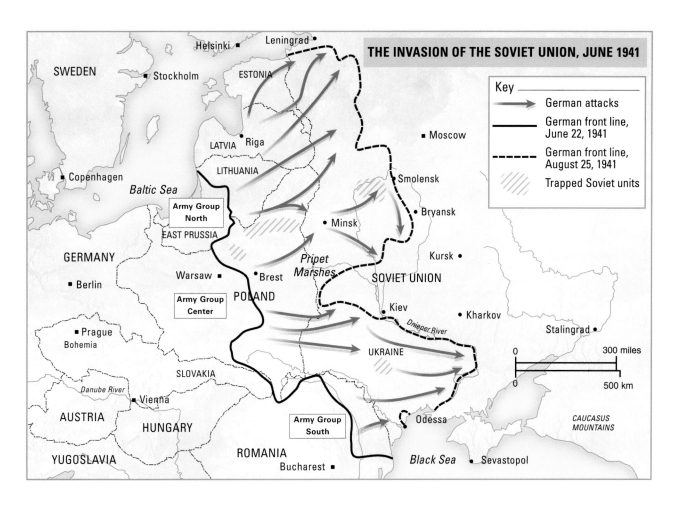

THE INVASION OF THE SOVIET UNION, JUNE 1941

Key
→ German attacks
— German front line, June 22, 1941
--- German front line, August 25, 1941
▨ Trapped Soviet units

▲ After the launch of Operation Barbarossa on June 22, 1941, the Germans made rapid progress along the whole 1,000-mile (1,600km) Soviet front.

◄ Soviet infantry wait to board a train to the front. The Germans were surprised by the seemingly endless supply of Soviet troops on which Stalin could draw.

81

▶ Soviet workers dismantle factory machinery ready to ship it east to the Ural Mountains, beyond the range of German bombers. Factories were rebuilt as quickly as possible to minimize the loss of production.

Soviet factories move east

The Soviets' removal of their industry east to the Ural Mountains—the traditional dividing line between European and Asian Russia—was a great planning triumph. As German forces advanced in the fall of 1941, the danger to Soviet industry was very real. Without the capability to produce tanks and other materiel in massive numbers, the Red Army would be unable to recover and launch an offensive.

Soviet industry packed up and moved. Entire factories were loaded onto railroad cars and transported to the Urals, out of range of German bombers. Up to 25 million workers were also forced to move east, where they often lived in the open until basic housing had been constructed. They unloaded machinery from the trains and went straight to work, even before factories had been built.

Once built, few of the new factories had any heating. Yet despite freezing winter temperatures, the production lines never stopped. They produced vast numbers of trucks, munitions, and tanks, in particular the T-34, which played a vital part in the efforts of the Red Army to reverse its losses and secure eventual victory.

◀ A T-34 tank rolls out of a factory. So many tanks were produced in the factories of Chelyabinsk in the Ural Mountains that the city became known as Tankograd.

preparing for a conflict with Germany, he certainly was not expecting it to take place as soon as it did.

Soviet forces

By spring 1941, there were 149 Soviet divisions along the country's western border. The troops almost matched the German invasion force in numbers, but they lacked their organization and equipment. In the second half of the 1930s Stalin had embarked on a purge of Red Army commanders he saw as disloyal. The purges greatly weakened the armed forces. They deprived the Red Army of its most talented leaders. The commanders who remained were either young and inexperienced or old and dedicated to doing and saying exactly what Stalin wished.

In addition to military unpreparedness, Soviet industry—which had grown remarkably since the 1920s—was mainly in the west of the country, and might be overrun in an invasion.

Hitler's lightning attack

The Red Army was taken by surprise when, at 3:30 A.M. on June 22, 1941, German artillery opened fire along the Soviet border. As German troops advanced into Soviet territory, Red Army and Air Force units were encircled and destroyed. As mechanized formations moved deep into the Soviet Union, the German chief of general staff Franz Halder wrote in his diary in July: "It is … not claiming too much when I assert that the campaign against Russia has been won in 14 days."

In the first weeks of Operation Barbarossa little happened that seemed to contradict Halder's optimism. In the north the 56th Panzer Corps covered 200 miles (320km) in four days, and by

the end of July, Army Group North was three-quarters of the way to Leningrad. Meanwhile, in late June, Army Group Center captured some 300,000 Red Army soldiers at Minsk. Less than three weeks later it took Smolensk, capturing another 300,000 Soviet troops and 3,000 tanks.

The German invasion appeared to be unstoppable. Soviet commanders were caught off guard. Afraid of punishments from Stalin if they appeared reluctant to fight—including being executed for cowardice—they sent huge numbers of untrained men into battle with little chance of success, when withdrawal might have been a more positive move.

The German advance slows

By mid-July, there were signs that the invasion was not going entirely Germany's way. After the fall of Smolensk, its initial objective, Army Group

▲ German heavy artillery opens fire on the Eastern Front at the start of Operation Barbarossa in the early hours of June 22, 1941.

83

Center had to wait several weeks before it could begin any possible push toward Moscow. German planners had not paid enough attention to the problem of transporting supplies over the vast distances of Russia, even though studies in 1940 had warned of possible supply difficulties if their lines were to stretch over about 320 miles (500km) in length. That distance would still leave German armies short of Moscow or Leningrad. The German High Command, however, had ignored the warnings. It based its supply and ammunition forecasts on the campaign in France, where very little prolonged fighting had taken place.

Additional problems

The condition of Soviet roads also added to German difficulties. They were usually little more than dirt tracks, which turned into muddy quagmires after rain. German military trucks were not designed for such conditions and quickly got stuck or broke down.

Another difficulty was that troops could not rely on finding food or fuel as they advanced. In a speech broadcast to the Soviet people on July 3, 1941, Stalin launched a "scorched earth" policy. He instructed civilians and retreating Soviet troops to destroy crops, fuel, and any other potentially useful resources to prevent them from falling into the hands of the advancing Germans.

Supply problems increase

As the three German army groups moved east, it became increasingly difficult to transport fuel, food, and spare parts to the front. Units from the various Axis countries involved in the invasion used different equipment, making an already difficult supply situation more complicated. Furthermore, while panzer divisions could cover around 50 miles (80km) a day, they frequently became detached from the rest of the army. The infantry could advance only about 20 miles (30km) a day.

▼ Soviet troops man a 203mm howitzer ready to defend Leningrad from German attack. In the first weeks of Operation Barbarossa the Soviet forces were so overwhelmed by the Germans that they lost more than 16,000 artillery pieces in seven battles.

The German Panzer Mark IV tank

The German Panzer Mark IV is an enduring symbol of World War II. Introduced in 1937, it was one of the most successful armored vehicles of the conflict. The Mark IV was relatively light and maneuverable, while its short-barreled 75mm gun was useful for supporting infantry. The combination of armor, armament, and reliability made the Mark IV the dominant tank in the early years of the war. German factories produced about 9,000 vehicles. Many models had special additions, such as air filters for desert operations or side skirts to protect the wheels and tracks.

The Germans used the Mark IV to great effect in the blitzkrieg campaigns in western Europe in 1939. In the Soviet Union, however, its short gun lacked the power to penetrate the armor of the T-34 tank. Later variants featured a long-barreled, high-velocity 75mm gun with better armor-penetration. As in earlier models, the tank's side armor was just 1.2 inches (30mm) thick; by the later stages of the war it could be penetrated by all Allied tanks. Still, the Mark IV could inflict great damage in the hands of a skilled commander.

On one celebrated occasion in 1944, SS tank commander Kurt Schumacher and his crew used a Mark IV to destroy 21 Soviet armored vehicles when they were vastly outnumbered by the enemy.

▲ A Panzer Mark IV goes into action. The Mark IV was crucial to German victories early in the war, but it was outclassed by the Soviet T-34 tank during Operation Barbarossa.

◄ Russian troops pose on a captured German tank. As the Germans got deeper into the Soviet Union and their supply lines became stretched, their advance slowed and they suffered more setbacks.

Eyewitness

❝The railroad stations were destroyed or in flames. The trains and the roads were … under air bombardment. I had not seen a single Soviet plane in the air. Because there were very few anti-aircraft machine guns, let alone anti-aircraft artillery batteries, the Luftwaffe reigned in the skies. Stukas were not only dropping bombs at targets of their choosing, but were often diving at and machine-gunning people after having scared them with their dreadful sirens. I saw people killed, some of the bodies twisted together. The wounded, especially the lightly wounded, were often crying for help, which was rarely available.❞

Gabriel Temkin, a Polish Jew enlisted into the Red Army, Gomel, Belorussia, July 1941

in August: "The whole situation shows … that we have underestimated the colossus of Russia…. When we destroy a dozen [divisions], the Russians simply establish another dozen."

More disagreement over strategy

Hitler and his generals continued to disagree about the main thrust of the attack. Hitler wanted to focus on the advances to Leningrad in the north and through Ukraine, toward the Caucasus, in the south. He ordered one of the panzer groups attached to Army Group Center to swing north and the other to head south. The order left Army Group Center with only infantry for its advance on Moscow.

Advance on Ukraine

On August 21, Hitler ordered his forces to concentrate on the advance through Ukraine. Von Rundstedt's Army Group South was to encircle the Ukrainian capital, Kiev, trapping large numbers of Soviet troops and capturing the city.

Kiev had been one of von Rundstedt's initial

▼ Soviet troops walk into captivity. The Red Army lost more than two million men in the first three weeks of Barbarossa.

It also became clear that the German High Command had not taken into account either the sheer number or the tenacity of the Red Army soldiers. By the end of June 1941 the Soviets had called up 5.3 million reservists. Franz Halder's optimism had turned to frustration. He wrote in his diary

◀ German troops set up camp in a village in Ukraine, in front of an arch set up by villagers to welcome them.

▼ German soldiers enter the Citadel, or fortress, in Kiev, after capturing the city in late September 1941.

targets, and he had come within 90 miles (145km) of the city by July 8. The offensive became bogged down, however. The 1st Panzer Group and the Sixth Army turned away from the city to deal with Soviet counterattacks.

The fall of Kiev

By early September, Army Group South had resumed its offensive, pushing east to the north and south of Kiev. On September 15, two panzer groups linked up 100 miles (160km) east of Kiev, encircling the city. Stalin insisted that the city be defended. He did not give his troops the chance to make a fighting withdrawal, which might have been more successful. On September 19, 1941, Kiev fell to the Germans.

In seizing the city, the Wehrmacht had captured 665,000 prisoners, along with many tanks and guns. The *Einsatzgruppen* went on to kill thousands of civilians, among them 34,000 Jews, who were massacred at a ravine outside the city, named Babi Yar.

Hitler called the encirclement of Kiev "the greatest battle in world history." Many of his commanders, however, saw it as a strategic error that distracted them from the advance to Moscow.

GERMANY'S ADVANCE

German troops pressed deeper into the Soviet Union through fall 1941. Kiev fell in September; German forces besieged Leningrad; and in October Hitler ordered a direct attack on the Soviet capital, Moscow.

Army Group North was advancing to take Leningrad on the Baltic coast. The city was important for symbolic reasons. Known as St. Petersburg, it had been the grand capital of the Russian empire for two centuries until 1918; it was also the location of the Russian Revolution in 1917. The city had been renamed in honor of the Bolshevik leader Vladimir Lenin. Leningrad was also economically important as the Soviet Union's second

city. It was a powerhouse of industry and its port was home to the Soviet Union's Baltic Fleet.

Advance through the Baltic States

Army Group North had overrun Lithuania in early summer. It now aimed to secure the other Baltic states—Latvia and Estonia—before heading to Leningrad. The Northwest Front—the Soviet army group defending the frontier near the Baltic Sea—could not resist the power of the Luftwaffe, the

German air force, and the rapid advance of German panzer, or armored, divisions. By June 28, the Northwest Front had lost 400 tanks, 200 artillery pieces, and thousands of men. On July 6, the Germans occupied Latvia and began the invasion of Estonia.

Assault on Leningrad

On July 9, the German High Command ordered Army Group North to send its panzer corps west and south of Leningrad. By July 20, German forces were within 60 miles (100km) of the city.

The authorities in Leningrad mobilized citizens to build barricades and ditches around the city. Soviet units behind German lines disrupted the attackers' supply convoys, forcing the Germans to send back detachments of troops to deal with them.

The German advance slowed in July and August. The woods and marshes of the Baltic region impeded the progress of the armored units. There were also delays as Hitler debated strategy with

his commanders. Many senior commanders were worried that an advance toward Moscow, which was being carried out by Army Group Center at the same time as that on Leningrad, was being deprived of resources.

On July 30, Hitler instructed Army Group North to continue its attack in order to encircle Leningrad and join up with the Finnish Army, which was fighting on the German side. On August 12 he ordered panzers from Army Group Center to help the offensive. By the end of the month German troops were on the outskirts of Leningrad.

By now Hitler had decided to concentrate his offensive in the south. He did not want to get dragged into a street-by-street battle for

▼ German soldiers fight alongside a Panzer Mark III tank as they advance into a Soviet town.

Leningrad, and ordered the city to be besieged. By September 8 communications between Leningrad and the rest of Russia were cut, signaling the start of a siege that was to last for 900 days.

Moscow and Operation Typhoon

By August 21, 1941, when Hitler ordered the Wehrmacht to concentrate on the offensive in the south, Army Group Center was just 200 miles (325km) from Moscow. The capture of the Soviet capital before winter was a key objective, and many commanders questioned Hitler's decision to divert panzer groups from Army Group Center. They doubted that the units could return in time for an advance on Moscow before the fall

The siege of Leningrad (September 8, 1941–January 27, 1944)

Leningrad had more than three million citizens in 1941. As German troops closed in on the city in the fall of that year, however, some 700,000 inhabitants were evacuated.

Food rationing began in August. To provide even basic rations, however, 510 tons of supplies had to reach the city every day by boat across Lake Ladoga to the northeast. Shortages set in, and people began to die of starvation. By January 1942 about 5,000 people were dying each day.

In January 1942, however, Lake Ladoga froze to such a depth that it became possible to drive trucks across it. The Soviets built a 20-mile-long (32km) road across the ice,

which they used to bring in supplies and to evacuate citizens. The route became known as the "Road of Life."

The Red Army tried but failed to lift the German siege several times. However, in January 1943 it made a breakthrough south of Lake Ladoga, and by mid-February supplies were reaching the city by railroad. The siege was finally broken in January 1944 after the Germans had been forced to retreat westward.

▼ The bodies of Soviet citizens, killed during a German bombing raid, lie on a street in central Leningrad. One million of Leningrad's inhabitants died during the siege.

Finland enters the war

Finland entered World War II on the German side in summer 1941, in what became known as the Continuation War. The Finns wanted to recover territories that they had lost to the Soviet Union in the Winter War (1939–1940). Hitler wanted the 400,000-strong Finnish Army to assist in the capture of Leningrad and the Arctic port of Murmansk. The Finns launched their offensive on July 10, 1941. The Soviets defended bravely around Leningrad, but were outnumbered two to one and pushed back. By September the Finns had regained their lost territory, cutting off access to Leningrad from the north. The Finns did not, however, attempt to advance farther.

▲ Horses draw supplies over the frozen Lake Ladoga on the "Road of Life" to Stalingrad.

rains turned all roads to mud and the winter started to set in; they were also anxious about supply problems and the exhaustion of their soldiers.

Despite the advances taking place in the north and south, however, on September 6 Hitler issued the order for Operation Typhoon, the campaign to seize Moscow. The operation's name highlighted the vital need for speed.

The plan called for Moscow to be enveloped in a double pincer movement from north and south. The outer pincers, however, were to be made up of panzer formations, so the offensive could not begin until the return of the panzer groups that had been sent to bolster Army Group South and Army

▼ German Panzer Mark III tanks advance on the Eastern Front.

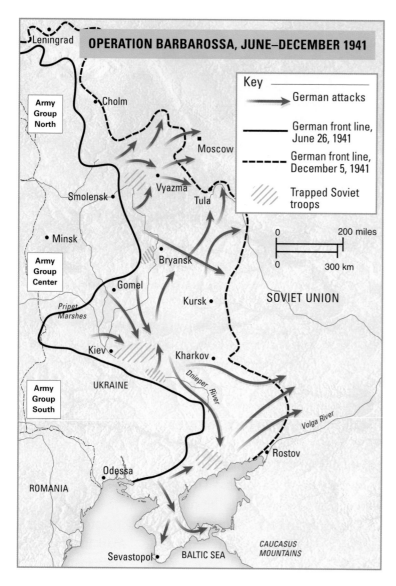

OPERATION BARBAROSSA, JUNE–DECEMBER 1941

Key

→ German attacks

— German front line, June 26, 1941

--- German front line, December 5, 1941

▨ Trapped Soviet troops

Leningrad

Cholm

Army Group North

Moscow

Vyazma

Smolensk

Tula

Minsk

Army Group Center

Bryansk

Gomel

Kursk

SOVIET UNION

Pripet Marshes

Kiev

Kharkov

Dnieper River

UKRAINE

Army Group South

Volga River

Odessa

Rostov

ROMANIA

Sevastopol

BALTIC SEA

CAUCASUS MOUNTAINS

0   200 miles
0   300 km

▲ The German advances made significant gains in the first six months of the invasion.

Group North. The 3rd Panzer Group had to come back from the Leningrad campaign, and the Second Army and 2nd Panzer Group from Kiev.

Kiev fell on September 19, and the German forces were in place by the end of September. Operation Typhoon began on October 3, when Army Group Center struck eastward on either side of the city of Smolensk. The campaign began well for the Germans. Within a week they had carried out two huge encirclements near Bryansk and Vyazma, taking another 600,000 Soviet troops prisoner.

By October 20, German troops were within 150 miles (240km) of Moscow. The Soviet government left the city and many citizens tried to flee. Stalin himself stayed in Moscow and ordered civilians to help defend the city.

Advantages for the Soviets

The weather was on Stalin's side: The fall rains set in at the end of the first week in October. They turned the roads into mud, bringing the German advance to a halt as men, tanks, and supply trucks got bogged down. The Germans planned to attack again when the frost came and the mud froze. Every day they lost, however, enabled the Soviets to bring up more reserves to defend Moscow.

The cold weather started in early November, and on November 15 the Germans attacked in force. Again the offensive began well. By November 27, the leading panzer units were just 20 miles (32km) to the north of Moscow.

▶ Soviet ski-troops pull a machine gun on runners over snowy ground. The Soviets were far better equipped for winter fighting than the Germans.

Meanwhile, the Soviets had learned from a spy in Tokyo that Japan, Germany's ally, was not planning to attack the Soviet Union, as the Soviets had expected. Instead, Japan was going to attack the United States in the Pacific. The news meant that Soviet forces based in Siberia to repel any Japanese invasion could be transferred to help defend Moscow.

It took several weeks to transport the men across the country. However, by late October they had begun to arrive, fresh and equipped for winter warfare. They were put under the command of Marshal Georgy Zhukov, the chief-of-staff of the Red Army, who took charge of the defense of Moscow.

By the beginning of December the Red Army had almost 720,000 troops, 1,700 tanks, 8,000 guns, and 1,400 aircraft around Moscow. The Soviets had several other advantages over the Germans. They had plenty of fuel, and broad-tracked T-34 tanks that operated well on ice and snow. Both Soviet equipment and troops had some protection from the elements, unlike the Germans. The majority of Soviet troops had warm winter clothing and white camouflage suits. They included specialized ski-troops who could move quickly over the snow-covered ground. There were also thousands of cavalrymen, including Cossacks who rode tough ponies that were accustomed to coping with cold weather.

Winter hits the German advance

While the onset of freezing weather enabled the Germans to renew their attack in November, it brought its own problems. The High Command had not made sufficient preparations for a winter war. To make matters worse, the winter of 1941–1942 was

▼ Civilians in the Baltic States greet German troops with salutes and waves. At first the people of Lithuania, Latvia, and Estonia saw the Germans as liberators, although Nazi rule soon proved to be as harsh as that of the Soviet Union.

▲ German troops struggle to move a StuG III assault gun along a Soviet road that has turned to mud during the fall rains of 1941. The heavy rains of fall and the sub-zero temperatures of winter stalled the German advance.

the coldest to hit the Soviet Union for half a century.

As temperatures fell as low as –13°F (–25°C), two thirds of German troops had inadequate clothing. Their weapons stopped working. Because there was little antifreeze, vehicles stopped running, and the narrow tracks of German tanks meant they sank into the snow.

German pilots, meanwhile, faced runways covered with snow and aircraft that had to be defrosted by lighting fires under their engines. The infantry could not expect the usual level of air support; for the first time the Luftwaffe was outnumbered by its Soviet counterpart.

The Wehrmacht's November drive stalled amid attacks from Red Army troops and civilian volunteers, called partisans. By early December some

155,000 German troops had been killed or wounded, or were suffering from frostbite. Field Marshal Fedor von Bock, commander of Army Group Center, informed Hitler that to continue the attack on Moscow would be highly damaging. The Soviets were better equipped and supplied, and had more soldiers. The Germans were depleted and exhausted, suffering from extreme cold and acute supply problems. On December 4, Hitler agreed to a withdrawal to a defensive line some 200 miles (320 km) west of Moscow.

Soviet counterattack

The order to withdraw came too late. The next day the Germans were taken by surprise by the terrifying noise of a new weapon: Katyusha rockets. The 130-millimeter rockets were fired in barrages of between 16 and 48 from a

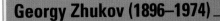

launcher nicknamed the Stalin Organ. The new weapon marked the start of a massive Soviet counteroffensive.

The German troops were spread along a 500-mile (800km) line in which there were two salients, or bulges into enemy territory, north and south of Moscow. The bulges were the focus of the main Soviet offensives, but the Red Army also attacked in the center of the line to prevent the Wehrmacht from diverting troops to bolster the salients.

From December 5, Zhukov smashed into the German defenses. With its fresh reinforcements, air superiority, and T-34 tanks, the Red Army drove the enemy back. The retreating troops were also attacked by partisans behind their lines.

German retreat

At first the Germans could not resist the offensive. Some units fell apart in panic, and Soviet tank units punched dozens of gaps in the German line, leaving the infantry to deal with any sustained German resistance.

The situation of Army Group Center became critical. Orders were confused or contradictory, as no one was sure what was happening. Every night

Georgy Zhukov (1896–1974)

Marshal Georgy Zhukov played a vital part in the Soviet victory in World War II. He had fought in World War I

▲ Zhukov was the most successful Soviet commander of the war.

and risen through the ranks of the Red Army. By May 1940, he was a general in charge of the Kiev military district. When the Germans invaded the Soviet Union in June 1941, Zhukov recommended abandoning Kiev, but Stalin refused. Zhukov offered to resign but Stalin did not accept the offer. Kiev fell anyway, and Zhukov took command of reserve forces east of Moscow. He was briefly sent to Leningrad to shore up the city's defenses, but was recalled in early October as the Germans neared the capital.

When the German attack on Moscow stalled, Zhukov launched a massive counteroffensive in December. His campaign not only saved Moscow, but also inflicted on the Germans their first strategic defeat of the war.

more poorly clothed troops froze to death. Supplies did not get through or were captured, and hundreds of vehicles were abandoned for lack of

◀ Soviet infantry counterattack near Moscow. Their white camouflage clothing and thick boots were specially designed for winter warfare.

fuel. After 10 days many German troops had retreated up to 100 miles (160km), although they managed to keep in an organized unit.

The retreat spelled the failure of Operation Typhoon and with it German hopes for a rapid victory in the Soviet Union. Many of Hitler's generals urged him to continue the retreat, to save as many troops as possible. Angry at what he saw as a defeatist attitude, Hitler fired his three army group commanders and 35 other senior generals and advisers. On December 19, he declared himself commander-in-chief of the Wehrmacht and forbade any further retreat without his permission. German units began to hold out in villages or towns. By the end of December a line had been restored.

Stalin broadens the offensive

Stalin had made himself supreme commander of the Soviet forces in August. Excited by the Red Army's achievements in December, he gave the order on January 5, 1942, for a general offensive to drive back the Germans along the entire front. It was to include attacks on Army Group South to regain Ukraine and the Crimea, and an onslaught against Army Group North to lift the siege of Leningrad. The main attack, however, was to be against Army Group Center.

Several of Stalin's senior officers were against extending the offensive, including Zhukov. He was concerned that the Red Army did not have enough resources for such a broad campaign and that the advance in the center would be weakened. However, like Hitler, Stalin would not listen to warnings about possible failure. The general offensive went ahead.

The offensive stalls

Outside of Leningrad, Army Group North resisted the Soviet counteroffensive. Although a large German force was cut off at Demyansk, most of the line around Lenin-

▼ Soviet troops, wearing white camouflage suits, advance past dead Germans in the Moscow area during the winter of 1941–1942. The battle of Moscow was the first great German defeat of World War II.

Supplying the Demyansk Pocket

When Hitler ordered the Wehrmacht not to retreat in the winter of 1941–1942, some units were cut off behind Soviet lines. Among them were 95,000 soldiers in Army Group North, who were surrounded in the town of Demyansk on February 8, 1942. The only way to supply the troops inside what became known as the Demyansk Pocket was by air.

Luftwaffe transport planes and supply gliders used the town's airstrip in an attempt to provide the troops and their animals with at least 200 tons of supplies each day. The target was sometimes achieved, but fog, blizzards, and ice often made it impossible to land or take off. On such days, supply containers were dropped by parachute.

The flight over the Soviet lines was short and few aircraft were lost to enemy fire. However, by the end of the siege the Luftwaffe had problems coping with worn-out aircraft and exhausted pilots. The half-starved troops in Demyansk were relieved on April 22, 1942.

grad held firm. Farther south the Red Army's onslaught against Army Group Center also soon slowed. By mid-February, as Zhukov had feared, the Soviet offensive had lost much of its momentum. Not only were the Germans beginning to fight back, but it was the Soviets' turn to suffer from overlong supply lines. Food, fuel, and ammunition were not reaching the front quickly enough to support the rapid advance.

Taking stock

In March 1942, the outcome of the German invasion was in the balance. Both sides had suffered losses on a scale that neither could sustain. German casualties totaled some 1,150,000, more than a quarter of the troops who had begun the campaign in June 1941. At least 4 million Soviet soldiers had been killed, wounded, or captured.

Large swathes of Soviet territory lay in German hands. Yet the delays in launching Operation Barbarossa had cost the Germans dearly, forcing them to fight in a harsh winter for which they were unprepared. By halting the

Eyewitness

❝ We could only advance step by step towards our final destination—Moscow. Fierce cold all around us—and all this with poor accommodation and insufficient food for the fighting troops.... Many of the soldiers had managed to steal Russian overcoats and fur hats and were hardly recognizable as Germans any more. All our winter clothing had been infested with lice and was impossible to wear. To keep the engines running, we had to light fires under the sumps. Some of the fuel had frozen, the engine oil had thickened, and we had no glysanthine to prevent the drinking water from freezing. ❞

SS-Unterscharführer Streng
Moscow, December 1941

German offensive and in many places pushing it back, the Red Army had saved the Russian capital and had showed that the Wehrmacht was not invincible. However, convinced of his own military genius, Hitler was undeterred. In spring 1942, he made plans for another major offensive in the Soviet Union.

PEARL HARBOR

December 7, 1941, stands in U.S. history as the "day of infamy" when Japan launched a surprise attack on the United States. The attack changed the course of World War II.

The attack on Pearl Harbor had its roots in growing tension between the United States and Japan. Japan had territorial ambitions in the Pacific and in China. It planned to create a "Greater East Asia Co-Prosperity Sphere." The United States had been involved in the Pacific since the late 19th century, when it took control of Hawaii and the Philippines. By 1940, the United States held naval bases across the Pacific.

The chief concern of the U.S. government was that a Japanese advance would threaten Allied, mainly British, possessions in Asia. That would weaken the British cause in World War II and aid Germany. Germany and Japan had signed a pact agreeing to come to each other's defense in the event of attack.

Roosevelt's strategy

The government of Franklin D. Roosevelt courted China as an ally. It thought the Chinese could help deter

Japanese aggression. The United States provided the Nationalist government in China with trade credits and supplies. In May 1940, Roosevelt also sent the Pacific Fleet to Pearl Harbor on Hawaii in the Central Pacific. He aimed to deter Japanese aggression against British and Dutch possessions in Southeast Asia. Pearl Harbor became the largest U.S. outpost in the Pacific.

Diplomatic negotiations

As tension grew between the United States and Japan, diplomatic movements continued. In February 1941, Japan sent a new ambassador to the United States, Kichisaburo Nomura. Nomura wanted peace, but later historians have questioned whether his government shared his commitment. In March, Nomura began talks with U.S. secretary of state Cordell Hull about China, which Japan had invaded in 1937. Hull demanded a Japanese withdrawal from China, and the talks made little progress. Meanwhile, the Japanese continued their military build-up. Many Japanese politicians believed war was inevitable.

Imposing trade restrictions

In July 1941, Japan agreed with Vichy France that it could station 50,000 troops in French Indochina. (Vichy France was the part of France not occupied by Germany.) This put the Japanese army and navy within striking distance of Malaya, the Dutch East Indies, and the Philippines. They belonged to Britain, the Netherlands, and the United States respectively.

Roosevelt responded by freezing all Japanese assets in the United States. On August 1, he placed an embargo on oil exports to Japan, which depended on imported oil. Roosevelt also ordered General Douglas MacArthur to return to active duty, creating a new U.S. Army Forces Far East in the Philippines. Faced with this tough U.S. stance, the Japanese tried to initiate high-level talks. The United States insisted that Japan stop its expansionist activities, and the talks broke down. Ultimately the oil embargo was one of the major factors that drove Japan to attack the United States in 1941.

Formulating a plan

When the embargo came into effect, the Japanese military had enough oil for only 18 months of combat. Prime minister Hideki Tojo considered options for a rapid campaign. He eventually decided on simultaneous attacks on the Philippines and Malaya, followed by an invasion of the Dutch East Indies to capture oil reserves.

The U.S. Navy remained a sticking point, however. Japan's war plans envisioned allowing the U.S. fleet to sail into the Central Pacific. There, the Imperial Japanese Navy would ambush and destroy it. Combined Fleet commander Admiral Isoroku Yamamoto thought the plan was bound to fail.

▼ Japanese sailors line the decks of an aircraft carrier as Mitsubishi A6M Reisen ("Zero") fighters take off for Pearl Harbor on December 7, 1941.

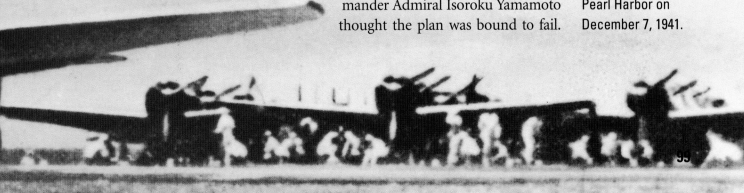

In early 1941 he proposed the "Pearl Harbor Plan," for a surprise attack on Hawaii. Yamamoto had been educated at Harvard and knew the potential industrial strength of the United States. He thought that Japan would be unwise to instigate a war. If it did, however, he saw the Pearl Harbor plan as the only way forward.

Buying time

Yamamoto planned a strike on the U.S. base at Pearl Harbor on Oahu Island. It would cripple the U.S. Navy, and delay any possible U.S. attack on the Japanese home islands by at least a year. The Japanese could then use the time to capture other U.S. bases and set up a defensive perimeter in the Pacific. The perimeter would allow them to exploit oil and rubber supplies in the "Southern Resource Area," centered on the Dutch East Indies. Tojo ordered the attack on December 4, 1941.

The operation begins

On December 6, Roosevelt made a final appeal for peace to the emperor. By now, however, the plan to attack Pearl Harbor was underway. Six aircraft carriers and two battleships had sailed from the Japanese Kurile Islands on November 26. They were commanded by Admiral Chuichi Nagumo. Maintaining radio silence to avoid detection, the task force sailed across the Pacific. It reached a position 230 miles (370km) north of Pearl Harbor. Everything was ready.

Historians still debate how much the Allies knew about the coming attack. Some argue that the Allies likely intercepted Japanese signals but failed to put them together into an overall picture. On November 30, U.S. intelligence decrypted a message from Tokyo to Berlin. It warned of imminent war: "There is extreme danger that war may suddenly break out between the Anglo-Saxon nations and Japan [and] this war may come quicker than anyone dreams." The message did not, however, contain any reason for U.S. military leaders to suspect that Hawaii was the target.

A final warning

Early on December 7, in Washington, D.C., U.S. Naval Intelligence intercepted a message from Japan telling

Isoroku Yamamoto (1884–1943)

Admiral Isoroku Yamamoto was one of Japan's leading naval strategists. Considering the possibility of war with the United States, he remarked, "If in the face of such odds we decide to go to war—or rather are forced to do so by the trend of events—I can see little hope of success in any ordinary strategy." Yamamoto had traveled extensively in the United States, both as a student and later as a naval attaché. Understanding the industrial power of the United States, he went to war in 1941 with great trepidation.

Yamamoto believed that the Pearl Harbor attack would buy Japan time to complete its conquests in Southeast Asia. He later set in motion the plans that led to the June 1942 Battle of Midway, where Japan lost naval supremacy in the Pacific. Yamamoto died when his aircraft was shot down in the Solomon Islands on April 18, 1943.

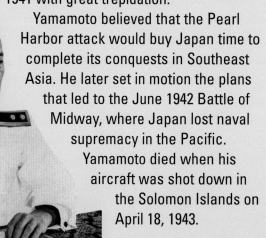

◀ Admiral Yamamoto had misgivings about entering into war with the United States.

Ambassador Nomura to break off negotiations with Cordell Hull. Army Intelligence decoded another message, sent at the same time. It ordered Nomura to submit his message to the State Department at precisely 1:00 P.M. (7:00 A.M. Hawaii time) and to destroy his code machines.

Army Intelligence concluded that a U.S. base in East Asia would soon be attacked. It tried to reach Army chief of staff General George C. Marshall. Marshall was not reached until two hours later; he issued a warning to all U.S. forces to be on the alert. The message to Hawaii was delayed, however. The War Department had to send it by commercial telegraph because radio communications with the island were out of service. The message only reached the U.S. Army commander in Hawaii, Walter C. Short, after the attack.

An easy target

Without a warning, the U.S. forces on Oahu were not ready to face an attack. They had not organized an effective defense. Several reports had identified an air raid as the most likely form of attack, probably in the early morning. Short and the U.S. Navy commander in Hawaii, Admiral Husband E. Kimmel, however, were more worried about the threat of sabotage. They had grouped ships together to make them easier to guard. For the same reason, the island's 400 aircraft were parked wing to wing on the airfields. However, this would make them an easy target for Japanese pilots. Both Short

▲ Japanese fighter pilots ready their planes on the aircraft carrier *Akagi*, 230 miles (370km) north of Pearl Harbor. They headed to Hickam Field to attack U.S. airplanes on the ground and stop them from getting into the air.

◀ Admiral Chuichi Nagumo, a key figure in tactical development in the Imperial Japanese Navy, commanded the Carrier Strike Force during the attack on Pearl Harbor.

101

▲ This aerial photograph of Pearl Harbor, taken during the attack of December 7, 1941, shows the inviting target the assembled U.S. warships offered Japanese pilots.

and Kimmel would lose their commands after the attack—unfairly, in the opinion of many historians.

Inside the anchorage at Pearl Harbor were 96 ships. They included the pride of the Pacific Fleet along Battleship Row: *Arizona*, *California*, *Iowa*, *Maryland*, *Nevada*, *Oklahoma*, *Tennessee*, *Utah*, *West Virginia*, and *Iowa*. The aircraft carriers *Lexington* and *Enterprise* were at sea, delivering aircraft to bases on Wake and Midway islands.

Incoming aircraft detected

The first part of the Japanese strike force took off from the carriers before dawn. It included 181 fighters, dive-bombers, and torpedo bombers. It was divided into four groups to head for the key targets: the anchorage at Pearl

Harbor itself, and the airfields at Kaneohe, Hickam, and Wheeler Field.

At 7:02 A.M., a radar station in the north of Oahu detected 137 inbound aircraft and reported them to the Army Operations Center. The duty officer, Kermit Tyler, was a fighter pilot with no radar experience. He and a switchboard operator were the only people on duty. Tyler believed the aircraft to be B-17 bombers due from the mainland. He told the radar operator, "Don't worry about it." The radar station then shut down for the day as scheduled.

Tora! Tora! Tora!

As the Japanese aircraft approached Oahu, the USS *Ward*, a destroyer on routine patrol, attacked a midget submarine at the entrance to Pearl Harbor.

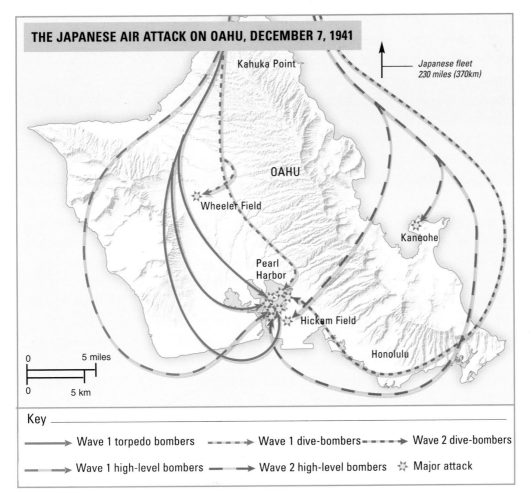

THE JAPANESE AIR ATTACK ON OAHU, DECEMBER 7, 1941

Kahuka Point

*Japanese fleet
230 miles (370km)*

OAHU

Wheeler Field

Kaneohe

Pearl
Harbor

Hickam Field

Honolulu

0   5 miles

0   5 km

Key

→ Wave 1 torpedo bombers   -- --→ Wave 1 dive-bombers - - -→ Wave 2 dive-bombers

→ Wave 1 high-level bombers   →Wave 2 high-level bombers   ✶ Major attack

◀ The paths taken by the two arms of the Japanese attack targeted the island's airfields as well as the harbor itself.

The craft was one of five intended to torpedo ships once the air attack had started. News of the incident reached Kimmel and his Pacific Fleet staff. They requested confirmation of the report.

Commander Mitsuo Fuchida led the strike force above Oahu. At 7:53 A.M., he radioed back to the fleet the code words "*Tora! Tora! Tora!*" ("Tiger! Tiger! Tiger!"). The message meant that the Japanese had achieved complete surprise. Fuchida could not believe what he saw. He later recalled: "I have seen our own warships assembled for review before the emperor, but I have never seen ships, even in the deepest peace, anchored at a distance less than 500 to 1,000 yards from each other.... This picture down there was hard to comprehend."

The attack began as soldiers, sailors, and Marines went about their Sunday-morning routines. Dive-bombers and

Eyewitness

❝❝It was just like the newsreels of Europe, only worse. We saw a bunch of soldiers come running full tilt toward us from the barracks and just then a whole line of bombs fell behind them knocking them all to the ground.... A bunch of soldiers had come into our garage to hide. They were entirely taken by surprise and most of them didn't even have a gun or anything. One of them asked for a drink of water.... He had just been so close to where a bomb fell that he had been showered with debris.❞❞

Ginger, U.S. schoolgirl,
Hawaii, 1941

fighters hit the air bases. The torpedo bombers headed for the fleet. They carried weapons specially redesigned for the shallow anchorage.

On Battleship Row, the *Arizona, California,* and *Oklahoma* suffered several direct hits, caught fire, and sank. More than 1,100 of the *Arizona*'s 1,500 crew were killed. Many were trapped below decks and drowned. The *West Virginia,* meanwhile, was holed and took on a huge amount of water. It tipped severely to one side. The ship's captain ordered the flooding of the other side of the ship, to bring it back upright. The maneuver allowed many of the crew to escape before the vessel eventually sank.

The air bases suffered similar destruction. Squadrons of flying boats at the Kaneohe Bay naval air base were destroyed on the ground. The same happened to fighters at Hickam, Wheeler, and Bellows fields.

The flight of B-17 Flying Fortresses due from the mainland arrived at the height of the attack. They had been stripped of weapons and ammunition for the long flight to Hawaii and had no defenses. However, the B-17s survived to land successfully at Hickam Field.

Mass destruction

The reaction of the U.S. forces to the attack was heroic but ineffective. The commander of the battleship *Nevada* got the ship under way as the attack began. It took only 45 minutes instead of the usual two hours. *Nevada* fired its antiaircraft guns as it steamed down the channel. On the *West Virginia,* African American cook Doris "Dorie"

▼ Smoke billows from the USS *West Virginia* after the Japanese attack. The ship sank, but was later salvaged. The *Tennessee,* beyond the *West Virginia,* was less seriously damaged; its crew fought to control fires on nearby ships.

◀ Rescuers stand on the upturned hull of the USS *Oklahoma* in the aftermath of the Japanese attack. A total of 429 sailors died when the battleship capsized. The USS *Maryland*, in the background, was also damaged, but not severely.

Miller manned an antiaircraft gun, for which he had no training. He won the Navy Cross for his brave action.

The attacked ended at 8:30 A.M. The island's defenders took the chance to improve their readiness. When a second wave of 170 planes arrived at 9:00 A.M., antiaircraft crews downed 20 of them. Many more got through, however, damaging ships in dry dock.

A devastating raid

When the attackers departed at 10:00 A.M., they left a scene of destruction. Five battleships were sunk or sinking. Eight more ships were damaged. Some 320 airplanes had been destroyed or damaged, and the runways of the air bases were cratered and littered with wreckage. Black smoke hung over the harbor and the airfields. There were 2,335 men killed and more than 1,000 wounded. Burning oil slicks covered the harbor. They hampered recovery crews who raced to

rescue men trapped underwater. Japanese losses, meanwhile, were between 30 and 60 aircraft, the five midget submarines, and fewer than 100 men.

"A date which will live in infamy"

It was early afternoon on the U.S. East Coast when word of the attack began to come in. Nomura had been unable

▼ Sailors abandon the USS *California* as it begins to sink. In the background, largely obscured by smoke, is the upturned hull of the capsized *Oklahoma*.

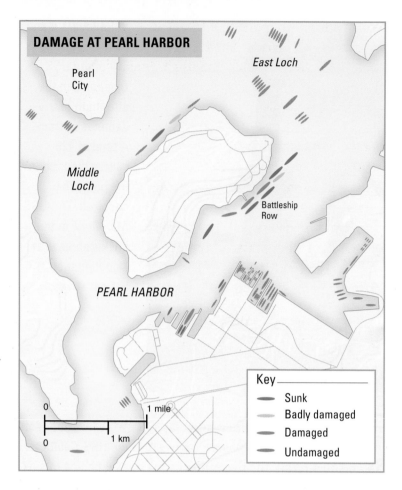

DAMAGE AT PEARL HARBOR

Pearl City

East Loch

Middle Loch

PEARL HARBOR

Battleship Row

0   1 mile

0   1 km

Key

Sunk
Badly damaged
Damaged
Undamaged

to deliver his message at 1:00 P.M., as his government had instructed. He arrived at the State Department only after the attack had begun. Roosevelt met with his military advisers. In the next 24 hours, they received reports of attacks on other U.S. and Allied bases in the Pacific: Guam, Wake Island, Hong Kong, and Singapore.

Roosevelt drafted a request for a declaration of war against Japan. He delivered the request in a six-minute address to Congress at noon on December 8: "Yesterday, December 7, 1941, a date which will live in infamy, the United States of America was suddenly and deliberately attacked by naval and air forces of the Empire of Japan." The Senate voted unanimously to declare war; in the House of Representatives, only Senator Jeannette Rankin of Montana voted against going to war.

▲ This diagram shows where U.S. vessels were sunk or damaged. Most of the five battleships lost were sunk in the first wave of the attack.

▶ A guard of honor fires a salute over a mass grave for victims of the Pearl Harbor attack at the air base at Kaneohe.

The reaction to Pearl Harbor in the rest of the country was initially one of panic. On the West Coast, in particular, many people expected an imminent Japanese attack. In San Francisco, the National Guard began patrolling the Golden Gate Bridge. People filled the streets. They fired guns at passing aircraft and smashed car headlights and street lamps to create a blackout. The Federal Bureau of Investigation (FBI) arrested Japanese American men and held them in prison for several days. There were also a series of unprovoked civilian attacks on individual Japanese Americans, or Nisei. Such attacks would be followed within months by the organized large-scale internment of Japanese Americans.

A change of tactics

The damage to Pearl Harbor and its facilities was severe, but the attack had not affected the Pacific Fleet as badly as the Japanese had hoped. The bombs hit none of the massive refueling facilities at Pearl Harbor. Neither did they seriously damage its dry docks and repair yards. The fleet would be

Wake Island

Wake Island was a small U.S. Navy outpost in the Western Pacific. The island was a coral atoll with a 5,000-foot (1.5km) airstrip. It was defended by 450 men led by Major J.P.S. Devereux, and a Marine fighter squadron.

Japanese bombers struck Wake on December 8, 1941. They destroyed most of the fighter planes, although the Japanese also lost many aircraft to coastal guns. When the Japanese tried to land on December 11, U.S. gun crews damaged or sank several ships. The Japanese troop convoy turned back. News of the successful defense elated the U.S. public.

The Japanese continued with daily bombings, however, while the arrival of a U.S. relief force was delayed. When the Japanese landing force returned on December 23, the defenders, outnumbered five to one, surrendered.

Control of Wake Island was strategically vital to the Japanese. It allowed them to set up a secure line of communication across the Central Pacific. This isolated the Philippines and exposed Douglas MacArthur's forces there to attack.

▲ On Wake Island, U.S. aircraft lie destroyed after the Japanese raid of 1941. Although U.S. troops fought off the first attacks, they were eventually forced to surrender.

operations. In effect, the attack forced the U.S. Navy to modernize its tactics. It could not depend on the big guns of battleships. The dominant weapon in naval combat for the rest of the war would be carrier-borne aircraft. The "flattops" and their pilots would stop the Japanese advance in the Coral Sea and win decisive victories at Midway, the Philippine Sea, and Leyte Gulf later in the war.

The United States joins the war

The most important legacies of the Pearl Harbor attack were strategic and emotional. Anger over the attack finally ensured that Americans abandoned their isolationism. They backed the country's entry into the war, two years after fighting had broken out in Europe. Jeannette Rankin's vote against war—she had taken a similar stand before the United States entered World War I—this time cost her her political career. "Remember Pearl Harbor!" became a rallying cry,

▲ Jeannette Rankin was the only Senator to vote against war. Her pacifism was out of step with the views of the public after the attack on Pearl Harbor.

able to use the yards throughout the war to repair damaged ships. More significantly, perhaps, the U.S. aircraft carriers had escaped the attack. That meant that the Pacific Fleet still had the ability to carry out long-range

▶ On December 8, 1941, President Roosevelt asks Congress for a declaration of war against Japan. The president's "Infamy" speech was broadcast around the world. Within half an hour, the United States was at war.

spurring industrial production and military efforts.

On December 11, meanwhile, Adolf Hitler declared war on the United States. Although Germany and Japan were members of the Tripartite Pact, there was no real reason Hitler had to declare war at this stage. His reasons for doing so remain uncertain. He probably believed that war with the United States was inevitable at some time. He was said to be elated when news came through of Pearl Harbor, because he saw the Japanese as strong allies.

Benefits to the Allies

Hitler's decision meant that Roosevelt was able to enter the war in Europe without encountering any domestic opposition. The benefit to the rest of the Allies of the full entry of the United States into the war was obvious. The "arsenal of democracy" brought the Allies new supplies of resources, industrial strength, vast reserves of personnel, and stronger political

What did Roosevelt know? _____

The greatest controversy surrounding Pearl Harbor concerns how much Franklin D. Roosevelt knew of Japanese plans before the attack. Several historians have suggested that Roosevelt ignored warnings about the attack from U.S. intelligence. They say he wanted an excuse to take the United States into the war.

One main controversy concerns the difference between Roosevelt having a sense that an attack might be imminent, which he may have had, and his having specific knowledge that Pearl Harbor was the target and not warning the military there, which is very unlikely. There were many rumors in Washington, D.C., that war was coming. The most likely explanation is that the president and his advisers did expect an attack, but that they believed it would be against British and Dutch colonies in East and Southeast Asia, rather than against the U.S. Pacific Fleet.

leadership. In a well-known—but probably inaccurate—story, British prime minister Winston Churchill, was woken up to learn the news of the attack at Pearl Harbor. He remarked, "Well, we've won then!" In a few hours, the attack had begun the process of turning the United States into the leader of the Allied coalition.

◀ The Pearl Harbor attack provoked a backlash against Japanese Americans, such as this girl waiting to be sent to an internment camp in 1942.

THE DEFEAT OF THE BRITISH AND DUTCH

The attack on Pearl Harbor was just the start of Japan's campaign of conquest in the Pacific. Its commanders launched a rapid onslaught against Allied forces to secure a series of conquests in the region.

Many Japanese officers understood that there were great risks in a long war against the United States and Britain. Admiral Isoroku Yamamoto was commander of the Combined Fleet. He thought that the Japanese might have the advantage for six months in the Pacific. Then the industrial power of the United States would come to bear on the conflict.

The Japanese developed a short-term strategy to achieve their long-term goals. They aimed to aquire territories that were rich in resources or strategically important. Their targets included the Dutch East Indies (now Indonesia) and the British colonies of Malaya, Singapore, Hong Kong, and Burma,

▶ British troops erect barbed-wire defenses along Hong Kong's rocky shore.

as well as the U.S.-ruled Philippines. They also aimed to create a line of defenses to protect the captured territory and the Japanese home islands.

The defensive perimeter was to stretch from the Kurile Islands south to Rabaul on New Britain. It would pass through Wake Island, the Marianas, the Carolinas, the Marshalls, and the Gilberts. From Rabaul, it would extend west to northwestern New Guinea, taking in the East Indies, Malaya, Thailand, and Burma.

The Japanese thought that the Allies would wear themselves out attacking this perimeter. They would eventually negotiate peace, and leave Japan in possession of its conquests. The plan depended on speed. For six months after the attack on Pearl Harbor on December 7, 1941, the Japanese forces swept all before them.

The first defeats

On December 8 (the same day as the Pearl Harbor attack, but on the other side of the international date line), Japan invaded Thailand and northern Malaya. It also attacked Hong Kong. Japanese infantry occupied some smaller islands in the Philippines. Aircraft launched attacks on the U.S. garrison on Wake Island, midway between the Philippines and Hawaii. By December 13, the Japanese had driven British defenders from the New Territories on the Chinese mainland to the island of Hong Kong. Overnight on December 18/19, the Japanese landed on the island. After hard fighting, the British surrendered on Christmas Day.

Strenuous defense

On Wake Island, meanwhile, the 450 U.S. Marines had put up a strong defense. When the Japanese sent a

The sinking of the *Prince of Wales* and *Repulse*

In October 1941, Britain sent a force of warships to protect the waters around Malaya and Singapore in the event of a war with Japan. British prime minister Winston Churchill sent the brand-new battleship HMS *Prince of Wales*, the battle cruiser HMS *Repulse*, and four destroyers. The force was named "Force Z." It was commanded by Vice Admiral Sir Tom Phillips. It arrived at Singapore on December 2. Only six days later, the Japanese invaded Malaya.

Phillips sailed his ships up the Malaya coast. He aimed to stop the Japanese from making amphibious landings to the north. It was a high-risk strategy: Force Z would have no air cover against Japanese attack aircraft and would be outnumbered by Japanese vessels.

On December 9, Force Z was spotted by Japanese aircraft. Phillips decided that the risks were too great and turned his fleet back. It was too late, however. A Japanese force of 52 torpedo planes and 34 bombers soon attacked. Torpedoes struck both the *Prince of Wales* and the *Repulse*; within hours, both had sunk. The losses were a huge blow to the pride of the British Royal Navy, for decades the world's most powerful navy. Churchill later said, "In all the war, I never received a more direct shock."

▲ British seamen scramble over the side of the torpedoed HMS *Prince of Wales* before the ship finally sinks on December 9, 1941.

landing fleet to the island on December 11, U.S. aircraft and artillery sank two destroyers and a transport ship. They forced the fleet to withdraw. Under heavy bombardment, the Wake Island garrison held out until December 23, when the Japanese put troops ashore.

By Christmas, Japanese forces had taken control of other Pacific territory, such as the Gilbert Islands. On the Asian mainland, meanwhile, they were about to inflict on the British one of the worst defeats in their military history.

Fighting the British

The Japanese attack began on the night of December 7/8 with two amphibious landings. One division landed in Thailand, just north of the border with Malaya. Another landed on Malaya's northeastern coast. The Japanese forces had about 60,000 men in total. They advanced in two columns. One headed down the east of the country, the down the west.

Facing the advance was a force of British and Commonwealth troops led

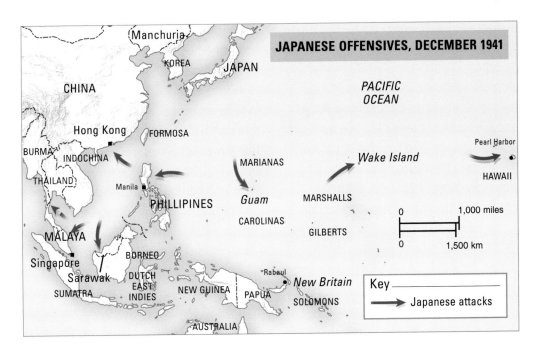

JAPANESE OFFENSIVES, DECEMBER 1941

◄ Japan launched a series of attacks across Southeast Asia in 1941 to seize strategic bases and economic resources.

by Lieutenant-General Arthur Percival. With 88,000 men, Percival had more troops than the Japanese, but the Japanese were better armed. They also had 459 modern aircraft and 80 tanks. The British had no armor and only 158 aircraft, many of which were old.

The Japanese troops were trained in jungle warfare, and included many combat veterans. By contrast the Allied soldiers had no special training. Be-lieving the jungle to be impenetrable, for example, the British set up road blocks to stop the Japanese. The Japanese simply moved off the roads and advanced through the vegetation.

Thailand and Malaya

North of the Malayan border, Japan secured control of Thailand, which surrendered on December 9. In Malaya, meanwhile, Japanese troops made

◄ Japanese soldiers advance along a jungle road with their supplies loaded onto bicycles. The use of bicycles greatly increased the mobility and speed of the Japanese advance in Southeast Asia.

Yamashita, the Tiger of Malaya (1885–1946)

General Tomoyuki Yamashita became known as "the Tiger of Malaya" after his eight-week victory over Allied forces there. He began his military career in 1906 as an infantry officer. His intelligence and resolve saw him rise through the ranks of the military and political establishment in Japan. Yamashita led units in Korea and Manchuria before being appointed commander of the Twenty-Fifth Army in November 1941. After his victory in Malaya in January 1942, he was promoted to full general. Prime Minister Hideki Tojo—a long-standing political rival—then posted him to Manchuria, far from the main conflict. After Tojo resigned in July 1944, Yamashita commanded the defense of the Philippines. He surrendered on September 2, 1945.

After the war, Yamashita was found guilty of war crimes committed by his troops in Manila, the Philippine capital. He was hanged on February 23, 1946. It is now widely accepted that he knew nothing about the atrocities.

▲ Tomoyuki Yamashita became a national hero in Japan after his victory over Allied troops in Malaya.

swift progress down the mainland. They gained control of oil fields in the north of the country. The Japanese were highly mobile. They covered ground quickly, even in thick jungle. They made a series of amphibious "jumps" along the coast to get behind the British front line. The destruction of a powerful Royal Navy force by the Japanese on December 9 meant that the British could not oppose these landings.

The Japanese took the town of Jitra on December 12. They swept south to break a line of Allied defenses along the Slim River. The British retreated south toward the capital, Kuala Lumpur, where Percival had his headquarters. Between January 1 and 10, 1942, more Japanese amphibious landings out-flanked the Allied defensive line near the town of Kampar. Kampar fell on January 3, and the Japanese came to within 20 miles (32km) of Kuala Lumpur. The British abandoned the capital, which fell on January 11.

Japan had conquered two-thirds of Malaya, a remarkable achievement. The rapid advance had resulted in the decimation of British air units. Around 100 British aircraft were lost in the first week. It had also brought the Japanese control of captured airfields. They extended their superior air cover south toward the end of the Malay peninsula and Singapore.

Local Allied resistance briefly helped to raise morale among the retreating Allies. It did little to slow the pace of the Japanese advance, however. The Allies were driven back toward Johor, the southern tip of Malaya.

Retreat to Singapore

Defeat in mainland Malaya was now a virtual certainty. Allied forces had only one place to retreat to: Singapore, just off the southern tip of the peninsula. Although only 266 square miles (683 sq km), the island was one of Britain's most important colonies in East Asia. It had become a British territory in 1824, and had grown into a thriving commercial and military port. The island gave Britain command of vital sea routes to the Dutch East Indies, India, and Australia.

Singapore's importance was reflected in the batteries of naval guns that protected it. However, the guns were

◀ Japanese troops advance through a rubber plantation in Malaya in 1942. Malaya was a major producer of rubber, a material crucial to Japan's industrial needs.

▼ A British infantryman surrenders during the Japanese advance in Malaya.

useless to repel the Japanese. They were set up to face a seaward attack. The Japanese assault came from mainland Malaya. More crucially, the guns and their ammunition were designed for firing at ships over long distances, not for antipersonnel use.

The British defense of Malaya ended on January 31, 1942. The last British troops crossed the Johor Strait to Singapore. The defeat had cost the British 4,000 dead and 21,000 prisoners, against Japanese losses of 2,000 dead and 3,000 wounded.

Defending Singapore

Percival allocated his men to defensive positions on Singapore. It seemed as if the British might now have the advantage. Percival had received reinforcements. At the beginning of February, his total troop numbers were around

▶ Japanese troops celebrate their rapid conquest of Malaya with a captured railroad locomotive.

▼ Japanese troops come ashore from a landing craft during the Malaya campaign. Their skill at amphibious landings was a key factor in their rapid progress.

85,000. The Japanese commander Tomoyuki Yamashita had only 35,000 troops, although he had greater air and armor resources. Yet British commanders were concerned about defending Singapore. Percival was warned about its defensive weaknesses by his superior General Sir Archibald Wavell, the Allied Supreme Commander in East Asia. Wavell was concerned about the northwest of the island. Understrength Australian battalions were guarding a long stretch of coastline there. Percival made a fatal error in his defensive plans, however. He concentrated his forces in order to defend naval and air installations on the east of the island. When the Japanese attacked, they came from the west.

Assault on Singapore

The Japanese assault on Singapore began on the night of February 8–9. Infantry of the Japanese 5th and 18th Divisions crossed the Johor Strait. They attacked the Australians in the northwest, as Wavell had feared. There was vicious fighting, often at close quarters. The Australians fought back the first two Japanese landing forces. However, a third force secured a beachhead and began to push the Allies inland.

The next night, troops of the Japanese Imperial Guards Division crossed the strait and attacked in the northwest. The first attacks were stopped on the beaches. A confused order from a local commander then led the Allied defenders to withdraw. They fell back to the Jurong Line, a defensive line across the center of the island. The mistake allowed Japanese troops to get ashore without resistance. They began to overwhelm the island.

The fall of Singapore

In Singapore City itself, civilians panicked under constant bombing and shelling. The Jurong Line was the last hope for an effective defense, but the Japanese broke through on February 11. They captured the island's main water reservoirs the next day. This gave them a crucial advantage. If they cut off water supplies, dehydration might cause many deaths.

On February 15, Percival met his senior officers. Unknown to them, Yamashita's forces had been weakened by the weeks of fighting. They possibly would not have had the strength to overwhelm the island's defenders had they put up a prolonged fight. After pessimistic reports at the

Eyewitness

❝ Dodging bombs and shells, I eventually approached the city [Singapore]. Hundreds of unburied dead almost blocked the streets, and the smell of putrefying flesh mingling with the bombed sewerage was appalling. A huge black pall of smoke from the blazing oil tanks on Pulau Bukum and the Naval Base hung over the city, and the rain drops were turning black as they reached the ground. Fires blazed everywhere, wrecked cars littered the streets with the dead, Jap planes bombed at will, and armed soldiers were wandering about bewildered; what unbelievable chaos. ❞

R.G. Curry, lieutenant commander, British Royal Navy
Singapore City, February 12, 1942

commanders' conference, however, Percival decided to surrender.

About 130,000 British, Commonwealth, and Malay soldiers were taken prisoner. They represented a large proportion of British military strength in Asia.

▼ The British surrender at Singapore on February 15, 1942.

Bushido: the way of the warrior

Bushido means "the way of the warrior." It was an ancient Japanese code of behavior. It was developed from the 11th to the 14th centuries by the class of knights called samurai. Bushido's values were complex, and many were not written down. They involved complete obedience to leaders, a total contempt for death and pain, and a mastery of military skills. The values of Bushido were revived during the 1920s and 1930s. The military leaders who became increasingly influential in Japan turned to them as the basis for a return to a former age of national pride.

The values of Bushido underlay Japanese military training and produced determined troops. Recruits were put through brutal training; they were also taught that death was preferable to surrender. That principle cost both the Japanese and the Allies heavy casualties during the Pacific War. It also underlay Japan's adoption of suicide tactics (kamikaze) toward the end of the conflict. General William Slim, British commander in Burma, wrote: "If 500 Japanese were ordered to hold a position, we had to kill 495 before it was ours—and the last five killed themselves. It was this combination of obedience and ferocity that made the Japanese army, whatever its condition, so formidable." Another by-product of Bushido was cruelty toward Allied prisoners and conquered civilian populations.

◄ Students in samurai armor parade at a *seinengakko*—a school where Japanese boys learned to fight, usually in preparation for military service.

Yamashita had suffered around 5,000 casualties. The victory was a spectacular achievement for the Japanese and an unmitigated disaster for the Allies.

Strengthening Allied territories

The British were not the only Allies to suffer defeats by the Japanese. South and east of Malaya lay the islands of the Dutch East Indies. They stretched across 2,000 miles (3,200km) of the Pacific Ocean. One of Japan's major war aims was to get control of the islands' oil and other resources. It also wanted the colony's ports as bases for naval actions in the South Pacific and the Indian Ocean.

The islands were protected by around 140,000 soldiers of different nationalities. The majority of the troops were local people who had little training and no experience of battle. Only 25,000 troops were Dutch. The troops were controlled by ABDACOM (American-British-Dutch-Australian Command), under the overall command of British general Archibald Wavell. ABDACOM was intended to coordinate Allied military and other resources in East Asia. In the case of the Dutch East Indies, though, these resources were relatively low. The most powerful force in the area was a flotilla of six cruisers commanded by Dutch rear admiral Karel Doorman.

The attack on the Dutch East Indies

The Japanese had made significant landings in mid-December 1941 in Sarawak on Borneo, one of the largest islands of the Dutch East Indies. Their main offensive began in January 1942. It involved three Japanese forces. Western Force would attack Sumatra, Java, and British North Borneo. Eastern Force would strike at the islands of Celebes and Amboina before advancing into the far south of the Dutch East Indies. Central Force aimed to take Borneo.

The offensive began on January 10, 1942. Initial operations went smoothly, despite some localized resistance. By the end of January, Japan had conquered the coastlines of almost all of the central and eastern islands. A landing at Balikpapan on January 24 brought most of Borneo's oil fields under Japanese control.

Futile resistance

In February the Japanese widened their operations. On February 14, Western Force began its attacks on Sumatra. It made extensive parachute landings around Palembang. British and Commonwealth defenders met the paratroopers with heavy anti-aircraft fire. The next day, the Allies launched an air attack against a Japanese amphibious landing. It sank one ship, killing dozens of men. The Allies wasted their successes, however, by making a premature withdrawal.

Java and the Java Sea

By the end of February, much of central and southern Sumatra was in Japanese hands. On March 1, Japanese forces made major landings along the northern coast of Java.

The decisive moment of the conquest of the Dutch East Indies was one of the largest naval battles since World War I: the battle of the Java Sea. On February 27, Doorman sent five cruisers and nine destroyers to intercept a Japanese invasion force off Java. Protecting the Japanese force were 4 cruisers and 14 destroyers.

The battle began in the late afternoon. Although the forces were relatively evenly matched, the Japanese were skilled at fighting at night. They also had stocks of fast long-range torpedos. The British cruiser HMS *Exeter* was hit by a Japanese shell, but remained afloat. Soon after, the Dutch destroyer *Kortenar* was hit by a torpedo. It blew up before sinking. The destroyer HMS *Electra* was hit by shells and sank.

By about 6:30 P.M., Doorman's force was greatly reduced. Four U.S. destroyers had to leave the combat area to refuel. Nevertheless, the rear admiral took his remaining vessels to hunt out the Japanese force in the darkness. It was a disastrous decision. HMS *Jupiter* struck a mine and blew

▼ On occupying a new area in the Dutch East Indies, Japanese soldiers set up a post office.

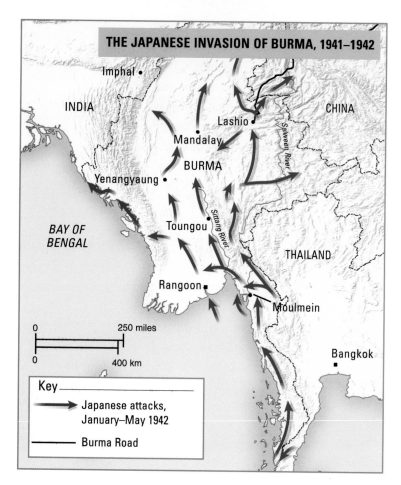

THE JAPANESE INVASION OF BURMA, 1941–1942

Imphal •

INDIA

CHINA

Lashio •

Mandalay •

BURMA

Salween River

Yenangyaung •

BAY OF BENGAL

Toungou •

Sittang River

THAILAND

Rangoon •

Moulmein •

Bangkok ■

| 0 | 250 miles |
| 0 | 400 km |

Key
→ Japanese attacks, January–May 1942
— Burma Road

Plans in Burma

In mainland Southeast Asia, the Japanese had invaded Burma in December 1941. They wanted to control the British colony to protect the Japanese invasion of Malaya. They would be able to stop British troops advancing from British India to the west. Burma would also provide a potential starting place for an invasion of India itself.

Burma was defended by about 27,000 troops, but many of them were of poor quality. The far north of the country was protected by the Chinese. Two Chinese divisions were led by the U.S. commander "Vinegar" Joe Stilwell. Allied air support was virtually non-existent. Nevertheless, the Allies expected the Japanese to make slow progress. Burma had mountainous jungles divided by rivers that would provide good defensive positions.

▲ The rapid Japanese advances through Burma drove the British back into India and the Chinese back into China.

up. When the Allies found the Japanese vessels, torpedo attacks sank the *De Ruyter* and the *Java*. Doorman died in the attack on *De Ruyter*. Five more Allied ships were sunk in the next two days. The disaster marked the virtual end of resistance to Japan's conquest of the Dutch East Indies. All the islands had surrendered by March 8.

The Burma campaign

In December 1941, Japanese forces invaded the far south of Burma from Thailand. They were followed on January 20, 1942, by the main invasion force. This was the Japanese Fifteenth Army. It comprised about 35,000 men led by General Shojira Iida. The Japanese overran the town of Kawkareik. They pushed north toward the

▶ The Dutch flagship *De Ruyter* was sunk in the Battle of the Java Sea. The action was disastrous for the Allied defense of the Dutch East Indies.

◀ Indian troops in the British Army advance through a plantation during the campaign in Malaya.

Burmese capital, Rangoon, which lay in the southern half of the country. By January 26, the Japanese had reached Moulmein. British resistance in the town collapsed on January 30.

Major-General John Smyth commanded the 17th Indian Division. He argued that all Allied troops should pull back to the Sittang River. The river would form a natural defense to break up the assault. The British high command hesitated. They did not agree to the plan until February 19. By then the Japanese had inflicted heavy losses on the British defenders around the Salween and Bilin rivers.

Fighting in the jungle

The jungles of Southeast Asia presented unique challenges for fighting. The dense foliage made travel difficult. The heat and humidity caused heat exhaustion and increased the need for constant supplies of water. Once off the few, unreliable roads, most supplies were carried by soldiers and mules. In the monsoon season, landslides and flash floods made the jungle even more treacherous.

Jungle fighting was confusing. Normal tactical maneuvers were impossible and it was difficult to keep visual contact with other units. Ambushes were a constant danger, and the dense foliage could deflect bullets and shells. But the most serious problem was disease. At one point in the Burma campaign, the British had 14 men sick for every one injured in battle; 90 percent of the sick suffered from malaria. Fungus and bacteria thrived. Even the smallest cut could become infected.

◀ Japanese soldiers in the Malay jungle support a makeshift bridge to enable their comrades to cross a river.

Japanese amphibious forces

A key element in Japan's rapid victories in 1941 and 1942 was amphibious warfare. Japan's commanders had developed equipment and tactics for landing forces from the sea, as they did, for example, during the invasion of China in 1937. One specialty was night landings, for which troops and vehicles were marked with luminous paint. The Japanese also had specialized equipment. Collapsible boats carried up to nine men, while larger landing barges carried up to 120 men or a small tank or artillery piece. For bridging rivers, troops each carried a pontoon float; when a number were put together, they formed an improvised bridge.

During the course of the war, the United States developed its own amphibious forces. Soon they outclassed the Japanese, with bigger landing craft and amphibious vehicles, and superior technology and tactics.

◀ Japanese amphibious troops run ashore on beaches in Borneo in January 1942.

The Allied retreat from Burma

When the Allied fallback did begin, both sides raced to reach the main bridge across the Sittang in the town of the same name. After hand-to-hand fighting around the river, the Allies managed to blow up the bridge before the Japanese could cross. The action also left thousands of Allies stranded on the wrong side of the river, however. The 17th Indian Division lost 5,000 men killed or captured.

Lieutenant-General Thomas Hutton, in charge of Burma, ordered that Rangoon be abandoned. Wavell disagreed. He replaced Hutton with Lieutenant-General Sir Harold Alexander. Alexander agreed with Hutton, however. "Burcorps," as the British and Allied forces were known, continued their retreat. Rangoon fell to the Japanese on March 8.

Reinforcements arrived from the Chinese Fifth and Sixth Armies, but they were defeated at Toungou on March 30. On May 1, the Japanese took Mandalay. The city was nearly 1,000 miles (1,600km) north of where the campaign had begun. Alexander realized that defending Burma was impossible. On April 25, he ordered Burcorps to retreat to India. The remaining Chinese forces would head back to their homeland.

The Allied retreat to India

The retreat to India was one of the longest in British military history:

Why did everyone underestimate the Japanese?

The Japanese conquests of 1941 and 1942 stunned the Allies. U.S. and British leaders had badly underestimated their foe, mainly on the basis of racial stereotypes. In the 1930s, Japanese forces were seen as fanatical warriors who could not match the discipline and courage of Western troops. One popular myth was that the short average height of the Japanese and the shape of their eyes made them poor fighters who could not aim weapons properly. Even after Pearl Harbor, an assumption remained that Allied troops would easily dominate in land fighting.

As a consequence, Allied defenses and training were neglected. The Allies also failed to appreciate Japanese advances in military technology and training. They particularly misjudged Japan's carrier airpower. The Allies paid a high price for their racist thinking. It was only when they started to respect their enemy that they began to work out how to defeat them.

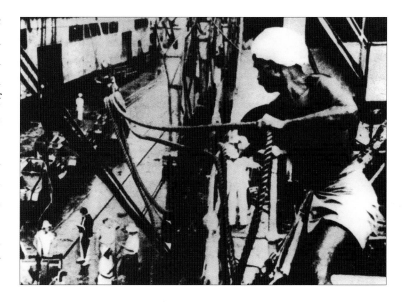

▼ U.S. tanks are unloaded at the docks of Rangoon at the start of the ill-fated Allied defense of Burma.

over 600 miles (1,000km) in nine weeks. The first Allied units entered India on May 19. They were weakened by aerial attack, ground combat, and disease. Burcorps had lost a total of 13,000 men in Burma, compared to 5,000 Japanese casualties.

In only six months the Japanese had won a stunning series of victories in Southeast Asia. The Dutch and British colonial empires had collapsed. In air, sea, and land warfare the Imperial Japanese forces had proved manifestly superior to their enemies.

◄ Smoke billows from burning oil refineries near the docks at Rangoon after the Allies retreated from the Burmese capital in March 1942.

123

THE FALL OF THE PHILIPPINES

The capture of the Philippines was a crucial part of Japan's strategy to secure an empire in the Southwest Pacific and to remove U.S. power from the region. Hours after Pearl Harbor, Japan attacked the islands.

The Philippines are a group of some 7,000 islands in the Pacific. They were of great strategic importance because they lay between Japan on one hand and Southeast Asia and the islands of the Dutch East Indies (Indonesia) on the other. Those territories were rich in resources that the Japanese needed, such as oil. With the region under its control, Japan could then move southeast to secure bases on New Guinea and the Solomon Islands. Japanese possession of the Solomons would limit communications between Australia and the United States. That would hamper Allied operations in the Southwest Pacific.

A U.S. colony

The Philippines became a U.S. colony in 1898, at the end of the Spanish–American War. The U.S. Navy began to use Manila Bay. Located off Luzon,

the largest and most northerly of the Philippine islands, the bay was one of the finest fleet anchorages in Asia.

By the mid-1930s, however, the U.S. Navy was short of funds. There were few ships at the naval base. The United States had also stopped building fortifications in the Philippines under the 1922 Washington Naval Treaty. The treaty was intended to reduce tensions in the Pacific. As a result, only the islands near the entrance to Manila Bay were well protected.

In any case, the U.S. government planned to withdraw from the Philippines. It could not defend a colony 3,000 miles (5,000km) from the nearest U.S. base on Hawaii. It gave the Filipinos some self-government in 1935, and promised full independence in 1946. In the meantime, defense of the islands would be handed over gradually to the Philippine government, despite its limited resources.

Growing Japanese power

Meanwhile Japanese power grew, isolating the Philippines. To the north Japan had colonized Formosa (Taiwan). To the east, it had taken over the Palau, Caroline, and Marshall islands as part of the Versailles Treaty of 1919. Japan's possessions east of the Philippines formed a chain broken only by two U.S.-controlled islands: Guam and Wake. In 1939 Japan struck west, across the South China Sea. Japanese troops occupied the island of Hainan in January. In July 1941 they entered southern French Indochina (modern Vietnam). By mid-1941, the Philippines were threatened on three sides.

▼ Japanese troops land on the island of Corregidor on May 6, 1942. Corregidor, the last U.S. stronghold in the Philippines, fell to the Japanese later in the day.

U.S response

As diplomatic relations with Japan deteriorated, military and political leaders in Washington, D.C., decided to reinforce the Philippines. They rushed to create defenses to counter a Japanese attack that was starting to seem inevitable.

In July 1941, U.S. leaders appointed General Douglas MacArthur to head a new command in the region. It was named U.S. Army Forces in the Far East (USAFFE). MacArthur was a famed but controversial commander who had retired from the U.S. Army. He was in the Philippines acting as a military adviser to the president, Manuel Quezon. To defend some 115,000 square miles (300,000 sq km) of territory, MacArthur had only 12,000 men of the Philippine Division, 4,000

men of the Philippine Army, and 20,000 Filipino "irregulars," trained militia. The number of recruits were significantly higher by December.

The Philippine Division was led by General Jonathan Wainwright. It comprised the U.S. Army-trained

▲ Filipino Scouts load a 10-inch gun on a U.S ship. The U.S.-trained Scouts were key to defending the Philippines.

Douglas MacArthur (1880–1964)

After graduating at the top of his class from the U.S. Military Academy at West Point in 1903, Douglas MacArthur served his first posting in the Philippines. His career advanced rapidly. By 1913, he was a member of the U.S. Army's general staff. After World War I, he became superintendent of West Point. He was again posted to the Philippines, but returned to Washington in 1930 to serve as the chief of staff. Although he retired in 1937, MacArthur was recalled in July 1941 to command the U.S. Army Forces in the Far East. Having said that he could defend the Philippines, MacArthur took

▲ General MacArthur was appointed head of forces in the Southwest Pacific in 1942.

Japan's invasion as a blow to his integrity. On Corregidor he made it clear that he was willing to fight on. However, the Allies needed a supreme commander in Southeast Asia to organize the fight against the Japanese. Roosevelt ordered MacArthur to leave the Philippines. He left for Australia on March 12, 1942. After a week-long journey, he arrived to tell reporters: "I have come through and I shall return." His men fought on for another two months. "I shall return" became a catchphrase for MacArthur, and a public declaration of his zeal to liberate the Philippines, which colored his view of strategic aims throughout the war.

Philippine Scouts, led by U.S. officers, together with the only U.S. Army unit in the Philippines, the 31st Infantry Regiment, which numbered some 2,100 men.

War Plan Orange

MacArthur inherited a defense plan for the Philippines known as War Plan Orange. It had last been updated in April 1941. The plan recommended defending only Manila Bay. The U.S. garrison in Manila, the capital, would withdraw to the Bataan Peninsula and the fortified island of Corregidor. The plan reflected Japan's strength and the weakness of the islands' defenses. U.S. military commanders had decided that most of the Philippines must be sacrificed if the Japanese attacked.

MacArthur, however, wanted to cancel War Plan Orange. He urged his superiors to adopt an ambitious program to build up the Philippines as a stronghold of U.S. power. MacArthur called for some 200,000 men. Because he had only limited naval resources available, he also called for the creation of a huge air force in the islands. Mac-Arthur wanted hundreds of the new Boeing B-17 bomber, which was later known as the "Flying Fortress." The bombers would to be able to attack Japanese bases on Formosa and any approaching invasion fleet.

U.S. chief of staff George C. Marshall gave top priority to reinforcing and equipping USAFFE. MacArthur hoped that the program could be in place by 1942. He did not take into account the logistical problems of building up and supporting large forces so far from the United States, however. A shortage of cargo space on military ships delayed shipments across the Pacific.

The U.S. Far East Air Force

MacArthur's plan to gain air superiority had influential support. Senior officers in the United States Army Air Force (USAAF) were eager to prove the value of high-altitude bombing. By the late summer of 1941, all new U.S. warplanes not earmarked for Britain and Russia in their fight against Germany were scheduled to go to the Philippines. By the middle of 1942, MacArthur would have four bomber groups of 314 aircraft and two fighter groups of 260 aircraft. The new force, the U.S. Far East Air Force, would be led by General Lewis H. Brereton. He arrived on Luzon in late 1941.

As warplanes arrived on Luzon, however, so warships left. The U.S. Navy's small Asiatic Fleet was

▼ U.S. defense of the Philippines was concentrated around Manila Bay on the northern island of Luzon.

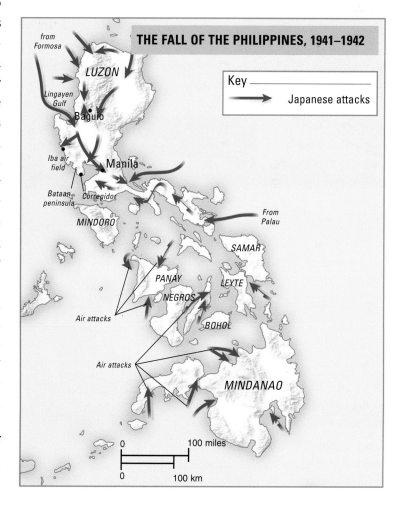

THE FALL OF THE PHILIPPINES, 1941–1942

from Formosa

LUZON

Lingayen Gulf

Baguio

Iba air field

Manila

Bataan peninsula

Corregidor

MINDORO

From Palau

SAMAR

PANAY

LEYTE

NEGROS

Air attacks

BOHOL

Air attacks

MINDANAO

Key

→ Japanese attacks

0   100 miles

0   100 km

The myth of invincibility

Before the fall of Singapore, many British and U.S. planners believed that Japanese soldiers would be too physically weak to beat Western troops. In fact, the troops of the Imperial Japanese Army were battle-hardened veterans. They had learned a strict code of warfare. Their officers had studied at jungle-warfare school. They learned concealment and how to infiltrate enemy flanks. In December 1941, when the Japanese attacked in Southeast Asia, the Allies were unable to withstand their offensives. Another myth soon developed that the Japanese were jungle-fighting supermen. The view began to change only in late 1942. By then, the Allies had won victories in New Guinea and on Guadalcanal. Allied troops now underwent jungle training and new units were created, such as U.S. Marine Raider battalions.

dispersed from Luzon south to Mindanao and to Borneo, in the Dutch East Indies, to avoid air attack. The naval presence on Luzon was reduced to a dozen patrol boats, although there were still 29 submarines, 32 patrol aircraft, and the 4th Marine Regiment.

A force to be reckoned with

By December 1941, MacArthur's army had grown in size to more than 19,000 U.S. soldiers and 12,000 Philippine Scouts. A further 100,000 Filipino militia were under training. MacArthur organized his troops in four groups: Northern Luzon Forces, under Wainwright; Southern Luzon Forces, under General George Parker; a Reserve Force to protect Manila; and a force to defend the southern Philippines.

MacArthur's air force now had about 270 aircraft. They included 100 modern Curtiss P-40 Warhawk fighters and 35 B-17s. He was expecting 128 more bombers by February. A convoy was

▲ Japanese soldiers were disciplined, skilled, and prepared to fight to the death.

▶ Douglas MacArthur (right) and General Jonathan Wainwright discuss the defense of Luzon.

also due to bring another 70 fighters, an artillery brigade, hundreds of vehicles, and thousands of tons of supplies.

The potential of the growing air force was limited, however. The islands lacked airfields and maintenance facilities. They also had poor antiaircraft defenses. That left aircraft on the ground vulnerable to attack. Despite such problems, MacArthur estimated that he would be able to meet any invasion by summer 1942.

The Japanese prepare to strike

MacArthur did not have that long. By November 1941, the Japanese had moved an invasion force of General Masaharu Homma's Fourteenth Army from China to Formosa. On December 4, a heavily defended convoy left Formosa carrying 43,000 men. Meanwhile the Japanese had assembled a powerful force of 500 aircraft on Formosa. They planned a surprise attack on Luzon to destroy Brereton's air force on the ground and clear the way for a landing.

The first Japanese air raids were scheduled for dawn on December 8. Given the time difference, that would be only three or four hours after the attack on Pearl Harbor, some 3,000 miles (4,800 km) away. However, heavy fog over Formosa prevented the aircraft from taking off.

▼ Japanese troops pass through a burned out Filipino town, one of many settlements wiped out in the fighting to conquer the islands.

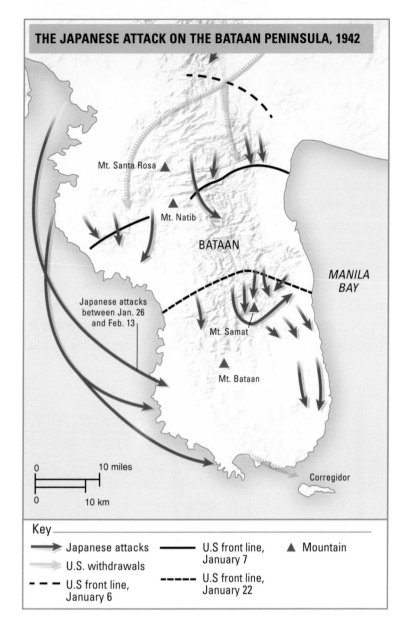

THE JAPANESE ATTACK ON THE BATAAN PENINSULA, 1942

Mt. Santa Rosa ▲

▲ Mt. Natib

BATAAN

MANILA
BAY

Japanese attacks
between Jan. 26
and Feb. 13

Mt. Samat

▲ Mt. Bataan

0   10 miles

0   10 km

Corregidor

Key

→ Japanese attacks   — U.S front line, January 7   ▲ Mountain

→ U.S. withdrawals

– – – U.S front line, January 6   – – – – U.S front line, January 22

▲ The Bataan
Peninsula was
mountainous and
covered with dense
jungle. The only
escape route was to
the tiny fortified
island of Corregidor.

Devastating aerial attack

By 3:30 A.M., news of the attack on
Pearl Harbor had reached MacArthur.
He ordered his troops to battle
stations. It was only much later in the
morning that he sent a reconnaissance
flight to Formosa, however. By the
time he authorized a bombing raid on
the Japanese bases at lunchtime, it was
too late. The fog over Formosa had
cleared hours earlier. Some 200 Japanese warplanes were now approaching
the B-17 base at Clark Field, 75 miles
(120km) north of Manila.

The Japanese caught 18 U.S. B-17s on
the gound and a number of P-40
fighters just taking off. Within an hour,
they had destroyed all the B-17s and
more than half of the P-40s. Elsewhere
the Japanese launched air raids against
Iba Field in northwest Luzon; Baguio,
the so-called summer capital of the
Philippines; and Mindanao. By the end
of the day, the U.S. Far East Air Force
had lost half of its aircraft.

Japanese raids began again next day.
Within 24 hours they had destroyed
seven more airfields and a naval base.
Brereton withdrew his remaining B-
17s to Mindanao to organize attacks
on Japanese convoys off Luzon's
northern coast.

Japanese troop landings

That same day, Japanese troops landed
on the north and northwest coasts of
Luzon. They were small forces sent to
capture airfields, but their effect on
the militia was devastating: The
Filipinos fell back in confusion. Their
retreat ended MacArthur's hope of
defeating the Japanese on the beaches.

The main Japanese landing took
place on December 22. Homma's 48th
Division came ashore at Lingayen
Gulf, 120 miles (195km) northwest of
Manila. Striking inland, it cut off the
northern part of Luzon and began to
advance on Manila and Bataan.

Withdrawal to Bataan

MacArthur ordered his troops to
withdraw into Bataan. On December
23, a second Japanese division landed
at Lamon Bay, south of Manila. It
advanced north. MacArthur's forces
were now cut off on two sides.

Communications began to collapse
as U.S. and Filipino units streamed

back toward the Bataan Peninsula. The command structure was kept in place by Wainwright and the commander of the Southern Luzon Force, George Parker. Parker fought a staged withdrawal. Homma held off some of his forces, because he thought he would have to fight for Manila. Instead, on December 26, MacArthur declared Manila an open city. He moved his headquarters onto the island of Corregidor and told his commanders that Plan Orange was now in effect.

Trapped on Bataan

The Japanese entered Manila on January 2, 1942. On January, 5 U.S. and Filippino forces completed their withdrawal into Bataan. About 80,000 troops and more than 25,000 civilians were trapped on a mountainous peninsula covered in jungle. Bataan was 14 miles (22km) wide and 30 miles (45km) long. It had no escape route.

▲ A landing craft full of Japanese soldiers approaches the burning city of Manila late in December 1941.

◀ Wearing British-syle helmets that were replaced later in the war, U.S. troops survey the damage caused by a Japanese air raid on the Philippine town of Paranaque in December 1941.

Corregidor

The island of Corregidor lies about 25 miles (40km) west of Manila and 2 miles (3.2km) east of the tip of the Bataan Peninsula. It covers an area of 3.5 square miles (9sqkm) and partly blocks the western entrance to Manila Bay. The United States began to fortify Corregidor as early as 1905. It was part of a chain of defenses to protect the bay and its anchorage from naval attack.

The U.S. Army transformed the rocky island into a stronghold they dubbed Fort Mills. By 1941, the defenses consisted of 14 gun batteries concentrated on the western side of the island. To the east rose Malinta Hill. An underground headquarters and hospital complex was built into the hill in 1938. Known as the Malinta Tunnel, it was 1,400 feet (425m) long and 30 feet (9m) wide. It had 25 secondary tunnels. East of the tunnel, the land rose to a small airfield known as Kindley Field. Elsewhere on the surface there were barracks, a parade ground, a power plant, and two docks. There was even a golf course and an electric railroad. The peacetime garrison was about 6,000 men.

▲ Bombs explode on Fort Drum, a fortified island defending Corregidor, in spring 1942.

In their rapid withdrawal, U.S. and Filipino troops had left behind most of their equipment. They had very limited supplies in Bataan. As a result of MacArthur's plan to defend all of the Philippines, food, ammunition, weapons, and medical supplies were widely dispersed. United States and Filipino troops in Bataan were on half-rations; within weeks they were eating mules.

United States and Filipino forces set up defenses across the neck of the peninsula. The west was defended by I Corps under Wainwright, and the east was held by II Corps under Parker. Between them lay Mount Natib, over 4,000 feet (1,220m) high. A second line was set up 8 miles (13km) south, in front of two more high points.

The campaign for Bataan

Japanese forces were weakened after their advance. Homma had suffered nearly 7,000 casualties, and a malaria epidemic had left 13,000 men sick. A division also had been transferred to the Dutch East Indies. He was reinforced by only one inexperienced brigade. Still, Homma launched his first attack on Bataan on January 9. He had promised that he could conquer the Philippines in 45 days. He would lose face if his campaign stalled.

MacArthur remained confident that his troops could hold out. On January 10, he left Corregidor to inspect the Bataan defenses. It was his only visit to the peninsula: His preference for staying on Corregidor led his troops to nickname him "Dugout Doug."

Bataan Death March

The Japanese took more than 12,000 American and 60,000 Filipino prisoners on Bataan. They were to be held at a camp more than 100 miles (160km) north. The Allies had been on starvation rations for months. They were exhausted and sick from malaria and dysentery. The Japanese forced them to march all day, without food or water, in 95°F (35°C) heat. Prisoners who fell behind were executed. What became known as the Bataan Death March began on April 10 and lasted a week.

The survivors were packed into airless railcars for an eight-hour journey. They were then marched another 8 miles (13km) to the camp. Of the 72,000 prisoners, some 18,000 died. General Homma, the Japanese commander who ordered the march, was arrested after the war. He was tried, found guilty of murder, and executed in April 1946.

Japanese progress

The first line of U.S. defenses held until January 15, when the Japanese found a route over Mount Natib. They attacked the flank of Parker's II Corps. They then infiltrated Wainwright's position from behind. The U.S. forces withdrew to the second defensive line on January 22. At the same time, Homma attempted three amphibious landings on the west coast of the peninsula behind the U.S. and Filipino positions. All three landings were thrown back with heavy losses.

▲ American troops await their fate after surrendering to the Japanese in Bataan on April 9, 1942.

▼ American prisoners leaving Bataan carry sick comrades in improvised stretchers.

▶ A Japanese assault team uses a flame thrower against a U.S. position during the attack on Corregidor.

The second defensive line held, but by the end of February the Bataan defenders were on starvation rations. Most were suffering from malnutrition, malaria, or dysentery. The U.S. government told MacArthur that his troops could not be rescued. Neither could they surrender, however. The government wanted to show a sign of U.S. determination to fight. At the same time, it did not want to risk having such an important commander as MacArthur captured by the enemy. He was evacuated to Australia on March 12, making a famous promise to the Filipinos: "I shall return." Wainwright took command of U.S. forces in the Philippines.

Meanwhile Homma received two new divisions of troops. His strengthened forces launched a fresh attack on April 3. Exhausted, the defenders finally broke. Wainwright withdrew to Corregidor to organize what few defenses remained in the Philippines. He left General Edward King to hold out as long as he could in Bataan. On April 9, despite a radio call from MacArthur ordering Wainwright to launch a counterattack, King accepted the hopelessness of the situation and surrendered his forces.

Eyewitness

❝ By the time we got to about the third day [of the Bataan Death March], we knew that they [the Japanese] were just hoping all of us would die. Hell, they hadn't even given us a drink of water. By then the people really started to fall out. A guy would jump into a ditch for a little bit of water. They'd run a bayonet through you, or shoot you, or hit you in the head with a shovel, whatever way they could to dispose of you. Behind us they had a cordon of tanks. If you stopped, those tanks would ground you into the dirt. The Japs also had this group we called the Buzzard Squad. They killed those that couldn't keep up. ❞

John Emerick, U.S. serviceman,
Bataan, Philippines

Corregidor stands alone

Corregidor now stood alone in the Philippines. Survivors from Bataan had increased its garrison to more than 11,000. Water, food, and medical supplies were running out. Homma could have waited and starved the defenders into submission. His pride drove him to take the island by force, however. Corregidor had been under air attack since the end of March. Homma now ordered an artillery bombardment from Bataan. On May 1, a huge artillery barrage wrecked what few defensive positions were left on the surface. Only underground defenses remained. During the night of May 3–4, a U.S. submarine arrived to remove the last evacuees.

Wainwright stayed on Corregidor. Early on May 6, Japanese troops and three tanks landed on the eastern end of the island. The fighting moved west,

around the entrance to the Malinta Tunnel, the U.S. headquarters. The defenders held the Japanese back until midday. Wainwright was concerned for the 1,000 wounded in the Malinta Tunnel. He surrendered.

Homma forced Wainwright to order all U.S. and Filipino forces in the islands to surrender. He threatened to kill the Corregidor garrison if he did not. On May 8 Wainwright broadcast the order across the Philippines. It was a humiliating end to a brave defense.

▲ Japanese soldiers celebrate their conquest of the Philippine islands in April 1942.

◄ General Jonathan Wainwright broadcasts news of the U.S. surrender on May 8, 1942. He later received the Medal of Honor for his part in the defense of Bataan and Corregidor.

NORTH AFRICA: ALLIED VICTORY IN THE DESERT

War continued to rage in the deserts of North Africa in 1942, as Axis and Allied troops fought to control the region. The fighting had seesawed back and forth, but by winter German forces were in retreat.

The Allies seemed to have the advantage in North Africa at the beginning of 1942. After almost a year of fighting in harsh desert conditions, they had forced Axis troops to retreat from the Libyan–Egyptian border west deep into Libya.

Rommel seizes the offensive

In January 1942, however, the German commander Major General Erwin Rommel prepared a new offensive. In the early weeks of January, German supply convoys got through to Tripoli, the Libyan capital. They brought Rommel fresh troops, tanks, fuel, and ammunition. With his forces strengthened, Rommel struck on January 21, while General Claude Auchinleck, commander in chief of the Allied Middle Eastern Command, was still preparing for a British attack.

Using antitank guns, tanks, and infantry in close coordination, German and Italian forces proved unstoppable. They pushed east along the Libyan coast, capturing key cities. By February 6, Rommel had advanced more than 400 miles (644km) east through Libya toward Egypt.

The British retreat to the Gazala Line

Auchinleck's army retreated to the Gazala Line. This defensive line stretched 50 miles (80km) south through the desert from the coastal village of Gazala. It comprised minefields and fortified strongpoints. Securely dug in, Auchinleck began to prepare for a June offensive.

Again, however, Rommel beat him to it. On May 26, Italian troops attacked the northern part of the Gazala Line, while combined German and Italian troops swept south. They planned to drive around the bottom of the line at Bir Hakeim then strike north to the coast. They wanted to encircle the Allies on the Gazala Line and to capture the port of Tobruk. Tobruk was heavily garrisoned and a key supply depot.

Rommel was unable to repeat the lightning advances of January, however. In the south his troops met determined Allied units armed with newly supplied U.S. Grant tanks. At the same time, supply shortages threatened the German advance in the north. Rommel shifted his focus to the center of the Gazala Line.

Rommel launched an assault against the British 150 Brigade. The ensuing battle was fought in a large oval-shaped depression that became known as the Cauldron. By June 1, Rommel's forces had destroyed 150 Brigade and established defensive positions, despite attacks from British aircraft and armor. German antitank and panzer fire inflicted heavy losses on the Allies. By June 6, the Allies had lost 230 fighting vehicles and four regiments of artillery, and 4,000 soldiers had been captured.

On June 11, Rommel broke out of the Cauldron and swept south. He captured Bir Hakeim, the southern end of the Gazala Line. He then swung north.

▼ British troops under fire at the first Battle of El Alamein, Egypt, in July 1942. The battle halted Rommel's advance, though in doing so the British Eighth Army incurred 13,000 casualties.

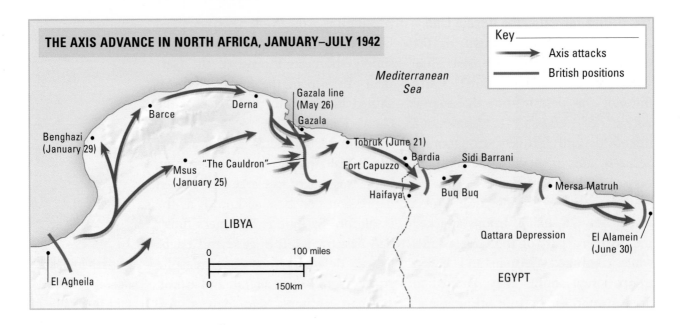

THE AXIS ADVANCE IN NORTH AFRICA, JANUARY–JULY 1942

Key
→ Axis attacks
— British positions

Mediterranean Sea

Gazala line (May 26)
Gazala
Derna
Barce
Benghazi (January 29)
Msus (January 25)
"The Cauldron"
Tobruk (June 21)
Bardia
Sidi Barrani
Fort Capuzzo
Haifaya
Buq Buq
Mersa Matruh
El Agheila
LIBYA
Qattara Depression
El Alamein (June 30)
EGYPT

0   100 miles
0   150km

▲ The Axis troops made significant advances in Africa between January and July 1942.

The Allies retreat

The Eighth Army—the Allied fighting force in North Africa—went into full retreat. As it withdrew into Egypt, it left Tobruk stranded. On June 21, after 24 hours of artillery barrage, the port and its valuable stocks of food and supplies fell to Rommel.

Perturbed by the British defeats, Auchinleck took direct control of the Eighth Army on June 25. He instructed it to gather on a new defensive line. The line stretched 30 miles (48km) south from the Egyptian coastal village of El Alamein to the Qattara Depression. Here soft sand made movement for

Hitler's failure to take Malta

The island of Malta, in the Mediterranean between Italy and Libya, was of immense strategic importance. A British possession, it was a crucial base for Allied attacks on Axis supply lines between Italy and North Africa. The attacks inflicted such serious damage that in 1941 Hitler ordered the Luftwaffe (German air force) to bombard the island into submission. What followed was one of the most prolonged bombing campaigns of the war. Malta's 300,000 citizens had to live in a network of caves, and suffered hunger and privations as the island was cut off from supplies. Against all odds, however, the Axis forces were unable to weaken the island's defenses sufficiently to attempt an invasion. That enabled Allied attacks to continue to decimate Axis shipping in 1942 and 1943.

▼ Army antiaircraft gunners in their positions as a destroyer enters Grand Habour, Malta, in January, 1942.

vehicles difficult. The line was just 65 miles (105km) west of the key British naval base in the Egyptian city of Alexandria. With Hitler pressing for the Axis capture of Egypt, El Alamein became the scene of three major battles.

The first Battle of El Alamein
On July 1, 1942, Rommel attacked the Allied line, beginning the first battle of El Alamein. His panzer divisions met stiff resistance. Rommel was also short of supplies. His nearest source of provisions was Tobruk, 250 miles (400km) away. Allied aircraft constantly bombed the narrow coast road that linked the port to the front line. By July 3, Rommel had only 26 tanks left. Allied counterattacks forced him to call off the offensive on July 22.

The British possessed Egyptian ports to their rear, and could rely on U.S.

supplies. Even so, their forces had proved unable to match the Germans in armored warfare, and the front line was dangerously close to Alexandria.

However, the British prime minister, Winston Churchill, was eager to strike a blow against the weakened Axis forces. He felt that Auchinleck was being too cautious. In August Churchill replaced Auchinleck as commander in chief of the Middle Eastern Command with General Harold Alexander. He also made General Bernard Montgomery commander of the Eighth Army.

The Battle of Alam Halfa
At the same time Rommel had finally begun to receive supplies and reinforcements, including an elite German parachute brigade and an Italian division. He again seized the initiative. On August 30, he launched a second

▲ British troops defending the Gazala Line fire a 25-pounder gun on June 18, 1942. The weapon was one of the best field guns of the war. It fired 25-pound shells—hence its name—and a variety of projectiles, including high explosives and armor-piercing shells.

Free French forces

After France's military collapse in June 1940, General Charles de Gaulle, a French army officer in London, formed the Free French Forces to fight against Hitler. The Allies recognized de Gaulle as the leader of the Free French government in exile. At first his force was small, drawn mainly from French citizens living in Britain and French colonies in Africa, but they assisted in British campaigns in 1941 and 1942. Free French forces fought very effectively at Gazala in June 1942, for example. De Gaulle's forces were strengthened after Operation Torch, the Allied invasion of Northwest Africa in November 1943. Thousands of Vichy troops defected to join them. About 100,000 Free French soldiers took part in the Allied invasion of Italy in 1943, and about 300,000 in the Normandy invasion in June 1944. The Free French First Army was given the honor of liberating the French capital, Paris, in August 1944.

▼ Soldiers of the 1st Free French Brigade stationed on the Gazala Line.

offensive against the El Alamein line in what became known as the Battle of Alam Halfa.

Rommel ordered diversionary attacks on the line in the north, while he advanced in the south to seize the Alam Halfa Ridge. The ridge lay behind Allied defenses. If Axis troops could seize it, they would be able to cut off the Eighth Army. Rommel's progress was slowed by minefields, however, and aerial bombardment. His troops were also running short of fuel and ammunition. They had to withdraw to positions just 6 miles (10 km) east of their starting point.

The Second Battle of El Alamein

Churchill urged an immediate attack on Rommel's troops. Instead, Montgomery took time to methodically plan a new offensive. He launched his assault on the night of October 23. The ensuing engagement, known as the Second Battle of El Alamein, was a turning point for the Allies not only in the North African campaign but in the wider war.

Owing to superior supply lines, the Allies had twice the men and resources of the Germans and Italians. Montgomery commanded 104,000 troops, 2,311 artillery pieces, 530 aircraft, and 1,029 tanks. The tanks included new, highly effective U.S.-built Sherman and Grant tanks. He faced 50,000 Axis troops, 489 tanks, 1,219 artillery pieces, and only 350 aircraft. Rommel himself had also been forced to leave North Africa to recover from illness.

Montgomery's relentless assaults

Montgomery's offensive, Operation Lightfoot, began with a massive artillery barrage on the German line. Meanwhile, infantry attacked the German defenses in the north and the south. They spearheaded an advance through the huge minefields laid by the Germans. Engineers followed them clearing passages wide enough for tanks to pass through. Under heavy fire, however, the Allied advance became bogged down in a bloody slugging match. Meanwhile, Hitler ordered Rommel back to take command of the front on October 25.

Montgomery ordered Australian units to push north to the coast on October 28. Again the Germans put up a dogged defense. Montgomery renewed the attack with British and New Zealand units in Operation Supercharge on November 2. His offensives succeeded in exhausting Rommel's troops. The Afrika Korps had lost 7,000 men and had fewer than 50 tanks. The Allies had 600 tanks and total air superiority.

On the evening of November 2, Rommel ordered his troops to retreat. Hitler ordered that they stand firm, but in the face of the overpowering Allied forces Rommel continued his

Eyewitness

❝ The battle commenced with a huge barrage, which for those days was tremendous. The sky was lit and fires of burning petrol dumps littered the desert. The engineers, who had moved in first to clear the enemy minefields, had made a path for us to pass through in our trucks. It was such a clear night you could actually see the bombs dropping from a lone Stuka raider.... Later, in the morning, we had numbers of Italian and German soldiers obviously shell shocked ... giving themselves up.... It was a shock to realize how young these soldiers were, and for me it was an indication of how bad things were for the Axis armies that they could send such youngsters into battle. ❞

Thomas Arthur Murray, British soldier
Second Battle of El Alamein, October 23–24, 1942

withdrawal. It eventually took him all the way along the coast to Tunisia.

America enters the desert war

Throughout 1942, the Allies debated what action to take against Germany. The Soviet leader Joseph Stalin urged the British and Americans to launch offensives in Western Europe to divert the Germans from their invasion of the

▼ The Eighth Army's Sherman tanks advance through the North African desert.

Field Marshal Viscount Montgomery of El Alamein (1887–1976)

Bernard Law Montgomery is one of Britain's most celebrated commanders. He began his army career in 1908, served in World War I, and by 1938 was a major general. Appointed commander of the British Eighth Army in in August 1942, he turned the tide of the war in North Africa with his victory at the Battle of El Alamein in October.

After the Axis surrender in North Africa, Montgomery led the Eighth Army in the invasion of Sicily in July 1943 and the Allied push through Italy. In early 1944,

▲ Montgomery wears a hat with the regimental badges of the Eighth Army units.

he took charge of the Twenty-First Army Group for the invasion of mainland Europe. He won victories in northern France, Belgium, the Netherlands, and northern Germany, before accepting the surrender of the German northern armies on May 4, 1945.

Montgomery was renowned for thorough planning, careful preparation, and caution. His approach and self-confidence inspired respect from his troops, but sometimes irritated other Allied commanders.

Soviet Union. George C. Marshall, chief of staff of the U.S. Army, and Dwight D. Eisenhower, deputy chief of the U.S. War Plans Division, wanted to attack occupied Europe through France.

The British, however, argued that Allied forces were not ready for such an attack. They felt that a second strike on the Germans in North Africa would be more likely to succeed. Such an offensive would assist the British forces fighting in the region and would force Hitler to divert troops from the Soviet Union. If successful, the offensive would secure Allied control of Africa. It would also open up the possibility of attacking Hitler's "Fortress Europe" from the south. After lengthy discussions, preparations for the offensive began in July.

▶ German soldiers captured by the British army in the desert in 1942 wait to be taken to a prisoner-of-war camp.

Operation Torch

Codenamed Operation Torch, the combined campaign was under U.S. control, with Eisenhower in overall command. The Allies planned a three-prong invasion. A Western Task Force of 24,500 U.S. troops would land near Casablanca, on the Atlantic coast of Morocco; a Central Task Force of 18,500 U.S. soldiers would land at Oran, on the western Algerian coast; and an Eastern Task Force of 43,000 U.S. and British troops would land at the Algerian capital, Algiers. The invasion forces would then move east to trap Rommel and meet up with the Eighth Army.

The success of Operation Torch would to some extent rely on the reaction of French troops stationed in Northwest Africa. Algeria, Tunisia, and most of Morocco were French colonies. After Hitler's defeat of France in June 1940, the colonies owed allegiance to the Vichy government, which collaborated with the Germans. The Allies tried to persuade Vichy French officials in North Africa not to resist the landings, but their efforts were hampered by the need for secrecy to achieve strategic surprise. Several French commanders agreed, but the situation remained unpredictable.

The Allied invasions begin

Operation Torch began on November 8, 1942. The Eastern Task Force secured Algiers with little resistance from the French. In a simultaneous landing at Oran, the Central Task

▼ U.S. troops bring ashore a gun on November 9, 1942, as part of the joint U.S.-British invasion of northwest Africa. British soldiers—some 23,000 of whom took part in Operation Torch—can be seen in the background.

143

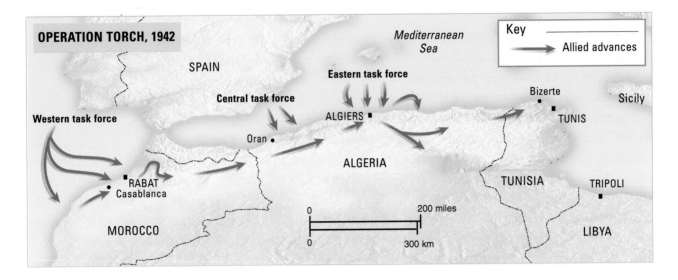

OPERATION TORCH, 1942

SPAIN

Mediterranean Sea

Key
→ Allied advances

Eastern task force

Central task force

Western task force

Bizerte

Sicily

ALGIERS

TUNIS

Oran

ALGERIA

RABAT
Casablanca

TUNISIA

TRIPOLI

MOROCCO

0 ____ 200 miles
0 ____ 300 km

LIBYA

▲ Operation Torch was a combined Allied operation to clear North Africa of Axis forces.

▼ A French soldier makes friends with British and U.S. servicemen in Algiers.

Force faced more resistance from French troops. The Western Task Force, led by General George H. Patton, had the toughest task; it took them four days of ground, naval, and air combat to subdue French forces in Morocco.

Admiral Jean-François Darlan, commander in chief of Vichy French military forces, was in Algiers when the Allies invaded. He ordered a cease-fire and switched allegiance. The next day,

November 11, Hitler ordered German and Italian troops to occupy Vichy France, bringing the southern part of the country under his direct control. Darlan and General Alphonse Juin, commander of French troops in Morocco, now committed their forces to actively side with the Allies.

The battle for Tunisia

Operation Torch led Hitler to order reinforcements to join Rommel's previously undersupplied forces. In November, 20,000 German troops, along with equipment including Tiger and Panzer Mark IV tanks, were shipped to Tunisia from Sicily, southern Italy. By early 1943, Axis forces in Tunisia numbered 250,000 men. Between November 2, 1942, and January 23, 1943, Rommel had retreated more than 1,000 miles (1,600km) from El Alamein to Mareth in Tunisia.

Meanwhile the Allied forces of Operation Torch pushed east along the North African coast toward Tunisia. On November 25, the Allied First Army began an offensive to seize the country. Progress was slow, however, and the newly reinforced Axis troops repelled the assault.

Afrika Korps

The Deutsches Afrika Korps (German Africa Corps) directed German mechanized divisions in Egypt and Libya in the first half of 1941. The name Afrika Korps is also often used more generally to describe the German forces in North Africa.

Major General Erwin Rommel took charge of the newly formed Korps on February 6, 1941, and embarked on a daring offensive against the British with a small but well equipped force. His Korps was bolstered by the arrival of the 15th Panzer Division in early summer.

When German forces in Africa were reorganized in August 1941, Rommel became head of the new Panzer Group Afrika, which included the Afrika Korps, additional German units, and two corps of Italian units. Rommel pushed the British back into Egypt, but by summer 1942 his forces were desperate for supplies and greatly understrength. He had fewer than 50 tanks and 71 guns. Hitler, whose main priority was the Germans' southern offensive in the Soviet Union, refused Rommel's requests for more resources.

Panzer Group Afrika was defeated at El Alamein and forced into a long retreat by the better supplied British Eighth Army. After the Allied invasion of northwest Africa on November 8, 1942, the German high command set up two new forces in Tunisia. However, it was too late to avoid defeat. Rommel was recalled from Africa on March 6, 1943. The decimated Axis forces surrendered on May 13.

The front line in Tunisia

By January 1, 1943, the front line in Tunisia ran from Sedjenane in the north to Rommel's strong defensive line at Mareth. The Allied front comprised three parts, with British troops in the north, French troops in the center, and U.S. troops in the south. Montgomery's Eighth Army continued to bear down on Rommel's Afrika Korps from the southeast.

A series of German counterattacks in January managed to strengthen the Axis position. The next month Rommel struck west at the U.S. forces. He intended to push north to cut off, or at least drive into retreat, a large part of the Allied force and to seize the Allied base at Tebessa. On February 14, his forces headed north and seized Sidi bou Zid, inflicting heavy losses on U.S. armor. Rommel's troops then thrust south to capture Gasfa. On February 18, the two forces converged and captured the Kasserine Pass, in the mountains of western Tunisia. Again, heavy losses were inflicted on its U.S. defenders.

From this point, however, the German offensive began to crumble, and Rommel's commanders began to disagree. On February 21, the British

▲ An Afrika Korps machine-gun team lies in wait. Their 7.92mm MG34 could fire at a rate of up to 900 rounds a minute.

The Battle of Kasserine Pass (February 19–25, 1943)

The Kasserine Pass through the mountains of western Tunisia was the setting for the first large-scale battle between U.S. troops and Axis forces. It resulted in a rapid defeat for the inexperienced U.S. soldiers.

U.S. troops had retreated to the pass after being attacked in their forward position. Rommel struck them on February 19, 1943, and in full force the next day. The battle-hardened German troops broke through U.S. lines within minutes. The U.S. response was hampered by poor command structures and communication lines; field commanders radioed their high command for permission to counterattack. As Rommel's forces surged northwest, morale among U.S. troops collapsed. The U.S. II Corps suffered about 10,000 men killed, wounded, or captured, and lost about 300 tanks.

Rommel looked set to seize Tebassa and cut off more U.S. troops, but he had overextended himself. Low on supplies and facing resistance from combined U.S., French, and British forces, he retreated to the Mareth Line. By February 25, the Allies had retaken the Kasserine Pass. The battle had taught the U.S. forces some costly lessons. A new commander was introduced, General George S. Patton. Changes were also made to the U.S. command structure, training, and equipment.

▲ Captured U.S. troops sit on the ground after their defeat at the Battle of Kasserine Pass in February 1943

First Army succeeded in halting the advance. Two days later Rommel gave the order for a general withdrawal.

Rommel now planned a strike against the Eighth Army in the east. Montgomery had anticipated an attack, however, and had heavily defended Allied positions facing the Mareth Line. When Rommel attacked on March 4, he lost more than a third of his 150 tanks to Allied minefields and antitank guns and was forced to withdraw.

◄ The people of Gabes, Tunisia, welcome British general Bernard Montgomery after the liberation of their town from Nazi rule.

Allied assault on the Mareth Line

Two weeks later, on March 20, Montgomery attacked the Mareth Line. The British 50th Division launched a massive frontal assault. Meanwhile the New Zealand Corps cut down through the Matmata Hills—which marked the southern end of the Mareth Line—before turning north and attacking behind the line. The Germans fiercely defended both advances.

Montgomery sent reinforcements to assist the New Zealand Corps. On March 26, they succeeded in breaking through behind the Mareth Line. Threatened with encirclement, the Germans retreated. Suffering from ill health, and with little prospect of reversing the Allied advance, Rommel returned to Germany.

German retreat and surrender

Starved of supplies and under attack from the Eighth Army in the south and U.S. forces in the west, Axis troops retreated into northeastern Tunisia. Rather than evacuate the troops to Sicily—thereby saving personnel and equipment—the German high command directed its soldiers to defend the last pocket of Axis-held territory in North Africa.

By April 1943, Axis defenses were ranged along a 100-mile (160km) front protecting the capital, Tunis, and the port of Bizerte. The Germans withstood assaults between April 20 and April 23, but on May 6, an Allied attack broke through the line. The next day British armored forces seized Tunis, and British and U.S. troops captured Bizerte. Between May 8 and 12, a final Allied push cleared enemy forces from Cape Bon, the northernmost tip of Tunisia, and Axis forces surrendered.

Costs and gains

Some 250,000 German and Italian soldiers surrendered on May 13. In North Africa the Axis had lost more than a million troops and thousands of armored vehicles and tanks for no territorial gain. The losses, combined with those on the Soviet Front, were a serious blow to Hitler's war effort.

The Allies had also suffered considerable casualties in North Africa. Set against the losses, they had secured control of Africa and the southern shores of the Mediterranean. U.S. forces had gained combat experience, and the British and Americans had begun to wage war together. In addition, the Allies were now in a position to attack Nazi-occupied Europe from the south.

▲ People throng the streets of Tunis to celebrate the Allied victory over the Germans in North Africa in May 1943.

THE INVASION OF SICILY AND ITALY

In 1943, the Allies put into effect their plan to invade Europe. Their first target was the island of Sicily. They hoped that occupying Sicily would knock Italy out of the war.

The surrender of nearly a quarter of a million German and Italian troops in Tunisia, in May 1943, shifted the balance in the Mediterranean. The Allies were already planning the next phase of their campaign.

In January 1943, Allied leaders gathered in Casablanca to decide on strategy for the coming year. At first the British and Americans could not agree on the priority of attacking the Axis "underbelly" in southern Europe. British prime minister Winston Churchill pushed for assaults on Italy and Greece to open up two new fronts against the German army. He hoped to knock Italy and Axis countries in the

▶ British troops land on the quay at Salerno, in southern Italy, in September 1943. They would later be engaged in a six-day battle to secure their position and drive out the Germans.

148

Balkans out of the war. American air commanders were also eager to set up bomber bases in Italy and Greece. They wanted to make air raids on German oil and other industrial facilities in southern Europe.

President Franklin D. Roosevelt and the U.S. military high command, however, saw the Mediterranean as a distraction from the buildup of forces for the invasion of northern France, planned for early 1944. They did not want valuable assets such as landing craft and air support—already in short supply—to be spread out in small operations across the Mediterranean. They wanted to mass them for an eventual invasion of northern France. Eventually this view prevailed. Allied operations in the Mediterranean would be aimed at diverting as many German troops from the defense of northwest Europe as possible.

Arranging the landing on Sicily

The first phase of the Allied offensive against Italy was Operation Husky. It would be an amphibious (land and sea) assault to capture the island of Sicily, off southern Italy. It would provide a base for a move on to the Italian mainland.

The Allied commander in the theater was U.S. general Dwight D. Eisenhower. During the initial planning stages for the invasion, he had proposed landing simultaneously on the southeastern end of Sicily, around the city of Syracuse, and the northwestern end of the island, near Trapani. However, the British ground commander, General Bernard Montgomery, complained that the plan would leave both forces vulnerable to counterattack. The plan was changed to allow the landing force to go ashore in a concentrated mass on the island's southern coast.

149

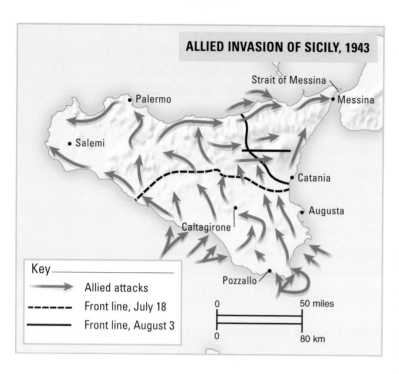

ALLIED INVASION OF SICILY, 1943

Strait of Messina
Messina
Palermo
Salemi
Catania
Augusta
Caltagirone
Pozzallo

Key
→ Allied attacks
------- Front line, July 18
—— Front line, August 3

0   50 miles
0   80 km

▲ Allied troops landed on the south side of Sicily.

▼ British troops make their way to the shore during the Allied invasion of Sicily in July 1943.

Strategy of deception

The initial landing force from North Africa included 115,000 British and Canadian and 60,000 U.S. troops. Waiting on Sicily were 230,000 Italian troops backed by two German armored divisions. The Italians lacked modern tanks and other weapons, commun-ications, and supplies. In addition, their morale was low after two years of defeats. German commanders on Sicily were already making plans to defend the island without Italian help.

The 500 Axis aircraft on Sicily were heavily outnumbered by 5,000 Allied fighters and bombers. They were unable to mount any effective resistance to the invasion. Without air cover, the large Italian fleet was confined to ports in northern Italy, unable to reach the action. In addition to their supremacy on land, at sea, and in the air, the Allies also embarked on a major series of deception operations to mislead the Germans and Italians about their intentions.

In preparation for the main attack, the Allies launched an air bombardment of the island fortress of Pantelleria, which dominated the straits between Tunisia and Sicily. After six days of bombing, the 15,000-strong Italian garrison surrendered.

"The man who never was"

Operation Mincemeat, the Allied deception effort before the landing on Sicily, culminated in the dumping off the coast of Spain of the body of a "fake" British officer. The body carried false plans that suggested the targets of Operation Husky were Sardinia and Greece rather than Sicily. Although officially neutral, Franco's Spain was sympathetic to the Axis cause.

The body was that of a vagrant recovered from a mortuary. He became a fictitious Major Martin of the Royal Marines, whose

"death" occurred in a staged aircraft crash in the Mediterranean. The body washed up on the Spanish coast, and pro-Nazi Spanish officials handed the contents of his briefcase to German intelligence. Within days the documents were in Berlin. The Germans were completely fooled: Hitler ordered extra troops to Sardinia and diverted two panzer divisions from the Russian front to Greece. Even after the landing in Sicily began, Hitler was still convinced that the threat to Greece was real.

Allied air and naval forces then turned their attention to isolating the Axis garrison on Sicily. For almost a month, aircraft dropped thousands of tons of bombs on airfields, ports, bridges, rail links, and supply depots.

Operation Husky

Early on July 10, landings by British and U.S. paratroopers and glider-borne troops marked the launch of the operation proper. The Italian troops defending the beaches around Syracuse and Comiso put up little resistance. Thousands soon surrendered.

The German defenders on Sicily, however, struck back at the Allied landings. Two panzer divisions advanced against the U.S. Seventh Army of Lieutenant-General George S. Patton around Gela. The U.S. forces were taken by surprise by the appearance of more than 100 German tanks, including units of powerful new Tiger tanks and fell back toward the landing beaches. United States Navy battleships and destroyers provided artillery support for the retreat. German advance came to a halt.

The battle for Sicily

German resistance was just as fierce in the British sector. A regiment of German paratroopers was dropped around a strategic bridge that had been captured by British paratroopers. The two forces battled for days until

▼ A German assault-gun crew grabs a meal before going into battle against Allied forces on Sicily.

Field Marshal Pietro Badoglio (1871–1956)

A veteran of Italy's colonial wars and World War I, Pietro Badoglio was made governor of Libya in 1928 and viceroy of Ethiopia in 1935. When Italy entered World War II in June 1940, he became chief of staff, but resigned that winter.

In July 1943, after Mussolini was deposed, King Victor Emmanuel III asked Badoglio to head a new government. He was one of the few officers who could hold together the army as Italy abandoned its alliance with Germany and disowned fascism.

▲ In September 1943, Badoglio negotiated the Italian surrender.

Badoglio declared martial law and put Mussolini under guard.

Badoglio began negotiating an armistice with the Allies. When the Germans occupied Italy, Badoglio and the Italian royal family escaped to the port of Pescara, where they set up a government under Allied protection.

On September 23, 1943, Badoglio and U.S. general Dwight D. Eisenhower signed the Italian surrender aboard HMS *Nelson* off the coast of Malta.

German reinforcements arrived and set up a strong position east of Mount Etna to halt the British advance. The Italian army had by now all but given up fighting.

Patton ordered his troops to race around the northern coast to seize the town of Messina and block any German escape back to mainland Italy. When Patton's troops ran into strong German rearguard positions, they bypassed them in a series of amphibious landings along the coast.

By July 23, Patton had Messina in his sights. A total of about 467,000 Allied troops were now committed to Sicily. Their superiority was beginning to show on the heavily outnumbered German defenders.

◁ Soldiers of the British Eighth Army look for pockets of German resistance on Sicily in July 1943. By mid-August, 102,000 Axis troops had evacuated the island across the Strait of Messina to the mainland.

▲ An American soldier leads a convoy of German prisoners in Sicily, 1944.

Fleeing to the mainland

Field Marshal Albert Kesselring, the German commander in the Mediterranean, realized he could no longer defend Sicily. He ordered his troops to retreat across the Strait of Messina to the mainland, guarded by hundreds of antiaircraft guns lining the channel. The Germans managed to move more than two-thirds of their 60,000 men and much of their heavy equipment back to safety. By August 17, the last German ferry had crossed to the mainland. Few Italian troops escaped from Sicily. Those that did not surrender simply threw away their uniforms and returned home.

The month-long battle for Sicily had cost the Allies 5,532 dead, 2,869 missing, and 14,410 wounded. This compared to 4,278 Italian and 4,325 German dead, and more than 132,000 Italians taken prisoner. Almost all the Italian and German aircraft on Sicily were lost. An Italian naval force that had tried to intercept the Allied landing fleet suffered heavy losses.

Eyewitness

❝ The first wounded began to crawl back over the ridge. They all told the same story. They fired their bazookas at the front plate of German tanks, and then the tanks swiveled their huge 88-mm guns at them and fired at the individual infantrymen. By this time the tanks could be heard, although I could not see any because of the smoke and dust and the cover of vegetation.... Cannonball had gone forward to command the attack. It did not seem to be getting anywhere, however, as the German fire increased in intensity and our wounded were coming back in greater numbers. ❞

General James M. Gavin,
U.S. 82nd Air Division, Sicily, July 1942

Italy surrenders

Soon after the Allied invasion of Sicily, as war threatened to turn Italy into a battlefield, many Italian politicians sought to escape from their alliance with the Nazis. In late July, senior military chiefs and cabinet ministers hatched a plot to force the fascist dictator Benito Mussolini to step down. On July 26, King Victor Emmanuel III relieved Mussolini of his post, and he was arrested by troops loyal to the new government. For the next six weeks the new government tried to avoid German intervention while it held negotiations with the Allies about a possible armistice, or cease-fire.

Hitler was furious about the removal of his ally Mussolini, and suspicious that the Italians would change sides in the war. He sent reinforcements to Italy, including the elite Waffen-SS Leibstandarte Panzer Division and a large contingent of paratroops. They were to prepare to seize key areas if the Italians went over to the Allied cause.

▲ The Italian dictator Mussolini (right) is escorted by Otto Skorzeny (center) to a waiting aircraft after his rescue by German troops in September 1943.

▶ Brigadier-General Giuseppe Castellano signs the armistice with the Allies on behalf of Pietro Badoglio on September 3, 1943.

The rescue of Mussolini

Hitler was outraged that Benito Mussolini was being held captive by Italy's new government and feared that his former ally would be turned over to the Allies. He sent Waffen-SS Special Forces officer Otto Skorzeny to Italy to find out where Mussolini was being held. After searching for over a month, Skorzeny located him at the Hotel Campo Imperatore, a resort high in the Gran Sasso mountains in central Italy.

General Kurt Student organized a daring rescue mission using gliders to land an assault force virtually at the main entrance of the hotel. Skorzeny led his paratroopers and SS men into the building past astonished Italian guards who did not fire a shot as the Germans surged past them.

Skorzeny smashed the garrison's radio and found Mussolini, who was then loaded into a light aircraft that had landed on the lawn outside the hotel. Mussolini and Skorzeny were flown to Vienna, where they received a heroes' welcome and a congratulatory phone call from Hitler.

▲ This picture shows the Hotel Campo Imperatore, in the central Italian Apennines, where Mussolini was detained in September 1943.

Italian talks with the Allies, meanwhile, led to secret negotiations in neutral Portugal in mid-August to sign an armistice. The Italians wanted Allied airborne and amphibious forces to land near Rome as the armistice was signed in case the Germans counterstriked. Eisenhower, however, did not have enough ships or planes for such an operation and was wary of putting Allied troops in such an exposed position. Instead he agreed only to limited landings in the south of Italy.

German contingency plans

With little choice, the Italians signed the armistice on September 3. The Germans then activated their plans, seizing key points in Rome, and in central and northern Italy. They also disarmed Italian garrisons in Yugoslavia, Greece, and Albania, sometimes massacring them.

German troops under the command of Field Marshal Erwin Rommel surged south across the Alps to occupy northern Italy. In Rome, Kesselring's troops occupied civic buildings, forcing the government and the royal family to flee. The Italian navy put to sea to join the Allies, but the army put up only token resistance to the Germans. Only on the islands of Corsica and Sardinia did the Italians force the German garrisons to retreat and eventually call for evacuation. The culmination of the German operation was a daring raid to rescue Mussolini.

The invasion of Salerno

As the Germans were completing their occupation, the Allies were finally ready to land on the mainland. An invasion fleet appeared off Salerno, to the south of Naples, on September 9, and two British and two U.S. divisions began landing.

At first the Allies took the weak German defenders by surprise and established a bridgehead (a fortified position in hostile territory). Although the Germans were badly battered, they managed to form an improvised defensive line on the high ground above the landing beaches. This kept the Allied troops pinned down. Kessel-

ring ordered five divisions against the bridgehead to drive it into the sea.

The six-day battle culminated in an all-out assault that threatened to divide the British from the Americans. The U.S. commander, General Mark Clark, committed all his reserves to the defense, including his regimental band, cooks, and clerks. Allied warships laid down supporting artillery fire. This turned the tide of the engagement by giving time for a regiment of U.S. paratroopers to be rushed to Salerno to shore up the position. Later, British armored columns pushed up from southern Italy.

Aware that his bid to crush the Salerno bridgehead had failed, on September 16 Kesselring withdrew his troops north. The Allies had

▼ British troops in North Africa wait to be loaded onto landing craft in September 1943. They were headed for southern Italy to reinforce Allied invasion forces.

prevailed, but the strong German counterattack had come as a nasty shock. Some 756 Allied troops died during the battle, and 2,150 were captured. Almost 3,000 Allied troops had been wounded.

Grinding to a halt

The German troops in southern Italy withdrew to a purpose-built defensive line to the south of Rome. The British and U.S. spearheads pushed north, but found themselves in terrain that favored their opponents. Dug-in antitank guns held up their tank columns for weeks, while machine-gun nests prevented their infantry from crossing fast-flowing rivers.

By October it was clear to the Allied high command that there would be no dramatic breakthrough in Italy until the following spring at the earliest. At the same time, London and Washington made a strategic decision to wind down resources allocated to Italy in favor of the buildup for the cross-Channel invasion of France. The Allies began to transfer divisions from the Mediterranean to Britain for Operation Overlord, as the invasion was now code-named. Eisenhower and Montgomery were also reassigned to the new invasion front.

▲ Two German soldiers of the Tenth Army, commanded by General Heinrich von Vietinghoff, prepare to fire on Allied troops landing at Salerno in September 1943.

▶ Marshal Badoglio (left) with Lieutenant General Mason-Macfarlane of the British Army during the planning of the new Italian government.

THE BATTLE OF THE ATLANTIC: 1942–1945

By 1941, the wolf packs of German U-boats in the Atlantic had proved themselves to be one of the greatest threats to the British war effort. In 1942, the United States would also experience the horror of the U-boat war.

In late 1941, the British were beginning to make some headway in countering the German U-boat threat. Merchant-shipping losses remained high, with about 400,000 tons sunk during November, but the figure had fallen from a peak of 900,000 tons during the summer.

U-boats, once nearly invulnerable, now faced real danger from rapid British convoy escorts using barrages of heavy depth-charges, or underwater bombs. New sonar technology known as ASDIC increased depth-charge accuracy. In addition, improved radar introduced in early 1941 enabled an escort to detect a surfaced U-boat up to 1¾ miles (3km) away.

Progress was also being made in deciphering the German Enigma military codes. As a result, more convoys could avoid wolf packs—groups of U-boats—and their escorts were better prepared. Convoys were also helped by air support from escort aircraft carriers and long-range antisubmarine aircraft. In addition, new convoy shipping provided by the U.S. Lend-Lease policy helped to turn the tables on the U-boats in the Battle of the Atlantic.

Operation Drumbeat

Until December 7, 1941, the United States was technically neutral in the war. However, the Japanese attack on Pearl Harbor and Hitler's subsequent declaration of war on the United States changed the Atlantic War entirely.

The commander of the U-boat fleet, Karl Dönitz, saw new opportunities. He started Operation Drumbeat, diverting much of his force from the central Atlantic to patrol the eastern coast of the United States. The U.S. homeland had so far been untouched by war, and a mixture of complacency and inexperience was to have tragic results. The merchant fleet that sailed along the U.S. coast was almost entirely unprotected.

On January 12, 1942, *U-123* ("U" indicates "U-boat"), commanded by Reinhard Hardegan, moved into waters off the northern United States. It sank the merchantman *Cyclops* off Nova Scotia; two nights later the tanker *Norness* was destroyed 60 miles (96km) off Long Island, New York.

Hardegan then took his craft deeper into New York waters—at one stage he could see the bright lights of New York City. Over subsequent months, U-boat commanders benefited from coastal lights, which had the effect of silhouetting targets clearly. The U.S. authorities initially refused to implement blackouts like those used in Britain. As losses mounted, they applied a "dim-out"—lights were dimmed rather than turned off. From offshore, however, any onshore illumination made targets stand out prominently enough to help the U-boats.

The return of the "Happy Time"

Spurred by Hardegan's successes (he sank another tanker on January 15), Dönitz deployed more U-boats to similar positions. Before long, 12 U-boats were on patrol along the East Coast at any one time. From January to June, a total of 327 U.S. ships were sunk in U.S. waters between Maine and the Caribbean. Some 1.25 million tons of ships were lost in the first three months of the year, and a similar total in May and June. More than 2,400 sailors lost their lives, and U.S. coastal communities experienced many dead bodies washing up on their shores.

Arguing from experience, the British advised the U.S. chief of naval operations, Admiral Ernest J. King, to group ships into convoys protected by heavy escorts. King instead tried ineffective measures such as antisubmarine patrols and decoy shipping. The rising losses were a convincing argument, however, and by July 1942, the United States had adopted convoy systems.

▼ A British ship burns after being hit by a Luftwaffe bomb on the Arctic convoy route. The convoys took supplies from Britain to Soviet Russia's northern ports, principally Murmansk.

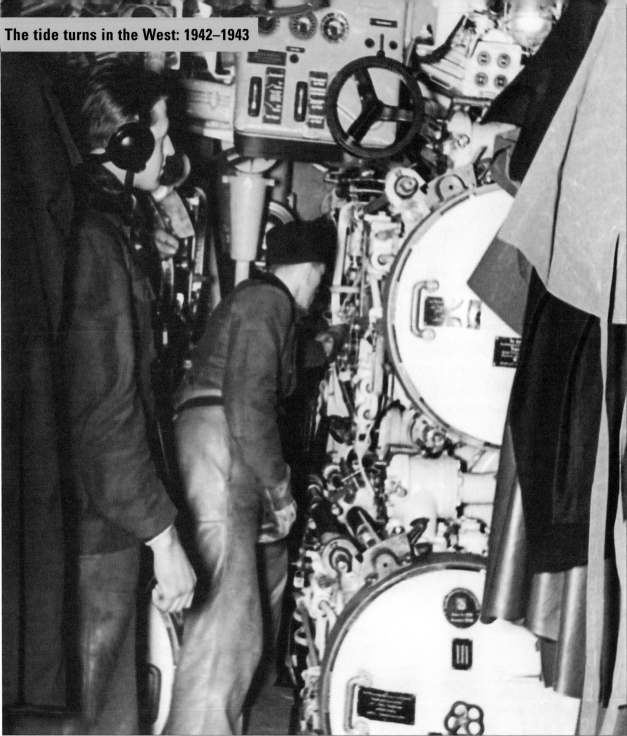

▲ This picture shows the cramped conditions in the forward torpedo room of a German U-boat, home to the boat's four bow torpedo tubes.

However, Operation Drumbeat and further attacks on convoys in the Atlantic resulted in between 6 million and 8 million tons of Allied shipping losses in 1942. The U-boat commanders referred to their success as their second "Happy Time" (*see Chapter 5, Volume 2*).

Exploiting the weak spots

The U.S. shipbuilding industry, however, had geared up to produce more ships than the U-boat fleet could sink. A "Liberty" ship—a standard, prefabricated merchant vessel—could be produced in three months or much less. The record was less than five days. By the end of October 1942, three Liberty ships or their tanker equivalent, the T10, were being completed almost every day.

In response to convoy tactics being used along the East Coast, in August

◀ The British tanker SS *Empire Gem* (carrying gasoline from the United States to Britain) sinks after being struck by a German torpedo south of Cape Hatteras, North Carolina, in January 1942.

▼ Crewmen from a German U-boat scan the waters for survivors from an Allied freighter they torpedoed the previous day.

1942, Dönitz switched his focus to the so-called Atlantic air gap, a large stretch of the ocean that lay beyond the range of Allied land-based antisubmarine aircraft. Over subsequent months, too, much Allied escort and merchant shipping was relocated to operations in North Africa, leaving the Atlantic convoys even more vulnerable.

Two huge packs of U-boats now patrolled just within the borders of the air gap, aiming to catch Allied convoys as they entered and exited. By March 1943, a total of 240 U-boats were in the central Atlantic. Their range was increased as specialist refueling submarines were developed. Meanwhile German naval codes were changing, and again defeating the Allied decoding efforts.

Defeating the U-boats

The level of merchant sinkings rose again, from 300,000 tons in February

The St.-Nazaire Raid

In the spring of 1942, in order to prevent the German battleship *Tirpitz* from operating in the Atlantic, the British planned to destroy the dry dock at St.-Nazaire in France, on which the battleship would rely. The plan was to ram the dock gate with an old destroyer packed with explosives armed with delayed fuses. Meanwhile, commandos would demolish key shore installations.

On March 26, 1942, HMS *Campbeltown*, packed with explosives, sailed for St.-Nazaire with 18 other vessels. At 1:34 A.M., on March 28, under fire from coastal guns, it rammed the dock gates. The commandos destroyed many installations, but the evacuation went wrong. Only 227 of the 611 raiders returned to Britain. At around 11:35 A.M., *Campbeltown* exploded with a huge detonation that killed 360 Germans and wrecked the harbor. The dock was unusable for the rest of the war.

▼ *Campbeltown* exploded 10 hours after ramming the dock at St.-Nazaire.

to 476,000 tons in March. In fact, however, the second Happy Time could not last. The U.S. convoy system steadily began to make life harder for the U-boats. About 15 U-boats were being built every month, but a similar number were being sunk.

The increased U-boat sinkings were the result of rapid developments in antisubmarine tactics and technology. Convoy escorts had received better weaponry since late 1942. In addition to depth charges, which sank 43 percent of all destroyed U-boats, many escort vessels were also armed with the "hedgehog." This weapon fired 24 small bombs that sank through the water in a circular pattern 130 feet

◄ A crewman struggles across the deck as his U-boat begins to sink.

(40m) in diameter; the bombs exploded on contact with an enemy craft. Later in 1943, the British introduced the "squid," a three-barreled mortar that fired fast-sinking bombs set to explode at a specific depth in a triangular pattern; the bombs hit a U-boat with shockwaves from every side. Escort destroyers also received improved radar and other submarine-locating systems, including "huff-duff," or High Frequency/Direction Finding (HF/DF) equipment. This located submarines by picking up their radio transmissions.

Technological advances

While shipboard weapons improved, so too did airborne antisubmarine tactics and firepower. Allied air power in the Atlantic War consisted mainly of Liberator bombers and Sunderland and Catalina flying boats. Armed with

▲ A mine scores a direct hit on a U-boat. U-boats traveling on the surface were vulnerable to air attack.

▼ Allied shipping losses during 1942–1943.

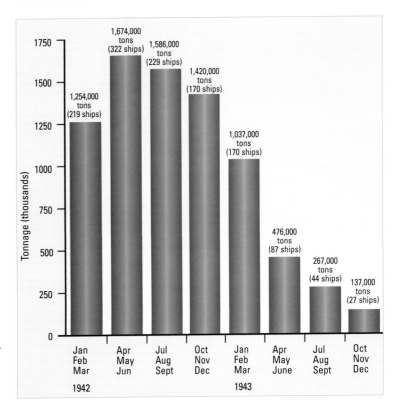

Eyewitness

❝There is a frightful crack, just as if the boat has been struck by a gigantic hammer. Electric bulbs and glasses fly about, leaving fragments everywhere. The motors have stoppod. Reports from all stations show, thank God, that there are no leaks—just the main fuses blown. The damage is made good. We are now using special breathing apparatus to guard against the deadly carbon-monoxide which may be in the boat. The rubber mouthpiece tastes horrible.❞

Midshipman Heinz Schaefer,
On *U-977*, as it is depth-charged in the mid-Atlantic, 1942

▼ The German battle cruiser *Scharnhorst*, at sea in February 1942. It could sail at a very high speed of 33 knots.

depth charges, machine guns, and cannons, the aircraft took a fearsome toll on U-boats within their range.

Aircraft initially discovered submarines either by visual reconnaissance or by radio information from escort ships. However, new centimetric radar systems were installed on board Liberators from spring 1942. They gave aircrew the ability to precisely locate a submarine on the surface.

In May 1943, Very Long Range (VLR) Liberators were introduced in the Atlantic theater. With a range of over 3,000 miles (4,800km), they closed the mid-Atlantic air gap. Escort carriers were also available in increased numbers, giving convoys air cover for the entire Atlantic crossing. From May 1943, Allied code-breakers again dominated the German naval codes, revealing the submarines' deployment. Even darkness could not conceal the U-boats: Allied aircraft were equipped with powerful search-lights that could illuminate the ocean once the U-boat had been detected by radar.

From April 1943, U.S. aircraft also began dropping the Mark 24 Mine, a revolutionary antisubmarine torpedo.

Once dropped into the water, the mine would guide itself to the target by homing in on the propeller noise. With a range of over 11,800 feet (3,600m), it was a devastating weapon.

The German reaction

Losses among the U-boats became catastrophic; 47 were sunk in May 1943 alone. With such unsustainable losses, Dönitz pulled his U-boat fleet back to France by the end of the year. After the invasion of France in June 1944, however, the Allies seized many submarine stations along the French coast as well as sinking a significant number of U-boats. Allied air forces also struck at the core of the U-boat production and transportation network, preventing new submarines from being built or delivered.

In response to their losses, the Germans invested in their own new technology. They introduced the "snorkel" air-breathing system. This sucked in air from the surface down a long tube, allowing a U-boat to remain submerged for longer. They also introduced their own homing torpedoes. In February 1945, a new submarine type, the XXIII, came into service. It had an exceptional underwater performance. However, these measures were too late: In May 1945, the navy surrendered with the rest of the German forces.

The U-boat crews suffered the highest percentage of deaths of any arm of service in the German military. Nearly 26,000 U-boat crewmen died out of a total of 40,900 who served; another 5,000 were taken prisoner.

The Arctic war

From August 1941, the Atlantic War was accompanied by another bitter naval conflict being fought to the north and west. This was the war of the

A U-boat in heavy seas in the North Atlantic in May 1943. May was a decisive month as the mid-Atlantic air gap was closed by very-long-range Liberator bombers.

The *Tirpitz*

The *Tirpitz*—like its sister ship the *Bismarck*—was a leading ship in the Kriegsmarine. It was launched in 1939 and named for Admiral Alfred von Tirpitz, an early commander of the German Navy. The battleship was 830 feet (253m) long, was powered by 12 boilers and three turbines, and could achieve a speed of over 30 knots. The *Tirpitz*'s armament was formidable, and included eight 15-inch main guns, more than 55 other guns and cannons, and 8 torpedo tubes. For most of the war the *Tirpitz* was confined to northern harbors because of Hitler's lack of confidence in surface vessels. Its threat to Allied convoys was more imagined than real, but the British pursued it until they destroyed it by air attack on November 12, 1944.

▲ The German battleship *Tirpitz* lies capsized in Tromsö Fjord, Norway, in November 1944, following an attack by RAF bombers.

Arctic convoys, which sailed from Britain and Iceland by way of the Barents Sea to supply the Soviet Union. While the Atlantic War was mainly a conflict between German U-boats and Allied surface vessels and aircraft, in the Arctic War the Germans used aviation, U-boats, and surface vessels.

The Arctic convoys were responsible for delivering vast quantities of U.S. and British goods to the Soviet Union. This had been supported by Britain following the German invasion of Russia in June 1941 (*See Chapter 2, Volume 3*). Over the course of the war, 4.3 million tons of jeeps, trucks, aircraft, tanks, weapons, boots, and other material reached Soviet forces by convoys that sailed to the ports of Archangel, Murmansk, and Molotovsk. The convoys delivered more than 22 percent of the Lend-Lease supplies sent to the Soviet Union and were vital to the Soviet war effort.

The first convoy sailed for Russia on August 21, 1941. Each was given a number and two letters: PQ indicated that the convoy was outbound, while QP designated homeward convoys.

Action in the Arctic theater

The first problem for the convoys was the environment. In the hostile Arctic waters, air temperatures were often below zero, causing the ships to ice up, and huge storms were common, especially in winter. On the other hand, enemy action remained relatively light until the spring of 1942, when the German land campaign in Russia ground to a halt. Then the Germans turned their attention to Russia's North Atlantic supply lifeline, launching all available resources against the Arctic convoys: U-boats, bombers, E-boats (fast torpedo boats), and large warships such as the *Tirpitz*, *Admiral Hipper*, and *Lützow*.

One of the first major encounters occurred on March 5, 1942. Convoy PQ12, supported by the battleship HMS *King George V* and the aircraft carrier HMS *Victorious*, clashed with the *Tirpitz* and three destroyers. Twelve torpedo planes attacked the *Tirpitz*, but two were shot down and the rest failed to make an impact. The *Tirpitz*, however, returned to base to avoid damage. It was the Arctic War's first indication of the limitations of the large German raiders.

U-boats and bomber aircraft, however, inflicted heavy losses on the convoys. In January 1942, PQ7 and PQ8 lost a merchant ship and a destroyer, while on May 27, seven ships from PQ16 were sunk by a massed aircraft attack. In July 1942, after some disastrous decisions by the British Admiralty, convoy PQ17 was broken up and destroyed by U-boats over several days. Twenty-six ships were sunk out of a total of 37. The next convoy, PQ18, which sailed after a nine-week suspension of Arctic convoys, was also heavily attacked, losing 13 ships. However, a beefed-up escort cost the Germans three U-boats and 22 aircraft.

The British improved their escort tactics in 1942. Losses were still high, but in the two convoys following PQ18 the Germans lost four U-boats and 41 aircraft. The second half of 1942 saw a reduction in Arctic convoy activity when Allied resources were channeled to the invasion of North Africa. It rose again, however, in December. That month convoy JW51B (JW was the new code for outbound journeys, RA for return journeys) was attacked by the heavy cruiser *Admiral Hipper*, the pocket battleship *Lützow*, and six destroyers.

The Germans became locked in an exchange of fire with the British escort, which included the cruisers HMS *Sheffield* and HMS *Jamaica*. Both sides suffered severe damage, and the Germans lost a destroyer. The German

Convoy PQ17

The destruction of PQ17 was the lowest point in the history of Arctic convoys. PQ17 sailed from Iceland on June 27, 1942, protected by a strong escort. It suffered several days of air attack from the Luftwaffe. Then, on July 4, Allied intelligence suggested that a surface force, including the *Tirpitz* and the *Admiral Hipper*, was preparing to attack the convoy. Admiral Sir Dudley Pound ordered the convoy to scatter, leaving the ships isolated from one another and from their escorts. German U-boats and bombers attacked, sinking 26 ships and causing severe supply losses to the Soviet Union. By the time the German surface force sailed, convoy PQ17 had already been destroyed.

▼ Survivors from the American steamer *Carlton*, one of the ships in the PQ17 convoy, sunk on July 5 by *U-88*.

Life on the Arctic convoys

For the crews who sailed on the Arctic convoys, the biggest problem was the cold. Daytime temperatures rarely climbed above 14° F (-10° C), and they dropped as low as -76° F (-60° C). Frostbite was common and eyelashes were covered with ice from freezing sea spray. Crews had to use axes and steam hoses to break ice off the decks and equipment. Anyone who fell overboard, or who entered the freezing water after a ship was sunk, died within minutes from hypothermia. Crew members wore numerous layers of thick clothing that, when wet, chafed the neck, wrists, thighs, and ankles. Meanwhile violent storms created waves up to 100 feet (32m) high for days on end, producing seasickness in even the most hardened sailors. Owing to the far northern climate and short winter days, the crews made many winter voyages in either pitch darkness or an eerie twilight.

▲ Crews on Arctic convoys braved freezing conditions in addition to enemy attacks.

ships returned to port, their commanders humiliated. Hitler forced the commander-in-chief of the Kriegsmarine, Grand Admiral Erich Raeder, to resign. He was replaced by Dönitz, who also retained command of the U-boats.

The tide turns in the Arctic

Worse was to come for the Kriegsmarine. The *Tirpitz*, *Scharnhorst*, and *Lützow*, which were anchored in Norway, still posed a major threat to the Arctic convoys. In September 1943, however, a force of British midget submarines called X-craft attacked the

◄ In March 1945, British warships HMS *Honeysuckle* and HMS *Trumpeter* dock in the Russian port of Murmansk. Murmansk was the destination of some 40 Allied convoys during World War II.

 An aerial view of the German battleship *Tirpitz* in Narvik-Bogen Fjord, Norway in July, 1942. *Tirpitz* was based in Norway from early 1942, where it posed a constant threat to Allied convoys.

Tirpitz at anchor, detonating over 13 tons of explosives beneath its hull. The ship capsized and was out of action for six months.

The next German warship to suffer was the battle cruiser *Scharnhorst*. In December it attacked convoy JW55B, which had a large escort of a battleship, four cruisers, and four destroyers. In the Battle of the North Cape, on December 26, *Scharnhorst* was hit by three 14-inch shells. British destroyers then put four torpedoes into the crippled ship's side. At 7:45 A.M., it sank, taking 1,932 crew into the icy waters; only 38 survived.

The *Tirpitz* remained under repair, but on April 3, 1944, a large-scale attack by British carrier aircraft caught it in Altenfjord and disabled it for a further three months. Between September and November, RAF Lancaster bombers, many carrying huge 12,000-pound (5,400kg) bombs, made several attacks against the anchored *Tirpitz*. On November 12, two bombs blew the *Tirpitz* apart, detonating its ammunition magazine. The pride of the German navy sank with 1,204 crew.

By the time the *Tirpitz* was sunk, the battle of the Arctic convoys had been effectively won by the Allies. By February 1945, an equivalent of more than one U-boat was being destroyed for every merchant ship sunk by the Germans. The convoy battles of World War II maintained the lifelines of the Allied war effort in Europe. As such, they may have been the most important campaigns of the war.

THE AIR WAR AGAINST GERMANY

Early in 1942 the British Royal Air Force launched a massive bombing offensive against German cities and industries. The United States Army Air Force soon joined the campaign to defeat Germany from the air.

During the summer of 1940, the Royal Air Force (RAF) turned the tide of the German air attack on Britain. Although Hitler had targeted British cities in his bombing campaign, Britain was slow to launch a similar offensive against Germany.

Early RAF strikes against Germany

The RAF had launched small daytime raids against German military targets in late 1939. It had suffered heavy losses as German fighter planes shot down its aircraft, however, and soon switched to nighttime raids.

During 1940 the RAF concentrated on destroying German factories that made oil from coal. Its aim was to cripple the German war economy, but it struggled to achieve its goal. Its bomber fleet lacked the means to navigate accurately at night, and accurate sights to aim bombs at targets. In addition, the Germans were improving a defensive network of fighters and antiaircraft guns directed by radar.

The switch to area bombing

During the fall of 1941, the British Air Ministry addressed the shortcomings of Bomber Command, one of three sections that made up the RAF. Pinpoint attacks on specific targets were now replaced with "area bombing," which targeted not just factories but large areas around them. It aimed to weaken German industry and morale by destroying the transportation net-

▶ American P-51 Mustang fighter aircraft take part in a daylight raid against Germany. Mustangs changed the course of the air war. They were able to fly more than 2,000 miles (3,218km) without refueling, and provided effective escorts for Allied bombers attacking Germany.

works and power and water supplies on which the factories relied, as well as the homes of their workers.

The strategy was, and remains, controversial. The bombing of civilian targets is against international law, which is why the British government was originally unwilling to undertake such attacks. However, growing numbers of politicians and military leaders began to reassess their positions in 1940, after the Luftwaffe bombed the British cities of London and Coventry, killing and injuring thousands of civilians. Supporters of area bombing have argued that the strategy ultimately saved lives by shortening the war.

Arthur "Bomber" Harris

On February 22, 1942, Bomber Command was invigorated by the arrival of a new commander-in-chief: Arthur "Bomber" Harris. Aggressive and single-minded, Harris set about transforming his command and redoubled efforts to perfect area bombing. He ordered thousands of four-engined heavy bombers, introduced new electronic equipment to defeat German radar defenses, and developed

Eyewitness

66 The raging fires in a high wind caused terrific damage and the grievous loss of human life.... The fires spread unhindered, causing fiery storms which reached heats of 1,000°, and speeds approaching gale force.... The fiery wind tore the roofs from the houses, uprooted large trees, and flung them into the air like blazing torches. The inhabitants took refuge in the air-raid shelters, in which later they were burned to death or suffocated. In the early morning, thousands of blackened corpses could be seen in the burned-out streets. 99

Wilhelm Johnen, Luftwaffe pilot,
Allied bombing of Hamburg, August 1943

new tactics to mass his aircraft against specific targets.

Harris first used area bombing against the German city of Lübeck on the night of March 28, 1942. Some 234 aircraft took part in the raid, which used incendiary bombs (bombs that start fires) to begin fires throughout the city. Although eight bombers were lost, 200 acres (81ha) of Lübeck were flattened. An attack on the port of Rostock on the night of April 23–24 resulted in similar devastation.

▼ Cologne Cathedral stands amid the city's ruined downtown. The RAF's 1,000-bomber raid on Cologne on the night of May 30, 1942, struck at both industrial targets and the city's historic center.

Hitler responded to the bombing of Lübeck and Rostock by launching a series of Luftwaffe raids on historic British cities. The attacks were called Baedeker Raids for a popular series of guidebooks, because they attacked destinations that were popular with tourists. Exeter, Bath, and York suffered particularly heavy damage.

The 1,000-bomber raid

After the success of the RAF attacks on Lübeck and Rostock, Harris started to plan a huge raid on the German city of Cologne using 1,000 aircraft. He devised new tactics and used new equipment for the attack. All the bombers would arrive over Cologne within 90 minutes of each other, to saturate German defenses and maximize the psychological impact on the city's population. Pathfinders—aircraft that flew ahead of the bombing force and dropped incendiary bombs to illuminate targets—were aided by a new electronic navigation device, Gee.

The raid took place on the night of May 30. It killed 469 Germans and destroyed or damaged 250 factories and 18,400 homes. Only 41 of the 1,087 bombers were lost.

Building up Bomber Command

After the raid Harris accelerated his efforts to perfect Bomber Command. He introduced Oboe, a more accurate version of Gee, and equipped the Lancaster bombers with H2S radar, which enabled their crews to pick out features such as river estuaries and cities. He formed and trained more Pathfinder units, and increased the production of Halifax, Stirling, and Lancaster bombers.

By the end of 1942, Harris was sending more than 260 four-engined bombers over Germany every night, and the aircraft hit their targets with ever-increasing accuracy. Harris aimed to amass a force of 4,000 to 6,000 bombers, with which he was confident that the RAF could destroy Germany.

The U.S. Army Air Force arrives

The United States's entry into the war in December 1941 set in motion events that further expanded the bombing offensive against Germany. On July 1,

1942, the first U.S. Army Air Force (USAAF) B-17 Flying Fortress arrived in Britain. The B-17 was a new heavy, four-engined, high-altitude bomber that was to be central to USAAF air strikes on Germany. By mid-August the USAAF's Eighth Air Force in Britain had three bomber groups with more than 100 aircraft. The Eighth Air Force and RAF worked together as the Allied Strategic Air Forces.

USAAF commanders had their own ideas about bombing strategy. They rejected area bombing and favored precision daytime strikes against individual industrial targets. They based their tactics on the B-17 and on an accurate new optical aid named the Norden sight.

Operation Pointblank

The British and Americans agreed on a campaign in which the RAF operated at night and the USAAF during the day. For spring 1943 they planned Operation Pointblank, a series of day and night raids against 58 German towns and cities. The attacks targeted the aircraft, submarine, oil, transportation, and armaments industries.

In the first half of 1943, while the USAAF was still building up its forces in Britain, the burden of Operation Pointblank fell on the RAF. Harris's first target was the German industrial region of the Ruhr, on which he planned a four-month offensive. The first raid of the so-called Battle of the Ruhr was launched on March 3, 1943, when 303 bombers attacked the city of Essen and the nearby Krupp armaments factory. Around 18,500 raids followed before July. They included the daring Dambusters Raid of May 16, in which the RAF used the newly

invented bouncing bomb to destroy key dams in the Ruhr.

The bombing of Hamburg

Harris's next target was Hamburg, an historic city and port on the Elbe River in north Germany. Harris planned a week of coordinated raids in July using fire bombs to obliterate the city. He code-named the attack Operation

▲ Arthur Harris (center in glasses) and his staff plan a bombing raid.

▼ The main targets bombed in the Allied air war against Germany from 1942 to 1945.

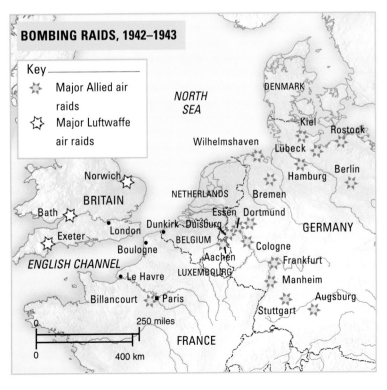

BOMBING RAIDS, 1942–1943

Key

✳ Major Allied air raids

☆ Major Luftwaffe air raids

NORTH SEA

DENMARK

Kiel
Rostock
Lübeck
Wilhelmshaven
Berlin
Hamburg
Norwich
NETHERLANDS Bremen
BRITAIN
Bath
Essen Dortmund
London Dunkirk Duisburg
GERMANY
Exeter BELGIUM
Boulogne Cologne
Aachen Frankfurt
ENGLISH CHANNEL LUXEMBOURG
Le Havre Manheim
Billancourt Paris Augsburg
Stuttgart
250 miles
FRANCE
0
400 km

The Dambusters Raid

One of the most daring bombing raids on Germany was the RAF strike on dams near the Ruhr industrial region on May 16, 1943. The attack used a bouncing bomb designed by British engineer Barnes Wallis to skip across the surface of water and explode while sinking to the base of the dam. The bombers had to fly a low, straight course over water toward their target, making them highly vulnerable to enemy antiaircraft fire. Of the 19 aircraft that took part, five were shot down before the attacks and three more after; 56 aircrew died.

The raid targeted four dams. The two main targets, the Eder dam and the Möhne dam, were both ruptured. The Möhne reservoir was the major source of supply for the Ruhr factories 20 miles (32 km) away. The destruction of the dam and its hydro-electric plant caused flooding and disrupted rail, road, and canal communications, as well as the supply of water and electricity. The damage was soon repaired, however.

◄ Water gushes through the broken Möhne dam on May 17, 1943, the day after the famous Dambuster Raid.

Gomorrah, for the Biblical city of the same name that was destroyed by fire because of its wickedness.

The first wave of 733 RAF bombers bombed Hamburg on the night of July 24. They were protected by a new device called Window that blinded the German radar defenses; only 12 of the aircraft were shot down. Just after dawn on July 25, 235 USAAF B-17s joined the attack. The RAF made four more large raids on Hamburg until the night of August 2. In all, some 3,000 British and U.S. bombers dropped 9,000 tons of bombs during Operation Gomorrah, for the loss of 89 aircraft.

The raids devastated Hamburg. The summer heat had dried out many of the city's wooden roofs, which were easily set on fire by RAF fire bombs. Strong winds fanned the flames and created firestorms that engulfed the city, sucking in waves of air that pulled people into the inferno.

By the end of the raids, the center of Hamburg was a smoldering ruin. Some 277,000 houses were destroyed, and some 45,000 civilians dead, about 10 per cent of total German civilian losses to bombing during the war. The survivors were in a state of shock. The German government was anxious that more similar attacks would destroy national morale, but the Allies did not yet have the resources to launch further offensives on such a large scale.

Deep-penetration raids

By late spring 1943, the USAAF's bomber force in Britain comprised more than 350 aircraft, including long-range B-24 Liberators, split into 11

▲ The bombing of shipyards at Kiel, Germany, by the 306th Bombardment Group of the U.S. Air Force in May 1943.

in the southern German cities of Schweinfurt and Regensburg were very costly. Of the 376 B-17s launched on the raid of August 17, German fighters shot down more than 60. A second raid on Schweinfurt in October again resulted in heavy losses. This time, of the 291 bombers, 77 failed to return and 133 were damaged.

Reorganization and a new offensive

Early in 1944 the USAAF reorganized and strengthened its European forces. At the same time the U.S. Eighth Air Force in Britain and the U.S. Fifteenth Air Force based in Italy began Operation Argument, a new offensive to destroy the German aircraft industry. Between them the two air forces had more than 1,000 heavy bombers.

In January, U.S. bombers began large-scale daylight raids on German factories. Again they suffered heavy losses, losing an average of 10 percent of the bombers taking part in each raid. The

groups. By July it had grown to more than 600 aircraft in 17 groups. USAAF commanders wanted to strike at industrial targets deep inside Germany, far beyond the range of fighter escorts. They believed that the B-17s could operate without fighter protection; Each bomber had 11 heavy machine guns to defend it from enemy aircraft.

The U.S. commanders proved over-optimistic. Bombing raids on factories

▼ Bystanders examine a B-17 Flying Fortress at a British airfield. The bomber was used by the USAAF to conduct high-level raids against Germany and became one of the most famous aircraft of the war. It was a heavily armored, four-engine bomber, well equipped with machine guns and able to carry up to 12,800 pounds (2,725 kg) of bombs.

USAAF had begun to receive new P-51 Mustangs, however; these aircraft carried external, disposable fuel tanks and so could provide fighter cover for bombing raids deep inside Germany. The Mustang was to have a huge effect on the air war, making Allied bombing raids more effective and destroying large numbers of Luftwaffe fighters.

Big Week

The USAAF intensified its bombing campaign in what became known as "Big Week." On February 20, 1944, the U.S. Eighth Air Force launched the largest aerial attack in the war to date: Some 941 bombers and 700 fighters took part in raids on aircraft factories in central Germany. All the target factories were hit with the loss of only 21 bombers. The RAF continued the attack on the night of February 20, sending 600 bombers to strike Stuttgart, another center of German aircraft production.

Heavy U.S. losses

On February 22, bombers from the U.S. Fifteenth Air Force in Italy set out to strike the Messerschmitt aircraft factory at Regensburg in southern Germany. At the same time the Eighth Air Force attacked aircraft production centers in the center of the country.

The Eighth Air Force action suffered bad luck, however. Thick cloud cover over eastern England caused several bombers to collide after takeoff; others

German air defenses

Germany's defenses against aerial attack grew in size and sophistication as the Allies stepped up their bombing campaign. They originally comprised heavy concentrations of searchlights and batteries of antiaircraft guns, also known as flak. However, as the RAF intensified its nighttime raids in 1941, the Germans turned to radar to direct searchlights and flak batteries against the bombers. A line of searchlights and guns was established along Germany's western coast and border to shoot down bombers before they reached their targets. Fighter aircraft were equipped with radar in 1942, to find enemy bombers in the dark.

When U.S. bombers started large daytime raids over Germany, the Luftwaffe began deploying large numbers of fighter aircraft to protect German cities. The process culminated in the deployment of the Me262, the first effective jet fighter, in 1945—too late to affect the outcome of the war.

▶ German soldiers operate an 88mm antiaircraft gun to shoot down RAF bombers and fighters in March 1941.

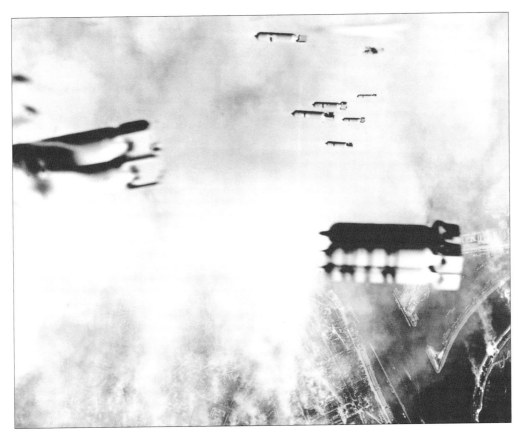

Incendiary bombs dropped by U.S. bombers fall on the German city of Hamburg on July 26, 1943. Incendiary bombs were designed to cause large fires that would engulf an entire city, thereby causing maximum damage and killing thousands of people.

A German 105mm anti-aircraft gun, which fired 10–15 rounds per minute, in Berlin. Some women and Hitler Youth members operated anti-aircraft guns in Germany during the war.

failed to get into formation, so two squadrons were instructed to return to base. The one squadron that continued was detected by German radar operators, who alerted the Luftwaffe.

German fighters surprised the U.S. pilots as they crossed the German border. The bombers had little fighter protection: Mustangs were not due to join them until they were nearer their targets, where the Luftwaffe usually focused its defensive action. The fighters shot down 44 of the 99 U.S. bombers before they could reach their targets. The Fifteenth Air Force was more successful, but it too faced heavy opposition from German fighters and lost 14 bombers.

Bad weather prevented any operations the next day, but on February 24, the two U.S. air forces again launched major raids. The Fifteenth Air Force struck the Daimler-Benz factory at Styria, in eastern Austria, while the Eighth Air Force bombed Schweinfurt and Gotha, as well as Tutow, Kreising, and Posen. A large RAF force also bombed Schweinfurt at night. Big Week ended

 A Flying Fortress bombs German positions in Italy during the Allied invasion of the country in 1943. The Allies faced little opposition in the skies over Italy.

with another day of heavy bombing on February 25. This time the two U.S. air forces converged on Messerschmitt factories at Regensburg and Augsburg. The Luftwaffe concentrated its fighters against the Fifteenth Air Force, shoot-

ing down 33 of the 176 bombers. The Eighteenth Air Force, however, protected by Mustangs, lost just 31 of its 738 bombers. The raids devastated their targets, destroying the Regensburg plant, although much of the factory's

▶ The German city of Hamburg still stands in ruins after its occupation by U.S. forces near the end of the war in 1945. The bombing of July 1943 destroyed 80 percent of the city's buildings and killed 30,000 people, 20 percent of whom were children.

178

vital machinery was repairable and in some cases undamaged.

Bombing Germany's capital

The British commander Arthur Harris believed that destroying Berlin would hasten the defeat of Germany. He had initiated a major RAF campaign of nighttime raids on the German capital, beginning on November 18, 1943. Sixteen major raids followed in the so-called Battle of Berlin. In 1944, U.S. bombers joined in, launching huge daytime raids on March 6, 8, and 22.

Results of the Allied bombing raids

Harris had predicted that bombing raids would force Germany's collapse by April 1944. Yet despite the destruction of cities and factories, Germany's war effort and the morale of its people were far from broken. Although the Allied attacks lessened their industrial capacity, the Germans continued to upgrade their armaments production and also managed to rebuild many bombed factories. Armament output rose significantly in 1943 and 1944.

The air war had put a severe strain on the German war effort, however. Hitler was forced to recall hundreds of fighter aircraft and nearly 600,000 troops from the Soviet Union to man air defenses, and 30 percent of artillery production was diverted to build antiaircraft guns. The Luftwaffe also lost large numbers of experienced pilots, who could not be easily replaced.

In April 1944, the Allied strategic bombing forces started a new campaign: to prepare the way for D-Day, the invasion of occupied France.

▲ An RAF Halifax bomber flies over the Ruhr industrial region of Germany during a daytime attack on a synthetic oil plant at Eickel in November 1944.

STALINGRAD

After being driven back from the outskirts of Moscow in December 1941, the Germans had narrowly avoided disaster during the bitter winter months that followed. By late spring 1942, they had sufficiently recovered and could renew their efforts to defeat Stalin.

As Hitler considered a new campaign, Stalin urged his generals to continue their faltering offensive. The Red Army's inexperienced officers and men made no headway, however. By April both sides had ground to a halt. The Red Army had failed in an attempt to liberate the German-held city of Kharkov, in Ukraine. Against the advice of his generals, Stalin ordered a second attempt in May 1942.

Meanwhile Hitler planned a summer offensive to conquer Ukraine and the Caucasus in the south. In the north, he wanted the siege of Leningrad brought to a successful conclusion: In fact, the city endured until January 1944, when a Soviet offensive lifted the siege.

The Caucasus offensive, Operation Blue, would be carried out by Army Group South. Before it began, the German High Command wanted to capture the naval base of Sevastopol in the Crimea and to eliminate the Barvenkovo salient—a bulge in the Soviet line south of Kharkov.

Soviet offensive around Kharkov

On May 12, the Soviet offensive to liberate Kharkov began with an attack by two armies southeast and north of the city. Within two days they had advan-

ced up to 20 miles (32km). General Friedrich Paulus, in command of the German Sixth Army, suggested withdrawal, but Army Group South commander Fedor von Bock had more aggressive plans. With Hitler's approval, on May 17 he launched the First Panzer Army against the south of the Barvenkovo salient, thus threatening the attackers around Kharkov. Two days later the Soviets called off the Kharkov offensive. By then it was too late.

Paulus attacked from the north, and by the end of May the Soviets had lost

▼ A Soviet soldier surveys ruined buildings in Stalingrad. Much of the city was destroyed during the conflict that engulfed it from September 1942 to the end of January 1943.

Sevastopol

Sevastopol was the main Soviet naval base on the Black Sea. Its position on the Crimean peninsula, behind the German advance, gave the Soviets a base from which to bomb the oil fields at Ploesti in Romania. Hitler ordered its capture before the start of Operation Blue. The task was given to Erich von Manstein, who began his offensive in May 1942. He swept Soviet forces before him and was soon besieging Sevastopol. The city was protected by trenches, bunkers, and miles of caves and tunnels manned by more than 100,000 soldiers, sailors, and marines.

The German attack began with shelling and air raids on June 7. For three weeks the Soviet defenders resisted relentless German progress. On June 30 Stalin ordered the evacuation of the city, which fell on July 4. Apart from partisan resistance in the mountains, all of the Crimea was in German hands by the middle of July.

▲ This cabin boy in the Soviet Black Sea Fleet was given the Order of the Red Star for his part in the battle for Sevastopol.

almost 300,000 men, two-thirds of whom had been captured; German casualties were only 20,000 men. In the Crimea, meanwhile, the Eleventh Army, led by General Erich von Manstein, was making good progress in its campaign to capture Sevastopol.

Launch of Operation Blue

The Germans now finalized Operation Blue, the Caucasian offensive, which was to begin with a drive from Kursk toward Voronezh. There would then be a pincer movement from north and south to encircle Soviet forces west of the Don River, before a final push toward the Caucasus. Stalingrad was just one of many targets on the map: There was no sign that it would become one of the most significant engagements of World War II.

The offensive began on June 28. The Red Army was taken by surprise when the German armies headed southeast of Moscow instead of toward it. Bock's first objective was Voronezh, but the city held out for longer than anticipated. It finally fell on July 7 as Soviet forces to the south retreated to avoid being encircled.

On July 4, Hitler dismissed Bock and reorganized Army Group South into Army Groups A and B. On July 23 Army Group A captured Rostov in the

◀ A German tank patrols in the city of Voronezh, which fell to Army Group South on July 7, 1942.

▼ Romanian troops look out for enemy forces near Sevastopol in 1942. Romanian, Italian, and Hungarian troops all fought in support of the Germans during their campaign on the Eastern Front.

south. Hitler ordered it to occupy the "entire coastline of the Black Sea" with the aid of Italian and Romanian troops. Farther north, Army Group B was to "thrust forward to Stalingrad, to smash the enemy forces concentrated there"; the advance would take control of the Don and Volga rivers and communications between them.

Soviet withdrawal

While Hitler remained ambitious, Stalin was persuaded to surrender territory to gain time by his new chief of the general staff, General A. M. Vasilevsky. Stalin agreed that the pointless sacrifice of men and equipment should stop, and on July 6 he ordered the withdrawal of Soviet forces in the corridor between the Don and Donets rivers. Behind them, German forces advanced steadily across the bleak, treeless terrain toward Stalingrad.

Preparations in Stalingrad

Stalingrad was an industrial city that stretched along the banks of the Volga River for roughly 25 miles (40km). No bridge spanned the river—over a mile

(1.5km) wide in places—but ferries carried people and goods across. The city was an important center for the distribution of oil and grain. Oil storage tanks and grain elevators were familiar landmarks to its population of more than

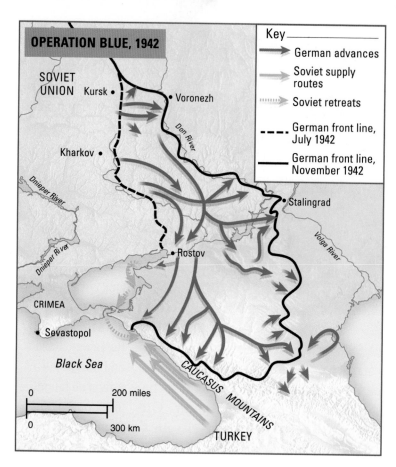

OPERATION BLUE, 1942

Key
→ German advances
→ Soviet supply routes
⇢ Soviet retreats
- - - German front line, July 1942
— German front line, November 1942

SOVIET UNION
Kursk • Voronezh
Kharkov •
Don River
Dnieper River
Dnieper River
• Rostov
CRIMEA
• Sevastopol
Black Sea
• Stalingrad
Volga River
CAUCASUS MOUNTAINS
TURKEY

0 ——— 200 miles
0 ——— 300 km

▲ The German push south into the Caucasus aimed to encircle Soviet troops west of the Don River.

▶ Soviet infantry ride on T-34 tanks as they advance into hostile territory; the troops would jump off to engage the enemy.

300,000—now almost doubled by the arrival of refugees.

On July 19, Stalin ordered Stalingrad to assume a state of war. The Stalingrad Defense Committee mobilized the population to dig antitank ditches, bunkers, and protective embankments around oil and petrol storage tanks. People living on the plain west of the city were ordered to leave their homes so that the army could use them for defense. Workers were given basic military training and organized into "Special Brigades."

First battles in Stalingrad

On August 23, a panzer corps of Paulus's Sixth Army reached the Volga north of Stalingrad. For the next 48 hours the Luftwaffe bombed the city, setting much of it ablaze and causing more than 35,000 casualties. The headquarters of the Southwest Front (the Soviet equivalent of an army group) moved to the Volga's east bank, along with the bulk of its artillery.

On September 13, the Germans began to advance through the shattered city. They met with stubborn resistance, but by September 21, troops of the Sixth Army had captured a major railroad station and the giant grain silo in the center of the city.

The Caucasus campaign

The main objective of the German campaign in the southern Soviet Union was to capture the oil fields of the Caucasus, the region between the Black and Caspian seas. In July Hitler sent Army Group A under Field Marshal Siegmund List to advance southwest to the Black Sea coast then east through the Caucasus Mountains to Baku.

List launched his offensive on July 25, and by August 9 he was in the northwest Caucasus, where he found the oil wells smashed. The Soviet forces began to regroup, and, with their supply lines stretched, the Germans struggled to get farther. On September 9 Hitler fired List and took control of the operation. The next day, the Germans captured the port of

▲ German troops and their mules make their way along a high pass in the Caucasus Mountains.

Novorossisk on the Black Sea.

A push east toward Grozny in late October failed despite heavy air support. There was only limited fighting during November and December, with the situation for the Germans becoming more perilous to the north. Finally, on December 28 Hitler ordered a retreat.

By January 2, 1943, Soviet troops were only 165 miles (265km) from Rostov in the northwest Caucasus; they threatened to cut off the German forces by severing routes north from the Caucasus. The German Army Group A split in two, with one retreating to Rostov and the other to the Taman Peninsula, east of the Kerch Strait. As they retreated, they destroyed roads and bridges to slow down the Soviet advance.

◄ German infantry take cover in a trench during the fighting in Stalingrad.

General Vasily Chuikov (1900–1982)

Born into a peasant family, Vasily Ivanovich Chuikov joined the Red Army in 1918, and by 1920 had become a regimental commander. He spent 13 years in the east of the Soviet Union and avoided Stalin's purges of the late 1930s to become commander of the Ninth Army in the war with Finland in 1940. Although the Soviets won, Chuikov's army suffered badly and he was sent to China as a diplomat. He returned in 1942 to command the Sixty-Second Army in its defense of Stalingrad. For its heroic efforts, his force was renamed the Eighth Guards Army. Chuikov led it in the battle for Berlin, where he accepted the German surrender on May 1, 1945. After the war Chuikov remained in the army, becoming a marshal of the Soviet Union in 1955.

▲ Chuikov is said to have told his troops at Stalingrad, "We shall hold the city or die here."

▼ Soviet infantry fight in the ruins of Stalingrad. The Germans called the street fighting "the War of the Rats."

Paulus now regrouped in preparation for an attempt to break through the Soviet lines to the Volga. Vasily I. Chuikov, commander of the Soviet Sixty-Second Army, launched a spoiling attack, but a German air assault held the Soviets at bay for more than two hours until the German attack began. By that evening the 24th Panzer Division had advanced almost a mile (1.5km) into the city.

Fighting among the ruins

For several days the fighting raged, and the Germans crept forward through streets full of dust created by incessant air and artillery bombardment. It was hard to tell friend from foe in the dust, and many soldiers were killed by their own side. Soviet artillery support was provided by gun batteries and Katyusha rocket launchers on the Volga's east bank. The screaming noise of the Katyushas and their German equivalent, the Nebelwerfer, unnerved the troops on the front lines, which were often less than 65 feet (20m) apart.

Soviet civilians who remained in the city lived in cellars and sewers, surviving on food they found in the pockets of the dead. Hunger sometimes drove them to work for the Germans in return for a meager ration. Soviet troops also deserted to the Germans in the hope of better food and a chance to be on what seemed to be the winning side.

Paulus's third major assault

By October 8, the second German attack had petered out. Just six days later, however, Paulus unleashed his third attack on the Soviet lines in the factory district in the north. In some places there was no clear front line, as men fought inside factory buildings among wrecked machines.

On the afternoon of October 18, the Germans reached the Volga. Two days later they captured one of the main factories. Paulus, however, was unable

▲ This posed photograph shows a German soldier preparing to fire a mortar during the campaign in the Caucasus.

to commit further units inside the city due to continuing Soviet attacks on his flanks to the north and south. He could not dislodge Soviet troops from the small areas of the city that they still held, despite almost continual bombardment. The German attacks grew less and less frequent, and—following a desperate final three-day effort—were all but over by November 12.

The Germans called the fighting *Rattenkrieg* (War of the Rats), where men scampered from ruin to ruin and sewer to sewer. Small, mobile Soviet assault squads often caught the Germans by surprise.

Operation Uranus

Outside the city, meanwhile, a major counteroffensive, code-named Operation Uranus, was being prepared by General Georgy K. Zhukov, Stalin's second-in-command. Zhukov gathered a force of more than a million men, 1,000 tanks, and 14,000 heavy guns. At 7:30 A.M. on November 19, he launched his first attack against the relatively weak Romanian Third Army, holding the line north of the city.

Sniping in Stalingrad

The ruins of Stalingrad were an ideal environment for snipers, expert marksmen who lay in wait to kill enemy troops from long range. Both armies provided "sniper school" training to their leading marksmen. The Germans did not allow women to fight, but the Red Army did; several women, such as Nina Petrova, became acclaimed snipers.

Working alone or in teams of two or three, the snipers would move into a hidden position and wait for a target, such as an officer, or a specialist, such as a signaler or machine gunner. Concealment was vital, and snipers went to great lengths to blend into their surroundings, lying immobile for hours peering through their telescopic sights. Their work, which was both physically and mentally demanding, was invaluable: They killed hundreds of enemy officers and created great fear in their opponents. They were rewarded with better food and quarters. The most famous Soviet sniper at Stalingrad was Vasily Zaitsev, who was featured in romanticized form in the 2001 movie *Enemy at the Gates*.

▶ The Soviet sniper Vasily Zaitsev (on the left) killed more than 200 German soldiers at Stalingrad.

Planning Operation Uranus

Operation Uranus was the code-name for the Soviet counterattack against the Sixth Army in the autumn of 1942. Planning began on September 12, when Stalin called Zhukov and other commanders to a conference in Moscow. The generals managed to persuade the Soviet leader to relieve Stalingrad by encircling the German Sixth Army. The plan involved two attacks: one to the north of the city and one to the south. The objective was to burst through the weak Romanian troops in those areas and link up at Kalach, where the capture of the bridge across the Don River would cut off the Sixth Army from its supplies. At the same time, Zhukov launched another attack, code-named Mars, against the German Army Group Center northwest of Moscow. The assault failed, but Zhukov claimed that it had been a screen all along to prevent Army Group Center providing support to the Germans at Stalingrad.

Success for Operation Uranus

The Romanians soon broke and T-34 tanks poured into the gaps. They headed for a bridge over the Don River at Kalach, 60 miles (95km) west. Paulus suspended operations in the city itself.

On November 20, the Red Army again broke through Romanian lines,

▼ An 80cm railroad gun, the largest gun ever built, stands ready for action at Sevastopol. It was one of two built for the invasion of the Soviet Union; the other was used at Stalingrad.

this time south of the city. Soviet tanks and cavalry headed for Kalach, but were slowed by fog and blizzards. As the Romanians struggled to hold the advance, the German Fourth Panzer Army began to retreat westward.

On November 22, Soviet troops captured Kalach. The next day Soviet forces from north and south linked up, encircling the Sixth Army and part of the Fourth Panzer Army. The circle was thin, and escape would have been possible. Hitler, however, ordered the 330,000 trapped Italian, Romanian, and German troops to stand firm. There was to be no retreat. Instead, the Germans would launch their own offensive, Operation Winter Storm. It was to be carried out by Army Group Don, formed on November 20 and led by Erich von Manstein.

Operation Winter Storm

Winter Storm aimed to break through to Stalingrad and link up with the Sixth Army, just outside the city. They would withdraw and be incorporated into Army Group Don. The withdrawal could only begin on the express order of Hitler. Winter Storm was planned to consist of two armored thrusts, but one was pinned down by Soviet attacks. Winter Storm was reduced to a single thrust, which began on December 12.

Meanwhile, the Soviets launched Operation Saturn, aimed at Rostov. If Rostov fell, Army Group A would be cut off and the German position in the whole southern Soviet Union would be in jeopardy.

Von Manstein's advance and retreat

Soviet attacks toward Rostov had achieved little by the time the Germans

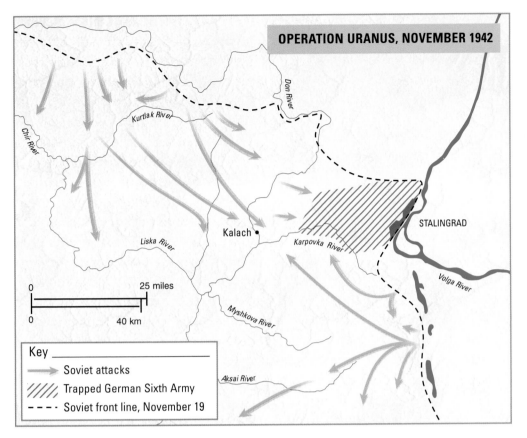

OPERATION URANUS, NOVEMBER 1942

Don River

Kurtlak River

Chir River

Kalach

Liska River

Karpovka River

STALINGRAD

Volga River

0   25 miles

0   40 km

Myshkova River

Aksai River

Key
→ Soviet attacks
/// Trapped German Sixth Army
- - - Soviet front line, November 19

◀ The Soviet pincer movement in Operation Uranus trapped the German besiegers of Stalingrad in a pocket to the west of the city.

launched Winter Storm on December 12. Von Manstein's forces made good progress, and by mid-December a panzer corps was within 35 miles (55km) of Stalingrad. Hitler, however, refused to allow the Sixth Army to withdraw.

On December 16 the Soviets began Operation Little Saturn, a counterattack against von Manstein's relief troops. The Italian Eighth Army started to collapse, and within 72 hours it was encircled. As the Axis front fell apart, Hitler called off Winter Storm. Four days later he authorized the retreat of Army Group A toward Rostov and Army Group Don to a line 150 miles (240km) west of Stalingrad. Paulus's Sixth Army would have to continue the siege of the city unaided.

The head of the Luftwaffe, Hermann Göring, promised his aircraft would keep the Sixth Army supplied, but the Luftwaffe proved incapable of supply-

ing even the minimum daily target of 550 tons of supplies; the most it ever managed in a day was 290 tons. By early December the troops in Stalingrad were starving, and short of ammunition and medicine. The situation worsened as the Soviet advance forced the Luftwaffe to use bases farther west, so that the planes had to carry more fuel and less cargo. Soviet

▼ German special forces wait on an airstrip to be evacuated from Stalingrad. Such highly trained troops were too valuable to leave to their fate.

▲ German aircrew look out through the nose of a Heinkel He III bomber over Stalingrad. The Volga River is just visible through the glass.

vive in temperatures that sometimes dropped as low as –22°F (–30°C). Even minimal rations of bread, fat, and horse meat were now a memory and they were forced to eat rats or search for scraps of food in the pockets of dead Soviet soldiers.

In the first week of 1943, the Soviets gave Paulus two chances to surrender, but he refused. On January 10 the Red Army launched a major assault around the perimeter of the Stalingrad pocket. Within six days the German positions in the west were collapsing. Soon the Germans were withdrawing into the center of the city; thousands died as the Soviet forces moved forward.

antiaircraft guns and fighters shot down many of the slow transport planes, and more crashed on damaged or icy airstrips inside the Stalingrad pocket. The airlift cost the Luftwaffe almost 500 transport aircraft.

As the year ended, the hungry and exhausted Sixth Army struggled to sur-

The end

On January 23, the Soviets captured the last airfield in the pocket, ending evacuation flights for the wounded. Reduced to 100,000 men, the Sixth Army was split in two by Soviet forces on January 26. Paulus had appealed to

▶ Soviet infantry advance cautiously through the ruins of Stalingrad. They are armed with PPSh submachine guns, ideal for combat at close quarters.

◀ German infantry keep guard on the snow-covered steppe outside Stalingrad. In the weeks following the success of the Soviets' Operation Uranus, the Germans suffered not only from lack of supplies but also from the intense cold.

Hitler four days earlier to be allowed to open negotiations with the Soviets, but Hitler had refused.

On January 30, Hitler promoted Paulus to field marshal. No German officer of such a rank had ever surrendered, and Hitler was signaling that he expected Paulus to commit suicide rather than surrender. Paulus ignored Hitler; on January 31, he surrendered.

Consequences of Stalingrad

Some 91,000 men followed Paulus into captivity, taking the total losses of the Germans and their allies during the Stalingrad campaign to more than 500,000 men. Many of the prisoners would later die from harsh conditions in captivity. To the south, meanwhile, the Red Army pushed on toward Kharkov and Rostov, which fell on February 14.

Both Army Group Don and Army Group A withdrew west to avoid immediate danger, but the southern flank of Germany's eastern front was still threatened with collapse. It would take a considerable effort for the Germans to repair the damage inflicted by the Soviets at Stalingrad.

▼ By making Friedrich Paulus a field marshal, Hitler was signaling that he should kill himself rather than give up. Paulus surrendered, however, and spent the rest of the war as a prisoner.

Eyewitness

❝ Stalingrad is no longer a town. By day it is an enormous cloud of burning, blinding smoke; it is a vast furnace lit by the reflection of the flames. And when night arrives, one of those scorching, howling, bleeding nights, the dogs plunge into the Volga and swim desperately to gain the other bank. The nights in Stalingrad are a terror for them. Animals flee this hell… only men endure. ❞

A German officer of 24th Panzer Division, Stalingrad, October 1942

IN THE BALANCE: KHARKOV AND KURSK

Between spring 1942 and summer 1943 a number of tank battles were fought around cities in the western Soviet Union. At Kharkov the Germans won their last victory on the Eastern Front.

Kharkov in Ukraine was the Soviet Union's fourth-largest city, an industrial center, important railroad junction, and strategic base on the Donets River. Kharkov had fallen to the Germans in late 1941 and was a key position as the German Army Group South advanced through Ukraine toward Stalingrad and the Caucasus region. Soviet leader Joseph Stalin was determined that the Red Army should recapture the city. He and the Soviet High Command planned a massive offensive to liberate Kharkov when the roads dried out after the spring rains.

Soviet plan to capture Kharkov

The Soviet plan called for a surprise attack by Marshal Semyon Timoshenko's Southwest Front. Two thrusts from the northeast and southwest would seal off the city. The Soviets had picked the strongest sector of the German line for their attack, however.

Throughout the winter the Germans had been moving men and equipment into the city ready for a drive into the Caucasus. Instead of facing 12 weak infantry divisions and one panzer division as they thought, the Soviets faced 16 infantry divisions, two refitted panzer divisions, and three infantry battle groups. The Germans also knew that the attack was coming: Their military intelligence had spotted the Soviet troop buildup.

Second battle of Kharkov

Despite the warnings, the initial Soviet attack on the city on May 12, 1942, caught the Germans by surprise, battering defenders northeast of the city.

The German Sixth Army mounted a strong defense and soon launched a counterattack with Luftwaffe support. The Soviets made more significant gains in the south, where the German High Command planned to withdraw in order to draw the Soviets forward into a position where they could be encircled and trapped. Hitler did not like to see German forces withdraw, however; he overrode the plan and insisted on an immediate counterattack.

On May 17, the Seventeenth Army of Colonel-General Ewald von Kleist launched the counterattack against the southern arm of the Soviet advance. Timoshenko reacted slowly, and by May 22 the Soviet forces were being encircled. More than 275,000 men were

▼ Red Army cavalry pursue the enemy on the steppe around Kharkov. The open countryside was ideal terrain for mobile warfare, both on horseback and in tanks.

encircled and killed, wounded, or taken prisoner, and 3,700 tanks and artillery pieces were lost.

The defeat cost the Soviets virtually all of their reserves in the southern part of the front. Joseph Stalin told Timoshenko: "Battles must be won not with numbers but with skill. If you do not learn to direct your troops better, all the armaments the country can produce will not be enough for you."

Soviets take Kharkov again

Having taken Kharkov, the Germans began Operation Blue, a drive southeast toward Stalingrad and the Caucasus region. The offensive led to the titanic Battle of Stalingrad in the fall

▶ German troops advance through a street in Kharkov in 1943.

and winter of 1942–1943, during which the German Sixth Army was surrounded and destroyed by a massive Soviet counterattack (*see Chapter 4*).

The counterattack carried the Red Army back toward Kharkov, where they arrived in February 1943. Huge tank forces quickly overran the German and Axis defenders of the city and drove on toward the Dnieper River, an important strategic position. The situation was critical for the Germans. Hitler ordered one of his most able commanders, Field Marshal Erich von Manstein, to recapture Kharkov and stabilize the front.

Germans recapture Kharkov

On February 21, Manstein ordered a counteroffensive to recapture Kharkov, spearheaded by three elite Waffen-SS divisions with Luftwaffe support. The German forces were outnumbered by seven to one, but they still had the advantage over the enemy: The Soviet advance had carried it beyond both its supply lines and its air support.

The Germans smashed through the Soviet Southwest Front 60 miles (100km) south of Kharkov, punching a gap for a German pincer attack on the city by the Fourth Panzer Army. After

Field Marshal Erich von Manstein (1887–1973)

Erich von Manstein, an outstanding commander, served in World War I before joining the German Army's general staff. He planned the ambitious German attack through the Ardennes in 1940.

▲ Manstein had a talent for armored warfare. He led Army Group South to success in the 1943 campaign to recapture Kharkov.

In 1942 Manstein led the Eleventh Army to victory in the Crimea. He was made a field marshal and placed in charge of Army Group Don, but failed to break through to relieve the German Sixth Army in Stalingrad. In his most famous action he led the counterattack at Kharkov in 1943. Hitler fired Manstein in March 1944 for criticizing orders. In the 1950s Manstein served three years of an 18-year prison sentence imposed by the Nuremberg War Crimes Tribunal.

three days of house-to-house fighting, the city again fell to the Germans on March 14.

Manstein's swift victory was a remarkable achievement. Defeat cost the Soviets 50,000 dead and 20,000 taken prisoner, while victory boosted Ger-

◀ Late in the war, the city of Kharkov displays the scars of being repeatedly fought over. Its citizens also suffered greatly under the German occupation.

The Waffen-SS

The Waffen-SS (Armed SS) formed the elite of the German Army but also represented the worst of Nazi excesses. It comprised three types: the Leibstandarte SS Adolf Hitler (Hitler's bodyguard), the "Death's-Head" battalions that ran the concentration camps, and the "Disposition Troops," the other SS fighting units. The SS also became home for troops from numerous satellite nations, as the Nazis set out to create a multinational force intended to combat Soviet communism.

Waffen-SS men underwent extensive training and acquired a reputation for courage and loyalty. While SS officers and sergeants were among the war's best small-unit leaders, senior officers were of uneven quality, because they were appointed more for their political reliability than their military skill.

The Waffen-SS cemented its fighting reputation in March 1943, when I SS Panzer Corps recaptured Kharkov in three days. Waffen-SS troops also fought well later that summer at Kursk. However, Waffen-SS units also carried out many atrocities. In May 1943 in Kharkov, for example, they set about systematically murdering more than 20,000 Soviet civilians.

◀ The Waffen-SS troops were easily identifiable by their distinctive camouflage smocks and helmet covers.

▶ Elite troops of the Waffen-SS speed across the open steppe near Kursk as part of Operation Citadel. Their offensive was blunted by well-prepared Soviet defenses.

man morale. Kharkov, however, was to prove the German Army's last operational success on the Eastern Front.

German forces depleted

On March 21, heavy spring rains brought the German counteroffensive to a halt. The recapture of Kharkov was little compensation for the loss of most of the territory the Germans had won in the summer offensive of 1942. A year of fighting had taken a toll on both sides, but was more damaging for the Germans. The Soviets had great reserves of manpower, whereas the

Germans were now clearly inferior in both numbers of men and the amount of equipment.

Plans to attack Kursk salient

The German army groups South and Center faced a difficult choice: Inaction would give the initiative to the Soviets, but offensive operations entailed great risks. In the end, Hitler decided to remain on the offensive. They proposed a limited attack on a salient (bulge) in the Soviet front north of Kharkov at Kursk. They wanted to stop the salient becoming a

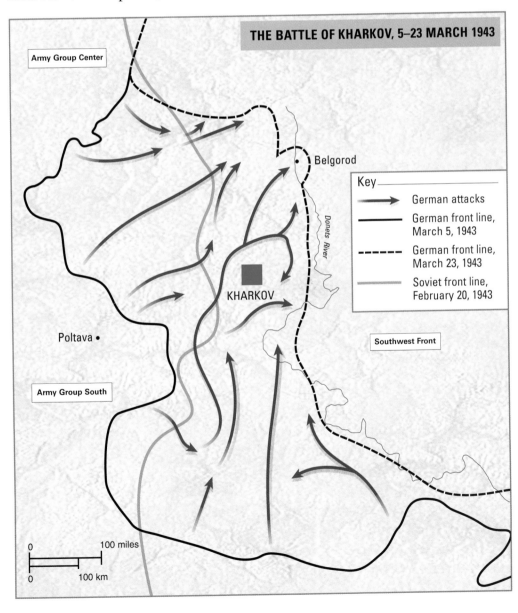

THE BATTLE OF KHARKOV, 5–23 MARCH 1943

Army Group Center

Belgorod

Donets River

Key
→ German attacks
— German front line, March 5, 1943
--- German front line, March 23, 1943
— Soviet front line, February 20, 1943

KHARKOV

Poltava •

Army Group South

Southwest Front

0 — 100 miles
0 — 100 km

The T-34

In 1941 the Soviet T-34 was described by German field marshal Ewald von Kleist as "the finest tank in the world." It was developed from fast U.S. tanks that were sold to the Soviet Union in the early 1930s after they had been declined by the U.S. military. Almost 40,000 T-34s were produced from 1940 to 1945, accounting for almost 70 percent of Soviet tank production.

Up to the end of 1941 the T-34 was faster, more maneuverable, and better armored than German tanks. It had a strong hull that sloped at such an angle that enemy shells often bounced off it. It also had a powerful 76-mm gun capable of penetrating any enemy tank. The T-34 had a top speed of 32 miles per hour (52kmh). Its tracks were 19 inches (48cm) wide: They spread the tank's weight and prevented it sinking in marshy or snow-covered ground.

The T-34 was highly influential; it was the model for the German Panther, developed in 1942–1943, and the gun of the German Tiger was designed to combat its armor.

▲ A T-34 goes into action. Its gun had a shorter range than some German tank guns, but it was the best all-round tank of the war.

possible springboard for a renewed Soviet drive in the summer. The attack on Kursk, code-named Operation Citadel, was to use a rapid and overwhelming pincer attack from Army Group Center in the north and Army Group South in the south that would trap the Soviet troops in the salient.

Hitler authorized Operation Citadel in mid-April, but there were difficulties in getting the panzer divisions up to strength and getting the new generation of Tiger and Panther tanks into operation. Despite the problems, Hitler insisted that Citadel must go ahead; but he pushed it back from May 3 to July 5.

Soviets set up defenses

Unknown to the Germans, Soviet intelligence was aware of the planned operation. The Red Army was setting up massive defenses near Kursk, with belts of trenches, barbed wire, and minefields in defensive lines 15 to 25 miles (24 to 40km) deep. The Red Army generals intended to inflict massive losses on the Germans in a gigantic battle of attrition.

By July two army groups—the Central Front under General Konstantin Rokossovsky and the Voronezh Front under General Nikolai Vatutin— were assembled in the salient. More than 1.5 million Soviet soldiers, 19,000 artillery pieces, 2,400 aircraft, and 4,500 tanks faced a combined German force of 900,000 soldiers, 9,900 artillery pieces, 1,800 aircraft, and 3,100 tanks. The German effort brought together 70 percent of their remaining armor and 65 percent of their aircraft.

Clash of giants

Operation Citadel began on July 5, 1943, but did not start as the Germans had planned. Troops from Army Group Center, who expected a supporting artillery barrage for the attack, instead found Soviet shells raining down upon them. The heavy bombardment disrupted German attack formations; when the offensive began, infantry had to use hand grenades and small arms to take each trench. They advanced no more than 12 miles (20km) in a week of heavy fighting.

To the south Manstein's force, which was the stronger of the two German wings, had more success. The Fourth Panzer Army, aided by elite Waffen-SS divisions, penetrated the Soviets' first defensive line along a 25-mile (40-km) front. However, it then got entangled in the second line, which Soviet deception had concealed from German planners. The advance petered out in

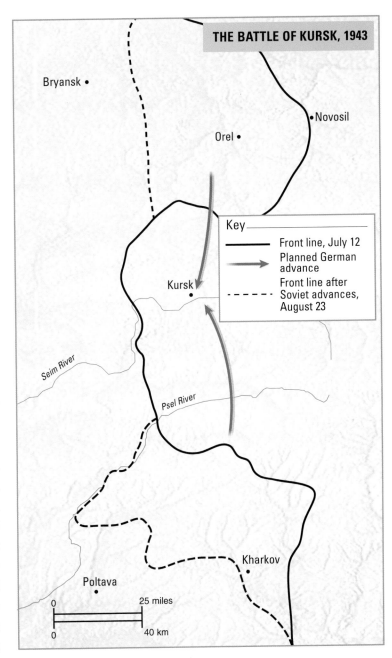

THE BATTLE OF KURSK, 1943

Bryansk

Novosil

Orel

Key
—— Front line, July 12
→ Planned German advance
- - - Front line after Soviet advances, August 23

Kursk

Seim River

Psel River

Kharkov

Poltava

0 ____ 25 miles
0 ____ 40 km

◀ Soviet T-34 tanks near the front during the Battle of Kursk. The Russians massed some 4,500 tanks to face 3,100 German tanks.

Day of decision: Prokhorovka

On the steppe around Prokhorovka, a railroad station 65 miles (100km) southeast of Kursk, German and Soviet forces fought the pivotal battle of Operation Citadel on July 12, 1943. As II SS Panzer Corps broke through Soviet lines and advanced from the south, the Soviet Fifth Guards Tank Army countered from the east.

German Tiger and Panzer Mk IV tanks clashed with Soviet T-34 tanks in the largest tank battle of the war. German general Heinz Guderian commented that he had "never received such an overwhelming impression of Soviet strength and numbers." Meanwhile, an air battle raged in the skies, as the Luftwaffe fought the newly improved Red Air Force.

Although the Soviets lost far more tanks and vehicles than the Germans, they secured a psychological victory. The battle showed that they could now fight the best of the German Army to a standstill.

ground turned to mud by heavy rain storms. By July 11, the two pincers of the German attack were still 75 miles (120km) apart.

Battle in the air

While fighting continued on the ground, an immense air battle raged over Kursk. The Red Air Force gradually gained superiority, largely because it had many more aircraft than its enemy. Luftwaffe crews flew 3,000 sorties on the first day of the operation alone, but could barely stem the tide. They also had to face the threat of Soviet antiaircraft defenses.

German hopes dashed

On July 11, Manstein gained room to maneuver in the south by encircling Soviet forces outside the village of Prokhorovka. The II SS Panzer Corps, with 400 tanks, broke through Soviet defenses and raced for Prokhorovka Station, triggering a Soviet counterattack. The resulting day-long tank battle was one of the largest in history.

The battle involved more than 1,200 armored vehicles, including 100 German Panzer VIs, or Tiger tanks. The Tiger had been developed in response to the Soviet T-34 tank, whose front armor could withstand the guns of earlier German tanks.

The Tiger tank had a long-barreled, high-velocity 88-mm gun, adapted from antiaircraft and antitank weapons that could penetrate the most heavily armored Soviet tanks at long range. However, even the Tiger tanks proved vulnerable to Soviet defenses at Kursk. Two-thirds of German tanks lost in the battle were destroyed by

▶ Soviet female crew stand in front of their biplane. The Red Air Force had three regiments of female fighter and bomber pilots, who were known as the "Nightwitches." They played a vital role in the fight to gain control of the skies over the Eastern Front.

mines. Others were destroyed by Red Army antitank guns.

End of the battle at Kursk

After Prokhorovka, German hopes of decisive progress toward eliminating the Kursk salient were evaporating quickly. They had been unable to gather momentum for a blitzkrieg operation, which depended on rapidly moving armored units supported by air power. However, the Red Army had also suffered enormous losses in tanks and their defenses were being stretched.

Manstein now proposed to use his last two fresh panzer divisions to break through to the town of Kursk. In Berlin, Adolf Hitler was facing problems on other fronts. The Allied invasion of the island of Sicily on July 9 threatened defeat for his Italian ally. Hitler knew that he could not both continue Operation Citadel and also meet this new threat. He concluded: "The Italians are not resisting and the island will probably be lost. As a result the western powers will be able to land in the Balkans or southern Italy. Hence new armies must be formed in the these areas,

which means taking troops from the Eastern Front, and calling a halt to Citadel."

Casualties and consequences

German forces had suffered more than 200,000 casualties at Kursk, the Soviets more than 800,000. The Germans had lost 1,500 tanks and Army Group South alone claimed to have destroyed 1,800 Soviet tanks. Neither side had won a clear victory, however, and that fact was far more serious for the Germans than for the Soviets. The Germans had lost vital tanks without gaining any ground. Despite their

▲ The Tiger was more powerfully armed than earlier German tanks, with an 88mm gun.

▼ German tanks and armored vehicles wait to go into action at the Battle of Kursk, one of the largest tank battles that has ever been fought.

Germany's foreign legions

Germany drew extensively on satellite nations to fill its armed forces. Its foreign legions came from countries as diverse as Albania, Armenia, Belgium, Croatia, the United Kingdom, Denmark, Hungary, and Switzerland. The Waffen-SS eventually had more foreign than German troops, in units grouped by nationality. The foreign contingents were of vastly varying quality. The Latvian and Estonian SS divisions fought exceptionally, but others did not perform as well.

Foreigners joined the Germans for various reasons. Some fought to win independence for their homeland, others simply to avoid becoming German prisoners of war; still others were opportunists who did not care what side they were on. Many Soviets fought for the Germans

because they hated living under Stalin's reign of terror. Western European volunteers joined for other reasons; some were fascists, some wanted to join an anti-Bolshevik crusade, and others simply wanted to be part of the elite Waffen-SS.

▶ Russian Cossacks, formerly of the Red Army, were among the foreign troops who fought for the German army.

◀ Soviet Yakovlev Yak-9 aircraft go into action against the Germans. The Soviet Union produced 18,000 aircraft in 1943 alone, helping its air force to gradually gain supremacy over the Luftwaffe.

heavy casualties, on the other hand, the Soviets were still close to their supply depots, and were able to repair many of their damaged vehicles. Rokossovsky sent a congratulatory message to the Soviet troops: "The soldiers of the Central Front who met the enemy with a rampart of murderous steel and truly Russian grit and tenacity have exhausted him after a week of unrelenting and unremitting fighting; they have contained the enemy's drive. The first phase of the battle is over."

Turning point on the Eastern Front

The two battles at Kharkov and Kursk were a turning point on the Eastern Front. More than any other engagements, they also clearly displayed the overwhelming difficulties facing any German attempt to secure victory on the Eastern Front. Neither the Wehrmacht's vast battle experience, nor its talented leadership, nor its superior equipment could overcome the immense spaces of the Soviet Union, with the challenges they posed to supply lines, or the extraordinary tenacity of their enemy. The Red Army and Air Force were both improving in skill and growing in sheer size.

By July 1943, the German Army and Air Force in the east were past their peak, having been weakened by losses in the previous year; they were still dangerous, however, and at the Battle of Kursk they had thrown everything they had at the Soviets. Yet they were turned back and the Soviets took the initiative. The stage was set for the decisive Soviet offensives of 1943, 1944, and 1945.

▲ A Waffen-SS crew loads an antitank gun at the Battle of Kursk; their weapon is a PAK 40 75mm antitank gun, of which more than 23,000 were built during World War II.

Nazi atrocities in Kharkov

When Soviet forces recaptured Kharkov in February 1943, they found evidence that during two years of occupation the Germans had killed more than 195,000 civilians. The victims had been shot, tortured to death, or gassed in mobile "gas vans." A wide variety of units had taken part in the atrocities, including regular infantry, elite Waffen-SS units, and *Einsatzgruppen,* who had the job of carrying out Hitler's program of racial purification.

After retaking Kharkov from the Germans for the final time, the Soviets staged a series of war crimes trials in the city in late 1943. Three Germans and a Russian were convicted of carrying out executions in specially equipped carbon monoxide vans. All four of the accused pleaded guilty, and on December 19, 1943, some 50,000 citizens turned out in Kharkov city square to see them hanged.

THE BATTLE OF THE CORAL SEA

By the spring of 1942, rapid advances in Southeast Asia and the Pacific had created a dilemma for Japanese military planners. Their split priorities brought them close to defeat in the Coral Sea.

After their attack on Pearl Harbor on December 7, 1941, the Japanese had enjoyed a string of victories. They had defeated British troops in Malaya and Singapore by February 1942, and U.S. troops in the Philippines in April 1942. They had secured the so-called Southern Resource Area, including the oil-rich areas of what are now Malaysia and Indonesia. The Japanese depended on these captured resources—particularly oil—to supply their forces.

The Japanese aimed to protect their gains with a defensive perimeter. It was to stretch from the Kurile Islands south through Wake Island, the Marianas, the Marshalls, and the Gilberts, to Rabaul on New Britain. From Rabaul, the perimeter would extend west to northwestern New Guinea. If the Allies could not breach the perimeter, the Japanese hoped, they would negotiate peace terms that would leave Japan in possession of most of its conquests.

Japan's aims change

After their rapid success, however, the Japanese were not sure of the next step. The Imperial Japanese Navy would dominate further actions. Its strategists disagreed among themselves. Admiral Isoroku Yamamoto, commander of the Combined Fleet, was anxious to defeat the aircraft carriers of the U.S. Pacific Fleet. The carriers had escaped the raid on Pearl Harbor. Yamamoto believed that they were the greatest threat to Japan's gains. He suggested a thrust into the Central Pacific, to establish forward bases on islands such as Midway. From there, Japan could draw the United States into an unequal battle that the Japanese would win.

Admiral Osami Nagano was head of the Naval General

▶ The carrier USS *Lexington* explodes in the Coral Sea on May 8, 1942. Hours after the ship was struck by enemy bombs and torpedoes, it was scuttled.

Staff. He wanted to damage communications between Britain and its dependencies, India and Australia. He wanted to push toward India, or to isolate Australia in order to prevent it from being used by the Americans as a base in the Southwest Pacific. To isolate Australia, Nagano proposed to win control of the Coral Sea. The Japanese would thrust out from their base at Rabaul in New Britain, south through the Solomon Islands and west to New Guinea. Japan's rulers adopted a version of Nagano's thrust toward Australia, code-named MO. They landed forces on the north coast of New Guinea at Lae, Salamaua, and Finschafen. They also planned an attack on the strategic harbor at Port Moresby on New Guinea's southeast coast.

A change in circumstances

In January 1942, Japanese forces captured Bougainville in the Solomons. They got ready to attack Guadalcanal, where they intended to build an airbase. Before Operation MO was fully put into action, however, a daring U.S. attack changed Japanese plans.

On April 18, 1942, U.S. bombers from the carrier *Hornet* attacked Tokyo and other Japanese cities. The Doolittle Raid was named for its commander, James H. Doolittle. It was a reminder of the potential threat from aircraft from U.S. carriers. The raid led the Japanese to adopt Yamamoto's plan. They would knock out the U.S. carriers after the occupation of part of the Aleutian islands off Alaska and Midway Island in the Central Pacific. Meanwhile, Operation MO was to continue with further advances in the Solomons, particularly the capture of an airbase at Tulagi.

Forces in the South Pacific

Yamamoto's eagerness to engage the U.S. carrier fleets reflected the apparent inequality between the forces in the southern Pacific.

The Doolittle Raid

Soon after the attack on Pearl Harbor in December 1941, U.S. officers planned to strike back at the Japanese. They planned a carrier-based bomber raid on Japan itself. The raid, which took place on April 18, 1942, was unofficially named for its commander, Army Air Corps lieutenant colonel James H. Doolittle.

Doolittle trained 16 crews in secret. Their bombers were converted and stripped down so that they could take off from carriers. They were fitted with extra fuel tanks to increase their range to 2,400 miles (3,850km). That would allow them to fly past Japan to friendly airfields in China.

The bombers took off from the carrier *Hornet* on April 18, 800 miles (1,290km) from Tokyo. Flying low to avoid Japanese planes, the crews bombed Tokyo before crash-landing in China. Eight men were captured by the Japanese, of whom three were executed.

The raid did little damage, but it had a great impact. It gave a major boost to U.S. morale at a time when the Japanese had the upper hand. It also panicked Japan's leaders into seeking a battle with the U.S. carriers—a battle they would lose.

◄ One of the 16 B-25s leaves the deck of the carrier USS *Hornet* heading for Tokyo. The bombers were stripped down to make them light enough to take off at sea.

The three fleets of the Imperial Japanese Navy had 10 carriers, including two new Shokaku class ships. They also had supporting vessels and over 200 carrier- and 160 ground-based aircraft. Their pilots' confidence was high after their early victories. However, Japan's forces were stretched by the decision to continue with Operation MO at the same time as the thrust into the Central Pacific.

On the U.S. side, the Pacific Fleet had four carriers. A fifth carrier, *Saratoga*, was damaged and temporarily out of action. The fleet also had support vessels plus 150 carrier aircraft and more than 500 ground-based aircraft. U.S. sailors and aviators were still learning the tactics of carrier warfare. Their senior officers, meanwhile, were learning to cope with the decision to split U.S. command in the Pacific between the army and the navy.

Army general Douglas MacArthur commanded the Southwest Pacific Theater, and all of its land-based Army Air Corps airplanes. All U.S. Navy ships and aircraft in the area, meanwhile, were controlled by Pacific Fleet commander Chester Nimitz. The clumsy command arrangement would cause difficulties for U.S. forces in the Pacific throughout the war.

Predicting Japan's plan

U.S. forces in the Pacific had one great advantage over their enemy. Late in 1940, the Office of Naval Intelligence had cracked the Japanese naval code, named JN-25. U.S. analysts could read about 10 to 15 percent of Japanese messages. They also used Radio Traffic Analysis to read signals. The technique examined the location, volume, and pattern of radio transmissions rather than their content.

By mid-April 1942, intelligence had convinced Nimitz that the Japanese would probably try to attack Port Moresby on New Guinea from their

---

Aircraft carriers

Aircraft carriers had been in use since the 1920s. Until the Battle of Taranto in November 1940, however, they were generally seen as playing a supporting role to battleships. At Taranto, British carrier-borne airplanes in the Mediterranean surprised Italian naval vessels in harbor while a carrier remained at a safe distance. The Japanese echoed the tactic with the December 1941 attack on Pearl Harbor. The raid was launched from carriers based over 230 miles (370km) to the north of Hawaii.

By the end of World War II in 1945, aircraft carriers had replaced battleships as the most important capital ships for the world's navies. They had a number of important roles.

Their regular duties included striking at coastal defensive positions before amphibious landings and providing cover to transport vessels carrying the troops to their landing sites. They were also important as a means of damaging enemy ships, particularly carriers, at a long range, such as at the Battle of the Coral Sea. Carrier-borne aircraft both dropped bombs and launched torpedoes at enemy vessels. The additional range that carriers gave aircraft also made them more effective for long-distance reconnaissance.

▼ The USS *Yorktown*, launched in 1937, fought in the Coral Sea but was sunk at Midway later in 1942.

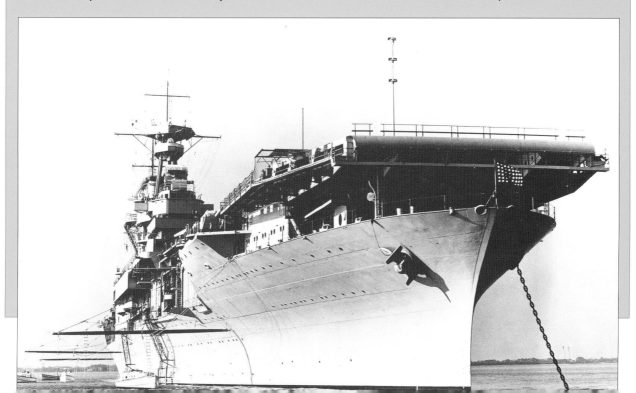

▶ A U.S. Avenger torpedo bomber launches its torpedo during maneuvers. At the Battle of the Coral Sea, many U.S. pilots fired their torpedoes from such a long range that Japanese vessels were able to outrun them in the water.

▼ Japanese air crew prepare to launch Zero fighters from the deck of the *Shokaku*. The Zero was the best fighter in the Pacific from 1940 until 1943.

base at Rabaul early in May. Nimitz wanted to use his carriers to prevent the operation, but neither *Hornet* nor *Enterprise* could reach the Coral Sea in time.

Nimitz could therefore send only two task forces to the area. Task Force 11 was based on the carrier *Lexington*, and commanded by Rear Admiral Aubrey

Fitch. Task Force 17, commanded by Rear Admiral Frank J. Fletcher, was based on the carrier *Yorktown*. Fletcher was put in charge of the whole operation. They were joined by U.S.–Australian Task Force 44 on May 4.

The next phase of Operation MO was supported by two Japanese naval forces.

Eyewitness

66 A few minutes later, twenty-one heavy bombers, escorted by eleven Zeros, attacked *Australia* from astern and up-sun at a height of about 18,000 feet. Bombing was accurate. Some twenty 500-pound bombs and several smaller ones were dropped, and we were straddled in all directions, and our upper decks were drenched with spray.

These aircraft had only just gone when three more, flying even higher at 25,000 feet, dropped bombs close to the destroyer USS *Perkins* which was just ahead of us.

Admiral Crace later reported that it was subsequently discovered that these aircraft were US Army B-17 Flying Fortress heavy bombers operating from Townsville. He also said in his report that they were good enough to photograph our force a few seconds after bomb release, thus proving that they had attacked their own ships. 99

Dacre Smyth, later commodore of the Australian Navy, on board HMAS *Australia*.

▼ Although the outcome of the Battle of the Coral Sea was inconclusive, the American forces succeeded in turning back Japan's force for the invasion of Port Moresby on New Guinea.

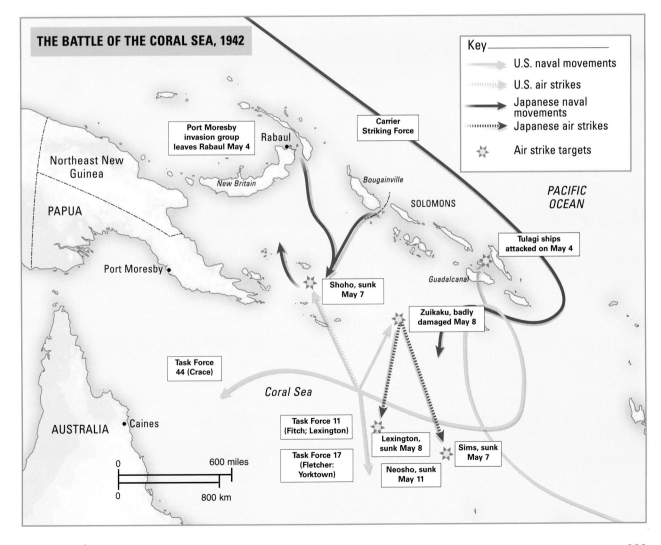

THE BATTLE OF THE CORAL SEA, 1942

Key
→ U.S. naval movements
→ U.S. air strikes
→ Japanese naval movements
→ Japanese air strikes
✳ Air strike targets

Northeast New Guinea

PAPUA

Rabaul

Port Moresby invasion group leaves Rabaul May 4

New Britain

Carrier Striking Force

Bougainville

SOLOMONS

PACIFIC OCEAN

Tulagi ships attacked on May 4

Port Moresby

Guadalcanal

Shoho, sunk May 7

Zuikaku, badly damaged May 8

Task Force 44 (Crace)

Coral Sea

AUSTRALIA • Caines

Task Force 11 (Fitch; Lexington)

Task Force 17 (Fletcher; Yorktown)

Lexington, sunk May 8

Sims, sunk May 7

Neosho, sunk May 11

0 ___ 600 miles
0 ___ 800 km

Chester Nimitz (1885–1966)

Admiral Chester W. Nimitz was one of the principal architects of Allied victory in the Pacific.

A Texan, Nimitz graduated from the U.S. Naval Academy in 1905. He commanded submarines during World War I (1914–1918) and in 1938 moved to battleships. He then occupied more strategic roles. Nimitz was promoted to commander-in-chief, U.S. Pacific

◄ Nimitz (left) with Raymond Spruance, the officer who commanded the U.S. fleet at the decisive Battle of Midway in June 1942.

Fleet, 10 days after Pearl Harbor. With typical energy, he set out to rebuild the fleet. He focused particularly on aircraft carriers and submarines.

Nimitz had a firm grasp of the logistical problems involved in Pacific naval warfare. He saw that the battleship was now merely a support vessel and no longer the heart of naval warfare. He also picked excellent subordinates.

At the end of the war, Nimitz signed for the United States at the Japanese surrender ceremony. In November 1945, he became chief of naval operations. As part of his role Nimitz began to adapt the U.S. Navy to the postwar world. He retired in 1947, served as a university regent in California, and died on February 20, 1966.

A smaller group based on the light carrier *Shoho* would protect transports taking troops to Tulagi and to Port Moresby. A larger force, meanwhile, took up position east of the Solomons. It included the large carriers *Shokaku* and *Zuikaku*. It would defend the landings against the U.S. carrier fleets.

Battle of the Coral Sea

On May 1, 1942, *Lexington* and *Yorktown* met up in the Coral Sea. Late the next day, Fletcher began looking for the Japanese fleet. On May 3, the Japanese landed on Tulagi, confirming U.S. intelligence. *Yorktown* launched four strikes against the Tulagi invasion force the next day.

The real battle began on May 7. The two carrier forces were on converging courses only 70 miles (112km) apart. Poor scouting by aircraft, however, meant that they remained unaware of each other's presence. Once the scout planes detected enemy ships, dive-bombers and torpedo bombers were launched. The Battle of the Coral Sea was a landmark of warfare: It was the first naval battle in which the opposing fleets did not come into visual contact, fighting only with aircraft.

Fighting at sea

The battle set the pattern for later carrier-based engagements: It was a confused affair. Groups of aircraft

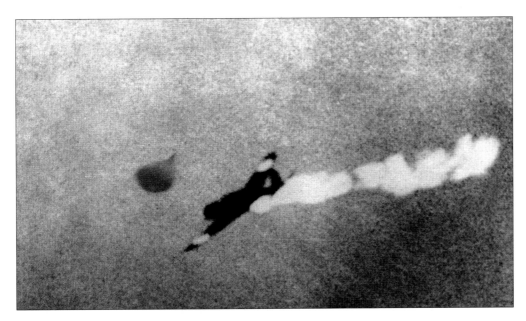

◀ A Japanese "Kate" bomber plunges from the sky after being shot down over the Coral Sea on May 8, 1942. Even more than the loss of aircraft, the loss of skilled pilots in the battle would have damaging long-term effects for the Imperial Navy.

swirled around opposing ships, commanders were never really sure where their enemy was. Both fleets launched all of their carrier aircraft, but neither could find the other's main force. Each mistakenly launched its maximum effort against minor targets.

A long day

Early on May 7, a Japanese plane spotted a carrier and a cruiser south of the main Japanese force. Eighty Japanese planes took off, but found and sank only a U.S. destroyer, the *Sims*, and damaged an oiler, the *Neosho*. Meanwhile, a force of 93 U.S. aircraft took off seeking two Japanese carriers. Instead they struck the force covering the Port Moresby invasion. The encounter brought the first big prize of the battle. The light carrier *Shoho* was sunk after numerous bomb and torpedo strikes. It was the first Allied naval success of the Pacific war.

The nature of the battle remained confused through the afternoon. The Japanese lost Fletcher's main fleet and instead focused on attacking a supporting force. The Allied ships escaped not only enemy bombs but also a mistaken attack by U.S. B-17 bombers flying from bases in Australia.

▼ This photograph shows the carrier *Lexington*, having already been damaged by Japanese attacks. Soon afterward the ship was destroyed by an explosion and a huge fire.

▲ Almost obscured by smoke, a destroyer waits alongside as the crew of the stricken *Lexington* abandon ship. The exercise was accomplished without the loss of a single life.

The loss of the *Shoho* left the Port Moresby invasion force without air cover. The Japanese ordered their two large carriers west to cover the invasion. At dusk, they launched 27 planes against Task Force 17, but they were intercepted by U.S. fighters. Ten were shot down, and 11 crashed into the sea as they tried to land in the dark.

The second day

On May 8, the fleets located each other soon after dawn. They each launched as many aircraft as they could. The Japanese carrier *Zuikaku* lost almost all of its aircraft, while *Shokaku* was hit three times. Unable to launch aircraft, it set out to Japan for repairs.

Japanese pilots attacked *Yorktown* and *Lexington*. Only 15 U.S. planes had been kept back to defend the carriers. They were handled poorly by inexperienced operations managers. The 70 Japanese fighters and bombers attacked almost at will. *Yorktown* was hit by bombs underwater, and *Lexington* suffered two tor-

pedo hits and a bomb hit. Firefighters stabilized the damage, and the carrier continued recovering aircraft. A few hours later, however, an explosion of aviation fuel led to a huge fire. The crew had to abandon ship; the *Lexington* was then torpedoed.

Fletcher knew that the Japanese still had at least one carrier. The loss of the *Lexington* convinced him to withdraw. Meanwhile, Japanese commanders believed their pilots had sunk both U.S. carriers. They thought they had won the action. The carrier *Zuikaku* was low on fuel and had fewer than 40 remaining aircraft. Its commanders ordered it to leave the area in case of attack by U.S. bombers from Australia. The lack of air cover forced the Japanese to turn the invasion fleet back from Port Moresby and abandon their landings.

Who won the battle?

The Battle of the Coral Sea was small in comparison to future clashes in the Pacific, but it shaped naval strategy for

Cracking Japan's codes

One of the continuing debates about World War II has been the extent to which the Allies owed their victory to the breaking of coded Axis signals. The Americans broke the Japanese diplomatic code, nicknamed Purple, before Pearl Harbor in 1941. U.S. codebreakers knew before Pearl Harbor that a Japanese attack was likely, for example, although they did not know where. By April 1942, U.S. analysts had also partially cracked the Japanese naval code, JN-25. That was enough to give them vital intelligence, particularly about the Battle of Midway.

The Japanese government and military were compartmentalized and secretive, and individual intercepts rarely contained decisive information. They provided clues that were gathered and analyzed by the U.S. Signals Intelligence Service (SIS). The scraps of data, however, still offered only a partial picture that allowed much room for error and uncertainty.

▼ Students at an Aeronautical Radio School take a class in deciphering coded Japanese messages. Although U.S. operators became better at breaking codes as the war went on, the partial nature of much of the information they gathered left considerable room for error.

the rest of the war. Both sides claimed victory. The Japanese had lost a small carrier while destroying a large U.S. carrier. The Americans, meanwhile, had prevented the landings at Port Moresby. That effectively ended Operation MO and protected Australia and its links with the United States. Today most historians judge the action a draw, but acknowledge that U.S. fortunes were at such a low ebb that the result seemed like a major victory.

Lessons of the Coral Sea

The battle taught the U.S. Navy valuable lessons. Firefighting received greater attention in training, to help avoid a repeat of the *Lexington* disaster. Radar operators and fire control officers learned to manage defensive air cover more effectively, while air commanders learned how better to combine torpedo bombers, dive bombers, and fighters. U.S. Navy pilots also learned that they could match their more experienced Japanese opposites.

The most important consequences of the battle lay in the long-term damage done to the Imperial Japanese Navy. The Japanese had lost valuable airplanes and even more valuable fighter pilots. Meanwhile, the two carriers that had been damaged or had lost most of their airplanes would not be available for the attack on Midway Island. They would be greatly missed.

THE BATTLE OF MIDWAY

Japan's thrust into the central Pacific was intended to destroy what remained of the U.S. fleet after Pearl Harbor and the Battle of the Coral Sea. Instead it was a disaster for the Imperial Japanese Navy.

▼ A squadron of U.S. Devastator torpedo bombers is readied for take off on the deck of the USS *Enterprise* during the Battle of Midway.

In spring 1942, Japan's military strategists had two priorities. They wanted to thrust through the Coral Sea to isolate Australia from Britain and the United States, and to defeat U.S. aircraft carrier forces in the Pacific. The commander of the Combined Fleet, Isoroku Yamamoto, intended to occupy part of the Aleutian Islands off Alaska in the North Pacific and Midway Island in the Central Pacific, 1,100 miles (1,760km) northwest of Hawaii. He would draw the U.S. carriers into an unequal battle, and defeat them.

When Yamamoto first put forward his plan, it was rejected. Japan's High Command decided to prioritize the thrust toward Australia. On April 18, 1942, however the so-called Doolittle Raid attacked Japan. U.S. aircraft flying

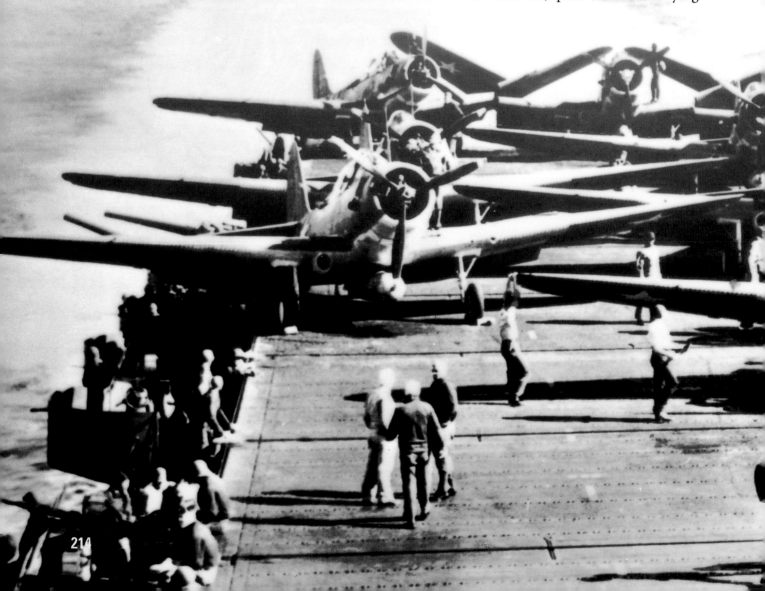

from carriers in the Pacific bombed Tokyo and other targets. The raid inflicted only minor damage, but it stunned Japan's leaders. Alarmed by the threat from carrier forces, they now adopted Yamamoto's plan.

Japanese carriers and their aircraft won at best only a narrow victory over U.S. carrier forces at the Battle of the Coral Sea in May 1942 (*see Chapter 1*). The thrust toward Australia stalled. The Imperial Japanese Navy's commanders decided to push ahead with the operation to seize Midway.

Speed was of the essence: The Japanese were anxious to achieve victory in the Pacific before the greater industrial strength of the United States could begin to influence the conflict. The decision set in motion a series of events that would result in the decisive naval clash of World War II.

The balance of forces

By late spring 1942, the Japanese fleet had an advantage over its enemy in terms of operational aircraft carriers. Its aviators were more experienced than their U.S. counterparts. They also had a superior aircraft, the Zero fighter. The Japanese advantage was offset, however, by the Americans' ability to read many encoded Japanese messages. U.S. commanders had some warning of enemy operations. In addition, while the Japanese thought they had sunk two carriers in the Coral Sea, they had only sunk one, the *Lexington*.

The Japanese Plan

In spring 1942 Isoroku Yamamoto sought to press home Japan's advantage in the Pacific. Moves on Ceylon and Australia were blunted by the Allies, so he planned a strike in the north and central Pacific. He believed that the U.S. Navy had lost two carriers in the Coral Sea and that he would be opposed by minimal airpower. Yamamoto gathered four large naval task forces. Three headed into the central Pacific. The other struck north to seize the Aleutian islands, off Alaska, as a diversion to draw off U.S. forces.

An amphibious force was then to make a surprise assault on Midway. The island was out of range of fighter cover from U.S. bases on Hawaii, so the Americans would have to resist an assault with the last of their precious fleet. At that point, Yamamoto would combine his forces into an overwhelming fleet and destroy the U.S. navy in the Central Pacific.

▼ Defeat at Midway meant the Japanese occupation of the Aleutian Islands became irrelevant.

The Japanese Combined Fleet left its home ports in the last week of May 1942 and headed into the Central Pacific. It was based on four main task forces, with a total of 165 vessels. It was the largest armada the Japanese had assembled; they would never again be able to send such a fleet into action.

Yamamoto's plan was complex. One of the task forces headed toward the

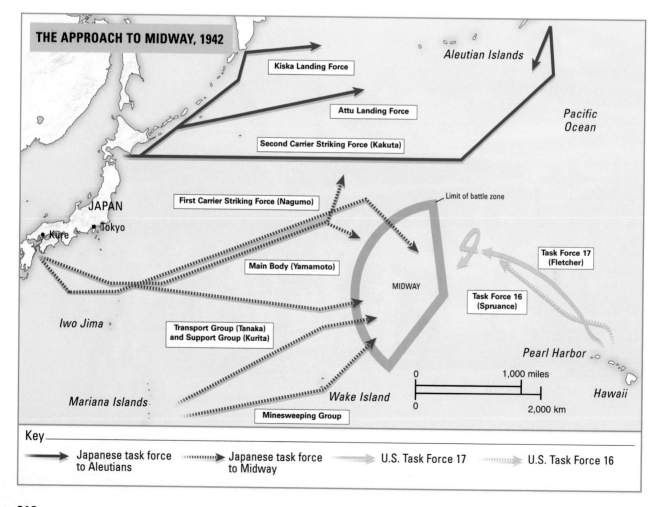

THE APPROACH TO MIDWAY, 1942

Kiska Landing Force

Attu Landing Force

Second Carrier Striking Force (Kakuta)

Aleutian Islands

Pacific Ocean

First Carrier Striking Force (Nagumo)

JAPAN

Tokyo

Kure

Main Body (Yamamoto)

Limit of battle zone

MIDWAY

Task Force 17 (Fletcher)

Task Force 16 (Spruance)

Iwo Jima

Transport Group (Tanaka) and Support Group (Kurita)

Pearl Harbor

0   1,000 miles

0   2,000 km

Hawaii

Mariana Islands

Wake Island

Minesweeping Group

Key

→ Japanese task force to Aleutians   ┈▶ Japanese task force to Midway   → U.S. Task Force 17   ┈▶ U.S. Task Force 16

Aleutians to try to divert U.S. naval and air forces from Midway. It was a large group of three heavy and three light cruisers, twelve destroyers, and two small carriers.

The primary task force was commanded by Vice Admiral Chuichi Nagumo. It boasted four large carriers, the *Akagi, Kaga, Hiryu,* and *Soryu.* Its 272 fighters, dive bombers, and torpedo bombers were to bomb U.S. defenses on Midway. They would prepare the way for an amphibious landing by about 51,000 assault troops in a third task force. A fourth task force, including three large battleships, was to block the approaches to Midway.

The Pacific fleet

Facing the Japanese was the Pacific Fleet of Admiral Chester Nimitz. It was split into two task groups. Rear Admiral Raymond Spruance's Task Force 16 was built around the carriers *Enterprise* and *Hornet.* Task Force 17, under Rear Admiral Frank J. Fletcher, had the carrier *Yorktown.* The three U.S. carriers could launch some 233

The Zero

The Mitsubishi A6M Zero-Sen was the premier naval fighter aircraft in the Pacific in the early years of the war. The first shipboard fighter capable of surpassing land-based aircraft, it outclassed any U.S. carrier-borne fighters. The Zero was deadly in a dogfight, and could outmaneuver enemy fighters.

With its maximum speed of 350 mph (560km/h), the Zero was the basis of Japanese carrier aviation during the Battle of Coral Sea and at Midway. More Zero-Sens were produced than any other wartime Japanese aircraft: A total of 10,938 were manufactured.

▲ Maneuverable and fast, the Zero gave the Japanese a real advantage in the air war in the Pacific in the first two years of the war.

◄ Japanese troops pull a field gun ashore during the landing on Kiska in the Aleutian Islands, on June 7, 1942.

▲ The Japanese flag flies on U.S. sovereign territory, on Attu Island in the Aleutians.

▶ U.S. Dauntless dive bombers fly above the coral reefs that ring Midway Island.

combat aircraft. They were supported by just over 100 fighters and bombers based on Midway itself, along with a garrison of 3,000 troops. None of the three carriers was near Midway, how-

ever. *Enterprise* and *Hornet* were still in the South Pacific, and *Yorktown* was in Pearl Harbor. The damage it suffered in the Battle of Coral Sea was scheduled to take three months to repair.

Code breaking

Yamamoto issued orders for his main task force to gather off Midway by June 4 to begin air raids on the island defenses. The order was deciphered by U.S. Navy listening posts on Hawaii. Nimitz ordered the admirals Spruance and Fletcher to defend the island. The *Enterprise* and *Hornet* sailed north from the South Pacific at maximum speed to try to reach the area before the Japanese. Pearl Harbor dockyard staff repaired the *Yorktown* in only three days, and it also put to sea. The U.S. carriers and their escorts sailed to positions north of Midway. They arrived before a Japanese screen of submarines, intended to

◀ Facilities burn at the U.S. airbase on Midway Island after a Japanese bombing raid.

detect movements out of Pearl Harbor, was in place.

Yamamoto had based his operation on the element of surprise. Instead, it was the Americans who had the advantage of surprise. The enemy had no idea that they faced three U.S. aircraft carriers.

First moves

On June 3, the Japanese Northern Area Force struck at the Aleutians. It seized the remote Kiska and Attu islands. It was the first time the Japanese had occupied sovereign U.S. soil. The Americans realized that the action was a diversion, however. They did not shift sizable forces to counter the landings.

The main Japanese landing fleet approached Midway on the morning of June 3. It was spotted by a U.S. Navy flying boat some 700 miles (1,250km) from the island. A formation of B-17 Flying Fortresses from Midway attacked the ships with little effect.

At dawn on June 4, Nagumo's four carriers arrived at their attack point 280 miles (450km) northwest of Mid-

Eyewitness ─────────────────

❝ There was a huge hole in the flight deck just behind the amidship elevator. The elevator itself, twisted like molten glass, was drooping into the hangar. Deck plates reeled upward in grotesque configurations. Planes stood tail up, belching livid flame and jet-black smoke. Reluctant tears streamed down my cheeks as I watched the fires spread, and I was terrified at the prospect of induced explosions which would surely doom the ship.❞

Mitsuo Fuchida,
Japanese sailor on board the carrier *Akagi*

way. They launched a strike force of 72 bombers and 36 fighters toward the island. Some 26 land-based U.S. fighters intercepted the attackers, while bombers tried to attack Nagumo's fleet. All but two of the U.S. aircraft were shot down or badly damaged. The Japanese lost only six aircraft. The remaining U.S. fighters were unable to mount an effective attack against the Japanese ships. A high-altitude attack by a squadron of B-17s also had little effect. Meanwhile, enemy bombers hit

▲ A Dauntless ditches in the sea alongside a U.S. carrier during the Battle of Midway, possibly because the aircraft's landing gear had been damaged by enemy fire.

Midway, damaging the island's airfield and shore defenses.

Nagumo had kept more than 100 torpedo bombers back. They were ready to strike at U.S. ships trying to defend Midway. With the island apparently defenseless, however, he decided to strike again. He took the torpedoes off the bombers and replaced them with high-explosive bombs.

U.S. counterstrike

At 8:20 A.M., a Japanese pilot located a U.S. carrier and its escorts northeast of Midway. Nagumo rearmed his planes to attack the new threat. In the rush the armorers left high-explosive bombs stacked on the hanger decks. Nagumo's carriers turned to meet the threat.

Unknown to the Japanese, three hours earlier the U.S. forces had pin-pointed the location of Nagumo's carriers. Frank Fletcher, the senior commander on the scene, ordered the three U.S. aircraft carriers to launch a strike against the Japanese vessels.

At 7:02 A.M., the *Enterprise* and *Hornet* launched 116 aircraft. Ninety minutes later the *Yorktown* launched a further 36 aircraft. The first dive bombers could not find the Japanese ships in the morning haze, and the attack became fragmented and disorganized.

At 9:30 A.M., 15 U.S. torpedo bombers at last found their targets. They began their attack runs against the carrier *Akagi* without fighter cover. A group of 50 Zero fighters was waiting. Within minutes all the U.S. aircraft had been shot down. A second wave of U.S. torpedo bombers also ran into the Zeros. Although six managed to fire their torpedoes, the weapons moved so slowly in the water that their targets were able to maneuver out of the way.

Nagumo's error

Nagumo believed that his fighters had driven off the U.S. attack. He changed his orders again; his armorers began reloading bombs onto their aircraft. Nagumo had miscalculated, however. A wave of dive bombers from the U.S. carriers, accompanied by several squadrons of fighters, was only just arriving over the Japanese fleet. Diving from an altitude of 20,000 feet (6,100m), the bombers took the Japanese fleet by surprise at 10:28 A.M.

The *Akagi* was ripped apart by bombs that exploded among the ordnance piled up in the loading bays. Within seconds the carrier was engulfed in explosions. Nagumo and his staff abandoned the burning ship to continue directing the battle.

A few miles away the *Kaga* shared a similar fate. Four bombs struck its

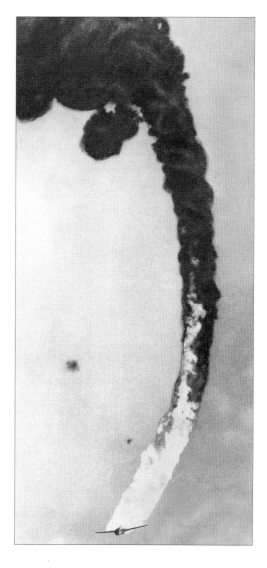

◀ A burning Japanese fighter falls from the sky after having been hit by U.S. antiaircraft fire during the Battle of Midway.

▼ Black smoke and splashes mark antiaircraft shells bursting among Japanese torpedo planes. A U.S. cruiser (left) is just visible in the distance.

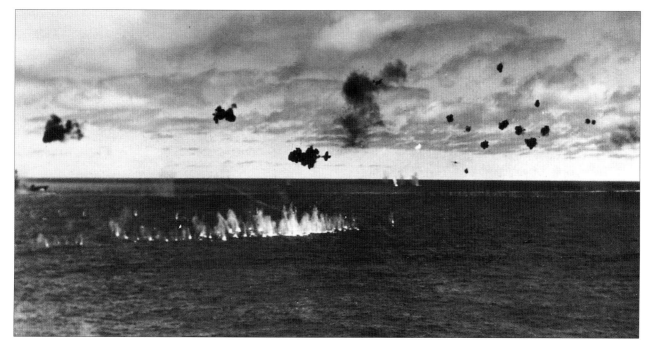

▶ The Japanese heavy cruiser *Mikuma* sinks after being damaged by U.S. bombers.

▼ The Japanese carrier *Akagi,* under attack by bombers diving from high altitude, blew up when explosions sparked bombs piled up in its loading bays.

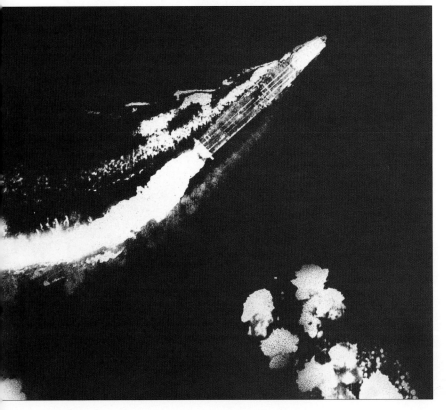

packed aircraft deck. The *Soryu* was also hit, at 10:40 A.M., and its rudder and engines were put out of action. Fires raged on both ships throughout the day. Three Japanese carriers were now out of action at a crucial point in the battle.

End game

Late in the morning Nagumo ordered his last remaining carrier, the *Hiryu,* to launch its reserve aircraft to strike back at the Americans. Just before midday, the first 18 aircraft dive-bombed the *Yorktown.* Twelve were shot down by U.S. fighters and antiaircraft guns. The others put two bombs on target.

A series of explosions struck *Yorktown,* and a second attack hit it with torpedoes. The crew abandoned ship. They included Frank Fletcher, who passed tactical command to Spruance for the remainder of the battle. Success cost the Japanese dearly, however: Only 15 aircraft survived the attack.

Late in the afternoon, Spruance's patrol aircraft spotted the *Hiryu.* He ordered dive bombers from the *Enterprise* to attack. They bombed the ship, starting a fire that raged among the aircraft parked on the ship's deck.

Yamamoto's last move

All four of Yamamoto's carriers were on fire or sinking as darkness fell. He now tried to take the offensive. He struck westward with his as yet un-damaged battleships and cruisers. He intended to engage the U.S. fleet in a surface battle. Spruance refused to take the bait, however. He ordered his two remaining aircraft carriers and support ships to sail to the east. They could avoid being surprised at night by the Japanese vessels.

The *Soryu* and *Kaga* sank just after 7:00 P.M. Many of the crew of the *Akagi* and *Hiryu* were lifted off by escort destroyers. When the order was given to sink the burning hulks, their captains returned to the ships and died with them.

The aftermath

The Japanese plan to seize Midway and decisively engage the U.S. fleet was now in ruins. Yamamoto ordered his two surviving carriers and all other surface vessels to turn for home. Two cruisers collided in the maneuver: One was subsequently sunk by U.S. planes, while the other later sank.

For two days, the Americans pursued the Japanese ships across the Pacific. When their fuel threatened to run low, they turned back to the base at Pearl Harbor. A Japanese submarine located the damaged hull of the *Yorktown* as it was being towed back to Hawaii for repairs. It fired two torpedoes at the stricken vessel, sinking the *Yorktown* and an escort destroyer.

Conclusion

The sinking of the damaged *Yorktown* was the last engagement of the Battle of Midway. In the course of the battle 307 Americans had died. Some 147 U.S. aircraft were lost, along with the *Yorktown*. The Japanese lost four fleet carriers, 332 aircraft, and 3,500 dead.

The casualties included many of the elite of the Imperial Navy's pilots. Although Yamamoto's northern task group had been able to occupy the undefended islands in the Aleutian chain, the defeat at Midway had made this a strategic irrelevance.

The outcome of the battle turned the tide of the war in the Pacific theater. The Japanese had failed to sink the last U.S. Navy carriers in the Central Pacific. They were left with a seriously weakened force. Having defeated the Japanese fleet in the Central Pacific, the United States had breathing space to build more carriers and other warships to replace the losses at Pearl Harbor, Coral Sea, and Midway.

▲ A Japanese aircraft took this photograph of the stricken carrier *Hiryu* on June 6, 1942, shortly before it was scuttled.

NEW GUINEA, GUADALCANAL, AND THE SOLOMONS

With their plans for the Southern Pacific disrupted by the actions in the Coral Sea and at Midway, the Japanese sought new advances. U.S. commanders planned their own offensive in the second half of 1942.

Following the U.S. victory in the Battle of Midway in June 1942, the Japanese and the United States faced choices in how to proceed with the war. Both of the strategies Japanese commanders had adopted in the spring had been disrupted. They planned a southward thrust from New Britain to New Guinea, intended eventually to sever Australia's communications with the Allies. The plan had been disrupted by an indecisive victory in the Battle of the Coral Sea in May 1942. Defeat at Midway ruled out the other plan, to extend a defensive perimeter through the Central Pacific and destroy the U.S. Pacific Fleet.

For the United States, meanwhile, Midway encouraged commanders to think in more offensive terms. Although U.S. Army and Navy planners disagreed over strategy, they reached a compromise. U.S. Navy and Marine forces would try to capture the strategically important island of Guadalcanal in the eastern Solomons. Meanwhile, U.S. Army forces would drive through New Guinea into New Britain, aiming to take the major Japanese base at Rabaul.

The Battle for New Guinea

Before the U.S. plan began, the Japanese made a new attempt to take New Guinea. They had decided that they needed to strike hard to make up for the reverses at the Coral Sea and Midway. They had landed in northeastern New Guinea earlier in 1942. They now targeted Port Moresby, the capital of Papua (New Guinea's southern, Australian governed territory) and a major Australian base.

On the night of July 21–22, 1942, the Japanese South Seas Detachment landed at Buna, on the north coast of Papua. They planned to push along the 100 miles (160km) of the Kokoda Trail. They would cross a jungle-covered mountain ridge in the middle of the island and assault Port Moresby by land from the north.

Most Allied defenders on New Guinea were Australian. They were a weak force numerically, as many Australian units were fighting in North Africa. The Japanese themselves faced a problem, however. Contrary to their intelligence, the Kokoda Trail was a difficult route. To move quickly, they could carry little apart from weapons and ammunition. They would rely for food on local produce, wild plants and animals, and captured supplies.

The invasion begins well

The Japanese advance began well. They drove back the inexperienced Australian and indigenous Papuan troops. Within a few days, they had crossed the Kusumi River 20 miles (32km) inland. The Japanese pushed on toward the Owen Stanley mountains. On July 29 they took Kokoda village—the midpoint between Buna

◄ A stricken Japanese transport ship lies half submerged off the beach at Cape Esperance on Guadalcanal after Japanese troops finally evacuated the island in February 1943.

The Kokoda Trail

The Kokoda Trail inflicted terrible punishment on Allied and Japanese soldiers alike. The "trail" was actually little more than a track that linked towns and villages in the rain forests of Papua. Some 96 miles (154km) long, it joined the northern and southern coasts of the island. It passed through the village of Kokoda on the northeastern slopes of the Owen Stanley mountain range. The trail was cut by fast-flowing rivers and wound through terrifying mountain passes, often rising nearly vertically. Diseases such as malaria and scrub typhus were common. During the campaign along the trail both sides suffered more casualties from the environment than from battle.

▶ Australian troops make their way through the rain forest along a muddy section of the Kokoda Trail.

▼ Indigenous Papuan troops volunteered to fight alongside the Allies in New Guinea.

and Port Moresby. The Australians at Kokoda fought fiercely against odds of 15 to 1, but withdrew when their commander was killed.

The capture of Kokoda gave the Japanese control of a nearby airfield. By late August they were ready to take Australian positions around Isurava. For four days 5,000 Japanese troops launched themselves on the 1,700 Australians in the town. The engagement was awful for the participants. Both sides suffered badly from disease. Many of the Japanese were starving, and some resorted to cannibalism. Despite huge casualties, the Japanese advanced to Templeton's Crossing through the mountains. By September 16, they were just north of Imita Ridge, only 12½ miles (20km) from Port Moresby. They could see the Coral Sea in the distance.

The Japanese collapse

The Japanese commander, Major General Horii Tomitaro, did not realize that disaster was building around him. The Australians had suffered 70 percent casualties during their retreat. They were now reinforced by five fresh brigades with artillery support. The stretched Japanese supply line was being bombed daily by aircraft from the United States Army Air Force. Furthermore, U.S. forces were preparing to land south of Buna. They would threaten the Japanese line with a crushing pincer movement from the east and west.

Although Port Moresby was in sight, Horii received orders to pull back. The Japanese High Command had switched its focus to events on Guadalcanal in the Solomon Islands, where U.S. troops had landed in early August. Horii's ragged army began a dramatic retreat. Starving and disease ridden, the Japanese moved back along the Kokoda Trail. They constantly fought bloody rearguard actions.

By October 15, the Allies had retaken Templeton's Crossing. On November 2, Kokoda and the nearby airstrip returned to Australian hands. The Japanese put up fierce resistance to the Australian advance: They lost 600 out

of their remaining 1,500 men. Horii himself was drowned while crossing a river. Meanwhile, elements of the U.S. 32nd Division landed south of Buna. They began fighting their way north.

Fighting on the coast

The survivors of the Kokoda Trail joined about 7,000 Japanese troops in defensive positions on the coast near Buna, Gona, and Sanananda. The Japanese kept up a stubborn defense through the winter monsoon rains. The Allies had to fight at close quarters with small arms and hand grenades to take hundreds of bunkers. Gona was finally captured on December 8. Buna fell on January 2, 1943, and Sanananda was taken on January 16.

Of the 7,000 Japanese defenders on the New Guinea coast, 6,000 died. That made a total of 12,000 Japanese dead in the 1942 Kokoda Trail campaign. The Allies had lost 2,165

▼ Map of the Kokoda trail

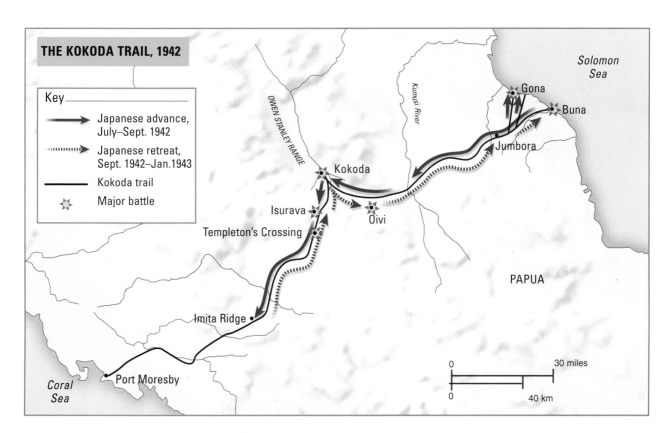

Australian and 930 U.S. soldiers, but 18,000 troops were suffering from malaria. For Japan, it was the first land defeat of the Pacific War.

Guadalcanal

Less than a month after the Japanese began their invasion of New Guinea, U.S. forces began their own advance in the Solomon Islands. It was this advance that had caused the Japanese to abandon the march on Port Moresby. The Americans wanted to seize the initiative after the victory at Midway. They were also concerned by reports that the Japanese were building an airfield on Guadalcanal in the Solomons.

On August 7, 1942, an amphibious task force landed the U.S. 1st Marine Division on Guadalcanal. The island was defended by about 2,200 Japanese. The Marines occupied the airfield, named Henderson Field for a U.S.

casualty at Midway. Marines faced greater resistance on the offshore islands of Tulagi, Gavutu, and Tanambogo. The Japanese launched suicidal "human wave" attacks against them. Massive U.S. naval firepower and aerial bombardment had ended the initial resistance by August 9.

Fighting continues

The battle for Guadalcanal was far from over, however. It continued on land and at sea. The Marines on the island were effectively on their own. They were surrounded by Japanese forces, who began receiving major reinforcements by sea from August 18. This supply route became known as the "Tokyo Express," and was the subject of a fierce campaign. The Marines at Henderson Field were also vulnerable because they had limited air cover. The only aircraft at the airfield

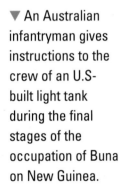

▼ An Australian infantryman gives instructions to the crew of an U.S-built light tank during the final stages of the occupation of Buna on New Guinea.

itself were 12 Dauntless dive-bombers and 19 Wildcat fighters. Naval support was also reduced, as the warships offshore clashed with vessels of the Imperial Japanese Navy. Under frequent Japanese naval gunfire and air bombardment, the garrison of 10,000 Marines reinforced their perimeter positions and waited for the attack.

The first attack came on August 21. A Japanese regiment of 800 men made a nighttime bayonet assault against part of the U.S. perimeter. The charging Japanese met a hail of bullets, artillery shells, and bombs. Those who survived dug in, but U.S. firepower killed virtually all of the attackers, against 35 U.S. losses.

Battle of the Eastern Solomons

On August 24, 1942, a U.S. task force with three aircraft carriers—*Enterprise*, *Wasp*, and *Saratoga*—located the Japanese carrier *Ryujo* and a large support group that was attempting to take supplies to Guadalcanal. The Japanese force was a decoy, however. It was intended to draw the U.S. carriers to be attacked by a striking force based on two carriers, *Zuikaku* and *Shokaku*.

When U.S. aircraft attacked and sank the *Ryujo*, they left their own carriers with little air cover. Japanese carrier aircraft were able to damage the USS *Enterprise*. The Japanese attack marked the end of the carrier battle. The next day, U.S. aircraft intercepted a Japanese convoy again heading for Guadalcanal. They damaged a cruiser and sank a transport vessel and a destroyer.

The Milne Bay Action

On August 26, 1942, the Japanese switched their focus to New Guinea. They landed 2,400 troops near Milne Bay on the eastern tip of Papua. They

▼ U.S. Marines charge from their landing craft during the landing on Guadalcanal on August 7, 1942. The initial landings were largely unopposed, in contrast to the fierce fighting that followed.

Eyewitness

" For some reason, I remember a Japanese slipped in on the motor section. Private Tucker woke up, saw the Japanese, as I recall, lurking around there…. The Japanese threw a hand grenade at him, but it didn't go off. I think Tucker shot the guy and finished him. After searching him, we found that he had taken some coffee, some sugar, and I think he had taken one of our American rifles and some ammunition. We buried him there in the motor section the next morning. He was probably starving… he was after anything which he could eat. We didn't have much food laying around so he didn't find much. "

James R. Garrett, U.S. Marine corporal, Guadalcanal, September 15, 1942

▲ U.S. coastguards unload supplies on Guadalcanal from landing craft in the shadow of a Japanese ship destroyed by a bombing attack.

aimed to capture Allied airfields whose aircraft had been harassing Japanese positions at Buna. From intelligence reports the Japanese expected only light resistance. Their enemy had been reinforced, however: They faced about 9,000 Australian and U.S. troops.

As the Japanese approached the shore, they came under fire from Australian Kittyhawk fighter aircraft. Ashore, infantry gunfire caused heavy casual-

ties. However, the Japanese marines managed to advance. During the night of August 27–28, they attempted to capture a key airfield. Despite the arrival of reinforcements, the Japanese

▶ The airstrip built by the Japanese on Guadalcanal was renamed Henderson Field after its capture by the Americans. It provided essential air support for U.S. operations in the Solomons.

◄ Exhausted and injured Japanese prisoners of war are guarded by Marines on Guadalcanal. Most of the island's defenders died rather than surrender.

▼ Sailing into port, sailors on the cruiser USS *Boise* study the record of their attacks during an engagement off Cape Esperance at Guadalcanal. In fact, their claims were exaggerated. The Japanese lost only one destroyer in the battle, although two cruisers

were unable to overcome the airfield's defenders. In one series of charges they lost another 500 men. Ultimately defeated by Allied numbers, the Japanese retreated east. The survivors were evacuated by sea in early September. They left behind about 1,500 dead and an Australian Army that was full of renewed confidence.

Bleak time for Japan

The failure at Milne Bay marked the start of a bleak time for the Japanese. On Guadalcanal, U.S. troops consolidated their perimeter around Henderson Field. At sea, the U.S. Navy now prevented daylight runs of the Tokyo Express to the island. A night raid by U.S. Marines on Japanese positions at Taivu inflicted much damage. It also gathered valuable intelligence about future Japanese plans.

The Japanese struck back on September 12 with a 2,000-man attack on U.S. positions just east of Henderson Field. The fighting was concentrated around a ridge about 1 mile (1.6km) southwest of Henderson Field. The site later became known as "Bloody Ridge."

▶ The U.S. defensive perimeter on Guadalcanal was relatively small, but it guarded the vital airstrip at Henderson Field.

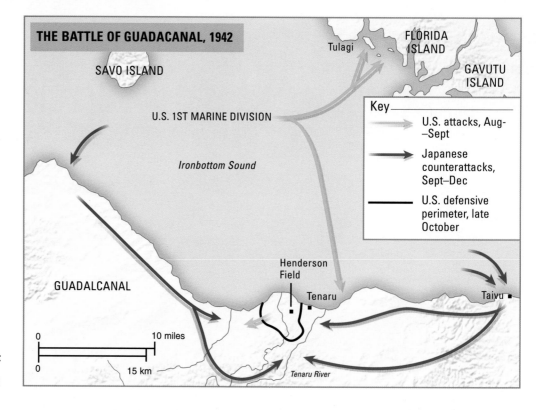

THE BATTLE OF GUADACANAL, 1942

SAVO ISLAND

FLORIDA ISLAND

Tulagi

GAVUTU ISLAND

U.S. 1ST MARINE DIVISION

Ironbottom Sound

Key

→ U.S. attacks, Aug–Sept

→ Japanese counterattacks, Sept–Dec

— U.S. defensive perimeter, late October

Henderson Field

Tenaru

Taivu

GUADALCANAL

0 — 10 miles

0 — 15 km

Tenaru River

▼ U.S. Gruman F4F Wildcat fighters on the airstrip at Henderson Field. The Wildcats were a good opponent for the Japanese Zero, although the Zero was more maneuverable.

Two days of fighting took the Japanese to within 1,000 yards (915m) of the airfield. They lost 1,200 casualties versus U.S. losses of about 300, however. The losses were so serious that they were forced to withdraw. Reinforcements arrived, taking the numbers involved to from 20,000 to 25,000 on each side.

End of the action

Fighting rumbled on until October 23. The Japanese then began three days of mass attacks on the north and west of the U.S. perimeter. As before, the attackers came close to success on several occasions. U.S. firepower eventually turned them back with 3,500 casualties.

The tide was turning against the Japanese. Their attacks had come to nothing. Their troops were now hungry and suffering from disease. Clashes lasted for about two months, but on January 14, 1943, the Japanese began a retreat. They headed to Cape Esperance, about 25 miles (40km) northwest of Henderson Field. The Imperial Navy evacuated them in the first week in February. The battle for Guadalcanal had cost the Japanese 9,000 dead.

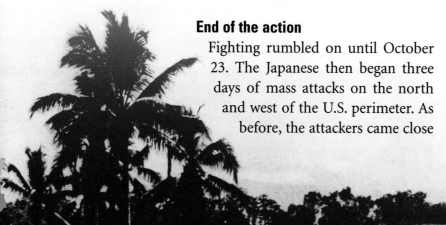

The naval war off the Solomons

The land fighting between August 1942 and February 1943 was matched by related naval actions in the waters around the Solomons. They were focused on the narrow gap between the East and West Solomons. The gap was a major route for Japanese naval traffic. It became known as "the Slot."

Within hours of the original U.S. landings on Guadalcanal on August 8, 1942, a force of Japanese cruisers set out to destroy the U.S. landing vessels. It met a U.S. defense group near Savo Island that same night. The Japanese crews were skilled at night fighting, and the Allied force was split up. The Japanese cruisers were able to get among its vessels. The U.S. cruiser *Chicago* and the Australian cruiser *Canberra* were badly damaged by tor-

pedoes and gunfire. The Japanese sank a total of four ships during the battle before the attackers moved away.

Naval success for the United States

The Allied defeat in the Battle of Savo Island was in some measure balanced by success in what is called the Battle of the Eastern Solomons on August 24. U.S. vessels sank a Japanese carrier, the *Ryujo*, and sank or damaged three other ships. The U.S. carrier *Enterprise* was also damaged. The Japanese now abandoned daylight supply runs to Guadalcanal: The "Tokyo Express" became the "Tokyo Night Express."

October 1942 saw two other major naval engagements. On the night of October 11–12, a heavily escorted Japanese supply convoy was intercepted by a U.S. cruiser and destroyer squadron

▲ In flames after being hit by fire from the USS *Wasp*, a Japanese Zero pluges toward the sea.

Coast watchers

The coast watchers were among the most useful tools in the intelligence war against the Japanese. They were mainly Australian military personnel and Polynesian locals who secretly reported on the movement of enemy shipping and aircraft. By 1941, coast watchers were active throughout the Pacific behind Japanese lines. They used their knowledge of the local terrain to conduct surveillance on shipping movements, weather, tides, and anything else that might help the Allies. They were particularly valued in the Solomons. They gave the U.S. Navy advance warning of Japanese troop runs to Guadalcanal and of approaching air raids launched from New Britain and New Ireland.

▲ Coast watchers pose in New Guinea at the end of the war. U.S. admiral "Bull" Halsey said, "The coast watchers saved Guadalcanal, and Guadalcanal saved the Pacific."

▶ White foam is generated by the propellers of one of two Japanese cargo ships as it attempts to escape after having been spotted by U.S. bombers near Bougainville in the Solomon Islands.

off Cape Esperance. The U.S. force knew of the Japanese approach from its radar, but was hampered by poor communications between vessels. In the chaotic engagement, however, U.S. guns sank a destroyer and damaged two cruisers. The U.S. force lost a destroyer and had a cruiser seriously damaged.

A major setback

October ended with a major setback for the United States at the Battle of Santa Cruz. A Japanese carrier group was supporting the land campaign on Guadalcanal. It met the U.S. carriers *Hornet* and *Enterprise* around the Santa Cruz islands to the west of Guadalcanal. In the ensuing battle on October 26, two Japanese carriers were badly damaged, but so were the *Enterprise* and the *Hornet*. The *Hornet* was abandoned and later sank. The U.S. vessels withdrew, but not before shooting down more than 100

Japanese aircraft and pilots. Such serious losses were difficult to sustain for the Japanese naval aviation wing.

Japanese attempts at reinforcement

The naval engagements in the Solomons were indecisive until November 1942. On November 12, a large-scale engagement between naval forces at Guadalcanal resulted in the Japanese losing one battleship and two cruisers. Numerous other ships were damaged. U.S. losses were one cruiser sunk and four destroyers damaged. Decisively, however, the Americans had prevented some 13,000 Japanese troop reinforcements being deployed to Guadalcanal.

With their situation on land getting more desperate, the Japanese attempted two more reinforcement runs. On November 14, they were turned back. They lost seven transports, two cruisers, a destroyer, and a battleship against two U.S. destroyers sunk and a battleship and a destroyer damaged. U.S. gunners used radar for accurate night shooting.

On the night of November 30, however, when another Japanese force tried to reach the island, U.S. commanders wasted their radar advantage. They made poor tactical decisions. An engagement took place in "Ironbottom Sound," named for the number of ships sunk there. The Japanese lost one destroyer. The Americans had a cruiser sunk and three destroyers badly damaged. The Japanese were still a force to be reckoned with.

Significance of the Solomons

The naval battles off the Solomons and the land campaign on Guadalcanal inflicted heavy losses on both sides. The Japanese losses were greater, however. Japan could not replace its men or materiel as easily as the United States, with its larger population and industrial output.

The Japanese evacuation from Guadalcanal in February 1943 was a turning point in the Pacific. From now on the United States would not only begin to gain dominance of the sea and air, it would also begin to claw back territory occupied by Japan. It was moving ever closer to the Japanese home islands.

▼ A Japanese dive bomber crashes into the bridge of the carrier USS *Hornet* during the Battle of Santa Cruz on October 26, 1942. The carrier was abandoned and later sank.

ON THE OFFENSIVE: 1943 IN THE PACIFIC

In spring 1943, U.S. forces prepared to go on the offensive in the Pacific for the first time. Their commanders disagreed about the best way to advance toward the ultimate target: Japan itself.

On March 28, 1943, the U.S. high command adopted a new strategy in the Pacific War. Japan was now pinned back, and the U.S. planners were trying to find the best route to the Japanese home islands.

U.S. planners disagreed, however, about the best direction of their advance. Admiral Chester Nimitz, U.S. Navy commander of the Pacific Ocean Areas, and General Douglas MacArthur, the U.S. Army commander of the Southwest Pacific Area, argued for different routes to Japan. They both planned to bypass most of Japan's strongpoints in the Pacific.

Nimitz wanted to drive west from the Central Pacific, aiming for the island of Formosa (now Taiwan). Formosa, off the coast of southern China, would act as a base for the invasion of Japan. MacArthur, on the other hand, wanted to drive north through the Solomon Islands to the Philippines. Such an advance had the advantage of cutting off the Japanese from the

◀ U.S. Marines take shelter behind a low sea wall on the beach at Tarawa, where the landing force was pinned down by Japanese artillery and gun fire.

Dutch East Indies (DEI). The islands' resources included vital supplies of oil.

Ultimately, the U.S. strategy included both options. Nimitz would push from the west and MacArthur from the south. Their thrusts would eventually meet at the island of Okinawa, south of Japan.

Operation Cartwheel

The first stage of MacArthur's plan was to neutralize the major Japanese naval and air base at Rabaul in New Britain. The plan was code-named Operation Cartwheel. It involved a two-pronged advance on Rabaul. U.S. forces already occupied Guadalcanal in the Solomons. U.S. and Allied forces would reconquer other islands in the group. Meanwhile, a simultaneous offensive would lead north through New Guinea to New Britain. The two arcs of the wheel would circle around Rabaul, and effectively seal off New Britain.

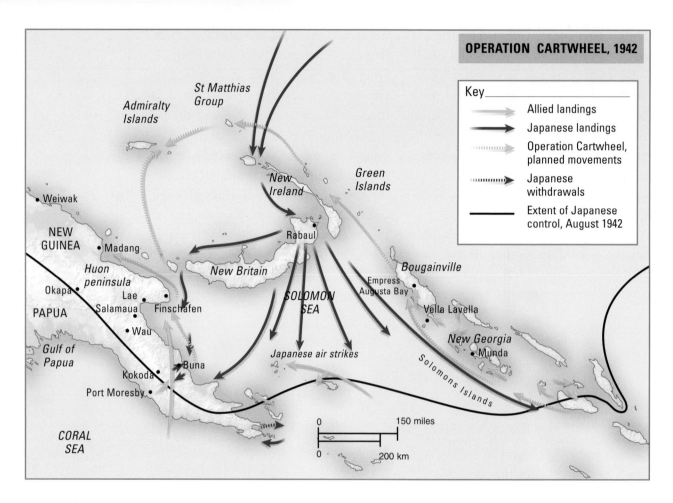

OPERATION CARTWHEEL, 1942

Key

→ Allied landings
→ Japanese landings
⇢ Operation Cartwheel, planned movements
⇢ Japanese withdrawals
— Extent of Japanese control, August 1942

St Matthias Group

Admiralty Islands

Weiwak

NEW GUINEA • *Madang*

Huon peninsula

Okapa • *Lae*
Salamaua • *Finschafen*

PAPUA

• *Wau*

Gulf of Papua

Kokoda

Port Moresby •

CORAL SEA

New Ireland

Green Islands

Rabaul

New Britain

SOLOMON SEA

Buna

Japanese air strikes

Bougainville

Empress Augusta Bay

Vella Lavella

New Georgia • *Munda*

Solomons Islands

0   150 miles
0   200 km

◆ Operation Cartwheel was a two-pronged approach that would encircle and isolate the key Japanese base at Rabaul.

▶ A U.S. light tank platoon is shelled by the Japanese as its landing craft bring it to shore in New Georgia.

Taking the Solomons

The right arc of Cartwheel was to be an advance through the Solomons. It was commanded by Vice Admiral William Halsey. It would involve a series of amphibious jumps through the islands of New Georgia and Bougainville, along with other minor islands.

The first objective was New Georgia. The island had a Japanese airstrip at the main town, Munda, on the southwest coast. Since February 1942, U.S. troops had occupied the Russell Islands, 30 miles (48km) southeast of New Georgia. Airfields there now provided air support. On June 30, 1943, U.S. Marines and infantry landed on Rendova Island. Artillery there could fire at targets on New Georgia. On July 2, U.S. infantry landed on New Georgia itself at Zanana Beach, about 10 miles (16km) from Munda. Other units also established footholds.

The Japanese defense

The 10,500 Japanese defenders on New Georgia were concentrated around

The death of Yamamoto

Admiral Isoruko Yamamoto, commander of the Combined Fleet, was one of Japan's leading military thinkers. On April 17, 1943, U.S. intelligence learned that he was due to fly to Bougainville the next day. He would be in one of two "Betty" bombers with a fighter escort. On April 18, 16 P-38 fighters flying low over Bougainville spotted Yamamoto's flight.

A twisting dog-fight ensued. The Japanese Zero fighters frantically tried to protect the lumbering bombers. However, one U.S. pilot managed to break away. He latched onto Yamamoto's plane, which was weaving just above the trees. Machine-gun fire destroyed the bomber's wing, and the aircraft crashed in the Bougainville jungle. Yamamoto's death was a huge blow to Japanese morale.

▶ The wreckage of the bomber in which Yamamoto died lies in the jungle near Bougainville.

Munda. Fighting began in earnest on July 6. It was so fierce that it took a full week for U.S. units to advance 1,000 yards (915m). They lost more men through battle stress than through injuries and death. The Japanese, however, suffered steady losses of hundreds of men. U.S. forces received reinforcements, flame-throwers, tanks, artillery, air strikes, and bulldozers. They finally captured Munda on August 5.

The Japanese navy made several unsuccessful attempts to land reinforcements. It was fought off by U.S. warships. Meanwhile, the survivors from Munda pulled back to the neighboring island of Kolombangara to the northwest. Japanese strength on Kolombangara grew to 12,000, but Halsey did not launch the expected attack. In-

▶ An Australian patrol moves chest-deep through water on Bougainville in the Solomon Islands

stead, on August 15, Allied troops landed on the more lightly defended Vella Lavella farther north. By October 3, Vella Lavella was in Allied hands. The New Georgian campaign had cost the Japanese nearly 3,000 dead. The United States had suffered 1,000 dead and 4,000 wounded.

Strategic change

By the time Vella Lavella fell, U.S. commanders had revised the goals of Operation Cartwheel. Allied war leaders met in Quebec, Canada, in the middle of August. They had decided not to attempt to attack and occupy Rabaul, but to bypass it. The forces at Rabaul would be isolated from reinforcements and supply routes. They would "wither on the vine." The same strategy would be used in many other places in the Pacific. By avoiding fighting for many strongly held islands, the approach would be an important element in minimizing Allied casualties in the advance toward Japan.

The capture of Bougainville

After Vella Lavella, the next Allied target in the Solomons was Bougainville. The large island was the only sizable landmass remaining between the U.S. forces and Rabaul. It was garrisoned by 65,000 Japanese soldiers of the Seventeenth Army.

On October 27 and 28, Halsey landed large U.S. and New Zealand forces on islands off the southern and eastern coasts of Bougainville. The landings drew the Japanese defenders into the east of the island. Halsey's landings were a feint, or mock attack, however. On November 1, the 3rd U.S. Marine Division landed at Empress Augusta Bay on the west coast of Bougainville, where it faced only light opposition.

The Japanese launched aircraft attacks from Rabaul, but they were repulsed with heavy losses. U.S. carrier and land-based aircraft, meanwhile, devastated a Japanese fleet heading for Bougainville from Rabaul on November 6, wrecking six cruisers.

▼ U.S. Marines leave their landing craft and dash up the beach at Bougainville. U.S. troops gained increasing expertise at amphibious landings as the Pacific conflict

Sporadic Japanese resistance continued on Bougainville until the end of the war. Serious resistance had been ended by December 1943, however. The U.S. beachhead contained more than 34,000 troops and three airfields. Empress Augusta Bay also became a major naval base. U.S. aircraft were flying regular raids against Rabaul itself. By now, a trap was closing on New Britain from another direction.

The New Guinea campaign

The Allied campaign to take New Guinea had begun well before Cartwheel was conceived. In 1942, Australian and New Zealand soldiers had been deployed at Wau, inland from the Huon Peninsula. Their task was to prevent an overland Japanese offensive toward Port Moresby, the Papuan capital, from coastal positions around Lae and Salamaua.

In January 1943, the Allied outpost had to resist a fierce Japanese assault. It halted the offensive after the arrival of

Nisei

During the war more than 120,000 Japanese Americans were interned, or confined in camps, even though many were U.S. citizens. Some 33,000 Nisei, however, were recruited for military service. They were second-generation Japanese Americans. Nisei served in duties from interpreting to cooking, but many also went into frontline combat units. Two of the largest Nisei combat units were the 100th Battalion and the 442nd Regimental Combat Team. They suffered nearly 9,500 wounded and 600 killed. Nisei received many decorations for bravery, including one Congressional Medal of Honor and 55 Distinguished Service Crosses. Such brave service helped reduce public suspicion of Japanese Americans in the United States.

an airlifted brigade of reinforcements. The Japanese continued to build up troop reserves on the eastern coast of New Guinea, however. The build-up continued despite the heavy loss of shipping and men in the battle of The bismarck Sea on March 3–4. In the battle U.S. forces sank eight transport ships and four destroyers taking troops to New Guinea. The Japanese lost more than 3,600 troops and sailors.

▲ A Japanese American battalion listens to a lecture on the use of hand grenades. Nisei battalions earned a reputation as fine fighters in the Pacific and other theaters of war.

The Battle of the Bismarck Sea

On February 28, 1943, a Japanese transport fleet sailed out of Rabaul harbor, New Britain. It was bound for Lae on New Guinea. U.S. intelligence had already warned the Allies about the approaching convoy. It was spotted by an aircraft in the Bismarck Sea off New Guinea. On the night of March 2, B-17 Flying Fortress bombers of the Fifth United States Army Air Force blew up two ammunition transport ships. At dawn, 97 U.S. and Australian bombers attacked. They sank four destroyers and all the transport vessels. The survivors were machine-gunned in the water and 3,660 died. Just over 900 shocked survivors made it to Lae.

Cartwheel in New Guinea

The New Guinea part of Operation Cartwheel began on June 29, 1943. The Australian New Guinea Force would make an overland advance from Wau up through the Huon Peninsula, in northeastern New Guinea. Meanwhile, troops of the U.S. "Alamo Force" would make coordinated amphibious landings at intervals along the coast. The Japanese would have to retreat to avoid the constant threat of being trapped between the two Allied forces.

The Australians' first objective was Salamaua, on the coast 35 miles (56km) north of Wau. An Australian brigade had actually begun a slow advance on April 24. Japanese resistance meant that it took two months to reach a position just south of Salamaua. On the night of June 29–30, however, a U.S. battalion landed just south of Salamaua. The combined Allied forces kept up pressure on the Japanese throughout July. The Japanese had to bring in reinforcements from Lae, along the coast.

The following month, the Allies also achieved a major victory in the air war in New Guinea. U.S. engineers had secretly built an airstrip in the jungle.

▼ An Australian patrol forces its way through heavy jungle during the advance on Lae in October 1943.

On August 17, U.S. forces launched a 200-plane attack on Japanese airfields near Wewak. They destroyed all but 35 enemy aircraft before they had time to take off.

On September 4, an Australian division made an amphibious landing just northeast of Lae. The following day more than 3,000 U.S. paratroopers dropped at Nadzab, northwest of Lae. They were joined by Australians airlifted from Port Moresby. The Japanese at Lae and Salamaua were now effectively encircled. They fought hard, but Salamaua fell on September 12, and Lae on September 16. Nearly 8,000 Japanese soldiers escaped the Allied trap. They fled northward across the Huon Peninsula.

Allied progress

Following their success, the Australian and U.S. forces now followed two distinct lines of advance. A mainly Australian force cut east along the

◀ U.S. Marines wade through 3 feet (1m) of water after landing at Cape Gloucester on New Britain in December 1943.

▼ U.S. troops fire a mortar in the jungle in the Solomons. The mortar's high trajectory made it ideal for using in jungle clearings.

Allied jungle weapons

The Allies in the Pacific had better small arms than the Japanese. The U.S. infantry had a self-loading rifle, the M1 Garand, which reloaded automatically every time the trigger was pulled. It helped them generate huge firepower to cut through jungle foliage. Submachine guns were also vital in close-quarter encounters in the jungle. Heavier machine guns like the U.S. M1917, M1919, and M2HB could hack down trees, suppress bunkers, and halt Japanese charges. Jungle warfare gave new status to flamethrowers. They were ideal for destroying bunkers by suffocating or burning the occupants. Infantry support often came from mortars. They fired shells up at a steep angle, making them easy to use in jungle clearings. Mortars were also light and easier to move than conventional artillery.

▲ A U.S. B-25 swoops across Rabaul harbor in an attack that sank 26 Japanese ships in November 1943.

▼ The landscape at Tarawa after the artillery barrage.

valley of the Markham River. Its target was Madang, just above the Huon Peninsula. Meanwhile, a combined U.S. and Australian force would work its way around the peninsula's coastline. When the two advances met up, they would cut off all Japanese forces in the Huon Peninsula.

This happened on April 17, 1944. The fighting had been terrible. There had been particularly stubborn Japanese defense around the mountainous Sattelberg Peak. However, the Allies had growing tactical confidence, air superiority, and heavy firepower. The weary troops made steady progress. During the fighting around the coastal town of Finschafen, U.S. aircraft had dropped the first napalm-type munitions. They were incendiary bombs made of slow-burning petroleum jelly. U.S. forces later used napalm widely in the Vietnam War (1964–1973).

Fighting on

The Japanese threat in New Guinea had largely been neutralized. A substantial force remained on the island. It eluded destruction or capture. Allied landings on the northern coastline around Aitape and Hollandia on April 22, 1944, trapped the Japanese in the New Guinea interior, however.

In July, more northerly Allied landings effectively sealed off the whole of the country. Despite being trapped, the Japanese troops fought on until the end of the war. Wewak did not fall to

The Aleutian Islands

The Aleutian Islands campaign is an almost forgotten aspect of the Pacific War. Lying in Arctic waters between Alaska and Japan, the islands are U.S. territory. In June 1942, the Japanese invaded. They occupied the Aleutian islands of Attu and Kiska, as part of a diversion to lure the U.S. Navy into battle around Midway (*see Chapter 2*). Poor weather limited the U.S. response to the invasions, but on May 11, 1943, the U.S. 7th Invasion Division landed on Attu to face about 2,500 Japanese. Despite being heavily outnumbered, the Japanese threw wave after wave of suicide charges against the U.S. guns. Within a few days the U.S. force had suffered more than 1,000 casualties from battle and cold, but the Japanese were running out of food and ammunition. They were pushed into the eastern part of the island, where on May 31 they were defeated. Only 28 surrendered. Kiska was then invaded on August 15. The U.S. and Canadian troops discovered that the Japanese had already evacuated the island.

▲ Part of the U.S. fleet rides at anchor at Atak Harbor during the campaign to regain the Aleutian Islands in 1943.

the Australians until May 10, 1945. Only the final surrender of Japan itself brought New Guinea under total Allied control.

Cutting Off Rabaul

The Allies consolidated their hold over the Huon Peninsula in late 1943. The Solomons were under their control to the east. They now moved to cut off the Japanese base at Rabaul. The island of New Britain was garrisoned by about 100,000 Japanese soldiers, however. Allied commanders wanted to avoid a large-scale battle.

On December 26, U.S. Marines landed in the coastal swamplands of Borgen Bay. That was farther east of Rabaul than the Japanese had expected. The landings took the Japanese entirely by surprise. After a bloody battle, the Marines occupied a Japanese airfield at Cape Gloucester. The U.S. forces then consolidated positions in the west of the island. Allied bombers pounded Rabaul itself.

In early 1944, Halsey's forces would take the Green Islands, Admiralty Islands, and St. Matthais Group to the south, north and northwest respectively. The Cartwheel trap was complete. Rabaul was isolated, along with another Japanese base in New Ireland to the north. Now the Allies could look north toward the Philippines.

▶ The U.S. landings on Betio, the main island of Tarawa, met determined resistance from defenders in three main pockets.

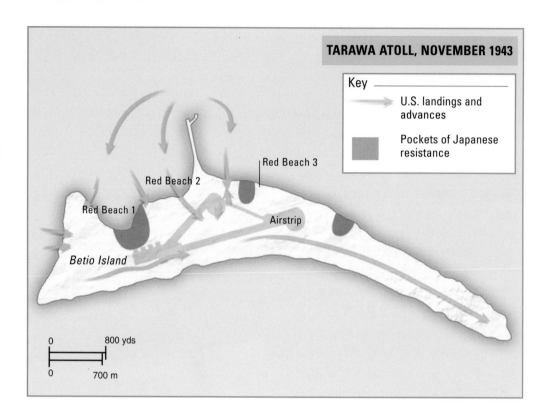

TARAWA ATOLL, NOVEMBER 1943

Key

→ U.S. landings and advances

◼ Pockets of Japanese resistance

Red Beach 2

Red Beach 1

Red Beach 3

Airstrip

Betio Island

0   800 yds

0   700 m

The Gilbert Islands

While Operation Cartwheel took place, the other major Allied thrust on Japan was also getting underway. This was Chester Nimitz's offensive toward Formosa. By October 1943, Nimitz had gathered huge naval and Marine resources. They included the Fifth Fleet, which comprised seven battleships and eight cruisers. He also had the Fifth Amphibious Force, and the Seventh Army Air Force.

The first stepping stone Nimitz targeted was the Gilbert Islands. They were coral atolls that would provide air bases for a move on the Marshall Islands to the north. The Gilberts were tiny. The only inhabited island, Betio in Tarawa, covered just 300 acres (120ha). The island was defended by 4,500 Japanese troops. U.S. forces launched a massive seven-day bombardment before making a landing. The Japanese were relatively unscathed. They sheltered in bunkers made of coconut logs and concrete.

Close fighting on Tarawa

On the nearby island of Makin, the bombardment seemed to have worked well. Infantry captured Makin in only

three days. More than 500 of its defenders died; only about 100 surrendered. On Tarawa, too, the landings on November 20 began well. The first Marines ashore, however, were soon pinned down by artillery and gunfire behind a 4-foot (1.2m) sea wall made from coconut logs. Meanwhile, the larger landing craft got stuck on coral reefs off the island. Hundreds of Marines had to wade a half-mile to shore. They were exposed to Japanese gunfire. Of the 5,000 Marines who tried to land on the first day, 1,500 were killed or wounded.

Despite the chaos, the U.S. forces built a defensive line. They could land more ammunition, tanks, and weaponry. Landings on the second day suffered heavy casualties, but U.S. forces on the island grew. They used their artillery, particularly howitzers, to drive the Japanese back into the east of the island. The island was secured early on November 23.

Lessons of Tarawa

The losses at Tarawa shocked U.S. military commanders and the public at home. More than 1,000 U.S. soldiers had been killed and 2,100 wounded in only three days. Equally shocking was the Japanese willingness to fight to the death. Fewer than 100 of the island's defenders had surrendered.

Tarawa provided valuable lessons for future amphibious landings. Preliminary bombardments would be improved. It would also be a priority to use stronger landing vehicles and get tanks ashore. Radio communications were also improved to increase the coordination of landings, which had been chaotic at Tarawa.

Infantry tactics were also refined. The best way to assault bunkers was for flamethrower teams, infantry squads, and demolition teams to work together. Such lessons would be put in place for the next target, the Marshall Islands in February 1944.

▲ Marines escort Japanese prisoners along a beach at Tarawa. Fewer than a hundred of the island's 4,500 defenders surrendered.

THE U.S. SUBMARINE CAMPAIGN

When the war in the Pacific began, the U.S. submarine fleet was small and largely obsolete. It expanded rapidly and proved vital in cutting off Japan's movement of supplies for its military campaign.

The U.S. Navy's submarine fleet had two main offensive roles in the Pacific. The first was to act as the eyes of the main surface fleet. Submarines detected and tracked Japanese warships, and sank them if the opportunity arose. The second, an often overlooked but vital role, was that of sinking the enemy's merchant fleet. Exploits like *Sailfish*'s sinking of the carrier *Chuyo* off the coast of Japan on December 4, 1943, grabbed the headlines. The routine and unglamorous sinking of merchant ships made a greater contribution to final victory.

Japan was acutely vulnerable to this type of submarine warfare as it had few natural resources of its own. Most of its raw materials had to be imported by sea. They included oil, rubber, and mineral ores. The Japanese also needed to resupply the various far-flung island garrisons they had established between December 1941 and May 1942, particularly in their Southern Resources

▼ The USS *Cavalla* was one of the Gato class, the standard U.S. submarines of the war; so many were produced that the U.S. Navy ran out of the fish names traditionally used for submarines.

Area. The conquered zone encompassed most of the Southwest Pacific and parts of Southeast Asian mainland.

Japan's merchant fleet

By 1941, Japan had a merchant fleet of some 6 million tons of ocean-going vessels and 1 million tons of smaller coastal and fishing vessels. However, this merchant fleet was never going to be large enough to satisfy the great military and economic demands of the Japanese empire.

A further 4 million tons of shipping were added to the fleet between December 1941 and August 1945. Shortages remained in key areas, however. This was especially true with regard to the oil tankers, whose cargoes Japan's war machine relied on. There were just 42 tankers in service at the outbreak of war. More were built, but there were never sufficient tankers to meet the demand for oil or to offset the tankers destroyed in U.S. attacks. Some 259 tankers were sunk between 1941 and

1945. Some were hunted down by aircraft, but many more succumbed to torpedoes fired by U.S. submarines.

The U.S. submarine fleet

Most of the U.S. Pacific Fleet's submarines were absent from Pearl Harbor during the Japanese attack on December 7, 1941. Only four older boats were in harbor for refits. None of them was damaged. Despite that escape, the U.S. Navy's submarine fleet was not at the time fit to wage war on the enemy's merchant fleet. It was a small force, and over half of its vessels dated from World War I. The submarines had been largely ignored by strategists and politicians during the interwar period.

The submariners' frustration was expressed by John Fyfe. He was an officer on *Dolphin* at Pearl Harbor: "*Dolphin* is part of my life I would like to forget. We spent more time fighting the ship than we did the Japanese. I was the chief engineer and … it was a constant struggle just to keep her operating. The

▲ This picture was taken through the periscope of a U.S. Navy submarine moments after it had torpedoed a Japanese transport ship in the Pacific. The ship burst into flames immediately.

boat leaked water in and fuel oil out, dove like she was built to fly, and you never knew whether she would start down stern first, or bow first, or just sink on an even keel."

Technical problems

The Asiatic and Pacific Fleets facing the Japanese had only 29 and 27 submarines each. They were originally designed to defend U.S. coastal waters. Few of them had the range to conduct operations far from the main U.S. Pacific bases at Pearl Harbor and in the Philippines. An S-class boat, for example, had a range of 3,420 nautical miles (6,330km), which made it unsuited to operations in the Pacific.

The navy's few ocean-going submarines had a range of 18,000 nautical miles (33,340 km). They were armed with six torpedo tubes and a pair of 6-inch deck guns. Their great length made them difficult to operate, however. They were so short of torpedoes that their captains were ordered to use them singly or in small salvoes.

Support in high places

Although the submarine fleet was in a generally poor state, it had support from senior commanders. Admiral Ernest King, chief of Naval Operations from March 1942, had helped develop the submarine force in the interwar period. Admiral Chester Nimitz, com-

Torpedoes

▲ A Mark XVIII torpedo is loaded onto a U.S. submarine in 1944. It was far more reliable than previous models.

The U.S. submarines' main weapon was the Mark XIV torpedo. It had a number of problems that were not resolved until later in the war. Its motor left a tell-tale wake that allowed enemy ships to follow its course and possibly avoid it. Its magnetic detonating system was unreliable, and many torpedoes never exploded when they hit their target. The torpedo was also prone to turning full circle and hitting the firing submarine. From late 1943, there was a gradual switch over to the more reliable electric-powered Mark XVIII torpedo. It was easier and quicker to make than its predecessor, although it traveled slightly slower through the water. The Mark XIII also left no wake. It was being used in about 65 percent of all attacks by 1945.

mander of the U.S. Pacific Fleet from December 1941, had served on submarines during World War I. The head of the Asiatic Fleet, Admiral Thomas Hart, also had experience with submarines. They all recognized the weapon's great potential and backed plans to expand and modernize the fleet. Vice Admiral Charles Lockwood, commander of the Pacific submarine forces from 1942, worked tirelessly to get his command better equipment.

Improving the fleet

To wage submarine warfare against Japan's supply lines and its merchant fleet, the navy was going to need many more—and more modern—ocean-going submarines. New models were introduced once war was declared. They included the well-armed Tench class, which had a range of some 11,000 nautical miles (20,370km). The

greater part of the expansion program produced the excellent Gato class of boats. So many were built that the navy ran out of existing names. Submarines were traditionally named after fish. The navy invented new

▼ The USS *Barb* is launched from an East Coast shipyard during the rapid expansion of the submarine fleet.

names that were later used by scientists to name new species of fish.

The navy also had to address the poor leadership qualities and seamanship of many of its available submarine captains. Most had never seen a shot fired in action. They had largely trained to operate in conjunction with the main surface fleet. There was no tradition of independent thought or aggressiveness. Many were unable to come to grips with the idea of long-range warfare against the enemy's merchant fleet. John Fyfe, engineering officer on the *Dolphin* and later a submarine ace in his own right, said of one of his commanders: "He was the classic example of the peacetime skipper who couldn't cut it when the chips were down."

Such difficulties meant that the submarine campaign did not get into full swing until the latter part of 1943. As the problems were overcome, however, the campaign soon built up an unstoppable momentum.

Ultra and radar

Finding targets was difficult in the vast areas of the Pacific. For the most part, Japanese merchant ships sailed singly or in small groups. They mostly used known sea lanes between predictable ports, however. That meant that the submarine captains had a general sense of where to find them. The submarines were also often aided by Ultra. This was the name given to intelligence gathered by U.S. and British cryptanalysts. They

▼ The Japanese destroyer *Yamakaze* sinks after being torpedoed by USS *Nautilus* close to the Japanese coast in June 1942. In addition to the damage they inflicted on Japan's merchant fleet, U.S. submarines also destroyed 214 warships in the Pacific War.

Commander Richard O'Kane

Submarine ace Richard O'Kane (1911–1994) graduated from the U.S. Naval Academy in May 1934 and served on surface warships before receiving submarine instruction. He served on the submarines *Argonaut* and *Wahoo* until July 1943, when he took command of *Tang*.

On five patrols O'Kane sank 24 Japanese ships. His fifth sortie remains the most successful of any U.S. submarine. He fired 24 torpedoes in four attacks, sinking 13 vessels. One torpedo malfunctioned, however, and turned back on *Tang* during a surface attack on the night of October 24–25, 1944. It hit the submarine at the stern and sank it. Of the 87 crew, only O'Kane and eight others survived. They were rescued by the Japanese and spent the rest of the war in captivity. O'Kane was awarded the Medal of Honor after his release, and continued to serve until he retired in 1957.

▲ A submarine crew proudly displays a flag recording a successful mission: each white symbol with a red circle indicates a sunk merchant ship; the three rising sun symbols stand for sunk warships.

had broken Japan's main naval code, JN-25, in early 1942. Although the Japanese frequently updated the code, Allied decoders provided vital intelligence about troop and supply movements.

Ultra intelligence informed submarines about the routes and departure dates of potential targets. It was radar, however, that finally allowed them to locate individual targets on the surface at long range. Sonar (SOund NAvigation Ranging) allowed them to do the same underwater. The U.S. Navy started investigating the potential of radar at its Naval Research Laboratory in the early 1930s. A version that could be used on warships, the CXAM, was introduced in

▼ The *RO55* was one of three Japanese submarines sunk by the USS *Batfish* over three days in February 1945.

▲ The USS *Puffer* is launched sideways into the Manitowoc River near the Great Lakes. As the submarine fleet expanded, shipyards in the Midwest were converted to submarine construction.

1939. Submarines started receiving modern radar in 1942, before which they had to rely on lookouts to spot targets. Radar meant it was also possible to "see" targets far away at night.

The submarine aces

As U.S. submarines improved, some very able commanders emerged. They earned reputations as aces. *Wahoo*, under Captain Dudley Morton, sank vessels totaling 20,000 tons in one patrol in October 1943. Former engineering officer John Fyfe became a lieutenant commander in charge of *Batfish*, and achieved a record that still stands. *Batfish* sank three Japanese submarines on three consecutive days in February 1945. The large, ocean-going

vessels were spotted while *Batfish* was cruising through the Luzon Strait in the Philippines. Fyfe received the U.S. Navy's highest award, the Navy Cross, and the crew gained a Presidential Unit Citation. Twenty-three other Japanese submarines were also sunk by U.S. submarines. Yet there were casualties, even among the aces. *Wahoo*, for example, was lost in late 1944.

The campaign

The U.S. submarine campaign gradually became more effective. In 1942, it lost seven boats to the Japanese. In 1943, it lost a further 15 vessels, but in return it sank 335 enemy ships totaling 1.5 million tons. The campaign peaked in 1944. Submarines sank more than

The Gato class

The first Gato class submarines, which became the backbone of the U.S. fleet, were built in 1941. Around 200 had been launched by 1945. The Gato had a range of 12,000 nautical miles (22,224km) at 10 knots. It had a top speed of around 20 knots on the surface and half that under water. The boats were roomy and air-conditioned, and when fully provisioned could stay at sea for around 75 days. Comparatively short and light, they were more maneuverable than the larger V class boats. Their armament consisted of one 5-inch (125 mm) gun, one 1.5-inch (40mm) gun, and up to 26 torpedoes. There were six forward and four rear torpedo tubes. A modified version, the Balao class, was largely the same but had a thicker pressure hull.

▲ A worker checks the hull of a submarine in a shipyard in Connecticut.

half of the 3.3 million tons of merchant shipping Japan lost that year. It also accounted for the last major Japanese warship to be sunk during the war. On November 21, 1944, the super-carrier *Shinano* was torpedoed by *Archerfish* off the coast of Honshu.

By spring 1945, the Japanese merchant fleet was effectively destroyed. The Imperial Japanese Navy, or what little was left of it, was so starved of essential oil it rarely ventured out from port. The greatest danger to U.S. submarines now was to avoid coming into accidental

◄ Crewmen line the deck of the submarine *Squalus* during a ceremony to rename the vessel *Sailfish* in May 1940. The *Squalus* had sunk a year earlier, with the deaths of 26 sailors. Although it was salvaged and served until 1945, the boat was largely made obsolete by more modern vessels during the war.

conflict with friendly vessels that failed to recognize them and opened fire.

The last wartime duty for a handful of submarines was to participate in the official surrender ceremony. Twelve boats were present when the Japanese signed the unconditional surrender on board the battleship *Missouri* anchored in Tokyo Bay on September 2, 1945.

Summary of the campaign

Submarines made up less than 2 percent of the U.S. Pacific Fleet's total strength, but made a remarkable contribution to the war effort. In some 1,700 separate patrols, they sank 1,178

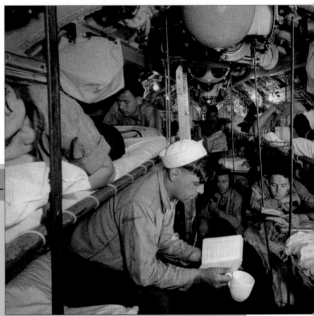

▲ Crewmen relax in bunks in the torpedo room of a submarine. Their hazardous duties were rewarded by higher pay and better food than other seamen received.

▲ A machinist on a U.S. submarine checks part of the diesel engines that powered the vessel on the surface. Submarines generally used their electric engines when submerged, because of the shortage of oxygen for combustion engines.

Submarine life

Although Gato class boats were comparatively roomy, space was always in short supply. There was little privacy. The captain had a cabin, but crews had to live among the stores and weapons for up to seven or eight weeks on patrol. The boats surfaced at night, but stayed underwater during daylight.

Outside periods of action, crews had a daily round of watch-keeping, sleeping, eating, drills, and routine maintenance. There was some leisure time to read, play games, listen to music, or watch movies. Boredom was fairly common. Air

conditioning prevented men from suffering heat exhaustion, but rough seas routinely made them feel sick. Accidents and minor injuries were fairly common, particularly in such rough weather.

Japanese merchant ships, or roughly half of the country's entire fleet. They also sank 214 warships, including one battleship, eight aircraft carriers, and 11 cruisers. The submarines fired 14,748 torpedoes, about 33 percent of which hit their target.

Success was bought at a high price, however, particularly in terms of the courageous crews of the vessels. Of the 288 submarines in service by 1945, 52 were lost through accident or enemy action. That was roughly 18 percent of the force. Crew casualties were also high. A total of 3,506 submariners died in the war. That total represented the highest loss in relative terms of any branch of the U.S. armed forces.

The morality of the submarine campaign

Since World War II, there has been intense debate about the morality of unrestricted submarine warfare. For its critics, it was an unfair and sneaky way of fighting. In both the U.S. campaign in the Pacific and that of the Germans in the Atlantic, most direct victims of submarine attacks were undefended merchant ships. They had no way of fighting back. Many thousands of crewmen died when their vessels were sunk. Often the ships' cargos were foodstuffs and other nonmilitary goods. Submarine warfare set out to increase the suffering of civilian populations by causing shortages. In total war, supporters of submarine warfare argue, merchant seamen and other noncombatants were legitimate targets to undermine the enemy war effort.

◀ The crew of the USS *Sealion* rescue British and Australian sailors after their vessel has been sunk by enemy fire in the Pacific in September 1944.

BURMA AND CHINA

The mountains and jungles of Burma were some of the most demanding environments for fighting in the whole war. Burma was strategically valuable, however: It guarded the supply routes to China.

By summer 1942 on the Asian mainland, Japanese troops had overrun much of Southeast Asia. They had conquered what is now Malaysia and Burma. The British defenders and their allies had retreated north and west into India. There the Japanese campaign stalled. Overstretched supply lines, difficult terrain, and growing Allied resistance prevented a Japanese attack on India.

For the Japanese, the campaign in Burma became inextricably linked to their attempt to conquer neighboring China, which they had invaded in 1937. Routes through Burma were the main way for the Allies to continue providing weapons and other support to the Nationalist Chinese government of Chiang Kai-shek.

The tough conditions in Burma made supplying armies difficult. The climate also had a significant impact on the war. The summer monsoon season brought large-scale military operations to a halt. Only in the dry season, from October to May, could air support be relied upon and supply convoys move easily along Burma's dirt roads.

Burma Road

Burma was a strategic prize for the Japanese. It had many valuable natural resources, including large oil fields, and Japan's victory in 1942 cut off the only land route into China from outside. The so-called "Burma Road" stretched north from the Burmese capital, Rangoon, into southern China. It combined a railroad with a winding track through the high mountains near the Chinese border.

By 1942, Japanese troops in China controlled the northern region, Manchuria. They were also in charge of a large swathe of territory between the major cities of Beijing and Shanghai and a series of coastal settlements, including Hong Kong and Canton. There were a million Japanese troops in China, but in such a huge country even that number could not win a decisive victory over the Chinese. The Chinese, in turn, were split between the Nationalist government of Chiang

▼ Supply trucks rumble along a twisting section of the Burma Road toward the mountains that mark the Chinese border in the distance.

Chiang Kai-shek

Chiang Kai-shek was the leader the Nationalist Chinese movement from 1925 until his death in 1975. The movement was known as the Kuomintang, or KMT.

Chiang underwent military training in Japan and Russia. He rose to high command in the KMT army, and took control of the movement after a power struggle. He then set about purging the KMT of the Communist sympathizers of Mao Zedong. The dispute sowed the seeds of a civil war in China that lasted nearly 25 years.

In 1926, Chiang launched a long military campaign to try to unify China. He defeated Mao, who in 1934 led his followers on the famous Long March to Shensi in northwest China, beyond the reach of the government Chiang established in Nanking (Nanjing).

When the Japanese invaded the heartland of China in 1937, Chiang was forced to move his capital from Nanking to Chungking. He lost control of the coastal regions and most of the major cities to Japan. In an effort to beat the Japanese, he agreed to collaborate with the Communists. The alliance was always tense, however, and there was little actual cooperation.

▼ Chiang Kai-shek (left) and Madam Chiang entertain Claire L. Chennault, commander of the "Flying Tigers" who provided air support to keep vital supply routes to China open.

Kai-shek and Communist guerrilla forces led by Mao Zedong.

The population had suffered during a decade of disease, starvation, and war. Chiang's government was hanging on only thanks to U.S. supplies. They had formerly been brought up the Burma Road, but now they were flown in over the "Hump," the pilots' nickname for the Himalaya mountains.

The war in China was at a stalemate. The Japanese believed that they had to keep the Burma Road closed if they were going to finally subjugate the Chinese. For the duration of the war, the Allies and Japanese would struggle to control the strategic communications route.

The First Arakan offensive

At the end of the 1942 monsoon season in September, the British began a counterattack from southern India into Burma. The four Japanese divisions in Burma were badly stretched. They had to defend borders with both India and China, as well as the country's oil fields and cities.

The object of the British offensive was the Arakan. It was a lightly defended coastal region in northwest Burma. Indian and British troops first sought to drive the Japanese back from the Indian port of Cox's Bazar. The region was a mix of high hills, narrow valleys, and large swamps. Supplies had to be carried on rivers on small boats, slowing the British advance.

Japanese resistance

Although they were outnumbered, the Japanese defenders were all combat veterans. That gave them an advantage over the British and Indian troops, who had limited training for and

The Flying Tigers

The Flying Tigers, also known as the American Volunteer Group (AVG), were U.S. pilots. They protected the vital supply routes into China in late 1941 and early 1942. They took their name from the distinctive fanged jaws painted on the noses of their P-40 Kittyhawks.

Recruited by retired U.S. captain Claire L. Chennault, the Tigers fought Japanese fighters above Burma and China. As Japan conquered Burma and the Tigers withdrew to China, Chennault fell out with the Chinese leader Chiang Kai-shek. Chiang

▶ AVG pilots run for their planes at an airfield in China. The Tigers' pilots were all experienced volunteers from the United States.

reserved fuel and ammunition for his ground forces rather than for the Tigers. In July 1942, the Tigers were incorporated into the U.S. Army Air Force. With only 75 pilots and about 50 aircraft, they had shot down 299 enemy aircraft and damaged many more.

▶ The British advance into the Arakan left its flanks exposed to Japanese counterattack. The operation was a disaster for the Allies.

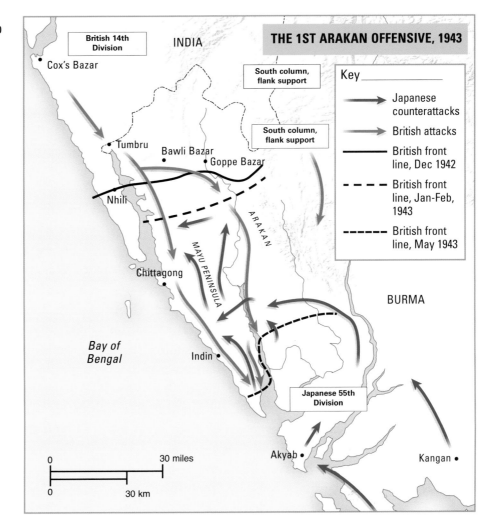

THE 1ST ARAKAN OFFENSIVE, 1943

Key

→	Japanese counterattacks
→	British attacks
—	British front line, Dec 1942
- - -	British front line, Jan-Feb, 1943
– – –	British front line, May 1943

British 14th Division

INDIA

Cox's Bazar

South column, flank support

South column, flank support

Tumbru

Bawli Bazar

Goppe Bazar

Nhili

ARAKAN

MAYU PENINSULA

Chittagong

BURMA

Bay of Bengal

Indin

Japanese 55th Division

Akyab

Kangan

0   30 miles

0   30 km

"Vinegar" Joe Stilwell

Joseph W. Stilwell was the senior U.S. Army officer assigned to the Chinese Nationalist leader Chiang Kai-shek. He played a crucial role in building an alliance against the Japanese in Southeast Asia. Stilwell spoke fluent Chinese and Japanese, but his "Vinegar Joe" nickname derived from his famous lack of tact and difficult personality.

Stilwell's relations with Chiang Kai-shek were strained partly because he wanted to bring Chiang's armies under U.S. control. He also wanted weapons supplied by the United States to be distributed among the Nationalists and their Communist allies to fight the Japanese. Chiang believed that arming the Communists might undermine his government.

After the attack on Pearl Harbor in December 1941, Stilwell urged the Nationalists to play a more aggressive role. Chiang largely left it to the Americans to take the fight to the Japanese.

As the campaign in Burma developed, Stilwell took command of the China Burma India Theater (CBI Theater). In October 1944, he was recalled to Washington owing to his disagreements with Chiang.

◄ Joe Stilwell (in dark jacket) clashed often with the Nationalist leader Chiang Kai-shek.

experience of jungle warfare. It took three months for the Allies to advance 60 miles (95km) across the border into Burma. As they pushed down the Mayu Peninsula in January and February 1943, they had to divert men from combat to guard their supply lines, which were growing dangerously long.

Even though the British had some medium tanks and air support from the RAF, the Japanese held them up at the bottom of the Mayu peninsula. This gave Japanese reinforcements time to march across the country through dense jungle to attack the Allies' flank. British

forward units were in danger of being cut off. The British high command ordered a retreat north.

Six weeks later, by the second week of May, the British were back on the Indian border and had lost 5,000 casualties. One Indian brigade had been virtually destroyed. Four other brigades had been badly shaken. The fighting reputation of the Japanese reached new heights.

Chindit strike

Allied morale was lifted by a dramatic commando raid deep behind Japanese lines. The commandos were dubbed the Chindits. They were led by the highly unorthodox British lieutenant colonel Orde Wingate. Two columns of troops pushed more than 100 miles (160km) into northern Burma, crossing the Chindwin and Irrawaddy rivers on February 14, 1943. Once behind Japanese lines, the Chindits had to rely totally on air-dropped supplies. Wingate's men had to fight a series of running battles against their Japanese pursuers in difficult jungle terrain.

The Chindits faced harsh conditions. Food was in short supply and disease was rampant. After more than six weeks behind Japanese lines, Wingate ordered a withdrawal back to Allied lines. The retreat took the Chindits 1,000 miles (1,600km) through the jungle to British India. The survivors arrived on April 30, after a journey of about five weeks. Out of some 3,000

▲ Chindits and their supply mules cross the Chindwin River in Burma at the start of their first operation. They were named for a mythical Burmese lion, the chinthe.

◄ Japanese infantry guard an oil field near the Burmese city of Mandalay. The Japanese relied on captured resources to support their campaign.

Orde Wingate

British officer Orde Wingate (1903–1944) was a pioneer of deep-penetration missions behind enemy lines. After experience leading Jewish commando raids on Arab bases in prewar Palestine, he was sent to Khartoum in the Sudan at the start of World War II. He formed the Gideon Force and led raids against Italian units. With only a few hundred men, Wingate bluffed 12,000 Italians into surrender.

Wingate later joined British forces in India. He was promoted to brigadier and given permission to form the Chindits, commandos trained in jungle raiding and guerrilla tactics.

Wingate convinced British prime minister Winston Churchill of the value of Long Range Penetration to disrupt enemy supply lines. Churchill made Wingate a major general and expanded the Chindits to six brigades. U.S. president Franklin D. Roosevelt decided to create a similar group. It was led by Brigadier General Frank Merrill, and became known as "Merrill's Marauders."

Wingate then planned Operation Thursday, a second Chindit mission in Burma. He died soon after it began. His plane crashed near Imphal, in eastern India, during a storm on March 14, 1944.

◄ Orde Wingate (center) believed that troops deep behind enemy lines could disrupt Japanese supply lines.

▶ British Churchill tanks armed with flame-throwers go into action in the Arakan peninsula in 1944.

men who set out on the expedition, only 2,182 returned; only 600 were ever fit for frontline service again. The Chindit raid did not really achieve its aim of disrupting Japanese communications. However, it was a great boost for British and Indian morale after the failure of the first Arakan offensive.

The British advance again

In October 1943, British prime minister Winston Churchill ordered a major shake up of the command arrangements in East Asia. He appointed Louis Mountbatten as head of the Southeast Asia Command (SEAC). Churchill ordered Mountbatten to launch offensive operations in order to pull Japanese troops away from China and the Central Pacific. Lieutenant General William Slim was put in command of all British and Indian land forces in the Burma theater.

Eyewitness

❝ The great metropolitan cities of China—Shanghai, Canton, Hong Kong… with their paved streets, treasures of ancient art, movie houses, race tracks and Western hotels—are all still in Japanese hands. What the GI sees of China today is really its back yard—its farm country and its third and fourth-rate cities, jam-packed with refugees, poverty, disease, and dirt. It is possible for a GI to spend 30 months of service back here and not once get out of his nostrils the smell of the human and animal manure with which the good earth of China has for centuries been fertilized. ❞

Lou Stoumen on U.S. troops in China,
YANK magazine, October 20, 1944

In fall 1943, the British struck again at the Arakan region; this time, however, Slim prepared them carefully for the task. He put them through a tough training program for jungle warfare. Slim realized that a Japanese counter-

▼ Landing craft carry Indian infantry along a river during the second Arakan offensive in Burma.

attack would have to rely on captured British supply dumps. He trained his troops to defend their bases, even if they were cut off by the Japanese; the bases would be resupplied by air.

The second offensive

The second Arakan offensive followed much the same pattern as the first. The British pushed steadily south and the Japanese then counterattacked against their exposed flanks. This time the British and Indian troops were not panicked by the infiltration attacks behind their lines.

The British supply bases were soon surrounded by the Japanese, but the bases were protected by a series of fortified positions. The Japanese tried to capture the supplies on which their counteroffensive depended. The Allied troops held out, and inflicted many casualties on the enemy. The British and Indians themselves suffered more than 3,500 casualties, but the Japanese suffered worse. They eventually had to

pull back when they could not capture the supply dumps. It was a major boost for Allied morale.

Operation Thursday

Farther north, the Allies planned to drive the Japanese from the northern Burmese city of Myitkyina. The city controlled the northern part of the Burma Road and an airfield. Its capture would open a new supply route into China.

In spring 1944, Chinese and U.S. units pushed south into Burma from China. They were led by Merrill's Marauders. The Marauders were U.S. troops trained in unorthodox warfare.

The Chindits behind enemy lines

Chindits were again dropped behind Japanese lines. Their leader, Orde Wingate, died in an air crash early in the operation. From March to June 1944, 9,000 Chindits dug in to fortified bases and raided enemy supply lines. They relied on air support from

▼ A U.S. Douglas Dakota transport plane takes off from the airfield at Myitkyina after the field was captured by U.S. and Chinese forces in August 1944.

◄ A detachment of Merrill's Marauders patrol through the Burmese jungle. Like the Chindits, the Marauders were trained in guerrilla warfare.

◄ Food and ammunition are dropped to support Chindit forces in their bases deep behind Japanese lines in Burma.

British and U.S. fighters and bombers. Transport aircraft brought in supplies and evacuated the wounded.

At the end of the mission, the 111th Chindit Brigade headed north to link up with U.S. and Chinese troops. Its wounded were evacuated by flying boats that landed on jungle lakes. Like their predecessors in 1943, few of the brigade were fit for combat after more than four months behind enemy lines.

Another Chindit brigade had been attached to the main U.S. and Chinese ground forces. It played a key role in an assault on Mogaung, south of Myitkyina. Chinese troops backed by Merrill's unit captured Mogaung at the end of June 1944. Mogaung was the first Burmese town recaptured by the Allies.

The Allies now possessed the strategic initiative in the Burma theater. Even though the Japanese would stage one last offensive, their rule in Southeast Asia was now threatened.

ITALY: 1944–1945

By the end of 1943, the Allies in Italy had worked their way 200 miles (320km) from Salerno, on the west coast, up the Italian mainland. They now faced a series of German defensive lines on the way to Rome.

The U.S. Fifth Army under General Mark Clark had made an amphibious landing at Salerno on September 9, 1943. It had almost been forced back into the sea. In the following weeks, however, Clark's forces pushed out of Salerno. They inched slowly north up the west side of Italy.

On the other side of Italy was the British Eighth Army, led by General Bernard Montgomery. The British advance through central and eastern Italy was also hard. The mountains, rivers, and valleys provided defensive positions for the Germans. They fought hard as they retreated.

Defensive lines across Italy

In 1943 the German forces in Italy were led by Field Marshal Albert Kesselring. He had supervised the building

of three lines of defenses across Italy from the west coast to the east coast. The Allies called the complete defensive system "the Winter Line." In fact, it included three separate defensive lines. The Barbara and Reinhard lines were strongest in central and western Italy. They protected the routes to Rome, Italy's capital. North of them, the Gustav Line snaked across the entire country.

Destination: the Gustav Line

The Gustav Line was a massive chain of defenses. In places, it was 10 miles (16km) deep. It followed the Garigliano River from the west coast, then crossed the Apennine Mountains to the east coast. The line was based on a series of strongly fortified positions. The forts were linked by minefields, machine-gun and artillery posts, and miles of barbed wire. The line was defended by 15 German divisions, including special mountain troops and a panzer corps.

The Allies' plans depended on breaking through the western side of the Gustav Line. It was the last main defense between them and Rome. The most important obstacles facing them were the defenses around the mountain town of Cassino. The defenses dominated the highway to Rome that ran through the Liri Valley.

For weeks the Allies fought their way north over the rugged ground. Their advance ground to a halt on October 8. Allied troops were stretched along the line of the Volturno River in the west to Termoli in the east. By now the Allies were fighting not only the Germans, but also appalling weather. The Italian winter had started early that year. It was snowy and bitterly cold.

The Allies' slow progress

Clark's forces resumed their offensive on October 12. U.S. and British troops crossed the Volturno River under heavy fire. They then advanced into the Reinhard Line. The attackers

▼ British Sherman M4 tanks move through the village of Imprunetta in August 1944, during Allied operations against the German Gothic Line.

Albert Kesselring (1885–1960)

Born on November 20, 1885, in Bavaria, Albert Kesselring joined the German Army in 1904. In the 1920s, he rose to the rank of colonel. In the 1930s, he moved to the Reich Aviation Ministry. In 1936, Hitler made him chief of the general staff of the Luftwaffe, the German air force. In December 1941, Kesselring was made Commander-in-Chief South. The position put him in overall charge of all Axis forces in North Africa and the Mediterranean.

After the German defeat in North Africa in 1943, Kesselring commanded Axis troops in Italy until March 1945. He then commanded German forces in western Germany. In 1947, Kesselring was sentenced to death for his part in the execution of Italian civilians. His punishment was then changed to life imprisonment.

▶ Albert Kesselring was a talented commander. He used the mountains of Italy to good effect in his defensive strategy.

suffered heavy casualties. They were only able to advance about 1 mile (1.6km) each day.

In the east, Montgomery's offensive was also going slowly. The British faced notably stubborn German defense and terrible weather—severe supply problems also delayed their advance. In mid-November, however, two corps finally crossed the Sangro River, just south of the Gustav Line. They kept moving forward and were able to fight their way through the easternmost part of the Gustav Line.

On December 27, 1943, Canadian forces captured Ortona. The strongly defended town lay about 5 miles (8km) north of the Gustav Line. Now Montgomery's exhausted troops came to a stop. Montgomery himself returned to England in preparation for the D-Day landings. In Italy, the war shifted to the west of the country.

Assaulting the Gustav Line

On December 1, the Allies began a huge offensive against the Gustav Line. They wanted to clear German positions south of Route 6, the highway that led to Cassino and Rome. The Allies used massive artillery and aerial firepower. Specialized teams of U.S. and Canadian mountaineers attacked positions high in the mountains that the Germans had thought unreachable. The Allies suffered many casualties. By the end of 1943, however, they had secured the mountains. Troops settled into the bleak positions. High in the mountains, frostbite and hypothermia were ever-present threats.

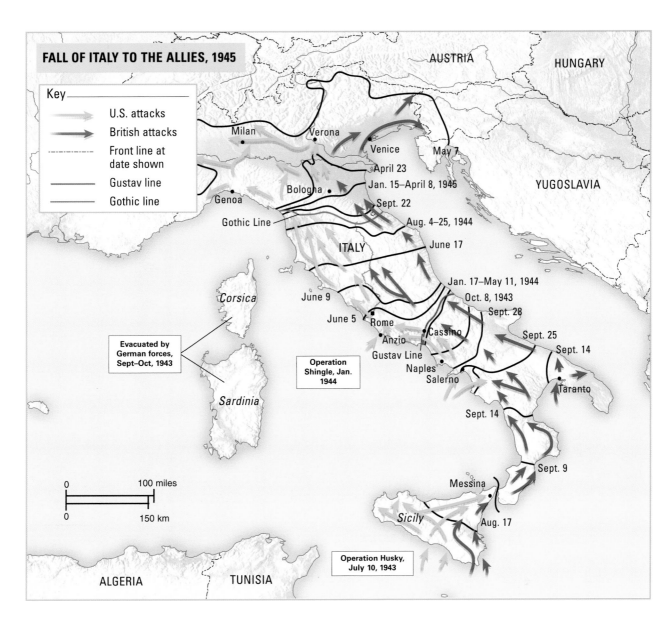

FALL OF ITALY TO THE ALLIES, 1945

Key

→ U.S. attacks

→ British attacks

– · – Front line at date shown

—— Gustav line

—— Gothic line

AUSTRIA

HUNGARY

Milan

Verona

Venice

May 7

April 23

Bologna

Jan. 15–April 8, 1945

YUGOSLAVIA

Genoa

Sept. 22

Gothic Line

Aug. 4–25, 1944

ITALY

June 17

June 9

Jan. 17–May 11, 1944

Corsica

June 5

Oct. 8, 1943

Evacuated by German forces, Sept–Oct, 1943

Rome

Sept. 28

Anzio

Cassino

Sept. 25

Operation Shingle, Jan. 1944

Gustav Line

Sept. 14

Sardinia

Naples

Salerno

Sept. 14

Taranto

Sept. 14

0   100 miles

0   150 km

Sept. 9

Messina

Sicily

Aug. 17

Operation Husky, July 10, 1943

ALGERIA

TUNISIA

▲ The main routes of the Allied advance through Italy.

◀ A Canadian patrol moves through the ruined streets of Ortona, on the Gustav Line.

271

▲ The monastery of Monte Cassino under Allied bombing. The ruins created a strong defensive position for the Germans.

The first attack on Cassino

It was vital to the Allies to capture Cassino. The town was dominated by a 1,693-foot-high (519m-) peak named Monte Cassino. An historic sixth-century Benedictine monastery stood at the top of the mountain.

Monte Cassino stood like a giant guard over Route 6. It was defended by battle-hardened German panzer troops and elite paratroopers. The Allied attackers included many nationalities. As well as British and U.S. troops, there were Poles and New Zealanders, Algerians and Moroccans of the French Expeditionary Force, Gurkhas from the Himalayas, and South Africans. At Cassino these troops fought what would be one of the bloodiest battles of the entire European war.

▲ A U.S. bomber flies over the hills around Monte Cassino. The decision to bomb the monastery remains controversial.

The first Allied offensive against the western Gustav Line at Cassino began on January 17, 1944. The Allies attacked the German defenders with machine-gun fire, tank shells, and mortar rounds.

The French Expeditionary Force managed to cross the Rapido River north of Cassino. It suffered huge casualties, however. The U.S. II Corps also endured a terrible experience. It was opposite Cassino itself. The Texas 36th Division spent three days attempting to cross the Rapido in assault boats. It suffered about 1,000 casualties before it called off the operation. By February 11, the whole Allied offensive had burned itself out. The Allies had suffered more than 14,300 casualties.

The Republic of Saló

Following the dramatic rescue of Mussolini from imprisonment in September 1943, Hitler created the Italian Social Republic (RSI) in German-occupied northern Italy. The new republic was also known as the Republic of Saló, because its capital was at Saló on Lake Garda.

Mussolini took charge of the RSI. He still had the respect of many Italians. His fascist beliefs appealed particularly to the young. However, it soon became clear that the RSI was a German puppet government. People quickly turned against both it and Mussolini. The RSI collapsed after the German defeat in 1945.

Eyewitness

❝ This kind of fighting has little coherence, no design that is easy to follow. For the New Zealanders [who were conducting an assault on the town] it was a mosaic of grim little fights over small distances: a lethal game of hide-and-seek in ditches, cellars, craters, mounds of rubble, sewers, and fragments of buildings that resembled stumps of teeth, but each of which concealed one or more abscesses in which a man, or a gun, or even a tank could be hidden. Enough of the prepared fortifications—reinforced cellars, gun emplacements, ground-floor bunkers—survived the bombing well enough to preserve a hard core of defense at the western end of the town, barring the way to the Liri Valley. ❞

Fred Majdalany,
officer in the British Eighth Army,
on fighting around Cassino

Two more attempts to take Cassino

The first battle was just the start of the fighting. In all, the Allies made four attempts to take Cassino. The second offensive took place between February 15 and 18. It began with a notorious act of destruction. Some U.S. commanders feared that the Germans would use the Benedictine monastery as a defensive position. They persuaded Clark to destroy it. U.S. bombers turned it into a pile of rubble.

▼ British Gurkha soldiers using a Bren machine gun at the Gothic Line.

▶ Goumiers in traditional dress man a machine-gun post in Cassino. The Goumiers came from Morocco and served in the French forces. Their skill at mountain fighting was vital to the Allied breakthrough on the Gustav Line.

▼ The town of Cassino lies in ruins beneath Monte Cassino after the Allied victory.

There were no Germans in the monastery at the time, however. Only monks and civilians died in the raid. But the rubble now created good defensive cover, and the Germans duly occupied the monastery.

The ground attack that followed was undertaken mainly by the New Zealand Corps. British, Indian, and New Zealand troops attacked Cassino railroad station and Monte Cassino. Meanwhile, French forces made an assault north of the town. The battle was another Allied disaster. Dug-in German panzers and infantry defeated most of the assaults.

Bad weather delayed a third Allied attack for four weeks. Then, on March 15, the Indian Division and the New

Zealanders once again attempted to take the town. This time the Allies fired 195,000 artillery shells and more than 900 tons of bombs at Cassino as preparation for the attack. The town was entirely destroyed. Plenty of Germans survived to fight among the rubble, however. By March 23, the battle had again ground to a halt, with few decisive achievements.

The fall of Cassino

Both Allied and Axis soldiers were suffering after weeks of fighting. Many were injured, shell shocked, or exhausted. However, the Allies managed to put together huge numbers of troops and masses of firepower for a final assault. Fourteen divisions of men would attack along a 20-mile (32-km) front.

On May 11, the Allies began a colossal artillery and air bombardment along the length of the German defenses. It was followed by infantry assaults. Nine thousand French North African troops climbed through the mountains to the south of Cassino. They began to swing north. They planned to sever Route 6 and cut off the Germans at Cassino.

Cassino town fell to British troops. On May 17, the Germans began to withdraw. Meanwhile, 50,000 Polish troops fought for six days on Monte Cassino itself. On May 18, they finally captured the summit.

The battle for Cassino was costly for both sides. About 45,000 Axis and Allied troops were killed or wounded. Yet now the Allies could resume their advance to Rome. They could join up with other Allied forces who had landed farther up the coast.

The landings at Anzio

A landing behind the German defensive lines had been part of the Allies' overall plan. Code-named Operation Shingle,

the plan was for U.S. VI Corps under Major-General John Lucas to make an amphibious landing near the town of Anzio. They would be 60 miles (96km) north of the Gustav Line. After landing, the troops would thrust inland. Their aim was to cut Routes 6 and 7, the supply routes from Rome to the Winter Line. The Germans on the Winter Line would be forced out of their positions or risk being trapped between Allied advances from north and south.

A strategic mistake

Lucas's men landed on January 22, 1944. They caught the Germans unprepared and the landings were a success. What followed, however, was an Allied disaster. Lucas had the advantage of surprise, but he was

▲ Helmets mark Allied graves near the Gustav Line. The fighting at Cassino alone cost the Allies about 25,000 casualties.

▶ U.S. large landing craft are docked in the harbor at Anzio after the Allied landings in January 1944.

Partisans and the Ardeatine Cave massacre

The German occupation of northern Italy led to the creation of a large partisan movement among the Italian people. Italian partisan forces were composed of a bewildering mix of social and political groups. The Committees for National Liberation (CLN) was an organization for communist partisans, but other partisan movements included Catholic groups, units of independent soldiers, and monarchists. Most partisans operated out of the mountainous Alps and Apennines, although there were some in the towns and cities, and they launched an effective war on the German occupiers and Italian forces of the Republic of Saló.

German reprisals for partisan attacks were horrific. Following the killing of 33 Germans in a bomb ambush in March 1944, 335 civilians were executed in the caves of Via Ardeatina, near Rome. Hitler himself had ordered that 10 Italians should be killed for each German life lost (the extra victims happened to be caught up in the massacre). In total, more than 10,000 Italians were killed in similar reprisal raids in World War II.

◀ These Italian partisans are armed with a range of British and Italian submachine guns.

afraid of a heavy German counter-attack. Instead of pushing straight inland, he decided to wait on the beaches while more troops landed to build up his strength.

Lucas's mistake gave Kesselring time to assemble 40,000 soldiers at Anzio. By January 26, the Germans had set up a defensive perimeter around the town. They began pounding the Allied positions with artillery and tank fire and aerial bombardment.

The Allies at Anzio were trapped. Between January 25 and 31, Lucas launched a series of attacks against the German perimeter. They failed, and at a terrible cost. The British 1st Infantry Division and the U.S. 3rd Division suffered 5,100 casualties in only six days.

The tide turns

By mid-February it looked as though the Germans would drive the Allies at Anzio back into the sea.

Meanwhile, however, Allied intelligence had gathered information about German plans. By this time, Lucas had also built up an overwhelming superiority in artillery and air cover. On February 16, German troops began an offensive that cut 1 mile (1.6km) into Allied lines. The Allies were ready, however. Over the next three days, the attack was halted by overpowering bomber raids and salvos from Allied ground and naval artillery.

A new commander

On February 22, 1944, Lucas was replaced by Major-General Lucien K. Truscott, Jr. From then on, the battle turned decidedly in the Allies' favor. Allied firepower halted another German offensive. The two sides settled into a siege that lasted until May. After the final Allied breakthrough at Cassino in May, the German position at Anzio was impossible to maintain.

◄ An American Sherman tank, in the service of British troops, is loaded onto the beach at Anzio in 1944.

By the end of the month Truscott had broken out from Anzio. He was beginning to advance north toward Rome.

The liberation of Rome

The German retreat from Cassino gave U.S. forces from Anzio the chance to drive east to trap Kesselring's Tenth Army. Instead, Clark decided to send VI Corps north to take Rome. Many people think that vanity was the main reason for Clark's decision. Although Rome was the Italian capital, it had little strategic significance. The decision arguably allowed the Tenth Army to escape to fight future battles.

Victory in Italy

Clark entered Rome on June 5, 1944. One day later, the Allies landed in Normandy, France, to begin the conquest of western Europe. The Italian campaign became secondary in the minds of Allied leaders. They sent men

and material from Italy to France. German resistance and winter weather made the rest of the campaign in Italy a hard slog.

As the German Tenth Army retreated north, the Allied advance slowed. Kesselring had time to gather his forces behind the Gothic Line. This defensive system ran across Italy from La Spezia in the west to Pesaro in the east. The British Eighth Army penetrated eastern parts of the line at the end of August 1944. The U.S. Fifth Army, however, did not break through for another month.

End of the campaign

By the start of 1945, the British and U.S. advance had ground to a halt. Allied forces were just short of Bologna. After a series of changes among Allied commanders, both sides strengthened their positions and waited for spring.

The final Allied offensive began on April 9, 1945. The Eighth Army drove

▼ U.S. troops pass the ancient Colosseum in Rome on June 5, 1944. The decision to liberate the city has been criticized. Some people say that it was taken because of General Mark Clark's desire for personal glory.

The death of Mussolini

Benito Mussolini' s death came at the hands of his fellow countrymen. With the Allies fast approaching his headquarters at Lake Garda, Mussolini attempted to flee to Switzerland with his mistress, Clara Petacci. They were intercepted, however, by pro-Allied Italian artisans on April 26, 1945, and shot two days later. Their corpses were taken to Milan and hung upside down in one of the city's squares.

◀ The bodies of Benito Mussolini and Clara Petacci are displayed in Milan after their execution on April 28, 1945.

toward Ferrara and the Fifth Army pushed for Bologna. The city fell on April 21.

The German forces in Italy were exhausted. On April 29, their commanders signed a surrender with the Allies. The Italian campaign was over. It had cost the Allies 312,000 casualties and the Germans 434,000. Italy had once been called the "soft underbelly" of Europe. In fact, it had proved very hard indeed.

◀ Members of a British anti-aircraft unit use a 3.7-inch gun to add firepower to the bombardment of the Gothic Line.

THE SOVIET UNION ON THE OFFENSIVE

During the late summer and fall of 1943, Soviet troops began to take the offensive on the Eastern Front. Within five months they recaptured much of the territory that had been seized and occupied by the Germans.

The defense of the salient (or bulge) in the Soviet line at Kursk was the first part of a three-part Soviet plan. After fighting at Kursk had exhausted the Germans, the Red Army would launch a series of offensives in the area. Finally, the offensives would be extended to the flanks of the German forces with the aim of reaching the Dnieper River and, if possible, advancing into Belorussia and Ukraine.

On July 12, after the Germans had run out of steam at Kursk, the Soviets began the second part of the plan. North of the city three Soviet fronts, or army groups, attacked the German Ninth Army, which was outnumbered two to one. After hard fighting the Western Front broke the German line north of Bolkhov, while the Central Front seized Kromy. The Ninth Army withdrew to avoid encirclement.

Operation Rumiantsev

South of Kursk the Soviets launched Operation Rumiantsev to destroy the Fourth Panzer Army and the Sixth Army by reaching the Black Sea Coast behind them. The offensive began on August 3, 1943. The Soviets opened a gap in the German line and on August 5 they liberated Belgorod, an important road and rail junction. Other breakthroughs soon threatened the German position at Kharkov. Erich von Manstein, commander of Army Group South, was determined to avoid another disaster like Stalingrad. Disobeying Hitler, he instructed his troops to evacuate Kharkov. The Red Army liberated the city on August 23.

German retreat to the Dnieper

In early September Hitler permitted Army Group South to withdraw to the Dnieper River. In theory the river was part of a 500-mile-long (800km) defensive system, but the only substantial fortifications were in the south, between the Black Sea and the Dnieper. Known as the Wotan Line, they were to be occupied by the Sixth Army.

As Army Group South retreated, it destroyed houses, factories, and railroad lines to slow the Red Army's advance. Ukrainian males, particularly those under 60, were forcibly evacuated to prevent them from being conscripted into the Red Army. Many civilians fled west to avoid retribution from the NKVD, the Soviet secret police, which was seeking out collaborators and anti-Soviet groups.

Manstein ordered the creation of a scorched-earth zone 10 to 15 miles (16–24km) wide on the east bank of the Dnieper to deny the Soviets any cover or natural resources. He also evacuated the Taman Peninsula, the Axis's last foothold in the Caucasus.

On September 10, Soviet marines landed at the Black Sea port of Novorossisk, on the right flank of the Axis position. In only a few weeks, more than 200,000 Axis troops and Soviet civilians were evacuated across the Black Sea to the Crimea.

◄ A Soviet T-34 tank moves past a knocked-out German Tiger tank. The soldiers riding on the T-34 are troops who jumped off when close to the enemy to fight, known as tank *desant* troops.

THE SOVIET ADVANCE, JULY–NOVEMBER, 1943

Key
→ German attack
→ Soviet advance
—— German front line, July 1943
‑ ‑ ‑ German front line, September 1943
.... German front line, November 1943

▲ The Soviet offensive pushed the Germans back into Ukraine and Belorussia.

▶ This German railroad car is equipped with a hook that tears up sleepers (parts of a track that keep a railroad in place) from the track. As they retreated, the Germans destroyed anything that might help the Soviet advance.

the first front crossed the river, followed over the next few days by two more. Manstein's scorched-earth zone had proved to be no obstacle.

The Soviet infantrymen who made the first crossings of the Dnieper—the river was up to a mile (1.6km) wide in places—did so at great risk. Using improvised rafts, inner tubes, or special inflatable rings, they crossed wherever possible, often under heavy fire. In places the waters ran red with blood. Behind them engineers labored to build rafts to carry tanks and guns to the opposite bank. A total of 12,000 men won medals for their bravery, including 2,000 who were made Heroes of the Soviet Union.

The bridgehead at Bukrin

To support a bridgehead on the west bank of the Dnieper at Bukrin, south of Kiev, the Soviets decided to drop about 9,000 paratroopers behind German lines. The troops would prevent the Germans attacking the bridgehead, allowing more Red Army units to cross the river.

During the night of September 26, the Soviets dropped 4,500 men. They were widely scattered, however, and

The Soviets cross the Dnieper

On September 18, Marshal Georgy K. Zhukov, Stalin's second-in-command, ordered the Thirty-Eighth Army to advance toward the Dnieper, south of Kiev. On the night of September 22,

Red Army reforms

When Germany invaded the Soviet Union, the Red Army was badly prepared for war and suffered many defeats. A process of reform, however, meant that by late 1943 it was much more capable of beating its enemies.

In January 1943, the Soviets formed five tank armies with more than 500 tanks each and about 50,000 men. The fast-moving armies were designed to exploit gaps created in the German defenses by the artillery and infantry. Heavy artillery divisions were also created to destroy defensive positions by sheer firepower. New equipment poured out of factories that had been relocated to the Ural Mountains. The Red Army also became expert at crossing Russia's numerous rivers with amphibious vehicles and pontoon bridges. Trucks imported from the United States made troop movement easier, and new uniforms introduced in late 1942 gave the troops a greater sense of pride. Finally Stalin began to trust his generals and he allowed them to plan more realistic offensives, which led to a string of German defeats in 1943 and 1944.

lost most of their equipment, including their radios. To make matters worse, they were dropped in an area full of German troops. Several groups of paratroopers managed to link up. They spent the next six weeks avoiding capture until Soviet ground forces made contact with them.

Soviet progress

As the Red Army's bridgeheads on the Dnieper became more established, Manstein reviewed his situation. It looked weak. The front was 440 miles (700km) long, and he had only 54 divisions to hold it. One of the enemy bridgeheads was now over 50 miles (80km) deep and 200 miles (320km) wide. Manstein had also been ordered to hold the Zaporozhye bridgehead on the eastern bank at all costs: Hitler hoped that it would be the jumping-off point for a future German offensive, and it also guarded the northern flank of the Crimea.

The next Soviet attack came on October 13. After several days of heavy fighting, the Soviet Eighth Guards Army broke through the line at Zaporozhye, forcing the Germans to retreat to the west. In another attack Soviet tanks reached the city of Krivoi Rog, many miles behind German lines, before a German counterattack retook the city and reestablished the line.

Dnepropetrovsk, with its enormous power plants and dams, was liberated on October 25, although the Germans had destroyed many of its installations.

▼ Soviet soldiers advance through swampland on their way to liberate the city of Melitopol in late October 1943.

▲ German infantry attack. Local German successes could not alter the fact that Soviet forces were far stronger across the whole front.

As Soviet forces linked up, they were becoming strong enough to withstand any possible German counterattack.

The Soviets liberate Melitopol

Meanwhile, farther south, the Soviet 4th Ukrainian Front (formerly the Southern Front) was ordered to break through the Wotan Line and capture Melitopol. Progress was slow as the troops advanced through swamps made worse by fall rains. After suffering many casualties, the Soviet Fifty-First Army liberated Melitopol, forcing the German Sixth Army back to the Nikopol bridgehead and defense line.

► The Soviet infantry in Kiev fought amid the ruins of the city for almost a full week at the beginning of November 1943 to recapture it from the Germans.

By taking Melitopol, the Ukrainians had isolated the German Seventeenth Army in the Crimea. Hitler wanted to hold the peninsula to prevent the Soviet Air Force from using it as a base from which to bomb Germany's last major oil resources at Ploesti in Romania. He denied the army the chance of fighting its way out. The situation of the Axis forces in the Crimea became more perilous when Soviet marines landed on the peninsula's eastern tip at Kerch.

Danger in Kiev

The Fourth Panzer Army, which was defending Kiev, was in even greater danger. The 1st Ukrainian Front (formerly the Voronezh Front) was preparing to liberate the city, the third largest in the Soviet Union and the capital of Ukraine. The attack would come from the bridgehead at Lyutezh, north of the city. In October the Soviets began to move men and tanks into the bridgehead in preparation for an attack. In pouring rain and under air and artillery attack, their engineers built extra bridges across the Dnieper.

The liberation of Kiev

The greatest bombardment to date on the Eastern Front began on November 1, 1943. More than 2,000 Soviet guns and mortars and 50 Katyusha rocket launchers pounded German positions. In the early hours of November 3, the Soviet Thirty-Eighth and Sixtieth armies attacked. Within two days the Kiev–Zhitomir road had been cut off, and fighting had reached Kiev itself. A Czechoslovakian brigade fighting alongside the Thirty-Eighth Army captured the railroad station in the center of the city.

The Katyn Massacre

In April 1943 in the Katyn Woods near Smolensk, in the Soviet Union, German authorities discovered mass graves containing the bodies of 4,443 Polish military officers. The Germans said that the Soviets had killed the Poles in early 1940 (*See Volume 2, Chapter 1*). Stalin denied the accusation, claiming that the Germans had shot the victims when they overran the area in August 1941. Investigations by the Germans and the Red Cross concluded that the Poles had been killed by the Russians. The Americans and British, not wishing to upset their Soviet allies, ignored the massacre. Half a century later, however, in 1992, the Soviet government released documents showing their forces had been responsible for the massacre on the orders of Stalin.

▲ The mass graves in Katyn Woods held the bodies of 4,443 Polish officers who had been shot in the back.

Stalin insisted that Kiev be liberated in time for the anniversary of the 1917 Bolshevik Revolution on November 7. The city fell a day earlier. Kiev had been occupied for 778 days. Some 60 percent of its 900,000 citizens had starved to death, been murdered, or deported to work in Germany.

Partisan fighters

The Red Army in the south was greatly assisted by Ukranian and Russian civilians who volunteered to fight as partisans. Many wanted revenge for Nazi atrocities. Some 17,000 men and women in about 20 bands operated on

▲ Smoke billows from a destroyed Panzer IV during a Soviet offensive.

▼ Soviet partisans ford a river during their operations to sabotage the German war effort. Partisans' activities included blowing up railroad lines and ambushing convoys of trucks.

the western bank of the Dnieper. Before the Soviet offensive began, the partisan bands infiltrated the rear of German troops. They disrupted transportation and carried out acts of sabotage, thereby diverting German troops from the front line.

The German position

The expansion of the Kiev bridgehead was rapid. Soviet units fanned out across the frosty steppe to pursue the Germans, capturing the key railroad junction at Fastov on November 8. The Fourth Panzer Army appeared to be disintegrating, which threatened the collapse of the entire German southern flank in the Soviet Union.

Manstein, however, was assembling reserves for a counterattack aimed at recapturing Kiev and stabilizing the frontline. His new troops included three well-equipped panzer divisions. He hoped that the Soviets would over-extend themselves as they had done at Kharkov in February. But the Red Army had learned its lesson; this time, too, the weather was in its favor.

Manstein's counterattack

Manstein's counterattack began in mid-November. The advance was soon bogged down in mud, which made it difficult for the heavy Tiger and Panther tanks to move, but the Germans got within 25 miles (40km) of Kiev, inflicting serious losses on the enemy. Although the Germans could manage local victories, the truth was clear: The Red Army had too many men, tanks, and guns.

As both sides waited for a change in the weather, Stalin ordered the Soviet

The Soviet experience of German occupation

The German plan for the treatment of conquered peoples in the Soviet Union was harsh. Jews and Communist Party members were to be executed almost at once. Other ethnic groups were to be used as slave labor, either on farms or in German factories, until they died.

However, the Soviet Union also included peoples who welcomed the advancing Germans and helped them. The Germans showed more leniency toward such people. In areas such as the Baltic States the locals were reasonably well treated and given a degree of freedom.

In places such as Ukraine, however, the German regime was brutal, and hundreds of thousands of people died of disease and hunger. Harsh treatment encouraged partisans to take up arms against the Germans, greatly aiding the Soviet war effort.

▶ German soldiers round up Soviet partisans from their hideout in a barn.

armies in the south on to the defensive so that they could prepare for the next stage of the campaign.

Operations in the center

After the fall of Kharkov on August 23, 1943, the Soviet Western and Kalinin fronts began an offensive against Army Group Center. They planned to take Smolensk and advance toward Belorussia. Soviet troops crossed the upper Dnieper River but made slow progress in the face of strong German defenses. At the cost of heavy casualties, the Red Army liberated Smolensk on September 25. Commanders then halted to reorganize and resupply both fronts.

The newly formed Belorussian Front was given the task of taking Belorussia. The Western Front would advance toward Orsha and Mogilev, while to its right the 1st Baltic Front (formerly the Kalinin Front) pushed forward to try to split Army Group North from Army Group Center.

If the Soviet fronts achieved their goals, they would open the way to the Baltic States, Poland, and eastern Germany. However, the advance faced tougher defenses than in the south, as well as many rivers and swamps that made tank operations difficult. They would have to rely on their artillery and infantry.

Another Soviet offensive begins

The attacks began in mid-October. Soviet troops liberated Nevel, but then ran up against a series of strongholds

▶ The message on this 1943 Soviet propaganda poster reads: "Hitler, Germany, and its vassals are facing a catastrophe."

where the Germans had assembled powerful reserve forces. Matters improved for the Soviets in the following month, however. On November 26, they liberated Gomel after savage street fighting.

The Polish Tadeusz Kosciuszko Division, fighting as part of the Red Army, suffered heavy casualties near Orsha. Its men had been prisoners of war in the Soviet Union but were now fighting to liberate their homeland from the Germans.

The Leningrad Front

Since the autumn of 1941, the important northern city of Leningrad (formerly and currently known as St. Petersburg) had been besieged by most of Germany's Army Group North. To the north of Leningrad, the Finns had reoccupied the territory that they had lost in 1940, cutting off a northern advance on the city. The Leningraders had suffered terribly: Tens of thousands died from cold, hunger, and disease, while more perished as the Germans kept up a relentless bombardment of the city.

During the siege Army Group North had been gradually stripped of men and tanks to replace losses elsewhere on the Eastern Front. The Germans built strong defensive lines to compensate for their reduced manpower. Beyond the defenses lay the three Baltic States—Lithuania, Lativa, and Estonia—whose populations were strongly anti-Soviet. Thousands of men from Latvia and Estonia, in particular, had volunteered to join the German Army and the Waffen-SS to fight the Russians.

Stalemate in the north

In late July, the Soviet Volkhov Front mounted an offensive against the German Eighteenth Army to capture an important railroad junction at Mga. At first the Soviet attacks went well, but the fighting against the German defenses soon degenerated into trench warfare. Soviet advances were measured in yards rather than miles. The operation was called off in late August. Soviet losses were just over 80,000 men for little or no gain. Undaunted, Stalin tried the same approach in September and suffered a similar bloody defeat.

The Germans had also suffered considerably during the attack. Their losses forced them to retreat and begin to build another defensive position named the Panther Line. The Germans planned to withdraw in stages. Hitler forbade retreat, however; he was convinced that the Red Army was near the end of its strength.

Year's end

The Soviet fall offensive had pushed the Axis forces in the south back hundreds of miles. Elsewhere results had not been so dramatic. In the center of the front, the Soviet commanders' aim for 1944 was to liberate Belorussia and push on into Poland. In the north the Red Army would prepare for an offensive to lift the siege of Leningrad.

The skies over the Eastern Front were meanwhile dominated by Soviet aircraft, since the bulk of the Luftwaffe had been withdrawn to defend Germany against bombers flying from Britain. German ground forces were given only sporadic air support, while Soviet Stormovik ground-attack aircraft attacked at will.

As the Red Army approached the borders of Romania and Hungary, Hitler's allies began to doubt his ability to deliver victory. Finland was on the verge of entering negotiations with the Soviet Union about ending the war. Italy had withdrawn its troops from the Soviet Union. By the end of 1943 Germany was clearly losing the war on the Eastern Front.

◄ A German antiaircraft gunner watches the skies. By late 1943 the Red Air Force dominated the skies.

▼ Women in Leningrad sit in the ruins of their home, which has been destroyed by German bombing.

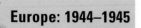

EASTERN FRONT: 1944

By 1943, the Russians had reclaimed much of the south of their country after a series of decisive battles. Now their goal was to drive the Germans from the rest of the Soviet Union.

The Soviet High Command decided that the first offensive of 1944 would aim to liberate Leningrad. The city in the Soviet northwest had been under siege by the German Army Group North since September 1941. There were two German armies outside the city: the Sixteenth and the Eighteenth. The first part of the Soviet offensive was code-named Operation Neva. It aimed to defeat the German Sixteenth Army and liberate the city of Novgorod, just 112 miles (180km) south of Leningrad.

Operation Neva

The German forces were not at full strength. During the second half of 1943, many of their units had been transferred to operations farther south, in Ukraine. Army Group North now had fewer than 500,000 men, fewer than 200 tanks, and about 2,400 guns and mortars. By contrast, the Soviets had built up their forces. By the start of 1944, they had assembled more than 800,000 men for Operation Neva. They had 800 tanks, and about 3,500 guns and mortars.

The Soviet offensive began on January 14 with air raids and a heavy artillery bombardment. After four days of fighting, the German defenses began to give way. The commander in charge of Army Group North, Field Marshal Georg von Küchler, asked Adolf Hitler for permission to withdraw. Hitler took some time to decide what to do next. Meanwhile, the Soviets advanced farther. They cut off a large number of German troops.

With his men in grave danger, von Küchler did not wait for Hitler. He ordered his men to retreat. On January 19, the Germans evacuated Novgorod. They blew up the city's buildings and bridges as they left.

The liberation of Leningrad

The next phase of the Soviet advance began on January 21. Von Küchler asked Hitler for permission to retreat to the Panther Line. This was a fortified position that followed the Narva River along the Estonian border. Hitler refused to let the troops pull back. However, he agreed to send von Küchler some reinforcements.

The Soviets faced stronger German defenses and severe winter weather. The retreating Germans also laid large minefields to slow down the Soviets. For a while, the Soviet advance stalled. After a short break, however, a new Soviet attack forced the Germans back

◀ A Soviet infantryman dashes to a new position while smoke rises behind lines of German defenses in the distance. The photograph was taken in summer 1944, during the Soviet Operation Bagration.

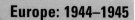

to the Panther Line. On January 27, 1944, Leningrad was liberated after a 900-day siege.

Soviet victories in Ukraine

From January to June 1944, the focus was on the central Soviet Union and Ukraine. At the Battle of Korsun in January and February, the Red Army made great advances against German Army Group South in Ukraine. In March, three Soviet army fronts began a series of attacks. They intended to push the Germans out of the region before the spring rains began. Once the roads became muddy, mobile warfare would become impossible. Within three weeks, the Soviets had reached the borders of Poland and Romania. Army Group South was in tatters.

The 4th Ukrainian Front headed south to liberate the Crimean peninsula on the Black Sea. The Soviets advanced on land and also through the shallow waters of the Shivash Lagoon.

The Axis defenses crumbled. The key port town of Sevastopol fell to the Soviets on May 9.

A time to take stock

In May 1944, the Red Army advance paused. Its men needed to rest. Worn out vehicles had to be repaired. Its overstretched supply lines had to catch up to the troops.

The Germans used the time to organize their own armies. Army Group Center controlled a large part of Belorussia. The area reached from the town of Vitebsk in the east to the Pripet Marshes on the border with Ukraine. Meanwhile, Army Group South had been split into two after its defeats in Ukraine in March. Army Group North Ukraine (AGNU) held positions from south of the Pripet Marshes to the Carpathian Mountains. Army Group South Ukraine (AGSU) defended the area between the Carpathians and the Black Sea.

▼ Russian troops in winter gear ride on tanks in January 1944, during the attack on the German lines at Leningrad. These tank *desant* troops had to be ready to jump off to fight the enemy on foot.

Finland

In Scandinavia, Finland had been at war with the Soviet Union since 1941. In early 1944, Finland asked the Soviets on what conditions they would end the war. The Finns felt that the Russian conditions were too harsh, however. They continued to occupy parts of Soviet territory.

The Soviet summer offensive pushed the Finns back to their own borders. A new Finnish president now agreed to the Soviet conditions. The fighting stopped. Finland was to lose some territory to the Soviet Union and pay compensation for the war. It would also help the Red Army drive the Germans from their positions near the Arctic Circle.

▲ German mountain troops retreat from Finland toward Norway late in 1944, after the Finns had made peace with the Soviet Union.

Preparations for Operation Bagration

The Soviets planned the next part of their advance. It was to be named Operation Bagration, after a famous 19th-century Russian general. The operation would take place between June and August 1944. There would be two main parts. The first offensive would drive Army Group Center out of Belorussia and advance into Poland. The second offensive would defeat AGNU, advance westward, and capture strategic points over the Vistula River.

The plan was based on the strength of the Red Army tank formations. The artillery, air force, and infantry would punch holes in the German lines. The tanks would advance through the gaps as far and as fast as possible. The Germans would have no chance to rebuild their lines. The infantry would then deal with any pockets of resistance.

Soviet forces

To camouflage the build up to Operation Bagration, the Red Army used a massive deception operation. They built false roads and crossings. They built dummy gun positions armed with dummy guns. They also placed wooden or inflatable tanks where the Germans would see them. The Soviets

▼ The Soviets overwhelmed Army Group Center with tanks and men.

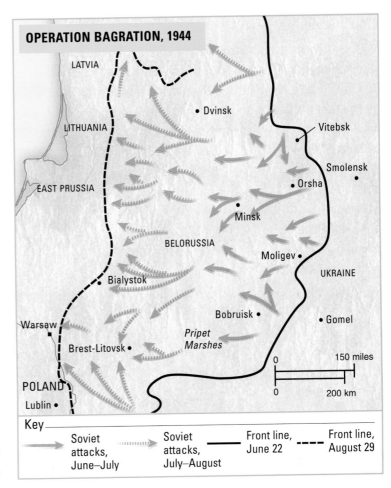

OPERATION BAGRATION, 1944

LATVIA
Dvinsk
LITHUANIA
Vitebsk
Smolensk
EAST PRUSSIA
Orsha
Minsk
BELORUSSIA
Moligev
UKRAINE
Bialystok
Bobruisk
Gomel
Warsaw
Pripet Marshes
Brest-Litovsk
POLAND
Lublin

0   150 miles
0   200 km

Key

| → Soviet attacks, June–July | ⋯ Soviet attacks, July–August | —— Front line, June 22 | ‐ ‐ ‐ Front line, August 29 |

Soviet river-crossing expertise

The Soviet Union and eastern Europe were crossed by a number of large rivers such as the Volga, the Dnieper, and the Vistula. These rivers were natural barriers and fine defensive lines. The retreating Germans blew up bridges and boats to stop the Red Army from crossing the rivers.

The Soviet infantry often had to cross rivers first and set up a bridgehead on the far bank. They improvised rafts to swim or float across, often under heavy fire. Meanwhile, engineers built rafts or used motorboats to tow barges across the river. The engineers also built underwater causeways for tanks using timber, stone, or even damaged vehicles. At times, T-34 tanks were waterproofed with putty and driven across the river bed.

▲ Russian reconnaissance troops use floats and makeshift paddles to cross a river. Such maneuvers were often carried out under heavy fire.

sent radio messages moving around fake units in the hopes that the Germans would intercept them.

Forces assemble

By early June, the four Soviet armies involved in the operation had gathered more than 1.5 million men. They had more than 4,000 tanks, including 85 JS-2 Stalin tanks that were able to take on the German Tiger tank. The Soviet forces also had 22,000 guns and mortars, 4,000 light antitank guns, and more than 2,000 Katyusha multiple rocket launchers. The Red Air Force also had more than 5,700 aircraft.

▼ Weary Germans march alongside a StuG-III assault gun as they retreat before the Soviet advance. Because of a shortage of other armor, the Germans used StuGs as antitank weapons, a role for which they were not designed.

German planning

Hitler had completely misread the situation. He believed that the Red Army was at the end of its strength. He thought that the Soviets would attack either the AGNU in Ukraine or Army Group Center in Belorussia. He did not believe that they would attack both. He therefore decided to focus German resources on what he saw as the most likely Soviet target: the weak AGNU positions in western Ukraine.

Hitler believed that Army Group Center was not in any real danger. Its defenses were based on "Fortified Areas." These were towns located on big rivers, including Vitebsk on the Dvina, Mogilev and Orsha on the Dnieper, and Bobruisk on the Berezina. Hitler thought they were strong enough to hold up any Soviet advance.

Despite Hitler's optimism, Army Group Center was in fact weak. Some of its men and weapons were sent to reinforce the AGNU. It had just 400,000 troops, 580 tanks, 540 aircraft, and 9,000 guns and mortars.

Taking the Germans by surprise

Before the start of Operation Bagration, Soviet partisans spent two days disrupting the German forces. They attacked fuel dumps, supply trains, and railroad lines. On June 22, 1944, exactly three years after the German invasion of the Soviet Union, the main operation began.

The 1st Baltic Front attacked first. Over the next two days, three more army fronts joined the attack. The staggered assault meant that the Germans could not tell the main direction of the attack. They were confused about where to deploy their reserves.

By June 25, Soviet armored forces had reached the important Smolensk–Minsk road and railroad. Their advance cut off the German Fourth Army's line of retreat. At roughly the same time, Soviet armored columns encircled Bobruisk, trapping 70,000 men. Orsha and Vitebsk fell on June 27. The next day, Mogilev fell.

Hitler had believed that the attack on Army Group Center was a bluff. Now

▼ A Soviet landing force pull a 76-mm fieldgun ashore in the Crimea in April 1944. In May, the Germans were forced out of the peninsula.

▲ Soviet infantry make their way past a German sign marking the edge of the German Reich, entering the area that was fomerly Poland.

that three out of four of the main fortified areas had been captured, he finally realized that the attack on Army Group Center was not a bluff. On June 28, he sent several divisions from AGNU to help Army Group Center.

The destruction of Army Group Center

The Red Army threatened to overrun Army Group Center. On June 27, a tank corps crossed the Berezina River. A substantial number of German troops were trapped on the river's east bank. At the same time, Soviet troops captured Baranovichi, an important rail junction 75 miles (120km) southwest of Minsk, the capital of Belorussia. The last of the German fortified areas, Bobruisk, fell on June 29. Nearly all of the 40,000 troops there were killed or taken prisoner.

The Soviets now threatened Minsk, the capital of Belorussia. It was the headquarters of Army Group Center. It was also a vital transport and commu-

nications hub. The Germans defended the city solidly, but they were overwhelmed. On July 2, Hitler gave permission to evacuate the city. Over the next few days, Soviet infantry and partisans overcame any final pockets of German resistance.

Baranovichi fell on July 8. Ten days later, Soviet troops crossed the border into what before the war had been Poland. On July 23, they captured the town of Lublin, followed by Brest-Litovsk. On July 31, the first Soviet troops reached the east bank of the Vistula River. They were now on the outskirts of the capital of Poland, Warsaw, across the river.

Attacking Army Group North Ukraine

On July 13, 1944, the second part of Operation Bagration began. It was the attack that Hitler had anticipated on AGNU in western Ukraine. The Soviets called this part of the offensive Operation Lvov-Sandomierz. It was led by the most powerful striking force in the Red Army, the 1st Ukrainian Front. The front had 1,600 tanks and assault guns; more than 15,000 guns, rocket launchers, and mortars; and 2,800 aircraft.

Some AGNU units had been moved to help Army Group Center. The loss of men had weakened AGNU. It was still a powerful force, however. It had 900 tanks and assault guns, 6,000 guns and mortars, and 700 aircraft. AGNU was able to fight off the first German attacks. Soon, however, it was pushed back. Its lines were broken. AGNU tried to launch a counterattack, but it ended in disaster.

On July 17, the 1st Ukrainian Front reached the gates of the city of Lvov. Reinforcements joined the attack, and

◀ A Soviet mortar crew prepares to fire its weapon during the advance through eastern Poland.

The Sturmovik

The Sturmovik was first designed in 1940 as a ground-attack aircraft. Its name meant "assault aircraft" in Russian. It was a strong, reliable, and simple aircraft that could take off and land on fields or roads. It was also relatively easy to fly and maintain, which made it very popular. As many as 36,150 Sturmoviks were built—more than any other type of Soviet aircraft. In 1942, a heavily armored fuselage was added. It protected the aircraft's engine, pilot, and gunner.

The Sturmovik could carry a variety of weapons, including eight air-to-ground missiles, bombs, and machine guns. It was not a fast aircraft, but it could fly at very low altitudes.

That made it difficult to shoot down from the ground. It could attack tanks and other vehicles from a height of just 65 feet (20m), and sometimes as low as 15–35 feet (5–10m). Such attacks were terrifying and also very effective. The Sturmovik's slow speed, however, made it easy prey for German fighter aircraft. Many were shot down.

▶ Soviet Sturmoviks fly in formation on their way to Berlin, Germany, in 1944.

Konstantin Rokossovsky (1896–1968)

Born in Russia, Konstantin Rokossovsky grew up in Poland. He was a cavalryman in the Russian Army in World War I. During the 1917 Revolution, however, he sided with the communists. Rokossovsky rose through the Red Army to become a senior officer. However, in 1937 he was accused of being a spy and was jailed until 1940. Chosen by Stalin to lead the Sixteenth Army, Rokossovsky played an important part in the defense of Moscow in 1941. Later, he was one of the generals who planned the German defeat at Stalingrad.

As commander of the 1st Belorussian Front, Rokossovsky was instrumental in the destruction of Germany's Army Group Center during Operation Bagration in 1944. He was rewarded with the rank of Marshal of the Soviet Union. When the war ended, he worked with the Polish Army. In 1956, he resigned and returned to the Soviet Union. He then worked in the Ministry of Defense. He is buried in Red Square.

▲ Konstantin Rokossovsky, on the telephone, survived Stalin's purges, despite being imprisoned for three years.

began heading for the Polish city of Lublin and the Bug River. One after the other, the Soviets took the strategic cities of Brody, Lvov, and Przemysl. They had now driven the Germans from the whole of Ukraine and eastern Poland. To celebrate the massive success of Operation Bagration, the Soviets paraded 57,000 German prisoners of war through the streets of the Soviet capital, Moscow.

The defeats of Army Group Center and AGNU had cost the German Army approximately 300,000 men, almost 300 armored fighting vehicles, and 1,300 guns. But the Soviets were determined to give the Wehrmacht no rest. One Red Army general said, "It is no longer important to capture such and such a position. The essential thing is to give the enemy no respite. The Germans are running to their deaths."

Next objective: the Baltic States

The Soviets were now ready to defeat Army Group North and recapture the Baltic States. They had four Russian army groups along the borders of the Baltic States: Estonia, Latvia, and Lithuania. There had been little fighting in the area since the end of Operation Neva and the liberation of Leningrad in January. Army Group North had had time to build strong defenses in the heavily wooded countryside of the region.

The Soviets had a simple plan based on their numerical strength. The four army fronts would all attack within a few days of each other, all heading west toward the Baltic coast. The fighting would be so heavy everywhere that the Germans would have no chance to move reinforcements around to face the different assaults.

Mixed fortunes on the Baltic front

Army Group North was now led by Field Marshal Walther Model. It had been weakened when some of its units had been moved to help Army Group Center. The Soviets hoped to cut it off from the rest of the German armies.

On July 5, the Red Army attacked the southern side of Army Group North. The German lines were strong, but there were not enough men to hold them. By early August, it seemed that Army Group North would be cut off near the German border.

Meanwhile, however, other Soviet fronts made slower progress. The Germans and their Estonian allies put up a strong defense near the city of Narva.

The Battle of Narva

Narva was a key position on the Estonian border. Early on July 25, Soviet guns opened fire on the German positions; shortly after, Soviet infantry started to cross the Narva River. By late morning, they had a foothold on the German bank. Soviet engineers built a bridge, and T-34 tanks began to cross the river.

A night of street fighting followed. By the middle of the next morning, the

Germans were pulling out of the city. The Soviets were now free to move into Estonia.

Advance on Riga

After a strong German counterattack in mid-August, the Red Army advance paused. The Soviets now planned an all-out attack to capture Riga, the capital of Latvia. The attack would isolate Army Group North once and for all. They began an offensive on September

◄ The crew of a Soviet antitank gun has a close escape as a German shell explodes nearby in a shower of earth.

▼ Troops from Soviet infantry and mechanized units advance into Poland in late July 1944.

14 along a 310-mile (500km) line. The three army fronts numbered almost one million men, 3,000 tanks, 2,500 aircraft, and 17,000 guns and mortars.

When the attack started, the Germans fell back from Estonia toward Riga. The Soviets captured Estonia's capital, Tallinn, on September 22. To avoid being cut off, Army Group North tried to get into a position where it could stay in contact with the rest of the Wehrmacht. However, the Soviets changed their attack in the south and reached the Baltic coast near the port of Memel (now known as Klaipeda). Army Group North was trapped. It was too weak to break through the Soviet lines.

By mid-October, the 300,000 men of Army Group North were cut off in a part of Lithuania known as Courland. They would remain there for the rest of the war. Riga fell to the Soviets on October 13.

The Red Army had reoccupied most of the Baltic States. That achievement, following the success of operations Bagration and Lvov-Sandomierz, confirmed the overwhelming success of Soviet operations in 1944. The Red Army had pushed the front line back by up to 350 miles (560km). Army Group North was almost cut off. Army Group Center and AGNU were fighting desperately to hold some sort of line.

The Warsaw Uprising

In 1944, the Red Army entered Poland, which had been occupied by Germany in 1939. The Poles feared that the Soviets would replace one occupation with another. In an attempt to secure independence, they decided to liberate themselves before the Soviets arrived.

Polish partisans had watched the Wehrmacht retreat as Operation Bagration pushed them out of eastern Poland. The Germans were in chaos. The partisans thought that this was their chance to liberate Warsaw.

On August 1, the partisans began their attack. Their most important targets were the bridges over the Vistula River and the German supply depots, which they needed for

ammunition. The partisan commander, General Tadeusz Komorowski, believed that the Germans would soon abandon Warsaw. Instead, Hitler sent reserves to the city. By the middle of August, the partisans were running short of food, ammunition, and medicine. Conditions were dreadful for the thousands of civilians caught inside the partisan lines.

The Germans attacked throughout August and September. The Red Army was stationed just across the Vistula River, but did not help the Poles. This refusal to help was highly controversial, even with the Soviets' allies. It meant, however, that the Germans destroyed any military force that might be able to oppose a Soviet occupation after the siege ended.

Komorowski surrendered on October 4. The Gemans then destroyed the city as they evacuated it. Warsaw was eventually liberated by the Soviets in late January 1945.

◀ Partisan machine gunners in action against the Germans during the Warsaw Rising of 1944.

The Balkans

By the summer of 1944, the Red Army had liberated Ukraine and was on the border of Germany's ally Romania. Beyond Romania lay the Balkans, which had been occupied by the Germans since 1941.

In late August, Romania surrendered to the Soviets. It then joined them to fight the Germans. By the beginning of October, the Red Army had reached the borders of Greece and Yugoslavia.

Hitler ordered his troops to retreat from Greece into Yugoslavia, so they would not be cut off. However, Yugoslavia had a large anti-Nazi partisan movement led by Marshal Tito. They were determined to liberate their country and fought alongside the Red Army. They freed the capital, Belgrade, in late October 1944.

Many Germans had already escaped from Greece. They were now preparing to defend northern Yugoslavia. It took many weeks of fighting to push them out. Yugoslavia was not freed until early 1945.

▶ Germans arrive in Bosnia, in Yugoslavia, in 1944, after the retreat from Greece.

Now the ultimate goal, Berlin, the German capital, was less than 400 miles (645km) away.

The July Bomb Plot

Germany's situation had grown more desperate as the year passed. The Eastern Front had collapsed. The Allies had landed in northern France. Germany's enemies were advancing on two fronts.

On July 20, 1944, a bomb exploded at Hitler's command post in East Prussia.

The so-called July Bomb Plot was the work of a group of army officers. With the war going badly, they wanted to remove Hitler and negotiate peace. Although a number of people were killed or wounded in the blast, Hitler was virtually unharmed. The attack reduced Hitler's faith in his senior officers even more. It also led him to rely more on his own instincts about the war rather than those of his generals. And Hitler's instincts were often wrong.

▼ Red Army infantry advance under cover of an artillery barrage. One carries a long-barreled antitank rifle.

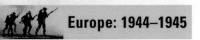

D-DAY: OPERATION OVERLORD

The D-Day landings on June 6, 1944, remain the greatest amphibious assault of all time. The landings undoubtedly speeded the defeat of Nazi Germany, but they were also an enormous gamble by the western Allies.

In early June 1944, southern Britain was a vast armed camp. Huge naval, air, and land forces prepared for the most complex military operation ever attempted. The operation aimed to land large numbers of troops on the other side of the English Channel. The shore was heavily defended by the battle-hardened German Army.

D-Day was the product of a long period of decision making and planning. In December 1941, Hitler had declared war on the United States, shortly after the Japanese attack on Pearl Harbor. To some Americans, it seemed natural to concentrate on Japan, the country that had directly attacked the United States. Two weeks after Pearl Harbor, however, Britain and the United States met at the Arcadia Conference in Washington, D.C. They agreed that they would concentrate on defeating Germany before they turned to Japan.

Britain drags its feet

The U.S. High Command worked out its strategy in 1942. The decision to defeat Germany first meant that the armies of the United States and Britain would have to invade northern Europe. What made this invasion more pressing was that during 1942 the Soviet Union was fighting a desperate campaign against Germany. Soviet leader Joseph Stalin appealed forcefully to President Roosevelt to engage major German land forces in northern Europe.

Britain's leaders, however, were reluctant to commit to an early invasion. There were many reasons for this. First, they argued that an amphibious landing was very risky. They pointed to the failure of the Dieppe raid of August 1942. The test landing on the French coast had been a disaster. The British believed that a huge force of landing craft would be needed for success.

The British preferred a strategy of deploying forces in the Mediterranean. They claimed that attacks via the "soft underbelly" of the Axis—Italy—would be very effective. Finally, the British argued that Germany could be defeated by bombing its industrial centers.

Britain managed to delay planning for an invasion for many months. Eventually, however, Britain's leaders had to back down.

A strategy is agreed on

The countdown to D-Day began in January 1943. It started at the Anglo-U.S. Casablanca Conference in Morocco. The Allies took several key decisions. They agreed to establish a new body known as COSSAC (Chief of

▼ British soldiers practice getting over barbed wire defenses on a beach in southern England. By D-Day, the Allies were far more experienced at amphibious landings than they had been earlier in the war.

Staff to the Supreme Allied Commander). The Allies also decided that the transfer of U.S. troops and equipment to Britain—an operation code-named Bolero—would take place as soon as possible.

COSSAC's plans

COSSAC was led by Lieutenant-General Frederick Morgan. His British and American team had a number of responsibilities. It had to prepare a plan for an immediate invasion of Europe. It was unlikely that a chance would arise to carry it out, but the Allies wanted to be ready in case there was an unexpected event, such as the assassination of Hitler. It also had to devise a plan that would divert German forces away from the real landing. Finally, the team also had to mastermind Operation Overlord, the actual invasion plan.

The key question for COSSAC was where to launch the attack. The target had to be within range of fighter aircraft from southern England. They would be needed to provide air cover. After the initial landings, it was also important to land follow-up troops at least as quickly as German reinforcements could arrive. Morgan initially thought the best plan was to capture a port. He soon realized, however, that the Germans would plan to destroy any ports as soon as an invasion began.

Northern France

If Morgan could not capture a port, his second choice was a long stretch of wide, gently sloping beach. COSSAC

Operation Bolero

The first U.S. service personnel arrived in Britain on January 26, 1942. They were a foretaste of what was to come. At the Casablanca Conference in January 1943, the Allied leaders decided to concentrate on the defeat of Germany before they combined to defeat Japan. The conference gave a high priority to the rapid build-up of U.S. forces in Britain, which were still small. The operation was code-named Bolero.

A few months later, the trickle of U.S. personnel across the Atlantic became more like a flood. By mid-January 1944, some 750,000 troops had sailed from Boston and New York. It took between five days and two weeks to make the crossing, during which time there was a danger of attack from U-boats. Over the next five months, a further 750,000 men and their equipment arrived and moved into barracks in Britain. Bolero was the largest cross-oceanic troop movement ever.

◀ U.S. troops march through the resort of Torquay before D-Day. The GIs faced resentment from some British troops, because they were better paid and supplied.

The Resistance

To support Operation Overlord, the Allies called on the help of about 100,000 members of the French Resistance. There were also some 40,000 affiliates of the *maquis*, a group of young Frenchmen who had gone into hiding to avoid being sent to Germany as forced labor.

Months before the landings, British and U.S. agents made their way into France, especially Normandy. They delivered arms and explosives to the Resistance, gathered intelligence, and carried out sabotage operations. Their main target was the rail system. Railroads were vital to the movement of German forces. In the event of an invasion, German troops would move by train to the point of attack.

The Resistance carried out raids on the railroads before, during, and after D-Day. Many railroad workers also staged permanent go-slows and did not cooperate with the Germans.

▲ Members of the Maquis and Free French troops study a map during the invasion of Normandy.

The Germans believed that it was this go-slow, rather than the Resistance or Allied bombings, that made France's rail system unworkable.

thought that the French coast in Normandy was promising. It had good beaches that were not very well defended. They were also very close to the port of Cherbourg. However, using Normandy as a target would also present some problems. It was quite far from the vital fighter bases. It was also on a wide part of the English Channel, so the invading troops would have to endure a long sea crossing. If the Allies did not quickly capture Cherbourg, it might also be difficult to land supplies and reinforcements. COSSAC planned to build two small artificial harbors, known as Mulberries. PLUTO (Pipe-

▼ Dozens of RAF aircraft line up to take off at an airstrip in southern England before carrying airborne troops to France.

Dwight D. Eisenhower (1890–1969)

Some people thought that U.S. general Dwight D. Eisenhower was an odd choice to command the greatest amphibious assault of all time. He had relatively little combat experience. Yet Eisenhower largely proved his doubters wrong. He had gained experience during the landings in North Africa in November 1942 and the subsequent capture of Tunisia in May 1943. He also put a lot of thought into his strategy. His decision to advance along a broad front in northwestern Europe in later 1944 is largely judged to have been correct. He also remained cool-headed when the Germans launched an offensive in the Ardennes in December 1944. The Allies soon took back the initiative from the Germans.

▲ Eisenhower studies a map of France in his London headquarters in January 1944, when planning for D-Day was beginning.

Headquarters Allied Expeditionary Force), under the command of U.S. general Dwight D. Eisenhower. He and other senior commanders modified the plans. Instead of landing on three beaches, they would land at five beaches across a 60-mile (96km) front. U.S. forces would target two beaches, code-named Utah and Omaha. The British would land at two others, Gold and Sword. Juno Beach was allocated to Canadian forces.

SHAEF rejected trying to stage such a large landing at night. They also believed that the artillery bombardments that would start the landings would be more effective in daylight. The main assault force would land at low tide. The beaches would be at their largest, and the German underwater obstructions most exposed.

The next decision was to fix a date for the landings, code-named Operation Neptune. Because of the threat of storms in the Channel, no landing could take place before early summer. The night before the landings, airborne troops were to land to protect the flanks of the landing beaches. They had a better chance of success if there was a full moon. Taking these factors into account, the best conditions would occur on June 5, 6, and 7. The invasion date was set for June 5.

Keeping the plans secret

It was vital that the Germans did not discover either the landings' location or timing. The British stopped civilians traveling to the Irish Republic, where there were many German spies. They also created a 10-mile (16km) exclusion zone along parts of the English coast where forces were being assembled. Only authorized personnel

Line Under the Ocean) would carry fuel across the Channel from England.

COSSAC's plan was approved by the Allied leaders at the Quadrant Conference in Quebec, Canada, in August 1943. In February 1944, COSSAC became part of SHAEF (Supreme

could travel within the zone. Meanwhile, diplomats from neutral countries were not allowed to enter or leave the country, in case they had got wind that something was happening.

False information also misled the Germans about the site of the landings. Fake radio signals convinced the Germans that the assault would take place at Pas de Calais, farther along the French coast from Normandy, in July.

German strategic debates

The Germans knew that an invasion would come, but disagreed about their best strategy. The Atlantic Wall, the name given to the defenses along

▲ The Allied High Command for D-Day. Front row (left to right): Air Chief Marshal Arthur Tedder, General Dwight D. Eisenhower, General Bernard Montgomery. Back row (left to right): General Omar Bradley, Admiral Bertram Ramsey:, Air Chief Marshal Trafford Leigh-Mallory, Lieutenant-General W. Bedell Smith.

◀ Landing craft move away from larger troop ships during a rehearsal for D-Day.

Europe's western coast, was commanded by field marshals Erwin Rommel and Gerd von Rundstedt. They had different views on how to defeat any landings. Rommel believed that the invasion had to be stopped on the beaches. Von Rundstedt predicted that the Allies would be able to get ashore. He argued that a large mobile force should be kept in reserve to strike at the Allies once they were inland.

German preparations

Hitler still believed the main Allied landing would come near Pas de Calais. He kept most of his forces there. Rommel received a few reinforcements, but von Rundstedt got none.

Rommel began strengthening the Atlantic Wall at once. He built new obstacles to prevent vessels landing from the sea, and blocked the exits from the beaches. He built gun positions at key points. Rommel's efforts were disrupted, however, by Allied air raids. The French Resistance also carried out acts of sabotage.

From early April, Allied aircraft dropped some 200,000 tons of bombs on northern France. They bombed railroads and airfields, coastal defenses, radar stations, and military compounds. By D-Day the Allies had air superiority over the beaches. This would hamper German counterattacks.

Eisenhower gives the "Go" order

On May 29, Allied troops began moving to the ports along the south coast of England where they would

The Funnies

The British 79th Armoured Division was a unit of specialized armored vehicles. They were designed to be able to cross a wide range of both man-made and natural obstacles. The unconventional tracked vehicles were nicknamed "Funnies." There were a number of variations. Most were based on modified British Churchill or U.S. Sherman tanks. They included the Sherman Crab, which had a rotating flail made of chains that could detonate mines or cut through barbed wire. The Centaur was a turretless tank fitted with bulldozer blades. The Ark was a turretless Churchill that had a hydraulic bridge. It lowered the bridge to cross antitank ditches and other wide gaps.

Other vehicles unraveled long strips of canvas from large bobbins. The canvas formed a roadway for other vehicles across soft sand. Another Funny fired trashcan-shaped shells to demolish concrete positions. One of the most useful was the Sherman Duplex Drive, which was an amphibious tank. The Funnies were among the first Allied forces to land on D-Day.

These Duplex Drive Sherman tanks are being used in the crossing of the Rhine River in 1945.

board their ships. By June 3, everything was ready. The next day, however, the weather changed for the worse, with high winds and low clouds. That evening Eisenhower's weather expert, Group Captain James Stagg, offered some hope. Starting on the afternoon of the next day, June 5, there would be an improvement in the weather. It would last for about 24 hours. On the morning of June 5, Stagg confirmed his forecast. Within a few hours, some 7,000 warships and landing craft were heading for Normandy.

Laying the foundations for the attack

Shortly after midnight on June 6, about 23,500 U.S. and British paratroopers landed along the edges of the landing beaches. Their mission was to seize vital bridges and communications centers. They also had to hold off any German counterattacks until they were relieved by the amphibious forces. The airborne landings were largely successful. Some U.S. troops missed their target and ended up scattered over the countryside. The fact that they were so spread out confused the local German forces, who did not know what was happening.

The main amphibious landings took place after an artillery bombardment from some 200 Allied warships at about 5:30 A.M. German positions also

▲ Loaded landing craft speed toward the Normandy coast. In the background is the heavy cruiser USS *Augusta*.

◄ Allied vehicles already line the shore as U.S. infantry land on Omaha Beach late on June 6, 1944.

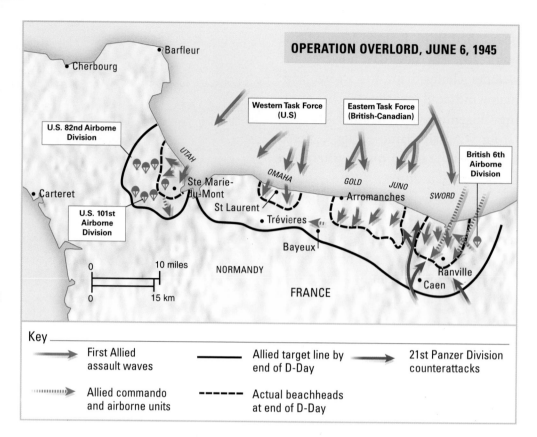

OPERATION OVERLORD, JUNE 6, 1945

Western Task Force (U.S)

Eastern Task Force (British-Canadian)

U.S. 82nd Airborne Division

British 6th Airborne Division

U.S. 101st Airborne Division

Barfleur

Cherbourg

Carteret

UTAH

Ste Marie-du-Mont

St Laurent

OMAHA

GOLD

JUNO

SWORD

Arromanches

Trévieres

Bayeux

Ranville

Caen

NORMANDY

FRANCE

0   10 miles

0   15 km

Key

First Allied assault waves

Allied target line by end of D-Day

21st Panzer Division counterattacks

Allied commando and airborne units

Actual beachheads at end of D-Day

▶ The five invasion beaches were all captured on D-Day. However, hopes of seizing an inland town or a port were not realized.

came under attack from Allied medium and heavy bombers. They were part of the 11,500 aircraft committed to D-Day. They bombed the Germans on and behind the five landing beaches.

Success on Utah Beach

U.S. troops landed on Utah Beach at 6:31 A.M. They were just a minute behind schedule. Strong currents and inaccurate navigation meant that they were a little away from their precise target. They landed about 1 mile (1.6km) south. The beach there was relatively undefended. The troops soon knocked out the only concrete gun position guarding the beach. Demolition teams cleared paths through the beach obstacles. By 9:00 A.M., the first tanks had crossed the Atlantic Wall. They fanned out into the countryside beyond to link up with the paratroopers. By nightfall on D-Day, some 23,000 men and 1,700 vehicles had

gone ashore. The beach had been highly congested for much of the day. The assault had cost 197 men killed and 60 presumed drowned.

The assault on Omaha Beach

Utah was a triumph. Ten miles (16km) to the east, however, Omaha Beach was nearly a disaster. The U.S. troops were unable to get off the beach to make room for later waves of invaders. The fight for Omaha was the most difficult of D-Day. There were better defenses there than on the other beaches, and the German defenders were more battle-hardened. They were positioned on high ground, from where they could pour fire down on the attackers.

The Allies also made mistakes. The naval bombardment ended too soon, and the bombers missed their targets. Commanders launched landing craft and amphibious tanks too far out from the beach. Many were sunk.

Many assault troops who reached the beach were seasick.

When the first amphibious assault wave landed at 6:30 A.M., it faced a barrage of fire. Within minutes, it was pinned down. By 9:00 A.M., some men were thinking of evacuation. However, inch by inch, small groups of troops began to make it off the beach to the high ground beyond. Others followed. By dusk, some 30,000 men were ashore. Most were still crowded on the beach. The high ground beyond was only thinly held by exhausted survivors of the first assault waves. Some 2,300 U.S. troops had been killed in the landings. The operation had come close to disaster.

▲ Men of the British 6th Airborne Division unload a jeep and other equipment from a glider on D-Day.

◀ These U.S. paratroopers on their way to France were some of the first Allied troops in Normandy. About 23,500 paratroopers were dropped to protect the flanks of the invasion beaches.

Eyewitness

❝ We were really just pinned down and couldn't really see anyone to shoot at. Around 10 o'clock things looked really hopeless on our part of the beach. They weren't bringing anyone else in because there was no use just piling them up on top of the ones that were already there. I saw a flat barge loaded solid with tanks. They were trying to get it in, and I guess the navy must have known just how far those mortar shells could reach, because that raft was moving parallel to the beach, back and forth and just out of range. I did see a half-track get in [to the beach], and there were several that got hit, and the one whole LCT [Landing Craft Tank] loaded with half-tracks caught fire and blew up. That was a Fourth of July fireworks. ❞

John Zmudzinski, assault engineer, describes breaking through German defenses on Omaha Beach, D-Day.

The English and Canadian landings

The three Anglo-Canadian beaches—Gold, Sword, and Juno—stretched for some 25 miles (40km). They were wide and open, and ideal for amphibious landings. The coast beyond the beaches was flat.

The first waves came ashore at around 7:30 A.M. The British on Gold and Sword quickly crashed though the Atlantic Wall. Their success was due partly to a range of specially developed armored vehicles known as Funnies. The Canadians at Juno had a tougher time. They faced rough seas and alert defenders. By late morning, however, they were also pushing inland.

How successful was D-Day?

Despite the horrors of Omaha Beach, overall Allied losses were far lower than

▶ U.S. troops help a wounded colleague after their landing craft was sunk off Omaha Beach. The Americans at Omaha suffered about 3,000 dead and injured.

◀ Blood arrives at a Normandy airstrip ready for U.S. troops injured in the campaign to break out from the beaches.

expected. Some 6,000 U.S. personnel were killed, wounded, or missing, along with 4,300 British and Canadian troops. German losses totaled between 4,000 and 8,000. By the day's end, some 128,000 Allied soldiers were ashore. Many more were on their way.

Despite this success, however, the invaders had failed in one goal for June 6. They had not pushed inland as far as they had hoped. They still had relatively little room to maneuver or to accommodate the reinforcements who were rapidly arriving. Worst of all, they had not captured any of the major towns immediately to the south.

Towns such as Bayeux and Caen were the focal points of Normandy's east–west transport arteries. The Allies hoped that Caen would provide a major base for further advances. British troops had gotten within 2 miles (3.2km) of the town, but their advance had been stopped by German defenders.

Those 2 miles would have great consequences. Caen went on to become the focus of the German response to the landings. The Germans fought back with great determination. They forced the Allies into weeks of bloody combat in which casualty rates soared.

▼ German troops enter captivity on June 6, 1944.

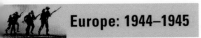

NORTHERN EUROPE: 1944

In the months after D-Day, the Allies experienced weeks of exhilarating progress alongside periods of agonizing deadlock. During this time, their fortunes alternated between major victories and costly defeats.

▼ Members of the 101st Airborne Division leave Bastogne in December 1944. The German Army had besieged U.S. forces in the town during the Battle of the Bulge.

In the days after the D-Day landings of June 6, 1944, the Allies had made reasonable progress in Normandy. However, despite promising progress, the momentum the Allies had gained on D-Day was fast ebbing away.

The Germans now threw some of their best units into the ongoing battle in Normandy. They wanted to keep the Allies pinned down in their long but narrow beachhead along the coast. Many of the German troops were combat veterans. Most of their Allied counterparts, however, had little or no experience of military action. Equally, the Germans had more skilled battlefield commanders and better quality equipment.

The local countryside also helped the Germans. The Normandy landscape in

the west is known as *bocage*. It is a network of small fields and narrow roads separated by tall hedge-covered banks. The hedges were ideal hiding places for German troops to ambush Allied forces.

Allied tanks found it difficult to move along the narrow lanes. When they tried to climb the banks, however, the maneuver exposed the thin bottom of the tank to antitank guns. The danger remained until U.S. sergeant Curtis G. Culin devised a plowlike device to fit to tanks that cut through the banks and hedgerows.

Weather slows the Allies

The Allied invaders also faced other problems. On June 19, a great storm blew up in the English Channel. It lasted for three days and prevented the shipment of vital military hardware from Britain. A total of 800 ships sank or were beached, with the loss of many supplies. The storm also destroyed one of the two artificial Mulberry harbors that were used for unloading supplies off the beaches.

The drop in the flow of supplies made it vital for the Allies to occupy the port of Cherbourg on the Cotentin Peninsula. U.S. troops took the port on

► In the days after the D-Day landings, supplies pour ashore from large landing craft to reinforce the Allied bridgehead. Barrage balloons fly overhead to deter German air attack.

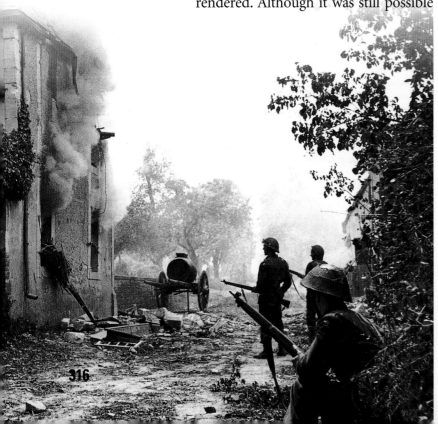

▼ British troops watch a farmhouse burn in the Normandy village of Christot in June 1944. The Allies had to fight hard to advance through Normandy.

June 29. The victory did not have as much of an effect as the Allies had hoped. The German garrison had destroyed the docks before they surrendered. Although it was still possible to beach and unload ships at Cherbourg, the main docks were not working fully until August 7.

By the end of June, the Allies had suffered close to 62,000 casualties. They had advanced just a few miles inland from the beaches through the *bocage*.

Attempts to take Caen

To the southeast of the landing beaches, the town of Caen was still in German hands. It was a hub of rail and road routes. British and Canadian troops had made several moves toward the town since D-Day without success. One advance was stopped when a handful of German tanks crushed an entire British armored column.

The next attack was code-named Operation Epsom. It involved 60,000 troops. It began west of Caen on June 24. It soon got bogged down, however.

Heavy rains turned the ground to mud. The rain also prevented any close air support. On June 30, British general Bernard Montgomery called off the operation. The Allies had suffered 4,000 casualties.

A new strategy

Montgomery tried to take the devastated town again on July 7. This attack, Operation Charnwood, began with a 450-bomber raid on the northern suburbs. After two days of fighting, the Anglo-Canadian forces finally captured Caen. The Germans retreated across the Orne River. They blew up all the bridges across the river, however. Again, the Allies came to a standstill.

The Allies now changed their plan. General Omar Bradley, commander of the U.S. First Army, suggested a way to break the deadlock: Montgomery should continue his attacks in Caen to draw in German reinforcements. This would keep them away from the base of the Cotentin Peninsula. Meanwhile, U.S. units would capture the German-held town of St. Lô. They would then make the main breakthrough attempt on a narrow front to the northwest of the town.

The Allied breakout

Anglo-Canadian efforts to keep the Germans focused on Caen began on July 18. Montgomery launched Operation Goodwood to the east of the town. Although the operation's main role was as a decoy, Montgomery still hoped to achieve a breakthrough.

Goodwood started with heavy bombing and a mass artillery bombardment. It failed to break the German defenses, however. After a heavy thunderstorm

▲ French villagers near the town of Bayeux listen to the news on a radio set mounted on a U.S. Army car in June 1944. The Germans had confiscated all radios in order to prevent the French from receiving news about the war from overseas.

► A German gunner waits beside his camouflaged 5-cm Pak antitank gun on the outskirts of Caen in July 1944. British and Canadian forces took weeks to overcome German resistance in the town.

▼ U.S. armor rolls through a ruined village during Operation Cobra, when the Allies finally broke out of their Normandy beachhead.

on July 21, Montgomery called off the operation. He had suffered 6,000 casualties and lost around 400 tanks. The Allies had pushed the Germans just 7 miles (11km) from Caen. The failure of Operation Goodwood led some critics to call for Montgomery to be fired. The fighting at Caen did prevent German reinforcements from being moved to St.

Lô, however. U.S. troops entered the town on July 22.

Operation Cobra had been postponed by a week owing to bad weather. It opened on July 25. A huge fleet of bombers struck at a narrow part of the German front. Bradley's units were ready to make the main effort to break through the German lines. After two days of sometimes bitter fighting, the U.S. Army had advanced 15 miles (24km). It was pouring south and west toward Brittany.

General Patton's bold plan

General George Patton now came to the fore. Patton was controversial but talented. He was an expert in fast-moving armored warfare. His Third Army had arrived in France after D-Day, and was fresh. Patton pushed his armored units south and west along the coast. The retreating Germans had no chance to establish a new front line.

Patton's men entered Brittany on July 30. On that same day, Montgomery

George Patton (1885–1945)

Patton first made his name during the Allied landings in North Africa in 1942. His career was controversial, however. His thirst for publicity led to clashes with other senior officers. In Sicily in 1943, he slapped two soldiers who had shellshock. Patton was sidelined and only returned to active duty in July 1944. From then until the end of the war, he led the U.S. Third Army in a series of fast-moving offensives. He reacted very quickly to block the German advance in the Ardennes. Patton's troops were also among the first across the Rhine.

At the end of the war, Patton was very outspoken about sensitive political issues. His opinions cost him control of the Third Army. He then took charge of the Fifteenth Army. Patton died from injuries after an automobile accident in 1945.

▲ Patton (left) talks to British commander Bernard Montgomery (right) and U.S. general Omar Bradley.

opened a new attack to the southwest of Caen. Montgomery's new attack was intended to prevent German units from moving westward to deal with Cobra.

Patton's armored units were now moving through Brittany without any real resistance. Patton now asked Allied commanders for permission to turn back to the east. He was ordered to drive behind the Germans toward the Seine River. The German forces on the Normandy Front would have to retreat to avoid becoming surrounded. By August 7, Patton's units had reached the Loire River, some 60 miles (96km) south of their starting point.

The German generals in Normandy argued for a retreat. Hitler instead ordered a counterattack against the town of Mortain. The town stood at the western edge of the fast-developing bulge in the German line. The Germans began Operation Lüttich on August 7. They soon captured Mortain. By the next day, however, the attack was over. The attackers could not overcome U.S. resistance backed by Allied ground-attack aircraft. The Allies could now push ahead with their plan to close the escape routes of the German forces.

The Falaise Pocket

The Anglo-Canadian force at Caen still faced considerable resistance, but it began to drive south on August 7. U.S. forces meanwhile drove north. The two Allied advances met at Falaise on August 19. They trapped some 100,000 Germans in a pocket measuring just 20 miles by 10 miles (32km by 16km).

Some 40,000 German troops managed to escape the trap and retreat, against Hitler's orders. When the

319

Eyewitness

❝ Back and forth the bomb carpets were laid, artillery positions were wiped out, tanks overturned and buried, infantry positions flattened, and all roads and tracks destroyed. By midday, the entire area resembled a moon landscape, with the bomb craters touching rim to rim …. All signal communications had been cut, and no command was possible. The shock effect on the troops was indescribable. Several of the men went mad and rushed dementedly round in the open until they were cut down by splinters. Simultaneous with the storm from the air, innumerable guns of the U.S. artillery poured drum-fire into our field positions. ❞

Fritz Bayerlein, commander of the Panzer Lehr Division, describing U.S. heavy bombing during the Allied breakout in the Normandy campaign, August, 1944.

fighting ended on August 22, however, the Allies had won a great victory. They had killed 10,000 German soldiers and captured 50,000, as well as 500 tanks and assault guns and 9,000 other vehicles. The defeat at Falaise was a huge blow to German morale. Now the Allies broke out from Normandy and poured toward the western border of Nazi Germany.

Landings in southern France

Allied morale, on the other hand, was high. It was increased by news that Allied troops had landed in southern France on August 15. Operation Anvil had been planned to take place at the same time as D-Day. It had been delayed, however. There were not enough landing craft for both operations.

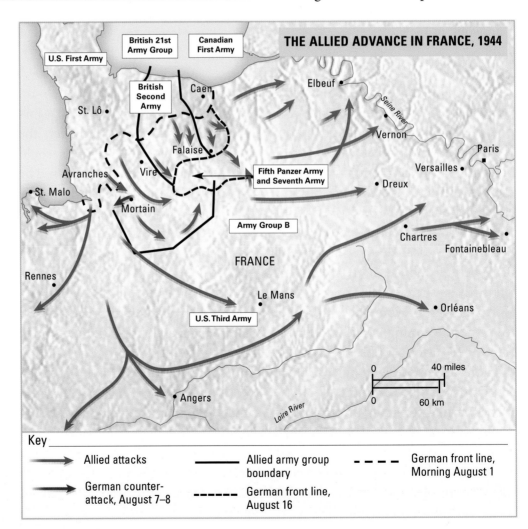

▶ Map showing the Allied breakout from the bridgehead in Normandy during the summer of 1944.

▼ British Royal Engineers patrol through the ruins of Caen to clear mines left by the retreating Germans. The town was a meeting point for 12 important roads, and a key transportation hub.

V-weapons

Hitler was enraged by the Allied bombing campaign in Germany. In response, he turned to a number of secret weapons. They included the *Vergeltungswaffen* (reprisal weapons). The V-1 was a flying bomb with a range of 250 miles (400km). It was first produced in late 1943. From June 1944, it began bombarding London and southeast England. The bombs were fired from mobile launchers along the northern coast of France and the Low Countries. As many as 9,520 bombs were launched, but about half were destroyed by antiaircraft fire or fast fighters. V-1 raids largely ceased once Allied ground forces overran their launch positions.

The V-2 was a supersonic rocket. It was too fast for the Allies to shoot down once it had been launched. About 5,000 were deployed between September 1944 and March 1945. Only 1,054, however, actually reached England. The two reprisal weapons killed about 7,000 people in England and injured more than 20,000.

▶ A technician makes a final adjustment to a V-2 rocket before firing. The weapon was far quicker and more accurate than the earlier V-1.

Operation Anvil aimed to protect the flank of the Allied armies in northern Europe. It was also planned to open the port of Marseilles as a supply base from the Mediterranean. The landings met with almost instant success. The German troops in the region were generally poor. By nightfall on August 15, some 95,000 troops had come ashore; only 183 soldiers had been killed.

The Allies forced the Germans to flee north up the valley of the Rhône River. By August 28, they had defeated most of the German troops stationed in southern France. They had suffered relatively few casualties themselves.

On September 11, the southern invasion force linked up with Patton's Third Army outside the city of Dijon. From then on, the Allies could drive toward the German frontier from the Swiss border to the North Sea along an unbroken front.

Paris is liberated

After Falaise, Montgomery's Anglo-Canadian armies started moving along the coast of northwestern France toward northern Belgium. U.S. forces followed a parallel course toward southern Belgium, Luxembourg, and eastern France.

The first big prize of the advance was Paris. On August 19, as the Allies approached, citizens in the French capital rose up against its German garrison. Five days later, the Allies entered the capital amid scenes of great joy. The first troops in the city were the Free French 2nd Armored Division.

The Allied advance stalls

In the excitement, some Allied commanders began to hope that the war might be won before the end of the year. By early September, however, the rush toward the German border was grinding to a halt. Allied troops were tired. Their worn-out vehicles were in urgent need of maintenance. The main problem, however, was keeping the armies supplied.

Liberation of Paris

On August 19, 1944, members of the French communist Resistance rose up against the German troops in Paris. The German commander, General Dietrich von Choltitz, tried to arrange a ceasefire. He did not speak to the communists, however, but to more moderate supporters of the provisional French president, General Charles de Gaulle. Von Choltitz also put tanks and troops on the streets, and more fighting broke out. The communists sought help from the Allies. The Allies had intended to bypass Paris to avoid fighting in which many people may have died. Now General Eisenhower sent the Free French 2nd Armored Division to liberate the city. The first Free French units arrived in Paris late on August 24. Two days later, De Gaulle made a triumphant entry into the liberated capital.

▼ Parisians line the Champs Elysées to cheer a parade of U.S. troops in August 1944.

The Germans had wrecked many ports as they retreated. Other ports, such as Brest in Brittany and Antwerp in Belgium, were still occupied by German forces. The Allies were therefore still being largely supplied from the Normandy beaches. The beaches now lay some 300 miles (480km) behind the troops. The huge strain on supplying the armies was unlikely to improve with the onset of winter weather.

The plan to conquer a usable port

Allied supreme commander, Dwight D. Eisenhower, wanted to avoid extending the war into 1945. He gave priority to Montgomery's drive through Belgium toward Antwerp. Because of the supply shortages, however, he halted the advance of the two U.S. armies to the south of the Anglo-Canadians.

Montgomery captured Brussels on September 3, and Antwerp itself 24 hours later. The port facilities were largely intact. Although the Allies now

▲ British troops take cover in Arnhem, Holland, during Operation Market Garden.

◄ German troops rush to leave Paris as the Allies approach in June 1944. One is pushing a car that has run out of gas.

323

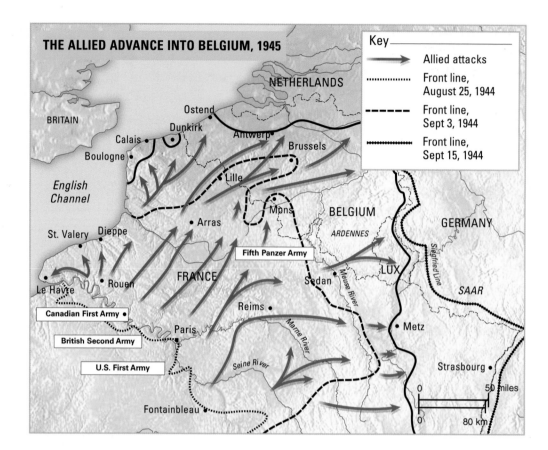

THE ALLIED ADVANCE INTO BELGIUM, 1945

Key

→ Allied attacks

······· Front line, August 25, 1944

– – – Front line, Sept 3, 1944

▪▪▪▪▪▪ Front line, Sept 15, 1944

BRITAIN

NETHERLANDS

Ostend

Dunkirk

Calais

Boulogne

Antwerp

Brussels

Lille

English Channel

St. Valery

Dieppe

Arras

Mons

BELGIUM

ARDENNES

GERMANY

Fifth Panzer Army

Le Havre

Rouen

FRANCE

Sedan

Meuse River

LUX

Siegfried Line

SAAR

Canadian First Army

British Second Army

Paris

Reims

Marne River

Metz

U.S. First Army

Seine River

Strasbourg

Fontainebleau

0   50 miles

0   80 km

▶ The Allied drive through northern France and Belgium in August and September 1944.

had a port near the front, it was useless. The Germans had laid mines in the Scheldt River, which linked Antwerp to the sea. German troops still occupied islands in the Scheldt Estuary. Access from the port to the sea was blocked.

Operation Market Garden

The Allies were close to the German border. They did not want to give the enemy time to reorganize. Montgomery and Bradley both told Eisenhower that they wanted all the available supplies. Each of them felt capable of making a single thrust into Germany to bring about victory.

Eisenhower decided to back Montgomery. The British general came up with a plan that was unusually bold. It was code-named Operation Market Garden. Montgomery planned to land Anglo-American and Polish airborne

forces in southeast Holland. They would create and then defend a corridor along the Eindhoven–Arnhem line to the German border. An armored spearhead would then drive along this

▲ Allied aircraft fly above a Dutch windmill during Operation Market Garden.

route. It would capture the important industrial area of the Ruhr. Without the Ruhr, Germany could not maintain its war effort.

The success of Market Garden depended on the airborne forces being able to capture bridges over major rivers before the Germans could destroy them. The ground forces also had to keep to a strict timetable to relieve the airborne troops.

Market Garden began on September 17. The odds were against success, however. There had been only a week to prepare for the operation, and the lightly equipped paratroopers were highly vulnerable. Near Arnhem, where there was a bridge over the Rhine, two panzer divisions happened to be refitting in the area. They put up stiff opposition. The ground offensive ended in failure after eight days.

Preparations for the spring offensive

Market Garden's failure ensured that the war would last into 1945. The Allies prepared for a spring offensive. Montgomery cleared the Scheldt at Antwerp, so the Allies finally had a port near the front. The first supply ships docked on November 27. It would still take some time to land the vast quantities of supplies that the Allies needed, however. Raids by V-1 flying bombs also made the work hazardous.

First moves into Germany

Two U.S. Army groups were getting ever closer to the German border. By October 1, the 12th Army Group was operating between Maastricht and Luneville. To the south, the 6th Army Group was advancing between Luneville and the Swiss border. The U.S. troops faced poor weather and sometimes strong German resistance. By October 3,

The July Plot

By 1944, it was clear to a number of people within Hitler's inner circle that the war was lost. They believed that the Nazi leader was the main obstacle to reaching an agreement with the Allies. Security around the dictator was tight, but some of his collaborators plotted to murder him. They included Count Claus Schenk von Stauffenberg. On July 20, 1944, von Stauffenberg took a briefcase containing a bomb into a conference with Hitler. He then left the room. When the bomb exploded, it caused considerable damage. Hitler, however, escaped with only minor injuries.

The plot quickly fell apart. Von Stauffenberg was shot, along with many of the suspected conspirators. Since several of the plotters were army officers, Hitler's distrust of his military advisers soared.

▲ Hitler shows the Italian dictator Mussolini the damage caused to the conference room by the July 20 bomb.

however, the Third Army was close to Metz. The German city of Aachen fell to the U.S. First Army on October 21.

Eisenhower now ordered an offensive against the remaining German forces west of the Rhine. The river was the last great barrier to an advance on Berlin itself. Eisenhower wanted to establish

The focal point of the attack was the heavily wooded Ardennes, in southern Belgium and Luxembourg. The hilly, forested landscape made fighting difficult, and the Allies did not expect an attack. That part of the line was held by a handful of weary and largely unproven U.S. divisions.

The Battle of the Bulge

The attack began on December 16. It caught the Allies by surprise. They were hugely outnumbered. Low clouds prevented them from using ground-attack aircraft. The Germans made early gains. They pushed back the Allies to create the bulge in the line that gave the battle its English name, the Battle of the Bulge. The Germans called the battle *Wacht am Rhine*, or Watch on the Rhine.

Although some U.S. units fled, others held their ground, mounting strong resistance around St. Vith and Bastogne. The resistance meant that the Germans lost the advantage of speed. The Americans also destroyed or moved their fuel dumps. That prevented the Germans from capturing fuel on which their motorized divisions relied. At the edges of the bulge in the line, U.S. forces largely held firm. The Germans had no chance to expand their attack front. The plan had failed.

Reversal of fortune

On December 19, Eisenhower sent British and U.S. troops to reinforce the sides of the bulge. There was heavy fighting around Bastogne. The Germans suffered great losses trying to capture the town. Hitler still persisted in attacking it until January 2, 1945. The Allies then gradually pushed his forces out of the bulge. The bulge itself had disappeared by January 18.

▲ A German King Tiger tank at the Battle of the Bulge. The Allies had thought that the forests of the Ardennes were not suitable for tanks, so their line was only weakly defended there.

bridgeheads across the river from where he could launch a spring offensive. Around Aachen, however, U.S. forces became bogged down in dense forest. German resistance held them up for the next month.

Operations farther south brought better news. U.S. troops took Strasbourg on November 23 and Metz on December 13. They reached the Rhine in two places that were separated by a German-held pocket around Colmar.

German fightback

By mid-December, the Allies were settling down to face the winter weather and prepare for spring. Hitler, however, launched an all-out offensive. He wanted to split the U.S. armies from the Anglo-Canadian forces to the north. He also wanted to recapture the port of Antwerp.

The Malmédy Massacre

On December 17, 1944, Battery B of the U.S. 285th Field Artillery Observation Battalion was overrun by a Waffen-SS unit near the village of Baugnez, southeast of the Belgian town of Malmédy. The SS troops herded the 64 unarmed captives, plus other U.S. prisoners, into a field. They then opened fire on them. Some Americans survived by running away or by pretending to be dead, but 86 men died. After the war, the SS commander Joachim Peiper was found guilty of a war crime. He was sentenced to death, but his sentence was then reduced to life imprisonment. He was finally released in 1956. In summer 1976, a French newspaper printed details of where Peiper was living. Two weeks later his home was firebombed. Sixty-year-old Peiper died in the fire.

▲ This photograph was taken as evidence of the Malmédy Massacre. The bodies are numbered for identification.

German losses in the battle were huge. About 120,000 men had been killed or wounded, or were missing. They had lost 600 tanks. Some had been destroyed and others abandoned owing to lack of fuel. They had also lost 1,600 aircraft. The Allies lost 7,000 dead, 34,500 wounded, and 21,000 captured or missing. Most of the casualties were American.

Hitler had gambled everything in the Ardennes. He had sacrificed his only remaining large body of reserves. Both he and Eisenhower knew that they could not be replaced. The fighting had merely delayed the Allies' final offensive against Germany by just six weeks.

▼ U.S. ammunition carriers make their way through a snowy wood during the Battle of the Bulge. The battle was fought in terrible winter conditions.

THE FALL OF GERMANY

By the beginning of 1945, the Third Reich was being crushed between overwhelming forces from both East and West. Armageddon was about to descend upon the people of Germany.

In February 1945, the Allies were finally in position to begin the conquest of Germany. In the west, the German offensive in the Ardennes had been defeated. U.S. and British armies were now preparing to drive to the Rhine River and into the German heartland. In the east, Soviet troops were massed along a huge front that stretched south across the continent from Lithuania to the Balkans. They would soon also enter German territory. Nevertheless, Hitler was determined to resist to the very end.

Plans for crossing the Rhine
The Allied advance to the Rhine was in some ways as much about personalities as military operations. The Supreme Allied Commander in Europe was U.S. general Dwight D. Eisenhower. His

forces were in turn led by three strong personalities. At the northern part of the Allied front line was the Twenty-First Army Group led by the British field marshal Bernard Montgomery. The center of the line was held by the Twelfth Army Group of U.S. general Omar Bradley. To the south, the U.S. Sixth Army Group was led by Lieutenant-General Jacob Devers.

By February 7, the Allied positions stretched from just east of Nijmegen in the Netherlands to the northern border of Switzerland. The Rhine River was the last significant obstacle barring the advance toward Berlin. Each of the Allied commanders wanted to be the first to cross it.

The Rhine arched out like a bow from the Allied line. Montgomery was the closest, at the top. Eisenhower's plan was that both Montgomery and Bradley would launch a general thrust toward the river. Montgomery would make the main crossing of the Rhine, between Emmerich and Düsseldorf.

Bradley, meanwhile, would back up Montgomery's operation. He would attack through the forested Eifel region and cross the Rhine near Koblenz. Then he would push outward to help Montgomery surround the Ruhr. The Ruhr was Germany's industrial heart. It contained the country's major coal fields and much of its heavy industry. Its factories included the vital Thyssen

▼ Soviet tanks enter the city of Berlin in 1945. The agreement made in February 1945 gave the Soviets the role of taking the German capital.

▲ Troops of the U.S Third Army keep low to avoid snipers, as they cross the Rhine River in an amphibious DUKW on March 26, 1945.

steelworks and Krupp armaments plants. Meanwhile, farther south, Dever's Sixth Army Group would move into the Saarland and attempt a Rhine crossing around the city of Mannheim.

Launching the Rhine offensive

On February 8, 1945, an artillery bombardment along Montgomery's front began the Rhine offensive. The Canadian First Army fought its way into the forested Reichswald area. It met stiff German resistance and had to cross difficult muddy terrain. The Canadians reached the Rhine by February 21. At the Rhine, the Canadians were scheduled to meet up with the U.S. Ninth Army, advancing from the south. However, the Germans blew

up dams on the small Roer River. The Ninth Army was delayed in the flooded countryside. It did not reach the Rhine until March 2.

Meanwhile, Bradley and Devers were fighting their way east. The U.S. First Army reached the Rhine on May 7, near Cologne. The Germans had by now blown up most bridges across the Rhine. In a surprise attack, however, the Allies captured an intact bridge at Remagen, just south of Cologne. The bridge provided the first major crossing point over the river.

Patton's dynamic strategy

The achievements of the First Army were somewhat overshadowed by those of the Third Army, which was part of the Twelfth Army Group. The Third Army was led by the controversial general George S. Patton. Of the Allied commanders Patton had the farthest distance to travel to the Rhine. He attacked the Siegfried Line, a defensive chain in western Germany. His infantry broke through to Koblenz, then headed south. Patton reached the Rhine between Mainz and Worms. The Allies had planned to cross the Rhine on March 23. Instead, Patton's Third Army crossed the river in an amphibious assault the previous night.

Patton had stolen Montgomery's thunder. Montgomery had reached the Rhine by the end of the first week of March. He had then, however, held back around the town of Wesel. Montgomery wanted to build up his forces for the crossing. He assembled

more than 250,000 men on the western bank of the river. After Wesel had been devastated by Allied bombers, Montgomery's troops crossed the river as scheduled late on March 23. The Allies had now succeeded in

▲ Engineers ferry one of the first tanks across the Rhine on a pontoon raft.

◄ White flags of surrender and confused civilians greet U.S. troops entering a ruined German town in the Rhineland.

Yalta Conference

From February 4 to 11, 1945, the three Allied leaders—Churchill, Roosevelt, and Stalin—met at a conference at Yalta in the Crimea, in the Soviet Union. They discussed a wide range of issues, including the strategy for the final defeat of Hitler. They also decided Germany's postwar future. The country would be divided into zones of occupation among the Allies.

The most significant discussions were about the political arrangements of postwar Europe. The Soviets would be left in control of much of eastern Europe. They agreed to allow free elections there. In reality, however, eastern Europe would be controlled by communist puppet governments. The failure of the western Allies to get better terms for eastern Europe led some later critics to call Yalta the "Western betrayal."

▲ Churchill (left), Roosevelt (center), and Joseph Stalin at Yalta.

▼ Tanks and trucks of the U.S. Third Army cross the Muhl River in Austria in May 1945.

establishing three large strategic points on the eastern bank of the Rhine.

In theory, the Allies still faced strong opposition in western Germany. Three army groups defended the German front line. In reality, however, the German troops were in a desperate state. After months of fighting, some units were at only a third of their normal strength. In order to boost unit numbers, poorly trained reservists had been sent to the front. They included both seniors and teenagers. Military typists and cooks were also pressed into action.

German command

In Berlin, meanwhile, Adolf Hitler was slowly losing his grip on reality. He could not accept Germany's impending defeat. He still tried to command his army as if it were at full fighting strength. Hitler had fired his commander in chief in the west, Field Marshal Gerd von Rundstedt. Von Rundstedt was replaced by Field Marshal Albert Kesselring. Kesselring was a talented commander, but he did

not have the forces to deal with the Allied advance. On a local level, however, many German units fought bravely and skillfully. They remained a formidable enemy.

Political influences

The next objective of the Allied western campaign was the River Elbe. The Elbe was only about 45 miles (70km) from Berlin itself.

The Allied commanders expected to push from the Elbe to the capital. Unknown to them, however, their advance would be halted by a political decision that had already been taken. When the Allied leaders met at the Yalta Conference in February 1945, they had agreed to divide Germany between the Western Allies. The Soviet Red Army would capture Berlin. Eisenhower had decided to halt the U.S. and British advance at the Elbe.

To the Elbe

The Allies first had to reach the river. Eisenhower now revised his strategy. He decided that the main advance toward the Elbe would be led by Omar Bradley's XII Army Corps. Bradley would also take control of Montgomery's U.S. Ninth Army. Montgomery would take the rest of his forces into the north of Germany. Devers's Sixth Army Group would meanwhile push out into southern Germany and Austria.

By the beginning of April, the Allied offensive was well underway. A large German force in a pocket on the Ruhr River was surrounded by U.S. forces on April 1. Cut off, it surrendered on April 18. Allied formations made rapid advances across the length of Germany.

Dresden

On the night of February 13–14, 1945, a force of 800 Allied bombers dropped nearly 3,000 tons of bombs on the historic German city of Dresden, on the River Elbe. The city was renowned for its architectural beauty. It had almost no war industries, however, and few air defenses. The bombing was so heavy that it started a firestorm. The individual fires started by the bombs combined to form a single blaze that burned at temperatures of up to 1,472°F (800°C).

Estimates of the death toll at Dresden range from 40,000 to 100,000. So many civilians died that people protested the bombing even in the Allied home nations. Some people began to question the morality of British air chief marshal Arthur Harris. Harris had developed the policy of carpet-bombing entire towns and cities rather than attempting to hit single precision targets. The controversy over the Dresden raid continues today.

▼ The bombing of Dresden became the subject of a famous U.S. novel, *Slaughterhouse-five*. The book's author, Kurt Vonnegut, Jr., was a prisoner of war in the city when the attack happened.

Heinrich Himmler (1900–1945)

Born in 1900 near Munich, Heinrich Himmler became an early member of the Nazi Party in the 1920s, and a close friend of Adolf Hitler. Himmler was appointed as head of the SS in 1929. In that role, he would be linked with some of the worst atrocities of the Nazi era. He set up the first concentration camp at Dachau in 1933.

After the outbreak of war in 1939, Himmler took charge of Nazi racial policy. He was the central figure in the development of the "Final Solution." That was the Nazis' attempt to kill all of Europe's Jews. Himmler rose to become second in authority only to the führer. In the last days of the war, Himmler tried to negotiate peace with the Allies. After the German surrender, Himmler tried to flee in disguise. He was discovered by British soldiers on May 23. According to official records, he took poison and died instantly, although conspiracy theorists believe he was killed by the British.

The Allies met fierce resistance. There were many instances where a small group of Wehrmacht troops was able to hold up far larger U.S. or British units. In the east, however, the Russian offensive was threatening Berlin itself. This disrupted supplies to the troops in the west. The German forces began to collapse. The Allies captured a total of 325,000 German prisoners in the Ruhr Pocket alone. By the end of April, the Allies had cleared almost all parts of Germany west of the Elbe. They had also defeated the Germans in the northern Netherlands.

Over to the Soviets

On April 25, 1945, a U.S. patrol met up with Soviet forces near Torgau on the Elbe. The Allies' eastern and western advances had come together. Eisenhower's commanders now urged him to continue the advance. They were certain they could reach and take Berlin before the Soviets. In accordance with the decisions taken at Yalta, however, Eisenhower stopped any advance farther east.

The Red Army's plan

The western Allied troops had suffered significant casualties in their campaign. On the Eastern Front, however, the losses were much greater. The advance through eastern Europe, from late 1944 until the fall of Berlin in May 1945, cost the Soviets more dead than the British and United States suffered in the entire war in all theaters.

By January 1945, Soviet dictator Joseph Stalin and his commanders had developed their plan for final victory. They would advance in two massive leaps. The first would take them from the Vistula River in Poland to the Oder River on the German border. The second leap would push from the Oder to the Elbe. On the way, it would capture Berlin.

▲ Himmler was one of Hitler's most loyal followers. In the last days of the war, however, he secretly tried to make peace with the Allies.

The *Volkssturm*

In September 1944, Hitler created the Volkssturm (People's Guard, literally "People's Storm"). He put the new organization under the leadership of his private secretary Martin Bormann and SS chief Heinrich Himmler. The Volkssturm conscripted all able-bodied German males between the ages of 16 and 60, who were not already in military service, into home-defense units.

Volkssturm soldiers had little military value. They could only train on Sundays, so that they could work the rest of the time, and they had few weapons and little ammunition. Nevertheless, Volkssturm members armed with Panzerfaust hand-held antitank weapons destroyed many Allied tanks. They played a major role in the city fighting in Berlin. It is estimated that as many as 200,000 Volkssturm soldiers died in front-line fighting.

▲ Volkssturm surrender. Many were forced to fight by the threat of execution.

The opposing forces

The Red Army assembled huge forces to launch its advance. Its divisions were arranged into fronts, which were the equivalent of Western army groups. From the Baltic Sea to Yugoslavia, there were 10 fronts in total. The four fronts that would strike directly into the heart of Germany comprised nearly four million men. The offensive would be supported by 10,000 aircraft, 3,300 tanks, and 28,000 artillery pieces. The drive to Berlin itself was to be handled by Stalin's two most capable military commanders. Marshal Georgy Zhukov led the 1st Belorussian Front, while Marshal Ivan Konev commanded the 1st Ukrainian Front.

Resisting the Soviets were four crumbling and battle-weary German formations. They were Army Group Center in East Prussia, Army Group Vistula in Pomerania, Army Group A in central Poland, and Army Group South in Czechoslovakia and Austria. The total German strength in East

▼ Soviet troops look out over Budapest. Hitler had ordered that the city be held "at all costs."

Prussia and Poland was only about 600,000 men. The Germans were further weakened by poor command. Hitler later placed Army Group Vistula under the command of Heinrich Himmler, for example. Himmler was the head of the SS, but he was not militarily experienced. Hitler put him in charge because of his political loyalty rather than his combat skill.

The Soviets enter German territory

The Soviet advance was the largest single offensive of World War II. It began on January 12, 1945. German resistance soon collapsed under waves of artillery fire, air and tank attacks, and infantry assaults. In East Prussia, Army Group Center was virtually wiped out.

East Prussia was the first German territory the Soviets entered. Several

million East Prussian civilians tramped west toward the Baltic coast, hoping to escape by ship from one of the ports. In the subzero winter conditions, up to a million of them died. Even those who got on board refugee ships were not safe. Soviet submarines sank many vessels. In only two such sinkings, more than 11,000 people died.

Farther south, the Red Army advanced through Poland. It captured the Polish capital, Warsaw, on January 17. Within two weeks, Konev and Zhukov were amassing troops along the eastern German border on the Oder River. Berlin lay only 35 miles (55km) to the west.

By February 24, Pomerania had been cleared. During February and March, the Soviets consolidated their position. There was little fighting apart from limited attacks into German territory. The focus of the war now shifted south into Hungary.

▼ Budapest was left in ruins after the Soviet siege.

◄ Red Army troops enter Vienna, the Austrian capital, in April 1945.

The taking of Budapest

The Soviets had captured eastern Hungary in October 1944. The capital, Budapest, however, was still in German hands. Stalin launched an attack to take Budapest on October 26. The city was defended by a garrison of 188,000 men. It took the Red Army two full months to surround it. The city was besieged.

In January 1945, Hitler made a decision that reflected how badly he had lost his grasp on military strategy. His army chief of staff, Heinz Guderian, urged him to send every available unit to the Oder. Guderian feared a Soviet thrust into Germany. Instead, Hitler ordered a panzer division from the western front to relieve the Budapest garrison. The panzers were held up by poor weather, however. They reached Budapest on February 13. On that same day, the city finally fell to the Soviets.

On March 6, Hitler launched what would be Germany's final offensive of the war. He believed that an offensive around either side of Lake Balaton to the south would retake Budapest. It would also establish a new defensive line along the River Danube. However, the troops and tanks available for the German offensive were dwarfed by Soviet firepower. By March 15, the Red Army was advancing north up the Danube Valley toward Vienna, the capital of Austria.

Eyewitness

❝ New command post in the subway tunnels under Anhalt railway station. The station looks like an armed camp. Women and children huddling in niches and corners and listening for the sounds of battle. Shells hit the roofs, cement is crumbling from the ceiling …. Water comes rushing through the tunnels. The crowds get panicky, stumble and fall over rails and sleepers. Children and wounded are deserted, people are trampled to death. The water covers them. It rises 1 meter [3 feet] or more, then it slowly goes down. The panic lasts for hours. Many are drowned. Reason: Somewhere, on somebody's command, engineers have blasted the locks of one of the canals to flood the tunnels against the Russians who are trying to get through them. ❞

From the diary of a German staff officer, describing conditions during the defense of Berlin.

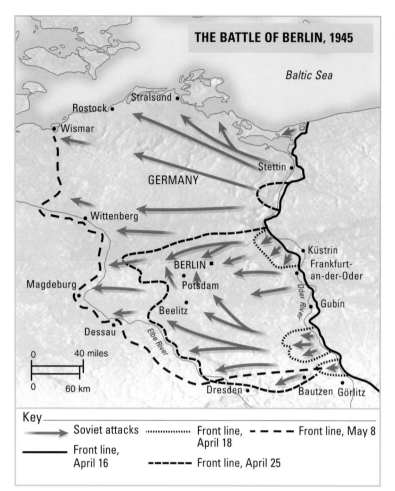

THE BATTLE OF BERLIN, 1945

Baltic Sea

Stralsund

Rostock

Wismar

GERMANY

Stettin

Wittenberg

Küstrin

Frankfurt-
an-der-Oder

BERLIN

Potsdam

Magdeburg

Beelitz

Gubin

Dessau

Oder River

Elbe River

Dresden   Bautzen Görlitz

0   40 miles

0   60 km

Key

→ Soviet attacks   ·········· Front line,   – – – Front line, May 8
April 18

——— Front line,
April 16

— - — - Front line, April 25

▲ The Red Army's taking of Berlin marked the final stages of the war in Europe, 1945.

▶ Russian troops look on as the Reichstag, the heart of German government, smolders after the fall of Berlin in 1945.

The fall of Vienna

The campaign to take Vienna began on March 16. Mountainous terrain and numerous rivers made it difficult to use armor. Using land maneuvers and amphibious actions, however, the Soviets reached the city on April 5. In eight days of fighting, much of Vienna's historic center was destroyed. The city fell on April 13, along with 130,000 German prisoners.

The strategy to take Berlin

The honor of taking Berlin was given to marshals Zhukov and Konev. Zhukov would attack west into the city from Küstrin, on the Oder. Konev's 1st Ukrainian Front was going to move into the south of Berlin. Another army front, meanwhile, would strike north of the city against Army Group Vistula.

Inside Berlin, Hitler had scraped together almost every available male to

Final days in the bunker

From April 20 to April 30, 1945, Hitler lived entirely in the *Führerbunker*. With him were his mistress, Eva Braun, a large number of high-ranking Nazi officials, and administrative and domestic staff. According to accounts by those present, by this time Hitler was physically and mentally broken. He was prone to furious rages. Even his closest allies began to desert him. On April 23, his close friend Hermann Göring sent a telegram from Bavaria saying that he would take over leadership of Germany if he did not hear otherwise from Hitler. Five days later, Hitler learned that another close friend, Heinrich Himmler, had been conducting secret peace negotiations behind his back.

On April 29, Hitler received reports that Russian forces were little more than a block away from the Chancellery above the bunker. He married Eva Braun. The next day, the pair went into a separate room and committed suicide. Braun took cyanide, while Hitler shot himself. Their bodies were later burned.

◀ One of the last photographs of Hitler shows him with members of the Hitler Youth in April 1945.

defend the city. The total defensive force came to about one million, but many of the defenders were poorly trained. They included, for example, 100 battalions of Volkssturm units, who were little more than civilians. The German defenders also lacked any armored vehicles.

Hitler himself had now retreated into the *Führerbunker*. The bunker was set deep underground beneath the Chancellery, the political center of Berlin. Hitler stayed in the bunker with his mistress, Eva Braun, and an entourage of his most faithful followers. He gave an order that the Soviets "must and shall fall before the capital of the Third Reich." It was a delusory hope. The Soviets had 2.5 million soldiers ready to attack the city. They had the equivalent of one artillery gun for every 13 feet (4m) of ground along 55 miles (90km) of front.

The battle of Berlin

A heavy bombardment on April 16, 1945, began the Battle of Berlin. Soviet

▼ A Soviet antitank gun and T-34 tank guard a bridge in Berlin in April 1945.

troops stormed forward, but they faced desperate resistance. The Russians were also slowed down by the conditions. The spring thaw made the countryside outside the city a muddy bog in many places.

Zhukov became stuck against the defenses to the east of Berlin for several days. It took him until April 20 to overcome all German resistance on the west bank of the Oder. Stalin ordered Zhukov to move around to the north of the city. Hitler, however, left his Ninth Army on the Oder while Zhukov began to maneuver. Meanwhile, Konev pushed up from the south.

By April 25, Berlin was surrounded. In ferocious fighting, the Red Army made its way into Berlin, street by street. Soviet aircraft bombed strongpoints around the clock. German resistance remained strong. Berliners feared the invaders. They also faced reprisals from their own army. Any male found not fighting risked being picked up by SS squads and hanged from a lamppost.

Last days of the Reich

After April 20, Hitler stayed permanently in his bunker. He was losing his reason. By April 27, the Germans held only about 15 square miles (38 sq.km) of the city. Hitler ordered that resistance must continue. By April 30, the Soviets were less than a half mile (800m) from the Chancellery. Hitler finally gave up. At 3:30 P.M., he and his mistress, Eva Braun, took their own lives in the bunker. Their bodies were then burned.

The Nazi leadership passed to the commander of the German Navy, Grand Admiral Karl Dönitz. The German High Command now tried to

▼ In one of the most famous images of the war, a Soviet soldier raises the Red Flag of the Soviet Union above the Reichstag in Berlin.

The surrender

The death of Hitler and the surrender of Berlin did not bring an immediate end to the fighting in Europe. Admiral Karl Dönitz, who now led Germany, tried to extend the war. He wanted to allow as many Germans as possible to escape Russian occupation. The surrender therefore happened in piecemeal fashion.

Dönitz sent Hans-Georg von Friedeburg to negotiate with Montgomery. On May 4, 1945, the German forces in northwest Europe laid down their arms. Von Friedeburg's next stop was northern France, where he met with Eisenhower's staff. Von Friedeburg tried to arrange a surrender in the west, while continuing war against the Soviets in the east. The Americans rejected the terms.

After negotiations, the Allies allowed Germans 48 more hours to move across into the U.S.–British western zone. At 2:41 A.M. on May 7, the Germans signed the surrender of all their forces. It became effective at one minute past midnight on May 9. Fighting went on until May 11 in places such as Austria and Czechoslovakia, but the Allies could now celebrate victory in Europe.

▲ New Yorkers celebrate Victory in Europe (VE) Day on May 8, 1945. Fighting in Japan would go on for another three months.

make a peace deal. Their first attempts failed because the Soviets demanded unconditional surrender, which the Germans rejected. On May 2, however, the commandant of Berlin, Lieutenant-General Karl Weidling, surrendered. The city had lost about 300,000 German and Soviet dead. Five days later, Germany signed its total surrender. The war in Europe was over.

▼ Field Marshal Bernard Montgomery (left) receives the German surrender in northwest Europe on May 4 at Luneberg Heath.

ISLAND-HOPPING IN THE PACIFIC: 1944

By the start of 1944, U.S. forces had begun their advance across the Pacific Ocean toward the home islands of Japan. Their goal remained thousands of miles away, however, protected by the vast ocean.

In October and November 1943, U.S. troops had captured the southern and central Solomon Islands and Tarawa in the Gilbert Islands. A band of islands across the Central Pacific still lay in Japanese hands, however.

The U.S. forces had until now not had enough warships, men, and equipment to fight Nazi Germany and wage a war on two Pacific fronts at the same time. By 1944, however, with support from Australia and New Zealand, U.S. commanders were ready to make two simultaneous thrusts in the Pacific.

Managing the Pacific theaters

American planners had previously divided the Pacific into a number of operational zones. In clockwise order, they were the North Pacific Area, the Central Pacific Area, the South Pacific Area, and the Southwest Pacific Area.

By the end of 1943, campaigning in the North Pacific was effectively over. The zones that were now vital to Allied success in the Pacific War were the Central Pacific and the Southwest Pacific. Operations in the Central Pacific were led by U.S. Navy admiral

Chester Nimitz. The Southwest Pacific Area was the responsibility of U.S. Army general Douglas MacArthur. The plan for the first half of 1944 was for Nimitz and MacArthur to make converging thrusts toward the Philippines. President Roosevelt and his top commanders would then meet to set their next priorities.

Strategy in the Southwest Pacific

Nimitz and MacArthur had the same ultimate objective. They both relied on amphibious assaults to get them there. However, they both fought their campaigns in entirely different ways.

MacArthur's Southwest Pacific Area covered Australia, New Guinea, the Solomon Islands, and the Philippines. MacArthur's main aim was to neutralize the key Japanese base, Rabaul. Rabaul lay on the east coast of New Britain, an island in the Bismarck Archipelago, northeast of New Guinea. MacArthur chose not to use a direct assault, however. He summed up his strategy as "hitting 'em where they ain't." He ordered his forces to bypass Japanese garrisons and isolate them. The garrisons would then wither for lack of outside support.

MacArthur's approach relied on surprise. His troops often landed on unguarded beaches. MacArthur also made secondary landings behind enemy forces who were already busy fighting off main landings to their front. Once an area was secured, Sea-Bees (Construction Battalions) built airfields from which aircraft could support the next assault and attack the isolated Japanese bases.

Halsey's support for MacArthur

MacArthur's main aim at the first half of 1944 was to conclude Operation Cartwheel and isolate Rabaul. That meant clearing the Japanese from New Guinea and the northern Solomons. MacArthur was supported by

▼ Marines take shelter from sniper fire during a landing on the island of Roi, in the Marshall Islands. In the background, smoke billows from a destroyed Japanese bunker that was full of torpedoes.

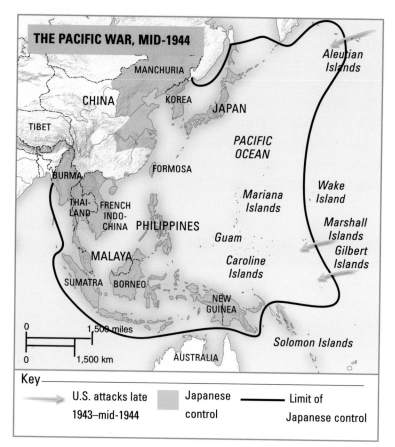

THE PACIFIC WAR, MID-1944

MANCHURIA
CHINA
KOREA
JAPAN
TIBET
FORMOSA
PACIFIC OCEAN
BURMA
THAI-LAND
FRENCH INDO-CHINA
PHILIPPINES
Mariana Islands
Wake Island
Marshall Islands
Gilbert Islands
Guam
MALAYA
Caroline Islands
SUMATRA
BORNEO
NEW GUINEA
0   1,500 miles
0   1,500 km
AUSTRALIA
Solomon Islands
Aleutian Islands

Key

→ U.S. attacks late 1943–mid-1944

■ Japanese control

— Limit of Japanese control

▲ Map showing the strategic position in the Pacific in mid-1944.

the commander of the South Pacific Area, Admiral William "Bull" Halsey. Halsey had responsibility for the northern Solomons, while MacArthur focused on New Guinea.

Backed by Halsey's Third Fleet, U.S., Australian, and New Zealand troops

completed the recapture of most of the northern Solomons in the first months of 1944. On February 14, New Zealand units occupied Green Island, to the east of New Britain. It was an ideal site for an airfield from which to attack Rabaul.

U.S. forces had another airfield within striking distance of Rabaul on the island of Bougainville in the northern Solomons. U.S. troops had held the airstrip area since November 1943. The U.S. airfields were protected against Japanese ground attack by a safe perimeter. Serious Japanese resistance was over by the end of 1943. However, sporadic fighting on the island continued to the end of the war, when 23,000 Japanese surrendered.

Halsey went on to seize the St. Mathias Islands to the north of New Britain in March. Its work over, much of Halsey's Third Fleet returned to the Central Pacific Area in June.

Clearing New Guinea

MacArthur started his own operations on January 2, 1944. His forces landed at Saidor, on the northern coast of New Guinea. Over the next two

▶ A U.S. B-24 Liberator makes a bombing run over Salamua in New Guinea. Its bombs burst in the lower left of the photograph.

344

Rabaul

Rabaul was on the eastern edge of New Britain, in the Southwest Pacific. It was taken from the Australians by the Japanese at the end of January 1942. The island had two large harbors and airfields, from where the Japanese could dominate New Guinea and the Solomons, and threaten Australia itself.

Neutralizing Rabaul became a top priority for the Allies. They believed that the island was too strongly defended to mount an amphibious operation against it. As a result, from October 1943, it became the focus of an intense air campaign. The campaign was supported by landings on Bougainville to the east and other islands. When captured, the islands were used as fighter and bomber bases. On thousands of missions against Rabaul, Allied bombers dropped about 30,000 tons on various targets.

U.S. Marines (later replaced by Australian troops) landed at Cape Gloucester on New Britain's east coast in December 1944 to isolate the Japanese further. There was never an all-out attempt to retake the island, but Rabaul was left isolated until the war's end. Finally, on September 6, 1945, some 60,000 Japanese troops and 20,000 civilian workers surrendered.

▼ An Allied bomber attacks vessels in the harbor at Rabaul in one of thousands of attacks on the port.

months, he also cleared the Admiralty Islands northeast of New Britain and expanded the Allied beachhead at Cape Gloucester, on New Britain itself.

The focus of the fighting now switched back to the northern coast of New Guinea. The Japanese there were preparing a major counterattack against Saidor. MacArthur's response was bold. He planned an amphibious assault against the main Japanese base at Hollandia, some 500 miles (800km) west of Saidor. The base was 150 miles (240km) beyond the range of U.S. fighters, so the landings would have no air cover. However, MacArthur knew it was only lightly defended. He also planned a simultaneous landing at

Aitape, between Hollandia and Wewak, but within range of the Saidor airfields. SeaBees would build airfields on Aitape, from where aircraft could protect the Hollandia force.

Clearing New Guinea

Operations began in late March with a prolonged bombardment of Japanese airfields. In early April, the Australians launched an attack toward Madang as a diversion. The Hollandia and Aitape landings began on April 22. American troops secured both targets before the end of the month. The surrounded Japanese units began to disintegrate. Many troops fled into the hostile jungle, where they stayed until the end of the war.

MacArthur also made a number of landings on offshore islands, most of which had valuable airfields. The operations were completed on July 30 with the capture of Sansapor. The north coast of New Guinea was now secure. MacArthur could begin to prepare to retake the Philippines.

The strategy for the Central Pacific

Unlike the Southwest Pacific, where there were numerous large islands in close proximity, the Central Pacific included smaller islands that were very widely dispersed. This meant that the Japanese would easily be able to predict where the U.S. forces would land.

American commanders knew that it would be virtually impossible to make a surprise landing. Their island-hopping campaign would invariably involve landings on heavily defended beaches. They therefore had to develop

▼ Tracked landing vehicles head for the beach during the U.S. invasion of Noemfoor Island, off the western coast of New Guinea in July 1944.

Tracked landing vehicles

Before the war, U.S. troops had staged amphibious exercises. The exercises showed that conventional flat-bottomed, propeller-driven landing craft had several failings. They often ran aground on the coral reefs that surrounded many Pacific islands. Once they ran up on the beach, they became effectively useless. When the forward-facing ramp was lowered, those inside were immediately exposed to enemy fire.

The solution to the problems was the amtrak (amphibious tractor), or LVT (landing vehicle, tracked). The LVT was based on a swamp-rescue vehicle. Its tracks allowed it to cross reefs and move inland. It had a rear-facing ramp, so that the troops could exit partly protected from enemy fire. The first LVTs were ordered in late 1940. Thousands eventually saw service in the Pacific. As well

▲ An LVT, or "Buffalo," heads for shore during the U.S. landings on Tinian in the Mariana Islands in July 1944.

as carrying troops, some LVTs hauled cargo. Others were fitted with rotating gun turrets to provide assault units with close-support fire.

---

techniques and equipment for conducting amphibious landings under heavy fire. The heavy losses they had suffered at Tarawa in November 1943 had shown how risky such landings could be.

Lessons in amphibious warfare

U.S. commanders had learned that successful amphibious landings depended on several factors. The target island had to be isolated from outside help. It also had to come under intense air and naval bombardment, which would protect the landing force.

For such complex missions to succeed, the U.S. Pacific Fleet had to be divided into four separate parts that would operate together smoothly. First, there were the large aircraft carriers and their escorts. They had the job of

isolating the target island by dealing with any enemy warships attempting to intervene in the battle. The carriers would also support the landings with air power. Second, the bombardment fleet had to pound enemy positions for days or even weeks. The third part was the amphibious fleet, which moved troops from island to island and undertook the actual landings. The final element of the fleet was the Fleet Train.

▼ The Fleet Train at work: landing craft unload supplies on Los Negros, in the Admiralty Islands.

Vice Admiral Marc Mitscher (1887–1947)

Wisconsin-born but Oklahoma-raised, Marc Mitscher was a pioneer of naval aviation and an expert on aircraft carriers. He commanded the carrier *Hornet* when it took part in the Doolittle bombing raid on mainland Japan in April 1942, and during the Battle of Midway the following June. In April 1943, he was made commander of the Fleet Air, Solomon Islands. He was based on Guadalcanal, from where his aircraft could support General MacArthur's drive northward through the Southwest Pacific. In January 1944, Mitscher returned to sea as commander of Carrier Division 3 (later Fast Carrier Task Force 58). After further service in the Southwest Pacific near New Guinea, he played a pivotal role in several major operations in the Central Pacific, including the battles of the Philippine Sea, Leyte Gulf, Iwo Jima, and Okinawa.

▲ Marc A. Mitscher watches operations from the bridge of his flagship in February 1945.

▼ U.S. Marines take shelter on Eniwetok, one of the outer atolls of the Marshall Islands, during the landings of February 1944.

The Fleet Train supplied the rest of the fleet. The Pacific Fleet was in virtually constant operation thousands of miles from home. It depended on a vast flow of supplies across the Central Pacific. Convoys sailed from the U.S. West Coast to an intermediate port, usually on a recently captured island. There cargo was transferred to the Fleet Train for transport to the operational area. Other train ships were converted into floating repair shops. They could repair anything short of major damage. This was not glamorous work, but the whole campaign would have ground to a halt without these ships and their crews.

Opening moves in the Central Pacific

The first thrust of Nimitz's advance in the Central Pacific was an attack on the Marshall Islands. Intelligence had revealed that the Japanese had transferred many troops away from the inner ring of islands—chiefly Kwajalein, Roi, and Namur—and stationed them on various outer islands. When the landings began on January 30, 1944, therefore, the U.S. armada targeted the three inner islands. Although there were a few problems with the

initial assault, there was no repeat of the heavy casualties the Marines had suffered at Tarawa in November 1943. The Marshalls were declared secure on February 7. American losses were 362 killed and about 1,000 wounded, while the Japanese garrison of 8,000 was almost completely wiped out.

Advantages of holding the Marshalls

The capture of the Marshalls had great strategic benefits. It brought a major Japanese base at Truk Atoll, in the Caroline Islands, within range of land-based U.S. bombers. That forced the Mobile Fleet, the Imperial Japanese Navy's main strike force, to retire northward to the Mariana Islands. This was a significant blow to the Japanese. The move north made it much more difficult for the Japanese Navy to intervene in the Southwest Pacific. That

added to the growing isolation of the troops stationed in the Solomons, in New Guinea, and on New Britain.

Next target: The Mariana Islands

After the success in the Marshalls, U.S. commanders brought forward an amphibious operation against the Mariana Islands by 20 weeks, to July. The stakes were growing higher for the Japanese. The Marianas lie roughly halfway between New Guinea and Japan. If the United States were able to establish airfields there, the Japanese home islands would be within range of U.S. long-range bombers.

In an attempt to prevent the capture of the Marianas, Japan launched Operation A-Go. The operation was intended to lure major elements of the U.S. Pacific Fleet into the area around Yap and the Palau Islands. There, they

▲ A Marine signal unit takes shelter in ruined buildings on Namur, one of the islets of Kwajalein Atoll, during the landings of January 1944.

349

▶ A Mitchell B-25 bomber flies a mission against Japanese positions on Wotje, in the Marshall Islands.

▼ U.S. attack aircraft during a raid in the Marianas in June 1940. The aircraft are TBM Avengers and SB2C Helldivers.

would be overwhelmed by land-based and naval air power. By May 16, the Japanese fleet was maneuvering into position for A-Go. It was unaware, however, that it was under surveillance from U.S. submarines.

The battle for the Marianas

The landings in the Marianas began with a landing on Saipan on June 15. Tough fighting lasted until July 13, by which time 29,000 Japanese troops had been killed. About 22,000 Japanese civilians also died. Some committed suicide rather than be taken prisoner. Many jumped off cliffs around the island's coast. Their deaths had a lasting impact. They made U.S. military planners concerned about the enormous number of civilian deaths that might result from a U.S. invasion of the Japanese home islands.

The next target was Guam. After a 13-day bombardment, Marines and army units landed on July 21. The defenses were largely overwhelmed by August 10. U.S. forces recorded 1,400 men killed and 5,600 wounded, while the Japanese suffered some 10,000 casualties. A few survivors fought on until the end of the war; one surrendered only in 1972.

The final U.S. landing came on Tinian. It was declared secure on August 2. About half of the 10,000-strong Japanese garrison had been killed. U.S. losses reached 389 men killed and 1,816 wounded.

The Great Marianas Turkey Shoot

The Mobile Fleet under Vice Admiral Jisaburo Ozawa steamed toward the Marianas as soon as the first Marines came ashore on Saipan. The U.S. Fifth Fleet under Admiral Marc A. Mitscher was waiting in the Philippine Sea. Ozawa had five large and four smaller carriers with 474 aircraft. Mitscher had seven large and eight smaller carriers, with 956 aircraft. The Japanese could also deploy about 100 land-based aircraft from Yap and elsewhere, but their crews were mostly inexperienced in actual combat.

The action began at daybreak on June 19. Ozawa attacked first, but things went wrong from the outset. U.S. submarines sank two of his carriers, while U.S. fighters downed most of the Japanese aircraft. The few that got through to the U.S. ships mostly fell to antiaircraft fire.

The action ended at dusk. It had been a disastrous day for the Japanese, who lost 346 aircraft to just 30 U.S. planes.

Ozawa tried to escape, but Mitscher caught up with him late on the afternoon of June 20. U.S. aircraft sank another of Ozawa's carriers, *Hiyo*, and two oil tankers. They also destroyed a further 65 aircraft. The Battle of the Philippine Sea was the largest carrier action of the war. It was so one-sided that the U.S. pilots named it the Great Marianas Turkey Shoot. Mitscher was criticized for not annihilating the Mobile Fleet. In fact, however, he had inflicted grievous damage. In one day, his pilots had effectively destroyed Japan's naval aviation arm. The lost aircraft could be replaced, but their highly trained pilots could not.

A heavy toll for Japan

The combined loss of the Marianas and the devastation of the Mobile Fleet were disastrous for Japan. The enemy had breached the ring of defensive

▲ U.S. troops evacuate Japanese civilians from a village on Saipan. Many civilians on the island chose to commit suicide rather than surrender to the Americans.

▶ U.S. Marines advance among palm trees during operations to capture Guam, in the Marianas, in July 1944.

islands in the Central Pacific Area. The Japanese home islands would soon become the targets of an ever-growing U.S. strategic bombing attack. In October 1944, Boeing B-29 Superfortresses flying from the Marianas launched their first attack on the Japanese capital, Tokyo. The repercussions went to the top of the Japanese government. General Hideki Tojo, who was both prime minister and army minister, resigned in July along with his cabinet.

Eyewitness

66 When he appeared, I … began squeezing off shots. As the first bullet hit him, his face contorted in agony. His knees buckled…. All the men near me, including the amtrak machine gunner, had seen him and began firing. The soldier collapsed…. Even in the middle of these fast-moving events, I looked down at my carbine with sober reflection. I had just killed a man at close range. That I had seen clearly the pain on his face when my bullets hit him came as a jolt. It suddenly made the war a very personal affair. The expression on that man's face filled me with shame and then disgust for the war and all the misery it was causing. 99

Eugene B. Sledge, U.S. 1st Marine Division,
describing the bitter struggle for Ngesebus,
one of the Palau Islands.

Preparations for the Philippines

U.S. commanders met at Pearl Harbor in July. MacArthur and Nimitz disagreed on the next step toward Japan. President Roosevelt rejected Nimitz's plan to move first against either Formosa (Taiwan) or China. Instead, he agreed with MacArthur that liberating the Philippines should take priority for both military and political reasons.

The final plan was for MacArthur to take Mindanao and Nimitz to capture Yap in the Philippines. Both would then turn on the island of Leyte. Once Leyte was secured, MacArthur would invade Luzon, the main Philippine island. Luzon was home to the capital, Manila. Meanwhile, Nimitz would head directly toward Japan, to the islands of Iwo Jima and Okinawa.

Prior to the Philippines operation, MacArthur thought it necessary to capture Morotai and some islands in the Palau group, between the Philippines and New Guinea. His forces took Morotai, but the Marines took severe casualties in the Palaus.

Ahead of plan

In the Central Pacific, Halsey's carriers made a largely unopposed sweep along the coast of the Philippines in September. U.S. troops landed on Ulithi Atoll on September 23. Its huge natural harbor became home to both the U.S. Third and Fifth fleets.

Halsey recommended the abandonment of the landings on Mindanao and Yap. He argued that the assault on Leyte should take place as soon as possible to exploit the weakened state

of the Japanese there. The landings on Leyte, which were planned for December 20, were brought forward to October 20.

U.S. air and naval forces started attacking Japanese air bases in the second week of October. By the middle of the month, the stage was set for the U.S. return to the Philippines.

▲ U.S. Marines are bogged down on Peleliu, in the Palau Islands, September 1944. The elite 1st Marine Division took heavy casualties in the operation.

◄ Vessels of the U.S. Fifth Fleet steam through the Philippine Sea during the Great Marianas Turkey Shoot in June 1944.

THE BATTLE OF LEYTE GULF

The naval battle around the Philippine Islands in October 1944 sealed the fate of the wartime Imperial Japanese Navy. A total of 29 Japanese warships were sunk in the engagement.

The capture of the Marshall and Marianas islands brought U.S. forces to a position from which they could assault the Philippines. The U.S. garrison on the islands had surrendered to the Japanese in May 1942. General Douglas MacArthur had been ordered to evacuate from the Philippines to Australia. He was now commander of the Southwest Pacific Area, and led one half of the U.S. thrust through the Pacific.

U.S. objectives

The first U.S. objective in the Philippines was Leyte, an island in the south of the group. The U.S. operation could call on huge resources: the Sixth Army plus two naval fleets comprising 800 ships. The Third Fleet was led by Admiral William F. Halsey. The Seventh Fleet was commanded by Vice-Admiral Thomas Kinkaid.

Japanese fleet movements

U.S. forces landed on eastern Leyte on October 20. The Japanese had a plan to defend the islands, code-named Operation Sho-1. It was highly complex. A large decoy force would sail toward the Philippines from the north. It would draw Halsey's fleet away from covering the landings at Leyte.

Meanwhile, two large attack forces would head for the Philippines. The First Attack Force would come from Borneo in the west. It would split into Force A and Force C. Force A included the two largest battleships in the world, *Yamato* and *Musashi*. It would sail to Leyte through the Sibuyan Sea and then the San Bernardino Strait north of Leyte. Force C would arrive through the Surigao Strait in the south. The U.S. landings would be caught in a pincer. The Second Attack Force would provide support for the First Attack Force.

▼ The USS *St. Lo* blows up in Leyte Gulf on October 25, 1944. The escort carrier was the first victim of a kamikaze suicide attack. The Japanese plane pierced the flight deck, starting a fire that ignited the ship's bombs.

It was an ambitious plan based on a huge fleet. The Japanese would use almost their entire navy for the operation. They were ready to sacrifice the decoy force for overall success. If the Philippines fell, then Japan would lose control of much of the western Pacific. The nation would be close to defeat.

Early disasters

By October 22, 1944, Japan's decoy force and the First Attack Force were heading for the Philippines. The First Attack Force split into Force A and Force C near Palawan Island, to the west of the Philippines. On October 23, however, two U.S. submarines spotted Force A near Palawan. The submarines fired spreads of torpedoes into the mass of warships. They sank the cruiser *Atago*. On board was the First Attack Force commander, Vice Admiral Takeo Kurita. He had to be rescued by a destroyer. The submarines sank another cruiser and severely damaged a third.

Air attack

The Japanese also had some success, however. They had aircraft based at Clark Field on Luzon, the large island in the north of the Philippines. They launched a 200-aircraft bombing raid

Eyewitness

❝ We circled the heavy cruisers for three turns to gain a cirrus cloud cover and attacked from out of the sun and through this cloud at about 09:05. We caught the second heavy cruiser in column completely by surprise as we received absolutely no antiaircraft fire. We completed all dives in about thirty-five seconds, scoring five hits amidships on the stack, one hit and two near misses on the stern and three hits on the bow. The third plane hitting the stern sent the cruiser into a sharp right turn. After pulling out of the dive, I observed the heavy cruiser go about five hundred yards, blow up and sink within five minutes. ❞

Commander R. L. Fowler,
describing attacks on Japanese ships
during the Battle of Leyte Gulf

William Frederick Halsey Jr. (1882–1959)

William Halsey, Jr., was born into a naval family in New Jersey on October 30, 1882. In 1900 he graduated from the U.S. Naval Academy. Throughout the 1910s and 1920s, Halsey served on a number of vessels, and won the Navy Cross during World War I. He later served as a naval attaché. After training as a naval aviation observer, he commanded the aircraft carrier USS *Saratoga*.

▲ Halsey was known as "Bull" for his aggressive tactics.

Halsey became a rear admiral in 1938 and a vice admiral in 1940. He trained air squadrons for the carriers *Yorktown* and *Enterprise*. His service in World War II was distinguished but controversial. He took commanding roles for operations in the Gilberts, at Guadalcanal, and at Leyte Gulf; he was criticized, however, for his conduct of the naval operation at Leyte. Halsey had overall command of the South Pacific Area from 1943. He was promoted to fleet admiral in December 1945, and retired two years later.

on the carriers of the U.S. Third Fleet, east of Luzon. Most of the aircraft were shot down by U.S. fighters. A 550-pound (250-kg) bomb holed the flight deck of the aircraft carrier *Princeton*, however. It set off a series of explosions. The carrier soon sank.

Attacks on Japan

The Japanese themselves soon came under air attack. On the morning of October 24, nearly 300 U.S. aircraft attacked Kurita's Force A in the Sibuyan Sea. Despite intense anti-aircraft fire, the attack seriously damaged both the *Yamato* and the *Musashi*. The *Musashi* sank in the late afternoon, after being hit by 20 torpedoes. A total of 1,023 crew died.

The day had been a disaster for Kurita. He turned and sailed away from the San Bernardino Strait. The Americans assumed that he was retreating, but they were wrong.

Taking the bait

One element of the Japanese plan was meanwhile falling into place. The Americans had spotted the decoy force led by Jisaburo Ozawa. Halsey swung

▼ U.S. gunboats lay a smoke screen to confuse enemy aircraft in Leyte Gulf on October 20, 1944.

the U.S. Third Fleet to the north to meet Ozawa. His commander, Nimitz, had ordered him to take any opportunity to crush the Japanese fleet. Halsey saw his chance. His departure, however, left the landings at Leyte more exposed. Although the Americans did not realize it, the landings were still under threat from Kurita's Force A.

In the darkness, Kurita had halted his withdrawal from the San Bernardino Strait. He was now turning around his remaining ships in the Sibuyan Sea. They were still a powerful force. Kurita headed back through the San Bernardino Strait. Japan's Force C and the Second Attack Force were also now approaching Leyte through the Surigao Strait.

The Seventh Fleet in danger

Kinkaid's U.S. Seventh Fleet was now vulnerable to the Japanese pincer plan. Kinkaid had sent Task Group 77 to block the Surigao Strait. It was a gunfire support group that included six battleships, eight cruisers, twenty-eight destroyers, and thirty-nine motor torpedo boats. The battleships were old but had updated radar and fire-control systems. They also had the advantage of surprise.

When Japan's Force C sailed in single file down the Strait, it was attacked by a 20-minute barrage of more than 4,000 naval shells and dozens of torpedoes. All but one ship was hit. Many sank, including the flagship *Yamashiro*. Force C's commander died in the attack. The

▲ The Japanese battleship *Yamato* comes under attack in the Sibuyan Sea. The ship was badly damaged by U.S. carrier aircraft.

► Led by the *Nagato*, Kurita's First Attack Force steams toward the Philippines in October 1944.

▼ Explosions surround the *Musashi* in the Sibuyan Sea. Hit 20 times by torpedoes, the Japanese battleship sank shortly afterward.

Second Attack Force was also driven back by U.S. ships and aircraft. The whole southern pincer of the Japanese plan had collapsed.

The northern pincer

On the morning of October 25, Kurita's Force A emerged from the San Bernardino Strait. It was in position to move against the Leyte landings.

Halsey, meanwhile, was fighting Ozawa's decoy force off northeastern Luzon. U.S. air attacks continued all day. Ozawa's carriers mostly had no aircraft of their own. They simply had the task of drawing Halsey north. On October 25, U.S. air strikes sank all four carriers.

Around Leyte, Force A threatened the vulnerable U.S. landing fleet. Halsey

had, however, promised to send back a group named Task Force 34 if the landings were threatened. Along the coast of Samar, an island northeast of Leyte, meanwhile, Force A met U.S. Task Force 3, nicknamed "Taffy 3." Taffy 3 was commanded by Rear-Admiral Clifton Sprague.

A valiant action

The U.S. force was far weaker than the Japanese. It had six escort carriers, three destroyers, and four destroyer escorts. Opposing it, Force A was far stronger. It still had four battleships,

six cruisers, and ten destroyers. A U.S. defeat looked highly likely.

U.S. commanders sent urgent messages instructing Halsey to return south. Admiral Nimitz himself sent a message: "Where is Task Force 34, the world wonders?" The final phrase was a filler added for code purposes, but Halsey assumed it came from Nimitz, and was furious. He sent some ships south, but the battle had already begun.

The U.S. engagement with Task Force A lasted 2 hours and 23 minutes. Sprague's force threw itself against the far-larger Japanese group. The U.S.

The Vought Corsair

The Vought F4U was a superb U.S. naval fighter plane. It was first flown as a prototype in 1940. The plane entered operational service in October 1942. It was soon showing its strength in combat with the U.S. Marine Corps on Bougainville in February 1943. Pilots found the Corsair powerful, maneuverable, and well armed. Its armaments could include six 12.7-mm machine guns, four 20-mm cannon, and

two 1000-pound (454kg) bombs or eight 5-inch (127mm) rockets. Corsairs were used as fighters or as attack aircraft against enemy land positions or ships. Its superiority as a fighter aircraft was such that it destroyed 11 Japanese fighters for every Corsair lost.

▼ Corsairs armed with 500-pound (227-kg) bombs prepare to take off from a Central Pacific base.

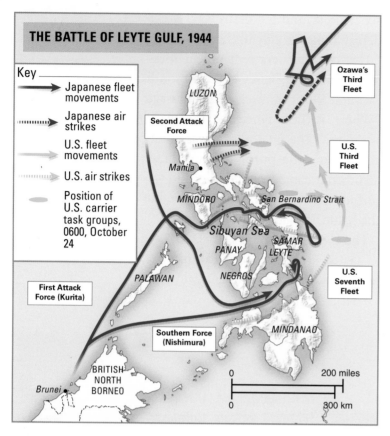

THE BATTLE OF LEYTE GULF, 1944

Key

→ Japanese fleet movements

┄► Japanese air strikes

→ U.S. fleet movements

┄► U.S. air strikes

⬭ Position of U.S. carrier task groups, 0600, October 24

LUZON

Second Attack Force

Ozawa's Third Fleet

U.S. Third Fleet

Manila

MINDORO

San Bernardino Strait

Sibuyan Sea

PANAY

SAMAR

LEYTE

First Attack Force (Kurita)

PALAWAN

NEGROS

U.S. Seventh Fleet

MINDANAO

Southern Force (Nishimura)

BRITISH NORTH BORNEO

Brunei

0   200 miles

0   300 km

▲ The Battle of Leyte Gulf, 1944, began the U.S. reconquest of the Philippines.

ships did receive some help from the weather. For short time a rain squall provided some temporary cover. It put off the Japanese gunners' aim. Otherwise, however, Japanese fire took a high toll.

Casualties on both sides

Taffy 3 lost the escort carrier *Gambier Bay*, the destroyers *Johnston* and *Hoel*, and the destroyer escort *Samuel B. Roberts*. They were sunk by huge shells from battleships and cruisers.

The U.S. ships also inflicted damage, however. Destroyers twisted toward the ranks of the Japanese ships, firing torpedoes and shells in great volumes. The aircraft from the escort carriers attacked the enemy until they ran out of bullets, bombs, or torpedoes. When they had no ammunition left, they buzzed near Japanese ships to draw their fire away from U.S. vessels.

Kurita withdraws

The Japanese lost three cruisers during the engagement. Kurita still had a huge advantage over the enemy in terms of numbers of ships and guns, but he was growing anxious that a major U.S. carrier fleet might arrive. He was also running low on fuel. He decided that his battered force had had enough. Even though he was only 45 miles (70km) from the Leyte landing vessels,

▶ Seamen injured in enemy attacks in Leyte Gulf use the wardroom of the USS *Suwanee* as an emergency sickroom, on October 25, 1944.

Kamikaze

Kamikaze means "divine wind." The word refers to a storm that saved Japan in 1281. The storm wrecked a Mongol invasion fleet. In World War II, the word was applied to suicide pilots of the Japanese air force. They flew their bomb-laden aircraft into U.S. ships, even though it meant certain death.

The kamikaze tactic was conceived by Vice-Admiral Takijiro Onishi. Onishi argued that suicide missions were ideal for Japan's inexperienced pilots. All the pilots had to do was fly the plane into the target. In addition, U.S. antiaircraft gunners had to completely destroy a kamikaze plane in the air to stop it. That was very difficult to do.

Kamikaze became an accepted tactic between October 1944 and August 1945. The pilots were volunteers. They were motivated by great patriotism. Coordinated mass raids began over the Philippines in October 1944. They reached their peak off Okinawa in March–June 1945, when 1,475 suicide planes targeted U.S. ships in 10 separate attacks.

▲ A kamikaze attack on the USS *Columbia* on January 6, 1945, during U.S. landings in the Philippines. The attack killed 13 sailors and started fires, which were soon put out.

Kurita turned his ships around. They passed back through the San Bernardino Strait and returned to their base.

A new tactic

Leyte Gulf was a great U.S. victory. For the Japanese, it was a crippling defeat. Not only had the Imperial Japanese Navy failed to stop the Leyte landings. It had also lost four carriers, three battleships, ten cruisers, eleven destroyers, a submarine, and 500 aircraft. The battle marked the end of the Imperial Japanese Navy as a significant threat in the Pacific. It was no longer capable of anything more than localized operations.

Other threats remained, however. The battle of Leyte Gulf saw the first major use by the Japanese of kamikaze suicide attacks. Pilots deliberately flew aircraft packed with explosives into U.S vessels. Between October 23 and 26, a total of 55 kamikaze aircraft attacked U.S. ships around the Philippines. They sank an escort carrier (the *St. Lo*) and damaged six others; they also hit 40 other ships, of which five sank.

Kamikaze was a terrifying new form of warfare. The Japanese would use the tactic increasingly as the conflict went on. There was no denying, however, that it was also a sign of growing Japanese desperation.

BURMA AND CHINA: 1944–1945

As 1943 drew to a close, Allied forces in Burma began to refer to themselves as the "forgotten army." They fought a war hidden away from the public eye in the jungles of Southeast Asia.

Burma remained strategically highly important in 1944. The Japanese had driven out the Allies in May 1942. For the British, Burma was a route to recapture their colonies in Malaya and Singapore. For the United States, it was an important base from which to supply Chiang Kai-shek's Nationalist army in China. The United States backed the Nationalist war against the Japanese, who had invaded China in 1937.

U.S. supplies were flown into China over the Himalayas. In December 1942, however, construction began on a road from India to southern China. It needed to pass through northern Burma, which had to be regained from the Japanese.

The British commander in chief in India was General Sir Archibald Wavell.

Throughout 1942 and much of 1943, he made limited attacks into Burma from India. The Japanese had fought off a probing invasion down Burma's north-western coast. British guerrilla units, known as Chindits, had operated deep behind Japanese lines after February 1943. They suffered 1,000 casualties and achieved few concrete gains. They did, however, give a much-needed boost to British morale.

Stilwell in China

Facing the Japanese to Burma's north-east were Chinese troops. They were commanded by U.S. general Joseph W. Stilwell, who was Chiang's chief of staff. Stilwell began operations to re-take northern Burma in October 1943.

▼ U.S. troops of the 124th Cavalry Regiment leave a camp in Burma on the way to join the fighting for the town of Myitkyina.

At the same time, the Allies set up a new South-East Asia Command (SEAC). SEAC was intended to strengthen the Allied command structure in the region. It was headed by Vice Admiral Louis Mountbatten of the Royal Navy. Stilwell was Mountbatten's deputy. British lieutenant-general William Slim became commander of the Fourteenth Army in Burma.

SEAC's plan

SEAC launched several major campaigns in Burma in late 1943. Its plan had two parts. Slim's Fourteenth Army would attempt another invasion of northwest Burma, in the area known as the Arakan. At the same time, Stilwell's North China Area Command (NCAC) would strike through northern Burma. It would be supported by a second Chindit operation. NCAC's target was Myitkyina (pronounced "mitchenaw"). The town contained a Japanese airfield and lay on the route from India.

The second Arakan invasion began in December 1943. British, Indian, and West African troops pushed down either side of the Mayu mountain range. Their target was Akyab, a coastal town that contained a major airfield and port.

Japanese resistance varied widely. In some places the Allies passed through deserted towns. In Razabil, however, the Japanese had built bunkers, machine-gun posts, and booby-traps. British forces spent two months there, and lost hundreds of dead.

An Indian division, meanwhile, set up a supply area of about half a square mile (1sqkm) at Sinzweya on the Ngakye-dauk Pass. The area was known as the "Admin Box." It received vital daily air-drops of supplies. That made it a natural target for the Japanese.

Japanese offensive

The Japanese were planning a major invasion of eastern India. Their first target was the Allied base at Imphal. To aid the invasion, they launched Operation Ha-go on February 3 against the British Arakan offensive. A large force headed directly north into the path of the British. Other columns threatened

Indian Forces in Burma

The bulk of the "British" forces in Burma were actually Indian troops serving in the Indian Army. Indians made up 700,000 of the million troops available to Mountbatten under his South-East Asia Command (SEAC). The Indian Eastern Army carried out the Arakan operations in Burma in 1942 and 1943. It later became the Fourteenth Army, under the command of Lieutenant-General William Slim.

Between 1942 and 1945, India contributed 10 divisions and four brigades to the Burma campaign. They effectively won the theater for the Allies. Britain had a difficult relationship with its Indian colony, however. At the start of the war, less than 10 percent of Indian Army officers were Indian. The rest were British. The Indian forces had also suffered years of underfunding. Nevertheless, the Indian divisions remained fiercely loyal to the Allied cause. About 40,000 died in action in Burma.

▼ Vice Admiral Louis Mountbatten, commander of SEAC, reviews Sikh troops of the Indian Army at Imphal in 1944.

the Allied flanks. Ha-go was designed to draw Allied reinforcements into the Arakan. That would leave fewer troops to defend Imphal.

For a time, it looked as if the Japanese plan would work. The Admin Box was soon under siege by more than 5,000 Japanese soldiers. Some Japanese units reached the sea at the Bay of Bengal. However, the main force was low on supplies. It did not have sufficient troops or aircraft to deliver a knock-out blow. British relief columns were now cutting down from the north. On February 24, the Japanese abandoned Ha-go. Building on their success, the British captured Buthidaung and Razabil by March 12.

Meanwhile, Stilwell was making progress in northern Burma. He had begun his push toward Myitkyina in October 1943. Japanese counterattacks halted him in November. Stilwell steadied his position. In February 1944, he was ready to renew the march. This time his Chinese troops were supported by 3,000 U.S. soldiers. Led by Brigadier-General Frank D. Merrill, they were popularly known as "Merrill's Marauders." They were tough veterans trained in guerrilla techniques. By May 16, Stilwell had captured Myitkyina airfield.

The Chindits

Supporting Stilwell's operation was a Chindit force of 26,000 men. Their commander, Orde Wingate, sent about half of his men to establish a series of strongholds in the jungle southeast of Myitkyina. They would be resupplied by air. Some Chindits advanced to the strongholds overland from India. Most, however, were deployed by glider and transport aircraft. By mid-March, more than 9,000 Chindits were in the strongholds. They began operations

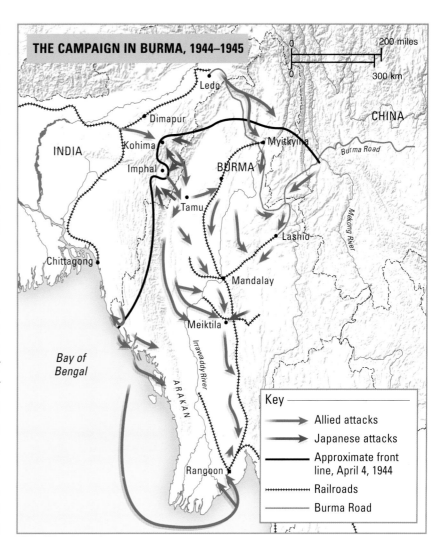

THE CAMPAIGN IN BURMA, 1944–1945

Key

→ Allied attacks
→ Japanese attacks
— Approximate front line, April 4, 1944
┅┅┅ Railroads
— Burma Road

▲ Between April 1944 and May 1945, the Allies were able to liberate Burma, save for small pockets of resistance.

◀ A U.S.-Chinese reconnaissance unit in Stuart M3 light tanks checks the Ledo Road in Burma, part of the land route to China.

Merrill's Marauders

Merrill's Marauders were formed as a result of President Franklin D. Roosevelt's wish to have U.S. troops similar to Britain's Chindit brigades. The Marauders were to spearhead Chinese Army operations in northern Burma. Their task was to disrupt Japanese supply lines and positions while an attempt was made to reopen the Burma Road.

Approximately 2,900 U.S. volunteers joined the 5307th Composite Unit (Provisional). The unit was popularly known as Merrill's Marauders after its leader, Brigadier General Frank Merrill. It gathered in India in late 1943.

In five major and many minor engagements, the Marauders defeated veteran Japanese forces that vastly outnumbered them. Their behind-the-lines operations culminated in the capture of Myitkyina Airfield, the only all-weather airfield in northern Burma.

Merrill's Marauders eventually became the 75th Ranger Regiment, which still has a role in behind-the-lines assault operations.

◄ Marauders lead a mule on a mission. Mules were vital for carrying supplies. They were landed from gliders.

against Japanese headquarters, troop movements, and supply lines.

The Chindit strongholds attracted massive Japanese infantry assaults. The Chindits became exhausted from resisting attacks, or fell sick with tropical diseases such as malaria. They also lost their leader when Wingate was killed in an air crash on March 24. By July, almost every Chindit soldier still alive was either injured or sick. They were also suffering from malnutrition. Stilwell demanded that the Chindits stay in place. The British, however, flew them all out of Burma by August 27.

Merrill's Marauders had had a similarly tough time. They were fatigued and their numbers had been

▶ Joseph Stilwell awards medals to exhausted troops from Merrill's Marauders after the capture of the town of Myitkyina in August 1944.

reduced. The town of Myitkyina fell on August 3, but operations in northern Burma had resulted in more than 5,000 Allied casualties. By now, moreover, the Allies had other worries farther west.

Imphal and Kohima

By early 1944, the Japanese knew that the British were building up forces in eastern India ready for a major land offensive to reconquer Burma. The Japanese wanted to defeat any offensive before it could begin. They planned Operation U-go. The operation had two main objectives. It would isolate and capture the Allied communications and supply centers at Imphal and Kohima in Manipur. It would also cut

the railroad through Dimapur to the northwest. The line provided the Allies in Burma with many of their supplies.

U-go was carried out by the Japanese Fifteenth Army led by Lieutenant-General Renya Mutaguchi. It began on the night of March 7–8, when 100,000 men began crossing the Chindwin River. One division headed for Kohima, two others for Imphal. Mutaguchi had to move quickly to beat the monsoon rains. He was also relying on capturing Imphal to resupply his troops.

Slim knew from intelligence reports that U-go was coming, but the experienced Japanese troops made rapid headway. Allied rearguard actions and an orderly retreat, however, meant that

▼ Japanese troops use a raft to cross a river at the start of the U-go campaign in eastern India.

William Slim (1891–1970)

William Joseph Slim entered military service at the outbreak of World War I in 1914. He rose to become a battalion commander. He was seriously wounded during the war, and won the Military Cross. After the war, he served in the Indian Army. By the start of the war in 1939, he was a brigadier.

Slim commanded the 10th Indian Infantry Brigade and the 10th Indian Division in Africa from 1940. In March 1942, he was sent to Burma to take charge of the Burma Corps. He was also promoted to lieutenant-general. Slim took charge of the Fourteenth Army. He rose to public prominence after he led the Allies to success at Imphal and Kohima.

Slim oversaw the final Allied victory in Burma. He became commander-in-chief of land forces of the South-East Asia Command (SEAC). After the war, Slim became a field marshal. He was governor-general of Australia from 1953 to 1960. He died in London on December 14, 1970.

▶ William Slim led a successful fighting retreat from Rangoon in 1942 and won celebrated victories at Imphal and Kohima.

▼ Japanese troops prepare to cross a Burmese river during the U-go advance in March 1944.

the Japanese were unable to destroy any Allied formation. In addition, Mountbatten organized a rapid airlift of troops from the Arakan to reinforce Imphal.

It still seemed, however, that the Japanese might achieve their primary goals. They cut the one road between Imphal and Kohima on March 29. On April 4, they isolated Kohima. The next day, Imphal was almost entirely encircled. Only one track was open into the town from the west. Both Imphal and Kohima were now effectively under siege.

Remarkable resistance

The Kohima garrison was tiny compared with the Japanese division surrounding it. It was spread thinly over a large number of hill positions in and around the town. The British XXXIII Corps was advancing from India to relieve the siege, but it had to be quick. Slowly the Kohima garrison lost many of its positions to the numerically superior enemy.

The Japanese also suffered many casualties. Their commanders were astonished by the strength of the resistance. The fighting was frequently hand to hand. Yet the Allied position was slipping. Soldiers of XXXIII Corps began to break into the town on April

14. It relieved the Kohima garrison on April 18, with only hours to spare.

The British moved to clear the area. XXXIII Corps trapped the Japanese 31st Division between advances from the south and north. Both sides suffered heavy casualties and supply shortages. The British had the advantage, however. They could airlift in supplies and reinforcements. They also had overwhelming artillery superiority. By the end of May, the 31st Division was beaten. The Japanese had lost 6,000 men around Kohima, the Allies 4,000.

The relief of Imphal

Now XXXIII Corps could push south to relieve Imphal, which was locked in its own desperate struggle. Imphal was better defended than Kohima, however. It had artillery to pound the surrounding jungle with huge barrages. It was also supported by tanks, against which the Japanese had no real defense. The Royal Air Force kept up an impressive supply lift. It delivered over 1 million gallons (4.5 million liters) of fuel for Allied vehicles.

On June 22, XXXIII Corps met up with forces from Imphal. The 88-day siege was broken. On July 18, most of the surviving Japanese forces began to retreat across the Chindwin. Operation U-go had cost them 65,000 dead from battle, starvation, or disease. The British had suffered 17,000 casualties, but they had effectively destroyed the Japanese offensive capability in Burma.

▲ British troops man a defensive position near Imphal. The defeat of the Japanese at Imphal and Kohima changed the course of the war in Burma.

369

Eyewitness

❝ In a moment Lieutenant Wright's India Sappers were up against the buildings, blasting in the walls. The men streamed in after them, shooting and bayoneting as they went. Then all was confusion, with cursing, sweating, struggling men killing each other in the narrow confines, among the piles of stores and crates and in amongst the ovens. Donald, who had led the attack into the first building, soon cleared it of the enemy and climbed up on the crates so that he could see what was going on around him. One by one he saw the buildings empty as his men came out, smeared with blood, with clothing scorched and torn, all exhausted after the nervous tension of the attack, the horror of the bayoneting, and the exertion of hand-to-hand combat. ❞

Arthur Campbell, British soldier, describing assaults on Japanese-held buildings at Kohima, 1944.

▲ Troops of the 17th Indian Division prepare to fire a mortar in the city of Meiktila in Burma.

▼ Alongside an M3 Grant tank, Gurkhas and British infantry advance toward the enemy at Kohima.

The road to Mandalay

The British pushed the Japanese into retreat. Allied troops began crossing the Chindwin on November 19. They soon met up with elements of Stilwell's NCAC advancing from the north.

The new commander of the Japanese Burma Area Army, General Hoyotaro Kumura, now tried to draw the advancing Allies into a trap. The Allies were heading toward Mandalay. Burma's second-largest city stood in the center of the country. Kumura hoped that the Allies would overstretch their supply lines. When they crossed the Irrawaddy River north of the city, his Thirty-third Army would destroy them.

Slim, however, second-guessed Kumura. He sent troops to cross the river south of Mandalay. They pushed forward to capture a vital Japanese communications center at Meiktila on March 3, 1945.

Burma reconquered

Kumura pulled his troops away from Mandalay. He began a bitter campaign to retake Meiktila. The Allies took Mandalay on March 20. Now XXXIII

Corps advanced to relieve Meiktila's defenders. Trapped between two Allied forces, Kumura ordered a retreat to the east.

Following the capture of Meiktila, the British began a rapid two-pronged advance down through Burma. Their target was the capital, Rangoon, in the far south. Burmese towns and cities fell in rapid succession. By May 1, troops were only about 50 miles (80km) from Rangoon. The next day, a division from the Arakan made an amphibious landing south of the city. Its Japanese defenders were trapped between northern and southern advances. The Japanese evacuated the city, which on May 3 fell into Allied hands.

The capture of Rangoon effectively brought the Japanese occupation of Burma to an end. Sporadic clashes continued, but no further major battles occurred. To the north of Burma in China, however, the fighting continued in earnest.

China's war

From the end of 1943, Japan was on the back foot in the Pacific and Southeast Asia. In China, however, it still had a clear supremacy over the Nationalist army of Chiang Kai-shek. Japan had now occupied most of eastern China.

China's southwest, however, was home to Allied airbases. U.S. and Chinese aircraft used the bases to strike at Japanese supply ships sailing from Indochina through the South and East China Seas. As the United States began to produce longer-range bombers, the airbases would become even more of a threat. The introduction of the B-29 Superfortress would bring the Japanese

▼ Allied troops shelter behind a wall during street fighting in Mandalay in May 1945.

▶ A member of the Japanese Fifteenth Army in Burma receives a welcome drink after surrendering to Allied forces.

Mars Task Force

Merrill's Marauders were disbanded in August 1944. They were replaced by the 5332nd Brigade (Provisional), also known as the Mars Task Force. The brigade was put together from the 475th Infantry and 124th Cavalry Regiments. It also included some former Marauders and conducted a similar range of operations as the earlier group.

Operating deep behind enemy lines, the task force harassed the Japanese in northern and central Burma. It blew up bridges and attacked enemy convoys and patrols. It also helped to clear the Burma road to China.

The task force included 24 Military Intelligence Service (MIS) linguists. The linguists crept through the jungle to hide close to Japanese positions. They reported the conversations they

heard. This intelligence helped the Allies to pinpoint Japanese supply bases. It also gave them advance warning of enemy troop movements.

▲ Members of the Mars Task Force in action in Burma.

homeland in reach of direct bomber strikes from the Chinese mainland.

The Japanese wanted to counter this threat. In April 1944, they launched one of their largest offensives of the war. The operation was code-named Ichi-go. It planned to use more than 400,000 soldiers to occupy southern China from the border with Indochina north to Changsha. The 500-mile-long (804km) stretch of territory held the key Allied airbases. It would also give the Japanese an unbroken rail link from Indochina up to Beijing in northeastern China.

Japan's victory

The Chinese army in the region numbered 300,000 men. To begin with, they were no match for the highly trained Japanese. Chinese resistance toughened around Hengchow, however. The city eventually fell on August 8, after a three-week siege that cost the Japanese 20,000 casualties.

By the end of the year, the Japanese had accomplished almost all of their objectives. They had captured five Allied airfields, from Hengyang to Nanning. They also threatened the Chinese Nationalist capital at Chungking. For a time it looked as if China was facing total defeat.

End of the offensive

By now, Japan's troops and supply lines were overstretched. By late 1944, China's army was also undergoing major reforms. Stilwell had fallen out with Chiang. He was replaced as chief of staff by Major-General Albert Wedemeyer. Under Wedemeyer, the Nationalist army re-equipped many of its divisions and improved training. It went on the offensive in December and clawed back many of Japan's gains.

Meanwhile, the Japanese withdrew to the Chinese coastline, to guard against a possible U.S. invasion.

In March and April 1945, Japan still had the strength to mount two large offensives in central China. They aimed to capture more U.S. airfields. These offensives had some success, despite the resistance of the Chinese Army.

Japan's Chinese possessions were looking increasingly threatened, however. On May 9, the Japanese High Command ordered its units to pull out of southern China. The imperial Japanese sun was setting over East Asia.

▼ U.S.-trained Chinese troops march toward a railroad station.

RETAKING THE PHILIPPINES: 1944–1945

General Douglas MacArthur had left the Philippines in March 1942, when the Japanese occupied the islands. He was determined to fulfill his promise to return. In fall 1944, his chance finally came.

The first U.S. landings in the Philippines took place on the island of Leyte on October 20, 1944. A desperate Japanese naval attack was defeated at the battle of Leyte Gulf, and the U.S. Sixth Army landed on Leyte, in the southern half of the islands. It was led by General Walter Krueger. Leyte was guarded by 22,000 Japanese troops. In one day, however, 134,000 U.S. troops landed, including MacArthur himself.

Japan had 224,000 troops throughout the Philippines. They were led by General Tomoyuki Yamashita. He was one of Japan's best military commanders. Yamashita had fortified large areas of the Philippines. There were not many Japanese guarding the coast, however. Yamashita's plan was to let U.S. forces land. His defenders would then attack them as they moved into the interior of the islands.

▼ U.S. infantry take cover during landings on the Philippine island of Cebu on March 25, 1945.

The first Japanese plan for the defense of the Philippines was named Sho-1. It concentrated most Japanese troops on Luzon. Luzon was the largest island, in the north of the chain. It contained the Philippine capital, Manila.

Changes to Sho-1

After the landings on Leyte, Yamashita changed Sho-1. He sent about 60,000 reinforcements to Leyte. As U.S. troops pushed inland, they faced strong Japanese defenses. The country was mountainous. There were many hidden bunkers and mines. The

torrential monsoon rains turned the ground to mud. It also kept U.S. aircraft on the ground and stopped U.S. engineers from building new airfields.

Fighting on Leyte was fierce. In November the Japanese even launched their own offensive. It was defeated. On December 7,

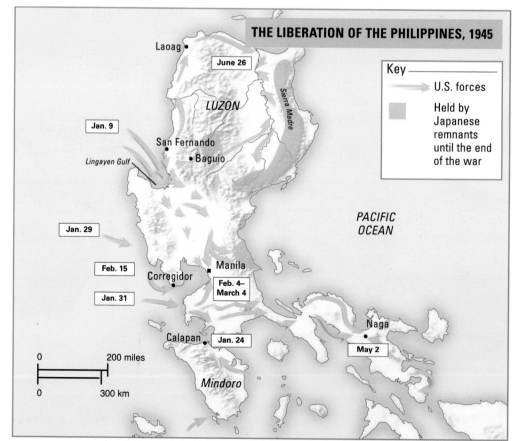

▲ After the first landings on Leyte, U.S. troops take cover as enemy fire passes overhead.

THE LIBERATION OF THE PHILIPPINES, 1945

Laoag

June 26

LUZON

Jan. 9

San Fernando

Baguio

Lingayen Gulf

Sierra Madre

Jan. 29

Feb. 15

Corregidor

Manila

Feb. 4–March 4

Jan. 31

Naga

May 2

Calapan

Jan. 24

Mindoro

PACIFIC OCEAN

Key

→ U.S. forces

▮ Held by Japanese remnants until the end of the war

0   200 miles
0   300 km

► The U.S. landings on Luzon and the liberation of the Philippines January–June 1945.

Krueger landed more troops at the coastal town of Ormoc. By the next day, Leyte was under U.S. control. The only pockets of Japanese defenders left were isolated in the mountains. They no longer represented a threat. The Japanese had lost 70,000 men. There were 15,000 U.S. casualties.

Mindoro and Luzon

MacArthur's next objectives were Luzon and a large island to its southwest, Mindoro. Mindoro was rocky, so it was perfect for building airfields. U.S. troops heading for Mindoro were attacked by kamikaze suicide aircraft. After they landed on the island on December 15, however, they soon captured it. They quickly built two airstrips.

Aircraft from Mindoro would support the capture of Luzon. Yamashita had more than 200,000 men on Luzon. Most were in the Sierra Madre mountains in the northeast and near Manila. Manila itself was occupied by only 17,000 troops.

On January 9, 1945, the U.S. Sixth Army began landing at Lingayen Gulf in western Luzon. American ships came under attack from Japanese aircraft. On land, however, the invading troops met little resistance.

Toward Manila

The U.S. offensive split into two. XIV Corps headed toward Manila. It made good progress to begin with. Meanwhile, I Corps spread out east and north. It advanced slowly through difficult terrain and hard fighting. Both sides suffered many casualties.

The advance on Manila slowed down after January 23. There were 30,000 Japanese troops guarding the outskirts of the city. U.S. forces captured Clark

Filipino guerrilla fighters

The Japanese occupiers of the Philippines faced strong resistance. Filipino resistance groups formed in the islands' jungle-covered interiors. They often included many former soldiers, as well as sympathetic civilians. There were numerous groups, which had different motives. All, however, wanted to end the occupation. They became an invaluable asset to the U.S. forces in the Pacific.

The Filipino guerrillas provided valuable intelligence to U.S. forces. They also committed acts of sabotage against the Japanese, and rescued downed U.S. pilots. During the U.S. military campaign in the Philippines, the guerrillas took over many mopping-up operations. This helped take pressure off battle-weary U.S. units.

▲ These young Filipino guerrillas fought with U.S. forces on Mindanao in 1945. About a million Filipinos died during the war.

Field airbase outside Manila, however. Several days later, more U.S. landings began around Manila Bay. U.S. troops now surrounded the Philippine capital.

By the end of the first week of February, U.S. forces were pushing into Manila. Yamashita ordered his forces to

▶ U.S. troops make a cautious advance in a plantation on Luzon. Dense vegetation made good cover for enemy defenders.

▼ While larger ships wait offshore, smaller landing craft carry troops to the beaches of Luzon on January 9, 1945.

leave the city. Instead, the local commander in Manila decided to fight to the death. For a month, battle raged in the streets of the old walled city in the center of Manila. The fighting destroyed much of the city. It cost more than 100,000 lives before the city was finally captured by the Americans on March 3.

The capture of Manila was far from the end the fighting on Luzon. Battles carried on throughout the island until the end of the war in August. The Japanese proved impossible to defeat in the mountains. Between February and April, however, U.S. forces seized the fortified island of Corregidor (*see box*). They also captured the huge concrete blockhouse at Fort Drum. On April 13, U.S. engineers poured 3,000 gallons (13,500 liters) of gasoline into the fort.

Corregidor

Corregidor was an island fortress that guarded the mouth of Manila Bay. Before the Japanese conquest in 1942, it had been the U.S. military headquarters in the Philippines. It now had to be taken back from the Japanese to secure the route through the bay.

On January 23, 1945, U.S. aircraft began bombing Corregidor. They were later joined by naval artillery. On February 16, U.S. paratroopers dropped onto the island. Meanwhile, infantry units landed from the sea on the east of the island.

Corregidor had 5,000 Japanese defenders, who put up stiff resistance. They took refuge in Corregidor's underground tunnel network. U.S. engineers blew up the mouths of the tunnels. Hundreds of Japanese soldiers were trapped inside and died. Sometimes the fighting in the tunnels blew up underground ammunition dumps. On February 21, a huge explosion blew up Malinta Hill on the island in a volcano-like blast. Corregidor was finally secured on March 1. The United States had suffered nearly 100 casualties in the action.

They set fire to the building, which was destroyed. The Americans now had control of Manila Bay. By the end of June, U.S. forces controlled most of the coast. About 50,000 Japanese soldiers were still stuck in the Luzon mountains. They had no way of getting reinforcements or supplies. They were still there at the end of the war. By then, many were starving.

Clearing up

The U.S. Eighth Army was led by Lieutenant-General Robert Eichelberger. Its job was to occupy the dozens of islands that made up the southern Philippines. Over four months, the Eighth Army made 52 amphibious landings. There was some fierce fighting. Most of the landings met only limited resistance, however.

◄ This view shows the devastated northwestern part of Manila in April 1945, a month after the city was liberated by U.S. forces.

379

▶ A machine-gun crew on Corregidor waits to fire on any survivors of a phosphorus charge set off by U.S. paratroopers against a Japanese fortification.

Rape of Manila

U.S. forces closed in on Manila in February 1945. Rear-Admiral Sanji Iwabuchi, the commander of the 17,000-strong Japanese garrison, ordered the fortification of the city. Despite orders to withdraw, he was determined to make a last stand. As U.S. forces began to enter the city, street-to-street and house-to-house fighting broke out.

The civilian population was caught between the opposing sides. Thousands died in crossfire, or as a result of the bombardment that destroyed many buildings. The Japanese also executed thousands of civilians as the Americans advanced. Encircled Japanese troops hid underground in tunnels and sewers. The Americans fought them with grenades and flamethrowers.

The fighting ended in early March. By that time, Iwabuchi's force of 17,000 men had suffered 13,500 dead. U.S. forces had suffered 6,500 casualties, including 1,000 dead. The death toll among civilians, however, was about 100,000. The old city of Manila was largely ruined. Liberation had proved a hollow victory.

◀ U.S. paratroopers patrol in the historic center of Manila, destroyed in the fighting.

▲ A U.S. column marches inland from the beaches on Mindanao.

It was a different story on Mindanao, the largest island in the southern Philippines. The fighting there was as difficult as it had been on Luzon or Leyte. The Japanese had about 43,000 men on the island who were determined to resist the invasion.

Battle for Mindanao

The main U.S. landings came on April 17, 1945, near Illana Bay on the south of the island. The landings met little opposition. However, as the U.S. troops moved across the island, they met great resistance.

They advanced nearly 200 miles east (320km) to the port of Davao. The advance led through hot, thick jungle that exhausted the troops. Many suffered from sunstroke or got sick with disease. They also came under attack from the Japanese.

U.S. troops took Davao without opposition on May 3. In the north of the island, however, fierce fighting went on until the middle of June. Pockets of Japanese resistance remained on Mindanao until the end of the war. By June 30, however, it was effectively in U.S. hands. That meant that the Philippines themselves were back in U.S. hands.

A promise fulfilled

In total nearly 200,000 people had lost their lives during the campaign for the Philippines. They included more than 100,000 civilians. MacArthur, however, could now say he had fulfilled the promise he had made to the Filippinos back in 1942—"I shall return."

381

TOWARD JAPAN: IWO JIMA AND OKINAWA

By the end of 1944, U.S. forces were nearing a position from where they could attack Japan itself. Nearing Japan, they took part in two battles that would be among the hardest and most costly of the Pacific War.

At the start of 1945, General Douglas MacArthur was fighting to liberate the Philippines. In the central Pacific, meanwhile, Admiral Chester Nimitz was preparing for a final drive that would bring U.S. forces within range of the Japanese home islands. The drive depended on the capture of two islands: Iwo Jima and Okinawa.

Iwo Jima

Iwo Jima is a tiny island of volcanic rock and black sand. It has no natural water supply and covers just 8 square miles (21.7sqkm). Its capture was vital to the U.S. war effort, how-

ever. It was one of the inner ring of islands protecting mainland Japan. It also lay almost exactly halfway between the Japanese home islands and the Marianas, which had been occupied by U.S. forces in mid-1944. The Marianas had important air

bases. From late fall 1944, long-range B-29 Superfortress bombers from the islands had launched attacks on the Japanese mainland.

A natural fortress

Iwo Jima had two completed airfields. Japanese fighter aircraft used the island to attack the U.S. bombers. The U.S. plan was to use the same airfields for long-range fighters to protect the bombers. The airfields could also provide emergency runways for damaged bombers. The capture of Iwo Jima would also be a huge blow to Japanese morale. The island was a Japanese territory, governed by the Tokyo Prefecture, part of Japan itself.

The island was shaped like a pork chop. Its terrain made it a natural fortress. In the south, the 500-foot (150m) Mount Suribachi, an extinct volcano, towered over the island. In the center was an area of volcanic sand that was difficult going for both infantry and vehicles. To the north, a series of deep ravines and rocky ridges made ideal defensive positions.

An amphibious landing would also be difficult, because of heavy surf and beaches that shelved steeply. The island had no natural harbor for landing troops or supplies.

The island was defended by 21,000 Japanese. The commander, Major-General Tadamichi Kuribayashi, had worked hard to

▼ U.S. Marines take cover from Japanese fire on a beach of black volcanic sand on Iwo Jima, March 5, 1945. Mount Suribachi rises behind them.

B-29 Superfortress

The U.S. B-29 Superfortress was the most technically advanced long-range bomber of World War II. The air force ordered it from Boeing in August 1940. A prototype took off in September 1942, but the aircraft only began flying combat missions in the middle of 1944.

A fleet of about 500 B-29s then began operations against Japan, largely from bases in the Marianas. Each aircraft had a crew of between 10 and 14 men. The Superfortress had a top speed of around 350 miles per hour (560km/h), a ceiling of 36,000 feet (10,973m), and a range of 5,830 miles (9,328km).

B-29s were in combat for around 15 months. Some 414 were lost, most through mechanical failure, along with 3,015 crew. In 34,790 missions, B-29s dropped about 170,000 tons of bombs. Their gunners were credited with shooting down 1,128 Japanese aircraft. In all, Boeing built about 3,700 B-29s. The last aircraft was finally retired from active service in the mid-1950s.

◄ B-29 Superfortresses fly in formation. The B-29s were attacked by enemy fighters based on Iwo Jima before U.S. Marines captured the island's air bases.

add to the natural defenses, especially around Mount Suribachi and in the north. He had built one of the most formidable defensive complexes of the war. It had miles of tunnels and trenches, hundreds of underground emplacements, antitank ditches, and minefields.

Desperate defense

Kuribayashi knew that the garrison had no hope of any outside help and could not withdraw from the island. He ordered his men to fight and die in their trenches. They should kill as many of the enemy as possible, using the network of tunnels to get behind the enemy. He also called for volunteers to join Human Combat Tank Destruction Squads. Joining a squad meant almost certain death. Kuribayashi chose not to oppose the initial landings on the beaches. He would lure the U.S. troops inland into the web of defensive positions in the interior.

U.S. Marine Corps

Marines are the U.S. Navy's amphibious soldiers. They also control their own air force. Marine units had a vital role in the Pacific campaign during World War II. At the start of the war in 1939, the corps had just 19,000 soldiers and 641 pilots. It also lacked the equipment and expertise necessary to conduct assault landings. In August 1942, however, it was Marines who launched the first counterattack against the Japanese when they landed on Guadalcanal.

The Marines fought throughout the campaign. They made their final assault on Okinawa in April 1945. The corps grew enormously during the campaign. By the end of the war, it comprised some 485,000 personnel. The corps suffered heavy losses because it was at the forefront of the bitterest fighting in the Pacific. Its 91,718 total casualties included 24,511 killed.

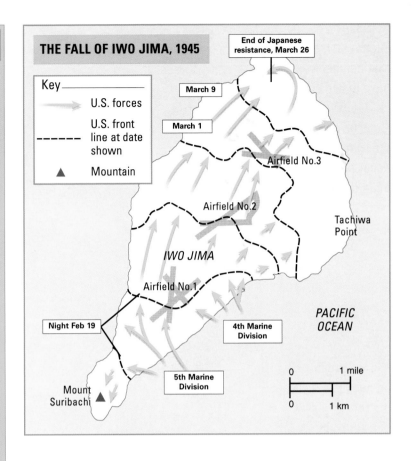

THE FALL OF IWO JIMA, 1945

Key
- → U.S. forces
- ----- U.S. front line at date shown
- ▲ Mountain

End of Japanese resistance, March 26

March 9

March 1

Airfield No.3

Airfield No.2

Tachiwa Point

IWO JIMA

Airfield No.1

PACIFIC OCEAN

Night Feb 19

4th Marine Division

5th Marine Division

Mount Suribachi ▲

0 — 1 mile
0 — 1 km

The U.S. invasion

The U.S. invasion was code-named Operation Detachment. It was planned for February 19, 1945. Preparations for the attack had begun in June 1944, when U.S. bombers began attacking the island. The bombing raids grew in intensity from December 8. For the next 72 days, Iwo Jima was bombed every day in what was the longest and heaviest aerial bombardment of the whole Pacific War. Three days

▲ U.S. Marines captured Iwo Jima's three airfields to establish an air base for the planned Allied attack on Japan.

◀ Marines rest in a command post only 30 yards (27m) behind the front line on Iwo Jima.

385

▶ U.S. Army infantrymen and a Marine check a cave in Iwo Jima for Japanese. The many lava caves of the island provided cover for pockets of Japanese who were determined not to surrender.

▼ The landings on Iwo Jima were the responsibility of V Amphibious Corps, led by Major-General Harry Schmidt.

before the landings, six battleships and five cruisers began pounding key sectors of the island around the clock.

The landings involved some 800 warships, manned by a total of 220,000 crew. About 110,000 troops were to take part in the initial assault or follow-on landings. The landings themselves were the responsibility of three Marine divisions under the command of Major-General Harry Schmidt. One was going into action for the first time.

The landing

The first assault wave hit the landing beaches on Iwo Jima's southwest coast at 09:30 A.M. on February 19. Confused, close-quarter fighting broke out. U.S. forces took the first airfield the next day, but their progress then slowed right down.

The 28th Marines were on the western flank of the landing beaches. It was their task to take Mount Suribachi. It took five days of intense combat before the first patrol reached the summit on February 23. They hoisted the Stars and Stripes, but the flag was too small to be seen by the troops still on the beaches. A larger flag was raised later in the day. The moment was captured in one of the war's most memorable photographs, taken by Joe Rosenthal (*see volume 10, page 57*).

The second airfield fell on February 27, but the fighting for the island was far from over. The Marines' slow advance north faced two of Kuribayashi's main defensive lines. Marine casualties mounted steadily, particularly among

Eyewitness

" After every Japanese volley, Corsair fighter planes streamed down on the mortar position, ripping their charges of bombs into the Wilderness…. Cracks in the earth run along the open field to the left of the Wilderness, and hot smoke seeped up through the cracks. Gains were counted in terms of 100 or 200 yards [90-180m] a day, in terms of three or four bunkers knocked out. Losses were counted in terms of three or four men suddenly turned into bloody rags after the howl of a mortar shell, in terms of a flame-thrower man hit by a grenade as he poured flame into a bunker. The assault platoon of flame throwers and demolitionists, spearheading the regiment's push through the Wilderness, lost two assistant squad leaders killed. "

Unidentified combat reporter,
at the "Wilderness," near No.2 Airfield, Iwo Jima

◀ U.S. troops unload supplies from huge landing craft at Iwo Jima. All supplies had to be shipped in: The barren island did not even have its own source of fresh water.

Simon Bolivar Buckner (1886–1945)

Simon Bolivar Buckner was born in Kentucky, the son of a Confederate general of the Civil War. He went to West Point, and from 1908 to 1918 he served in the military in the United States and the Philippines. In the 1920s and 1930s, he worked in military administration and instruction. He spent the first years of World War II in Alaska, but was made commander of the Tenth Army for the landings on Okinawa in 1944.

Buckner did not live to see the island secured. Early on June 18, he went to see the progress being made by the 8th Marines. At the front, he was spotted by enemy artillery. He was killed in an explosion, either by a shell splinter or by a fragment of coral blown off a boulder.

Buckner had been criticized for how he was leading the battle. Some other U.S. commanders suggested that, rather than batter away at strong Japanese defense lines, it would have been less costly in lives to have mounted a further amphibious assault behind those lines, on the south coast of the island.

▼ Buckner came under considerable criticism for his campaign on Okinawa. Critics dubbed the operation a "fiasco."

junior and noncommissioned officers. One position, a ravine only 700 yards (650m) long, took 10 days to capture. The Marines named the place "Bloody Gorge." By mid-March, however, the Japanese had largely been driven into the northern tip of Iwo Jima.

A famous victory

The island was declared secure on March 26. The 36 days of fighting had taken a terrible toll on both sides. Some 5,931 Marines had been killed and 17,372 wounded. There were also about 2,800 naval casualties. Many had been caused during a kamikaze attack on February 21. Nimitz wrote that: "Among the Americans who served on Iwo Jima, uncommon valor was a common virtue."

The precise number of Japanese dead is not known. Only 216 men surrendered during the fighting, although another 900 or so surrendered later. The rest of the 21,000 troops died.

Strategic advantage

Iwo Jima's strategic value to the United States was huge. Seabees (Construction Battalion engineers) had begun improving its airfields while the fighting was still going on. By early March, the first damaged B-29 had made an emergency landing there. The 15th Fighter Group also arrived to act as escorts for the Superfortresses.

The intensity of the fighting for Iwo Jima worried U.S. commanders and politicians. The Japanese had been willing to die almost to a man to protect a tiny part of their homeland. They had inflicted severe losses on the U.S. forces. How many more casualties would result from an invasion of the Japanese home islands themselves?

◀ A U.S. Landing Craft Infantry (LCI) approaches Okinawa on March 31, 1945. Behind it, a warship fires a salvo of rockets toward the beach defenses.

▼ The might of the U.S. armed forces: Tanks move inland on Okinawa as landing craft approach and leave the beach in the background.

The battle for Okinawa

The next U.S. step toward Japan was Okinawa. The island is the largest in the Ryukyu group. It lay between Kyushu, the most southerly of Japan's home islands, and Formosa (now known as Taiwan). The island would serve as a forward base for the first stage of the invasion of the home islands, which was planned for November.

The amphibious landings on Okinawa were code-named Operation Iceberg. Preparations began in mid-March 1944. U.S. and British carrier aircraft began attacking Japanese airfields on Kyushu and Formosa to isolate Okinawa. The Japanese struck back with kamikaze attacks against the carriers and their escorts. They had only limited success, however.

In the last week of March, Okinawa itself came under naval bombardment and air attack. The assault on the island was to be a joint Army–Navy operation.

The main landing force, General Simon Bolivar Buckner's Tenth Army, had five army and three Marine divisions, a total of 182,000 men. It was supported by a vast armada of warships.

389

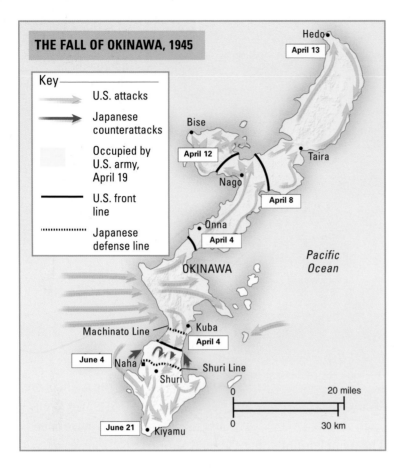

THE FALL OF OKINAWA, 1945

Key

→ U.S. attacks

➡ Japanese counterattacks

Occupied by U.S. army, April 19

━━ U.S. front line

┈┈┈ Japanese defense line

Hedo • April 13

Bise

April 12

Taira

Nago

April 8

Onna

April 4

OKINAWA

Pacific Ocean

Machinato Line

Kuba

April 4

June 4 Naha

Shuri Line

Shuri

0   20 miles

0   30 km

June 21 • Kiyamu

Iceberg begins

The landings began on April 1. The first U.S. troops ashore faced little resistance. The Japanese commander, Lieutenant-General Mitsuru Ushijima, wanted to draw the Americans inland. There his 130,000-strong garrison manned three defensive lines in the southern half of the island.

On April 4, U.S. forces reached the Machinato Line. It took nearly three weeks to batter a way through. On April 28, they ran into the even stronger Shuri Line. Again, they made slow progress and suffered heavy casualties.

After a major Japanese counterattack, the Tenth Army made an all-out attempt to break the line on April 11. Despite terrible weather, Buckner's men had broken through by the end of the month. The Japanese were penned behind their final defensive line across

▲ Map showing the fighting on the island of Okinawa, April 1–June 21. U.S. troops faced stiff resistance from the Japanese.

► Infantrymen watch as a flame-throwing tank burns out enemy defenses on a hill in Okinawa. Flame throwers were highly effective against an enemy dug in to tunnels and caves.

▲ Japanese prisoners of war await questioning on Okinawa on June 21. Only about 1 in 10 Japanese on the island chose to surrender.

the southern tip of the island. It took until June 22 to declare Okinawa secure. Buckner himself had been killed by an artillery shell four days earlier.

Kamikaze raids

The fierce fighting on Okinawa was matched at sea. The Japanese launched Operation Ten-go, an air and naval kamikaze attack against the U.S. warships supporting the landing. Hundreds of aircraft were supported by the great *Yamato*, which had enough fuel to reach Okinawa, but not to return.

Yamato itself did not even reach the battle area. It was sunk by carrier aircraft, along with five of its nine escorts. Kamikaze attacks continued against the U.S. fleet. In all, kamikaze pilots flew some 2,000 sorties off Okinawa. They sank 21 warships, badly crippled a further 43, and damaged another 23.

The reckoning

The fighting on Okinawa had resulted in higher Allied casualties than any other campaign in the Pacific War. The Tenth Army had lost its commander. Another 7,613 other men were dead or missing, and 31,800 were wounded. The U.S. Navy lost about 5,000 men killed and an equal number wounded.

Estimates suggest that about 100,000 Japanese civilians and troops on the island died. Perhaps as many as 10,000 more had been entombed in caves where they took up defensive positions. The Americans blew up the entrances to the caves. About 10,000 Japanese were taken prisoner.

The Japanese had thrown away much of their remaining air and naval power at Okinawa, but no one was left in any doubt that they would fight to the bitter end to protect their homeland.

THE SURRENDER OF JAPAN

With their forces nearing Japan itself, U.S. military planners faced a dilemma. Any invasion of the home islands would likely cause huge casualties, among both U.S. troops and Japanese troops and civilians.

On June 22, 1945, U.S. forces declared Okinawa secure. The occupation of the island marked the end of their long drive across the Central Pacific. They were on Japanese soil, within striking dis-tance of the Japanese home islands. Both sides were planning for what seemed an inevitable U.S. invasion of Japan. They expected this invasion to be the most bloody of the war, with casualty rates reaching new heights.

Japan's defensive preparations

Since April, the Japanese had been carrying out Operation Ketsu-go. The plan distributed about two million regular soldiers to defend the four home islands and Korea. The Japanese also tried to increase their ground forces. On June 23, a new law created the People's Volunteer Combat Corps.

The corps organized civilians into local defense units. They included men aged from 17 to 60 and women aged 17 to 40. There was a shortage of guns, so many units trained to fight any U.S. invaders with bamboo spears and wooden clubs. Propaganda reminded the recruits of their duty to "Defend the National Polity." It also called for them to fight to the end. It would be better, the propaganda argued, to be a part of the "Glorious Death of One Hundred Million," rather than suffer the humiliation of living under U.S. occupation.

Navy and air force

The Imperial Air Force and Navy were also part of the defensive plan. They were greatly weakened, however. The Air Force High Command believed that they would have 800 fighters and bombers available. They formed new kamikaze units that would largely use obsolete aircraft. The U.S. invasion was expected in June. By then, the air force hoped to have trained 3,000 volunteer pilots.

The navy, meanwhile, had 19 destroyers and 38 submarines fit for service. It was so short of fuel that any operations would have to be mainly confined to waters close to home. The surface warships were to operate around Kyushu and southern Honshu. The longer-range submarines were scheduled to attack U.S. naval bases at Ulithi, Leyte, and Okinawa. The shorter-range boats were to attack U.S. supply lines near Japan. The navy also had about 3,295 smaller craft, such as midget torpedoes and explosive motorboats. They were virtual suicide weapons for their crews.

American invasion preparations

U.S. planners drew up a timetable for a two-stage amphibious assault on Japan. Other elements of the armed forces, meanwhile, continued their operations to cripple the enemy's means to wage war. U.S. Navy submarines went on sinking merchant vessels that brought supplies to Japan's industries. Long-range B-29 Superfortresses carried on with their destructive strategic

▼ U.S. personnel crowd the decks of the battleship USS *Missouri* to watch the signing of the Japanese surrender on September 2, 1945.

▲ Members of the People's Volunteer Combat Corps dig defensive ditches in a Japanese city. Both sides expected a U.S. invasion of Japan.

bombing offensive against industrial centers. They also dropped mines to block Japanese ports.

Bombing campaign

The first B-29s of the Twentieth Air Force's XX Bomber Command had arrived at bases in Calcutta, India, in April 1944. They made their first raid, against Japanese targets in Thailand, on June 5.

Under its commander, Major-General Curtis LeMay, the bomber force was soon able to strike Japan itself. It had five lengthened runways built near Chengtu, in western China. On June 15, 68 B-29s from Chengtu struck a steel plant on Kyushu, the most southerly of the Japanese home islands.

The bombers were not based in China. They flew from Calcutta to Chengtu with as much fuel as they could carry. This lessened the bomb load they could carry. From Chengtu they raided targets in southern Manchuria and Formosa (Taiwan), which were under Japanese occupation. Within Japan, they struck targets on Kyushu and in southern Honshu, the largest home island. Tokyo, the Japanese capital, was in central Honshu. It lay beyond the B-29s' range.

New bases

The bomber offensive expanded after the capture of the Marianas in mid-1944. From bases on the islands, B-29s could now strike Tokyo itself. On November 24, 1944, more than 100 B-29s hit an aircraft factory near Tokyo. For the rest of the year, formations of more than 100 Superfortresses attacked Japan's home islands every 5 to 10 days.

The bomber fleets usually sustained losses to Japanese fighters stationed on Iwo Jima, the island halfway between the Marianas and Japan. Those losses stopped after U.S. Marines took the island in March 1945. The skies over Japan were also well defended. By the end of 1944, bomber losses were 6 percent per raid. That was 1 percent over the acceptable maximum level.

Re-evaluating strategy

In January and February 1945, U.S. planners re-evaluated the strategic bombing offensive. It was not proving as effective as they had hoped. The losses were too high, and the accuracy of the attacks was low. The crews were suffering from poor morale.

The bombers' chief problem was the weather. At 30,000 feet (9,144m), high winds often forced them off course. Fog often made accurate bombing impossible, and radar was not very effective at finding targets if visibility was low. Ice formed on the B-29s' wings and windshields, making the aircraft unstable and limiting visibility even more.

The U.S. review resulted in several changes. XX Bomber Command was

Curtis LeMay (1906–1990)

At the outbreak of war, Curtis LeMay was regarded as the U.S. Air Force's leading expert on strategic bombing. He first saw action in 1942, when he was sent to England to command a bomber group making precision bombing raids on Nazi-occupied Europe. LeMay developed the combat box tactic, in which bombers flew in tight formation for protection against enemy fighters. He also adopted pattern bombing, in which planes dropped their bombs together to

▲ Major-General Curtis LeMay (center, with other airforce commanders) developed mass fire raids on Japan.

increase the likelihood of hitting the target.

From August 1944, LeMay led the bombing offensive against Japan. He developed low-level nighttime bombing with incendiaries that devastated Japan's cities. LeMay held numerous senior posts after the war, including that of head of Strategic Air Command, the Cold War bomber force that carried nuclear weapons.

◄ The crew of a B-29 prepare for a mission. The high-altitude bombers had a crew of between 10 and 14 men.

▶ U.S. ground crew on Saipan island in the Marianas watch a B-29 take off on the first bombing raid from the island against Tokyo on March 9, 1945.

▼ U.S. bombers fly past the snow-capped peak of Mount Fuji, one of Japan's main national symbols.

largely relocated from India to the Marianas to join XXI Bomber Command. The combined force was led by Curtis LeMay, the most experienced U.S. bomber commander. LeMay changed bombing tactics. He largely dropped the high-level daylight raids with high-explosive bombs. Instead, the bombers would make low-level night-time attacks. They would drop incendiary bombs designed to start fires.

A new type of bomb

The decision to change bomb type reflected the difficulties of bombing accurately with high explosive. It also reflected the way Japanese industry was organized. It depended on small small firms, with as few as 10 or so workers. The businesses were scattered throughout the major cities, rather than being grouped into industrial zones. The tiny sites were difficult to target with high-explosive bombs.

Most of the structures in Japan's cities were built largely of wood. That meant that raids with incendiaries did not need to be accurate in order to be massively destructive. If high winds helped to fan the flames, the separate blazes would combine to create fire-storms with extreme temperatures. By keeping low, the B-29s could also carry three times as much ordnance as before.

Japanese cities burn

The first raid using the new tactic was made on the night of March 9–10, 1945. Superfortresses flying at just 7,000 feet (2,134m) started firestorms that destroyed 15 square miles (39sqkm) of Tokyo. B-29s flew 1,595 sorties in total over the next five nights. They dropped more incendiaries in just four raids on Tokyo, Nagoya, Osaka, and Kobe than they had delivered in the previous 14 weeks. About 32 square miles (82sqkm) of Japan's most important and well defended industrial areas were destroyed, with the loss of only 22 aircraft. The raids were on such a scale that LeMay ran out of incendiary bombs by March 21. The B-29s did not fly similar missions for some two months.

Back to daylight

On April 7, after the capture of Iwo Jima and its air bases, long-range P-47 Thunderbolts and P-51 Mustangs began accompanying the bombing raids. The bombers now expanded their operations to medium-level daylight raids with high-explosive bombs. By May, the escorting fighters had virtually absolute air superiority above Japan.

The bombers could operate at will during the final months of the war. They leveled huge areas of Japan's six major industrial centers: Kawasaki, Kobe, Nagoya, Osaka, Tokyo, and Yokohama. Estimates suggest that U.S. raids destroyed about 102 square miles (259sqkm) of these cities, around half of which were in Tokyo. From early

The Tokyo Fire Raids

On July 23, 1945, the Allied leaders met for dinner at Potsdam outside Berlin. Soviet leader Joseph Stalin proposed a toast to their "next meeting in Tokyo." U.S. general Henry Arnold responded that the bombing campaign against the city was so intense that "there would be nothing left of Tokyo to have a meeting in."

Arnold's prediction was not far from the truth. The first great incendiary raid on Tokyo took place on the night of March 9–10. Some 279 B-29s based in the Marianas dropped 2,000 tons of incendiaries. The resulting firestorms destroyed 25 percent of the capital's buildings, killed some 83,000 people, wounded 41,000 others, and left one million homeless. The B-29s returned on May 23, and again two days later. Just three raids detroyed more than half the city, or some 50 square miles (129sqkm) of streets and buildings.

▲ Armorers load M-69 incendiary bombs onto a B-29. The incendiaries carried chemicals that burned at extremely high temperatures, destroying buildings and generating firestorms.

▲ After Japan's surrender, observers visit the ruins of an aircraft plant in Nagoya devastated by B-29 bombing raids.

June, the B-29s attacked smaller cities and towns. Over the next two months, they destroyed or badly damaged 60 of them. Some 300,000 civilians died in the strategic bombing raids, a further 500,000 were wounded, and around 8.5 million lost their homes. By the end of July, U.S. intelligence services were finding it hard to locate any more worthwhile targets.

Japanese morale

The morale of Japanese civilians began to crumble. Food and shelter grew scarce, and the country's infrastructure collapsed. The shortages were made worse by U.S. mine-laying operations. In the last four and a half months of the war, U.S. aircraft dropped about 12,000 mines at the entrances to

Japan's main harbors and in the Inland Sea, between the home islands of Kyushu, Shikoku, and southern Honshu. The movement of supplies around Japan's coast virtually came to a halt. The Japanese garrison in Manchuria in China was essentially cut off.

Despite the destruction, it appeared that the military-dominated Japanese government was still willing to fight on. Emperor Hirohito, however, contacted the Allies. His ambassador in Moscow passed on the emperor's desire to end the war. Japan's leaders believed that the thought of the heavy casualties that would result from any landings on mainland Japan would convince the Allies to agree to peace talks.

President Roosevelt had demanded unconditional surrender by Japan. The

◀ In the aftermath of the war, a Tokyo resident drinks from a broken water pipe. More than half the city lay in ruins after repeated Allied bombing raids.

Japanese rejected such terms. After Roosevelt died on April 12, they hoped for better terms from his replacement, Harry S. Truman. Truman was comparatively unknown. In his first days in office, however, he declared his commitment to unconditional surrender.

Truman confirmed his views at the Allied Potsdam Conference in July, after the defeat of Germany. The leaders of the United States, Britain, China, and the Soviet Union declared that they would not negotiate peace. They would only accept Japan's unconditional surrender.

How to end the war

The B-29 raids and the U.S. submarine attacks on supply routes at sea were seriously reducing Japan's ability to wage war. Admiral Chester Nimitz, commander of the Central Pacific Area, and General Douglas MacArthur of the Southwest Pacific Area, pressed on with their invasion plans.

The first landing was code-named Operation Olympic. It was planned for November 1, and was to be directed against southern Kyushu. It was to be carried out by the 500,000-strong U.S. Sixth Army under General Walter Krueger and more than 3,000 warships. The second operation was code-named Coronet. Its target was the Tokyo area of Honshu. It was set for March 1, 1946, but the final timing would depend on the progress of Operation Olympic.

Both landings were to start with heavy attacks on the bases that housed Japan's naval and air kamikaze units. Even so,

Harry S. Truman

Franklin D. Roosevelt won a fourth presidential election victory in November 1944. His running mate as vice-president was a former lawyer from Missouri, Harry S. Truman (1884–1972). Truman had already demonstated political skill as chair of the Senate Special Committee investigating corruption within the National Defense Program. He had never held executive office, however. Some critics doubted he had the capacity to do so.

Truman became president after Roosevelt's death on April 12, 1945. He largely relied on Roosevelt's advisers and stuck to established plans. For example, in his first speech as president on April 16, he backed the Allied policy of unconditional surrender. As the war drew to a close, Truman's chief concerns were the shaping of the postwar world and the increasingly difficult relationship with the Soviet Union.

▲ Harry S. Truman wrote in his diary that he had made a decision to use the atomic bomb against "purely military targets."

▼ Spare B-29 engines at an air base on Guam. By the end of the war, the U.S. Air Force had taken delivery of more than 3,000 Superfortresses.

U.S. commanders and politicians feared that the landings would result in many casualties, among both U.S. personnel and Japanese civilians. In the recent battles at Iwo Jima and Okinawa, almost all of the Japanese defenders had died rather than surrender. Japanese resistance would likely be even more fierce on their home islands. Some people predicted that the landings would result in at least a million U.S. troops becoming casualties.

A new threat

A very few people in the United States knew that the landings might not be necessary. There was now another way to bring about a swift end to hostilities. The Potsdam Declaration had included an ominous warning to the Japanese. One passage stated that failure to surrender immediately would bring about "the inevitable and complete destruction of the Japanese armed forces and … the utter devastation of the Japanese homeland."

The declaration said nothing about the nature of the threat, but it was very real. After years of secret research, the United States had tested the world's first atomic bomb at Alamogordo in New Mexico on July 16. A special B-29 unit,

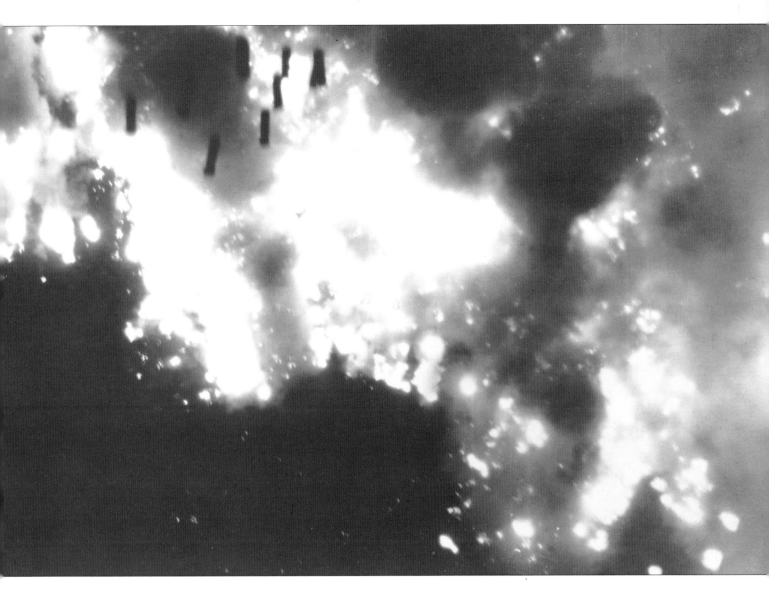

the 509th Composite Group, was completing its training in the Utah desert to deliver the new weapon.

The Manhattan Project

The program to develop atomic weapons was code-named the Manhattan Project. The immense scientific and technical undertaking had begun in December 1941. It cost about $2 billion and employed more than 600,000 people at one time or another. They included U.S. and foreign scientists, and staff at many universities and industrial sites. The key facility was at Los Alamos, New Mexico. It was directed by physicist J. Robert Oppenheimer. There were other facilities at Oak Ridge, Tennessee, and Hanford, Washington.

The new weapon had the destructive power of a raid by 2,000 B-29s. Some politicians and military commanders who knew about it were not sure it should be used. Some argued that it would cause too many civilian deaths. Others, mainly in the air force, felt that Japan was already on the verge of collapse. There was no need to use the new bomb.

Instead, the Joint Chiefs of Staff and a group of senior politicians headed by

▲ Fires blazing in the port of Takamatsu silhouette bombs that have just been dropped from a B-29 flying at high altitude.

401

▲ Colonel Paul W. Tibbets waves from the cockpit of *Enola Gay* before taking off on the mission to drop the first atomic bomb.

that Japan still had some four million troops under arms at home, across the Pacific, and in China. It would take the deaths of a huge number of Allied soldiers to defeat them.

Truman's decision

At Potsdam, Truman decided to use the bomb if the Japanese did not surrender unconditionally. The Japanese, however, dismissed the Allies' warning. Tokyo radio announced, "there is no other recourse but to ignore it and resolutely fight for a successful conclusion of the war."

Truman's decision was sent to the air force. The order to deploy was sent to the Twentieth Air Force in early August. The 509th Composite Group, now based on Tinian in the Marianas, began final preparations for its mission.

Japan's road to surrender

The first atomic bomb was code-named Little Boy. It was dropped on August 6 by a B-29 named *Enola Gay*, flown by Colonel Paul Tibbets. Its target was Hiroshima, a city of some 245,000 people on the southeast coast of Honshu. In an instant, some two-thirds of the city was destroyed. About 66,000 people died from the blast, from the resulting fires, or later from

Henry L. Stimson, the secretary of war, advised Truman to use the bomb. They argued that it would shock Japan's leaders into surrender. The Japanese had no defense against the new weapon, so the surrender would be an honorable one. The U.S. committee also argued

▶ "Little Boy," the atomic bomb dropped on Hiroshima, had an explosive power equivalent to about 15,000 tons of conventional explosives.

radiation sickness. Nearly 70,000 others were injured, many seriously.

American radio broadcasts and leaflet drops warned that Japan must surrender immediately, or more atomic bombs would be dropped. Still, no Japanese surrender came. Japan's leadership was divided. Hirohito told his foreign minister, Shigenori Togo, that Japan had to accept the Potsdam Declaration. The decision lay with the Supreme War Council, however. It was split, and could not immediately be summoned to discuss the ultimatum.

A second bomb

With no clear response from Japan, U.S. leaders ordered the 509th Composite Group to use a second atomic bomb. The next target was the city of Kokura, but on August 9, the day of the attack, it was obscured by fog. The bombers flew on to the secondary target, Nagasaki, a city of around 230,000 people on the southwest coast of Kyushu. The bomb, Fat Man, caused somewhat less destruction than the first due to the local geography. Still, about 40,000 people died and 25,000 were injured.

War with the Soviet Union

Japan's government argued about how to react to the atomic bombs. They had no way of knowing that the United States had no more of the weapons. Meanwhile, the Japanese had to face a new enemy: the Soviet Union. The two countries had signed a Neutrality Pact in April 1941, and had avoided conflict

▼ Months after the blast, Hiroshima still lies in ruins. The bomb flattened an area of about 4.5 square miles (11.65 sqkm) in the heart of the city.

▲ A mushroom cloud rises above Nagasaki after the atomic bomb attack of August 9. The cloud is caused by tons of dust sucked into the explosion at ground level.

since. Unknown to the Japanese, however, the Soviet Union had agreed to a request from the other Allies at the Yalta Conference in February 1945 to enter the Pacific War after the defeat of Nazi Germany. The Soviets had been preparing for conflict since May. They declared war on August 8.

The Red Army targeted Japanese troops in China. The 925,000-strong Kwantung Army looked imposing on paper, but was a mixture of local conscripts and inexperienced Japanese. They faced a battle-hardened Soviet force of a million men, 5,000 armored vehicles, 26,000 guns and mortars, and 5,000 aircraft. The Red Army invaded Manchuria on August 9. In only a week, the Japanese suffered some 80,000 men killed; Red Army losses were 8,219 killed and 22,264 wounded.

The surrender

The two atomic bombs and the Soviet declaration of war forced the Japanese leadership to act. Hirohito and Togo

Eyewitness

“ The technical school, a large two-storied wooden building, was on fire, as were many houses and the distant ordnance factory. Electricity poles were wrapped in flame like so many pieces of kindling. Trees on nearby hills were smoking, as were the leaves of sweet potatoes in the fields. To say that everything burned is not enough. It seemed as if the earth itself emitted fire and smoke, flames that writhed up and erupted from underground. The sky was dark, the ground was scarlet, and in between hung clouds of yellowish smoke. Three kinds of color—black, yellow, and scarlet—loomed ominously over the people, who ran about like so many ants trying to escape. What had happened? Urakami Hospital had not been bombed—I understood that much. But that ocean of fire, that sky of smoke! It seemed like the end of the world. ”

Tatsuichiro Akizuki, doctor, Nagasaki, August 9, 1945

Emperor Hirohito's broadcast

On the night of August 14, 1945, shortly before Japan's unconditional surrender became public knowledge, Emperor Hirohito recorded a radio broadcast. He announced the country's defeat and told his subjects that it was both his and their painful duty to surrender without causing further bloodshed. He warned them to "beware strictly of any outbursts of emotion."

The broadcast was a remarkable event. Hirohito had godlike status in Japan. He had never before spoken directly to his people, many of whom had never heard his voice. The speech was broadcast at noon on August 15. Hirohito spoke of the people's need to accept defeat with calmness and dignity, no matter how painful it might be.

A few militarists tried but failed to destroy the recording before it was transmitted. They also failed in an attempt to seize power. Hirohito's speech helped the transition from war to peace to go more smoothly than might have been expected.

finally convinced the military to accept defeat on August 10. They declared that Japan would accept the Allies' demand for unconditional surrender so long as it did not seek to limit the power of Emperor Hirohito. The Allies agreed, although in fact Hirohito would become a figurehead leader. Despite attempts by some militarists to disrupt the surrender, a ceasefire came into effect on August 15.

Hirohito addressed his people directly for the first time by radio. He told them they had to "bear the unbearable." The first troops of a mostly U.S. occupation force landed on August 30. They would remain until 1952. Across the Pacific, surviving Japanese garrisons gradually gave up to Allied forces.

Closing act

The formal surrender was signed on the U.S. battleship *Missouri*, anchored in Tokyo Bay, on September 2. MacArthur, who was in charge of the occupation, was the main Allied signatory. The Japanese delegation was headed by the new foreign minister, Mamoru Shigemetsu. At the end of the signing, MacArthur brought the ceremony and World War II to an end with the words: "Let us pray that peace be now restored to the world and God will preserve it always. These proceedings are now closed."

▼ GIs in Paris celebrate news of the Japanese surrender on August 10, 1945.

THE COST OF THE WAR

The destruction caused by World War II was on an immense scale. Millions of people had been killed, injured, or made homeless. Towns and cities were left in ruins. Whole nations became bankrupt.

By the end of the war in August, the conflict had spread around most of the globe. Fewer than 15 of the world's nations remained neutral throughout the war. Some combatants had made only a minor contribution to the war. They included many Latin American nations. A number of countries also joined the war in its late stages. They hoped to benefit from the peace settlements at the end of the fighting.

The major combatants, however, lost millions of lives. Almost all of the heavily populated areas of Europe and Asia became war zones. So did much of Africa. The conflict was so vast that it remains difficult to assess the total casualties and battle damage.

Keeping records

Some countries kept more accurate casualty figures than others. The United States, for example, kept precise records of all its losses. It was able to do so partly because there was no fighting on home soil. Great Britain also kept a careful tally of its losses. However, fighting destroyed the records of some

nations, such as Germany. When countries were occupied, new governments destroyed records or kept them in different ways. Some less-developed countries, such as the Soviet Union, had no accurate records in the first place. Throughout Europe and Asia, millions of deaths took place out of sight of any official record keeper.

The most common estimate for the conflict's total death toll is around 56 million people. Some estimates fall as low as 35 million, however. The highest rise to 70 million. The vast majority of the dead came from a few countries.

The human cost

World War II saw the mobilization of entire societies for war. Many countries were almost stripped of their young men for the armed forces. Around 120 million people entered military service between 1939 and 1945. At the height of the war, in early 1945, 12.5 million Soviet citizens were in uniform. At the same time, there were 12.25 million U.S. service personnel. German forces numbered nearly 11 million. Britain and its empire had 8.7 million people in uniform. Japan's armed forces had just over 7 million members.

Conscription

In all countries, the vast majority of soldiers were conscripts. They were not members of the regular army. They were drafted into service, and had no choice. The vast majority were men, although women were also called up in some countries.

For conscripts, the war was a massive disruption to their lives, even if they survived it uninjured. Conscription dragged them away from their homes,

▼ U.S. troops march through the ruined city of Saarbrücken in Germany in March, 1945. Allied bombing and troop combat left many German cities in utter ruins.

▶ German military graves in snow-covered Russian soil. The majority of German combat deaths occured in the fierce fighting on the Eastern Front.

▼ A German priest leads prayers during the postwar reburial of 800 slave laborers. The dead workers were murdered by the SS.

parents, families, and jobs. They were often away for years. For many of the draftees, the first time they had been abroad was when they climbed off a ship or truck in a war zone.

Military casualties

In terms of military deaths, the nations of North America and western Europe came off lightest. The one exception was Germany. The United States lost 292,100 military personnel. Britain lost 271,311 dead, France 210,671, Belgium

9,561, Austria 380,000, Italy 279,820, Denmark 4,339, and Norway 4,780. Taken together, the figures total nearly 1.5 million lives.

Such numbers are dwarfed by the losses in eastern Europe and the Soviet

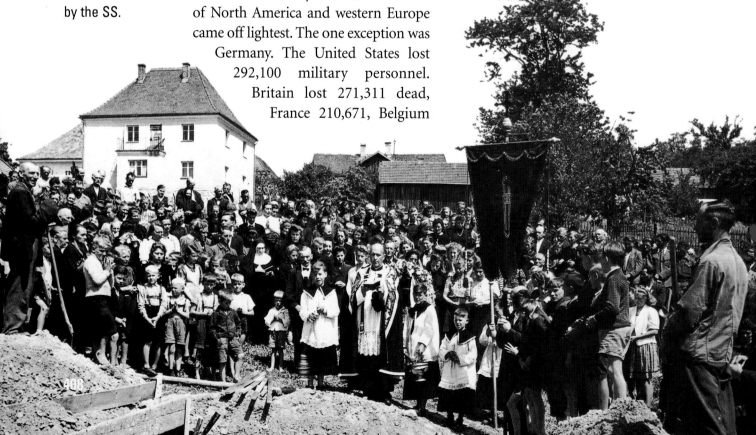

Union, and in East Asia. Poland, for example, lost 600,000 military dead, and Romania 200,000. Soviet military dead, however, totaled a remarkable 8.7 million. The high figure was partly the result of the ferocity of the fighting on the Eastern Front. It also reflected the disregard for human lives of the Soviet dictator, Joseph Stalin. China lost around 3.5 million troops.

The two countries most responsible for the war, Germany and Japan, also paid heavily. Japan suffered 1.7 million war dead, while Germany lost over 4 million troops. The bulk of German losses were on the Eastern Front and in Soviet prisoner-of-war camps.

Civilian death figures

The military death tolls give nothing like a complete picture of the cost of World War II. Civilian fatalities in the conflict far exceeded military deaths. There were many reasons for this. Civilians died in the area bombing of cities or when artillery was used in city battles. They were murdered as a result of persecution and execution. Millions of people also died from famine and disease created by wartime conditions.

The Soviet Union suffered well over 7 million civilian dead. Some estimates put the figure as high as 16 million. In China, up to 10 million civilians may have died in the war against Japan. Yugoslavia lost 1.7 million people during the German occupation and civil war. That was a similar proportion of losses to the Soviet Union. Both nations lost about 10 percent of their populations. Hungary lost a total of 750,000 civilian dead and Romania 465,000.

The country that suffered by far the worst civilian deaths in proportion to its population was Poland. During six years

The fate of prisoners of war

The war ended with millions of servicemen and women held prisoner. The treatment of POWs depended on their nationality and that of their captors. More than a million French POWs were used as forced labor throughout German territories between 1940 and 1945. On the whole they were not actively abused by the Germans, unless they were Jewish. The Germans treated Soviet POWs savagely, however. Four million Soviet POWs died in prison camps through starvation, overwork, or execution.

Meanwhile, Stalin decreed that any Soviet soldier who was captured, or who surrendered, was an enemy of the state. So a further 1 million Soviet soldiers would die in Soviet prison camps after the war. A similar number of German soldiers also died in Soviet POW camps. Of the 90,000 German soldiers captured at Stalingrad, only 5,000 returned home.

Allied soldiers imprisoned by the Japanese in East Asia also underwent a horrific experience. The death rate among prisoners was 25 to 30 percent. The survivors were often crippled by malaria or diseases that were caused by malnutrition. Others returned home with severe mental disorders.

▲ German prisoners of war march through Moscow in 1943. Only a small proportion of German POWs survived the harsh conditions of Soviet POW camps.

Psychiatric casualties

The experience of battle left hundreds of thousands of soldiers suffering psychological damage. There were many casualties suffering "battle fatigue" or "shell shock." A total of nearly 1.4 million U.S. troops were treated for psychiatric disorders during the conflict. Over 30 percent of those had to be discharged from duty.

In Europe and the Pacific, one in four of all casualties suffered mental trauma rather than physical injury. During the Battle of Okinawa alone, 26,000 front-line U.S. troops were evacuated because of mental breakdown. Many such casualties were suffering from what today is known as "post-traumatic stress disorder" (PTSD). They often had great trouble adjusting back into civilian life.

PTSD casualties had recurrent nightmares. They lost confidence and found it difficult to socialize. They could not control their temper. Such victims lived for the rest of their lives with the consequences of being in the war.

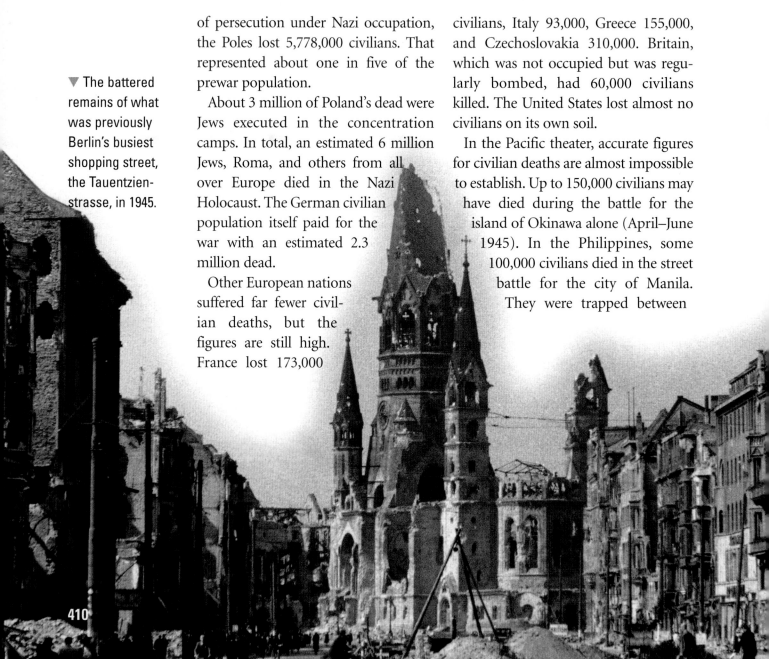

▼ The battered remains of what was previously Berlin's busiest shopping street, the Tauentzien-strasse, in 1945.

of persecution under Nazi occupation, the Poles lost 5,778,000 civilians. That represented about one in five of the prewar population.

About 3 million of Poland's dead were Jews executed in the concentration camps. In total, an estimated 6 million Jews, Roma, and others from all over Europe died in the Nazi Holocaust. The German civilian population itself paid for the war with an estimated 2.3 million dead.

Other European nations suffered far fewer civilian deaths, but the figures are still high. France lost 173,000 civilians, Italy 93,000, Greece 155,000, and Czechoslovakia 310,000. Britain, which was not occupied but was regularly bombed, had 60,000 civilians killed. The United States lost almost no civilians on its own soil.

In the Pacific theater, accurate figures for civilian deaths are almost impossible to establish. Up to 150,000 civilians may have died during the battle for the island of Okinawa alone (April–June 1945). In the Philippines, some 100,000 civilians died in the street battle for the city of Manila. They were trapped between

U.S. and Japanese troops. Across the whole theater, civilian dead certainly numbered in the millions.

The proportion of deaths

The death tolls reveal a lot about how World War II was fought. Of the total of 56 million deaths, more than 40 million were sustained by only four countries: the Soviet Union, China, Poland, and Yugoslavia. By contrast, U.S. and British losses together amounted to no more than 650,000. This total was exceeded by the individual death tolls of smaller countries such as Hungary, Romania, and Czechoslovakia.

The vast bulk of deaths took place in the fighting between the Soviets and the Germans and between the Japanese and the Chinese. The Soviets, for example, lost more people in the battle of Stalingrad than the combined U.S. and British death tolls for the whole war.

The huge numbers cloud the individual suffering. Each death represented a devastated family, and for every fatality there were usually three or four wounded. More than 200 million people had to adjust to the reality of life with damaged bodies.

Wrecked societies

Another human cost of the war was homelessness and displacement. The problem was particularly acute in Europe. Occupation, aerial bombing, and the movement of armies displaced millions of people. Some fled the fighting. Others had their homes destroyed. At the end of the war, mainland Europe lay in ruins. Approximately 30 million people were refugees. Some 10 million of these people had originally been deported from their home countries to provide forced labor.

The dispossessed roamed around countries that had been stripped of homes by bombing and fighting. Poland lost 30 percent of its buildings, including 60 percent of its public buildings. It also lost up to 35 percent of its industrial facilities. Around 30 percent of British homes were destroyed or damaged. Urban Germany was almost erased from the map.

More than 5 million Germans were homeless at the end of the war, and 2 million homes had been destroyed. U.S. Strategic Bombing Survey figures show that 39 percent of homes were destroyed in Germany's largest cities.

The problem of displaced people was worst in the last year of the war and in the war's immediate aftermath. Millions of people choked the roads of Europe. Some were fleeing the fighting.

▲ A displaced German family travels from eastern to western Germany with its few belongings. This family was lucky enough to have transport.

Divorce

One emotional cost of World War II was a huge increase in divorce rates immediately after the conflict. In the United States, for example, the divorce rate in 1941 was 2.2 per 1,000 people. By 1946, it had nearly doubled, to 4.3 per 1,000.

The causes of the rise were complex. Soldiers had been away from their wives for long periods. In that time, some wives had found new partners. Less commonly, soldiers might have found new partners. Also, the experience of years of war greatly changed the soldiers. They returned home as different people. Their wives had also changed. Many women found a new independence through war work. They could support themselves financially. They were therefore less dependent on their husbands when they returned. The huge numbers of returning soldiers led to high unemployment in some places. That increased tensions in the home.

▶ French prisoners of war in Germany celebrate as they are released. They would be returning home to a society that had changed markedly.

▼ Displaced people in Berlin, 1945, assemble to be taken to another camp in Munich, southern Germany.

Others were trying to return home. Just after the war, for example, up to 5 million Russian prisoners of war headed home. They joined other refugees heading for eastern Europe. In East Prussia and eastern German territories, meanwhile, some 8 million people fled their homes in the winter of 1944–1945. They were escaping the Soviet advance. Between 1 and 2 million German civilians died of exhaustion, hypothermia, or enemy action during the panic. It was one of the worst refugee crises of the entire war.

Dealing with refugees

Dealing with refugees in postwar Europe was largely the responsibility of the new United Nations Relief and Rehabilitation Administration. It set up refugee camps and food distribution points in 17 nations. Between 1945 and 1947, it handed out a total of 25 million tons of food to refugees and homeless people. Allied occupation forces helped rebuild towns and cities.

East Asia also experienced severe problems of displacement. The U.S. Strategic Bombing Survey found that 66

Japanese cities had suffered 40 percent destruction of urban areas. About 30 percent of the entire nation was homeless. In rural Asia, famine and disease were rife. The situation was made worse because many hospitals and water systems had been destroyed during the fighting. Only huge investment from the West and the Soviet Union helped much of Europe and Asia recover.

Financial costs

All the combatant nations had to cope with the financial cost of World War II. The conflict was massively expensive. It cost about $1 trillion, not including economic losses through war damage. It brought countries close to bankruptcy. France, for example, lost about 46 percent of its national wealth during the war. Such losses were not unusual.

The United States spent about $340 billion on the war. However, it ended the conflict financially stronger than it went in. It had sold equipment to its Allies, or provided it through the Lend-Lease system. Its former allies now owed it for the equipment. Germany spent $272 billion on the war, the Soviet Union $192 billion, the United Kingdom $120 billion, and Japan $56 billion. Such costs were too high for many countries to bear. They helped profoundly alter the postwar balance of global power. European nations in particular found it difficult to recover their prewar economic prominence.

By the end of the war, Europe had lost an estimated 70 percent of its industrial output. European governments had to cut costs to repay their huge debts and to finance reconstruction. That was one reason why Britain and France steadily got rid of their global colonies. They had lost their great power status to the United States and the Soviet Union.

German looting

Wartime firepower destroyed millions of historic artifacts and buildings across the world. Looting was another major cause of cultural loss. The Nazi regime had a highly organized policy of looting Europe's treasures. For example, they removed more than 14,000 paintings from museums in Warsaw, Poland, during the occupation. The Nazis sent nearly 22,000 art treasures and artifacts to Germany.

Some 1.2 million pieces of art were stolen during the war—20 percent of Europe's artworks. The Nazis also took $625 million of gold from European banks. They used it to finance the German war effort.

Much of the stolen art was retrieved after the war. At least 100,000 artworks still remain lost today, however.

▶ U.S. soldiers examine a famous painting by the French artist Edouard Manet discovered in a Nazi vault.

POSTWAR EUROPE

After the war ended in Europe in May 1945, both the victors and the vanquished faced the task of restoring order to a shattered continent. In addition, the Allies worked hard to bring war criminals to justice.

On May 8, 1945, word of the German surrender spread across North America and Europe. In the victorious nations, people rejoiced. Revelers crammed into New York's Times Square and London's Piccadilly Circus to celebrate.

While Europe was celebrating, however, fighting went on in the Pacific. American, British, and Australian forces were still fighting Japan. May 8 became known as Victory in Europe (VE) Day. On that same day, the U.S. Tenth Army was fighting a bloody battle for the island of Okinawa. The war against Japan still had three more months to run.

Uncovering the Holocaust
The joy of victory was also tempered by the emerging evidence of the extent of Nazi crimes during the conflict. For

most of the war, the Allies had only a dim understanding of the Holocaust that was taking place in Nazi-controlled Europe. The full horror of the systematic extermination of the Jews became apparent during the Allied advance into Germany in 1944 and 1945. The U.S. and British troops had experienced little to prepare them for what they found in the large concentration camps.

American troops liberated Dachau and Buchenwald concentration camps in southern Germany in April 1945. The British entered Bergen-Belsen in the north of the country in the same month. Meanwhile, Soviet troops uncovered the huge extermination camps in the east. They liberated Auschwitz, in southern Poland, in January 1945.

Many U.S. and Allied troops were accompanied by film crews, photographers, and reporters. They sent home newsreels, images, and reports of emaciated camp survivors and piles of dead bodies. U.S. general Dwight D. Eisenhower was the overall commander of the Western Allied armies. He encouraged U.S. and British troops to visit the liberated camps. He believed that the camps showed that the Allied cause had been just. Eisenhower himself visited the camp near Buchenwald in April 1945. He announced, "The things I saw beggar description…."

The Allies forced German civilians from nearby towns to visit the

▼ Crowds celebrate in Times Square, New York, on Victory in Europe Day, 1945.

415

▲ Members of Congress examine a pile of bodies at Buchenwald concentration camp. The politicians were flown to Germany at the request of Eisenhower to see evidence of the Nazi atrocities.

Eyewitness

❝And then, of course, the Americans opened the gate and we had to scream at them. "Don't touch the wires!" They had no idea because they didn't know the camp was there; they found it by accident, we were told later. And they had to bring the Corps of Engineers to take the electricity off those wires. Then they found that there was typhoid in the camps, so now they said, "Wait a minute, you guys can't get out of this camp," because they didn't want the American soldiers to be infected with typhoid, it would have been devastating. So they closed the camp again. And one day, after about a week or two, five of us, we got out; we conned one of the soldiers into letting us out because we could work. We got out and went to the next town, the town of Dachau.

We went to the first house, which was a nice home, we needed food and clothing. We looked like hell, and we were hungry and more so. This German wouldn't open the door, so one of the guys just took his foot and opened the door. So we got inside and we took what we needed.❞

William Lowenburg,
prisoner in Dachau concentration camp

concentration camps. They wanted to show the Germans the scale of the atrocities that had taken place in their neighborhoods. The Allies also forced the Germans to help in the mammoth task of burying the dead and caring for the near-dead.

A divided Germany

In the spring of 1945, the Western Allies advanced into Germany from the west and the Soviets from the east. They were following a plan established at the Yalta Conference of February 1945. The Allied leaders had agreed to divide post-war Germany into temporary occupation zones. The Allies would help to govern and rebuild the country. Broadly speaking, the zones represented the areas where the respective Allies had done most of their fighting, and where their armies were when the war ended.

According to the agreement, the Soviets would control east-central Germany. Their zone included the provinces of East Prussia and Saxony and the cities of Leipzig and Dresden. The British zone covered most of northwestern Germany, including the cities of Cologne and Hamburg. The French took areas directly bordering France, in the Saarland and on the west bank of the Rhine, including the cities of Saarbrücken and Baden-Baden. The U.S. zone covered south-central Germany. It included most of Bavaria and the cities of Frankfurt, Munich, and Nuremberg.

Potsdam conference

The arrangements were finalized at another conference held at Potsdam, near Berlin, a few weeks after the defeat of Germany. The Allied leaders also agreed that all territories conquered by

the Nazis were to be returned to their former governors. Their populations were to be allowed free elections.

Poland presented the Allies with a problem. The Soviet leader, Joseph Stalin, argued that the Soviets should receive territory in the east of Poland. The territory had been taken from the Soviets after World War I, in 1921. He also wanted to make sure that the Polish government would be "friendly" to the Soviet Union.

Stalin's intention was to create a zone of Soviet influence in eastern Europe. That zone would act as a buffer between his country and any future potential invaders from the west. The British and French had initially gone to war with

▲ German civilians and former POWs read about the end of the war in Hamburg. The newspaper was printed under the control of the Allied Military Government.

▲ German civilians leave a screening of a film on Nazi atrocities. The Allies tried to force ordinary Germans to confront the actions carried out in their name.

the Soviet zone, the occupiers moved whole German industrial plants to the Soviet Union. The factories would compensate for the damage caused to Soviet industry in the war.

Allied Control Council

The German capital, Berlin, lay deep within the Soviet occupation zone. The Allied leaders agreed to divide the city. Each of the four occupying powers took control of part of the city. The Soviet Union guaranteed to keep open the road, rail, and air links from Berlin to western Germany.

In theory, an Allied Control Council would set up rules to cover the whole of occupied Germany. The council included representatives from each of the four powers. The Allied Control Council proved something of a failure, however. It was weakened by increasing tension between the Soviets on one hand, and the British and Americans on the other. In practice, each of the Allies was left to run its own sector.

The British had a long history of ruling an empire. They soon developed working relationships with the German authorities. American servicemen were the wealthiest of the occupying forces. Their relative wealth encouraged them to break rules forbidding social interaction with ordinary Germans. The Soviets were the most vengeful occupiers. As one German observer put it, "One was freest in the British zone, best off in the American zone, and most at risk in the Russian zone."

Germany's fate

With the Soviets and the Western Allies now in control of Germany, the question turned to the fate of Germany's

Germany over the issue of Poland's independence. Now that the war was over, however, they were unable to guarantee that same independence.

Another subject discussed at Potsdam was the issue of reparations. These were payments imposed on Germany as a fine to pay for war damage. Under the influence of Stalin, the Allies agreed to impose reparations. Postwar Germany was in chaos, however. The Allies abandoned any effort to set a precise figure on reparations. Instead, the occupying powers would take reparations from their separate zones as they saw fit. In

surviving Nazis. They included a number of the regime's leaders. There were also many soldiers and other followers who carried out war atrocities. The Soviets proposed executing about 50,000 of the regime's political and military leaders. The U.S. secretary of the Treasury, Henry Morgenthau, put forward an alternative plan. It did not call for mass executions. Morgenthau proposed to strip Germany of all of its industry. The country would be "pastoralized." In other words, it would be reduced to a nation of farmers.

President Franklin D. Roosevelt died in April 1945. Before his death, he had

▶ A builder begins the arduous task of rebuilding Berlin, brick by brick.

The Potsdam Conference

The final meeting of the Allied leaders during the war took place in July 1945 in Potsdam, near Berlin. The alliance had just won the war in Europe. It was strained to the breaking point, however. The Allies met to plan the occupation of Germany and the postwar world. Each nation was motivated largely by self interest.

The United States was represented by new president, Harry S. Truman. British prime minister Winston Churchill left the conference midway through. His party had been defeated in a general election. The new prime minister, Clement Attlee, took his place.

In many ways, Soviet leader Joseph Stalin was the winner at Potsdam. He managed to shift the Soviet border west into Poland. He also strengthened his influence over eastern Europe. The other Allies had little choice but to let him do this.

▶ Clement Attlee (left), Harry S. Truman (center), and Joseph Stalin (right) attend the Potsdam talks.

The Allies also discussed how to end the war with Japan. The Americans told Stalin that they had a "new weapon" to use against Japan. The weapon was the atomic bomb. The Allies issued an ultimatum to Japan demanding its unconditional surrender. Japan refused, and the first atomic bomb was dropped a few days later. At Potsdam, Stalin also agreed that Soviet forces would attack Japan. They did so on August 8–9.

▶ Suspected Nazis fill in a questionnaire about their political activities at a British Army detention center, in May 1945.

▼ A U.S. soldier examines the papers of two German civilians accused of shooting and killing a Russian slave laborer. The accused were handed in by a civilian policeman (right) appointed by the U.S. military.

given some support to Morgenthau's harsh approach. New president Harry S. Truman backed away from it, however. In place of mass executions and forced pastoralization, the Western Allies settled on a policy of "de-Nazification." Each Allied power would implement different policies in its occupation zone. Those policies, however, shared the same aim. They intended to dissolve support for facism, remove Nazi officials from public office, and restore democratic government.

Prosecuting the offenders

German soldiers who had committed atrocities were tried and punished in military courts. A system of improvised "de-Nazification" courts tried Nazi political officials. They also tried other Germans who had given support to the Nazi regime. The defendents in the trials had little or no legal representation. The Allies wanted the process to be quick. They did not follow the time-consuming practices of British or U.S. courts.

The U.S. military government tried to assess how much support and partici-

pation the Nazis had received from Germans before or during the war. It sent out some 12 million questionnaires as part of its survey. That was one for every adult German living in the U.S. zone of occupation.

Tens of millions of Germans had worked or voted for the Nazi Party. Only about 170,000 people faced any form of punishment in the "de-Nazification" courts, however. The Western Allies realized that they would need to keep some German academics, industrialists, and bureaucrats in place. Otherwise, they would have no chance of restoring economic order to Germany.

The Nuremberg trials

The surviving high-profile Nazis had more formal trials. They were held in the southern German city of Nuremberg. In the 1930s, Nuremberg had been the home of huge Nazi rallies. The Allies chose it as a highly symbolic location for the postwar trials.

The Nuremberg trials began in November 1945. Twenty-one Nazi leaders were charged with "crimes against humanity." The crimes included conspiracy to wage aggressive war, the Holocaust, and the barbaric treatment of civilians and prisoners of war. The charges were new in the history of international justice. The leaders of a defeated nation had never before been subject to criminal prosecution.

The Allies also broke with tradition by rejecting two basic principles that had previously been accepted in law. The first was that leaders did not have to take personal responsibility for actions taken by their governments. The second was that leaders were not personally responsible if they were following orders from their superiors.

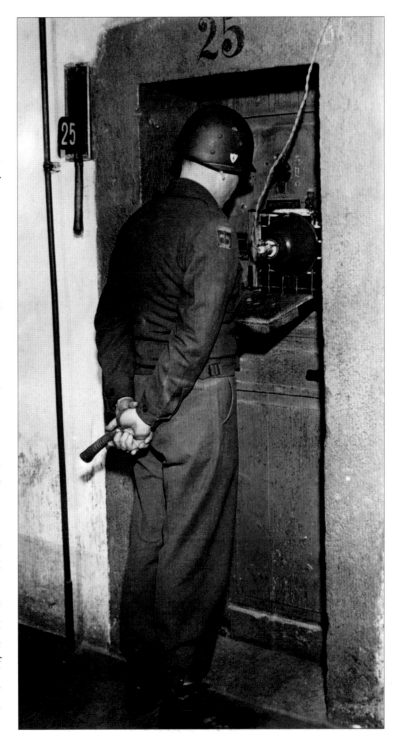

The Nuremberg defendants included Germany's army chiefs, Alfred Jodl and Wilhelm Keitel, and the navy chiefs, Karl Dönitz and Erich Raeder. Politicians on trial included the Nazi foreign minister, Joachim von Ribbentrop, and the economic ministers Albert Speer and Hjalmar Schacht. Also in the dock were

▲ A guard at the war crime trials in 1945–1946. The defendants were held in cells in the jail at Nuremberg.

▶ Hermann Göring was sentenced to hang at the Nuremberg trials, but cheated the executioner by committing suicide with a cyanide pill.

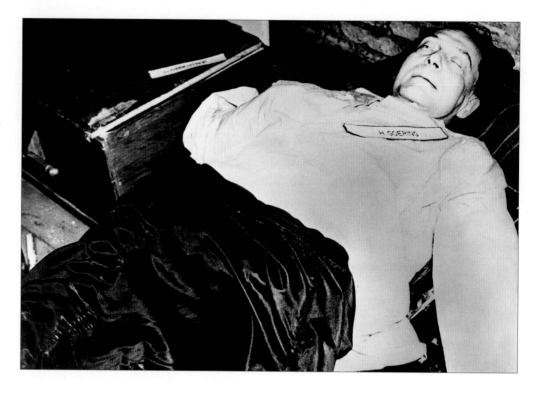

▼ Adolf Eichmann on trial in 1961 for his role in the planning of the Holocaust. Israeli secret agents had kidnapped him from South America in 1960.

Alfred Rosenberg and Konstantin von Neurath, who led the Nazi occupation of eastern Europe, and the former Nazi deputy führer Rudolf Hess.

One of the highest profile defendants was the air force chief Hermann Göring. Göring had long been an ally of Adolf Hitler. He was the most outspoken of the defendants. He showed no remorse for his actions. He made careful arguments in his own defense at the trial.

At the trial

The defendants at Nuremberg had similar rights to those found in U.S. courts. They included the right to defense attorneys. The Allied powers also had teams of lawyers and investigators to prosecute their case. The U.S. team included 700 people. It was led by chief prosecutor Robert Jackson. The panel of judges had members from each Allied nation.

The prosecution showed film of the liberation of the concentration camps. They produced so much eyewitness testimony of Nazi crimes that the final transcript of the trial totaled 10 million words. The proceedings were translated simultaneously into English, German, Russian, and French.

The first round of trials ended in October 1946. The court acquitted three defendants, and sentenced seven to prison. Speer received a 20-year sentence. Hess was imprisoned for life. The court passed the death sentence on 11 defendants. They were hanged on October 16. Hermann Göring cheated the executioner. He took poison before his scheduled execution.

Some of the defendants acknowledged their guilt. Hans Frank was the governor of occupied Poland. Many atrocities had taken place under his command. He became a Catholic during his imprisonment. Before his execution, Frank said: "A thousand years will pass, and still this guilt of Germany will not have been erased."

The United States led a further set of trials at Nuremberg. They lasted from 1946 to 1949. The defendants this time included SS officials involved in running the concentration camps and members of the SS *Einsatzgruppen* death squads. Industrialists and senior amy leaders were also tried.

Those that escaped

The policy of de-Nazification varied greatly. The system had been set up very quickly. It had many flaws. People accused of minor crimes sometimes received harsher sentences than more

▲ Defendants at the Nuremberg trials in 1945–1946. The Nazi leaders sit in two rows in the dock, guarded by Allied military personnel. The defendants include Hermann Göring (at left in dock, in light jacket and dark glasses) and Rudolf Hess (next to Göring, with his face in his hand).

serious offenders. Several of the captured Nazi leaders had helped plan the Holocaust. They were released without trial, however. There was not enough evidence against them. Young SS officers were often able to escape any formal punishment. One was Kurt Waldheim. He later served as president of Austria and secretary-general of the United Nations before his war record was exposed.

Living in a shattered world

For the vast majority of Germans, the trial of their former leaders was the least of their concerns. The country's transportation system was wrecked, and its economy was all but non-existent. Few Germans had jobs, and food shipments from the countryside to the cities slowed to a trickle. In the winter of 1945–1946, the average income for German families fell to about a dollar a month. Only a booming black market kept many Germans alive. They traded any valuables they had to Allied soldiers in return for food, gasoline, and cigarettes.

The situation in the urban areas was bleak. In Germany's great cities, some 20 million people were homeless. More than 16 million Germans from the east

▼ A street sign in the Russian zone of Berlin gives place names in both German and Russian.

Treatment of collaborators

At the end of the war, many nations had to decide how to treat citizens who had cooperated with or even fought for the Axis powers. It was a dilemma, because the nature of collaboration was sometimes difficult to define.

Some 2 million men from occupied Europe served in the German military during the war. They included 30,000 Dutch volunteers who fought on the Eastern Front. One of the last "German" units fighting the Soviets in the Battle of Berlin in April 1945 was the SS Nordland Division. It was made up of Norwegian, Danish, Dutch, and French volunteers.

There was no official Allied policy on the treatment of collaborators. Each nation punished its citizens as it saw fit. The United States imprisoned the U.S.-born radio broadcaster known as "Tokyo Rose." She had broadcast pro-Axis propaganda from Japan. The British executed William Joyce, known as "Lord Haw-Haw." He had broadcast propaganda for the Nazis. Norway had been under Nazi occupation for five years. The Norwegians punished 48,000 collaborators, executing 45.

Of the occupied nations, France had one of the most visible responses to collaborators. Officials in the Nazi-puppet government in

▲ These French women, accused of collaborating with their Axis occupiers, have had their hair shaved off.

Vichy went on trial as traitors. The courts found 120,000 people guilty of treason. Of 4,785 people sentenced to death, nearly 2,000 were executed. Women accused of having romantic relationships with German soldiers had their heads shaved. They were publicly paraded in the streets of their hometowns.

had become refugees. More than 12 million of them found refuge in the western zones.

Europe in ruins

Germany was not the only country left in chaos at the end of the war. Much of the rest of Europe was also in ruins. Road, rail, and canal networks were destroyed. In 1945 a severe drought combined with shortages of labor and machinery. The agricultural harvest fell to half of its prewar level across the continent. In Britain, bread rationing was introduced in 1946. Bread had never been rationed during the war. Now, however, it was necessary in order to feed people in the British-occupied zone of Germany. In Hungary and Greece, the currency collapsed.

In all countries, the first priority after the end of the war was to restore basic services, so that people could resume normal lives. In the next few years, U.S. aid would play a vital role in western Europe's reconstruction.

EUROPE DIVIDED

At the end of the fighting, differences soon emerged between the Soviet Union and its former allies. The tension between them dominated Europe and much of the world for 40 years.

At the end of World War II in 1945, the Allies faced the problem of what to do with the defeated powers. Germany and territories that had seen much fighting, such as Poland, were in ruins. Their economies were shattered. Millions of discharged servicemen had to fit back into civilian life. Millions more people were homeless refugees.

In contrast, the United States ended the war as one of the world's two greatest powers. The other was the Soviet Union. It could not match U.S. economic strength, particularly not after suffering severe damage during the war.

It was the strongest of the European nations, however. The Red Army had driven the Axis forces from deep within the Soviet Union to Berlin itself. The advance left it in occupation of much of eastern Europe.

The two great powers had cooperated during the war.

They made an alliance to defeat a common enemy, even though Soviet communism was directly opposed to the capitalism of the United States and its allies. The Soviet Union was a one-party state in which Joseph Stalin ruled as a dictator. When the war ended, tensions between the two powers soon came to the surface.

Dividing Europe

The military division of Europe reflected the decisions made by the main Allied war leaders: Stalin, U.S. president Franklin D. Roosevelt, and British prime minister Winston Churchill.

In February 1945, the "Big Three" met at Yalta, in the Crimea. Victory was now inevitable. They agreed to accept only Germany's unconditional surrender. The decision would leave the country with no real government. The leaders agreed on new borders for Poland, and Stalin promised to allow democracy in the countries of eastern Europe. The other Allies had already determined that those countries would be under Soviet influence. They accepted that this was the price of Stalin's support in the war. Churchill also hoped to use Stalin's support to resist U.S. demands for the breakup of the British Empire.

Potsdam

After the defeat of Germany, the Allied leaders met again at Potsdam, outside Berlin, in July 1945. Harry S. Truman had become president after the death of Roosevelt in

▼ Red Army troops pass the Brandenburg Gate in Berlin in a victory parade in May 1945. The gate later became a symbol of the divided city: It was a major crossing point between the Soviet and Allied sectors of Berlin.

April. During the conference, Clement Attlee was elected to replace Churchill as prime minister in Britain.

The Allies split Germany into four zones, or sectors, occupied by the main Allied powers: the Soviet Union, the United States, Britain, and France. The capital, Berlin, lay in the Soviet sector. Berlin was further divided into four zones of occupation. In effect, the country and capital were split into two: the Soviet sector and the western sector.

Truman left the conference alarmed. Roosevelt had reluctantly accepted that Soviet influence in postwar eastern Europe was inevitable. However, Truman was suspicious that Stalin would not fulfill his promise at Yalta to permit democratic states in eastern Europe.

Some historians believe that Truman's suspicions partly explain his decision to drop the atomic bombs on Japan the month after Potsdam. They say that not only did he want to defeat Japan, he also wanted to show Stalin the U.S. ability to resist the expansion of Soviet influence in Europe.

A clearer division

Within six months of the end of the war, the lines between the two superpowers had become clearer. Soviet leaders argued that they had to protect their nation. As the center of world com-

▼ A British official and a Soviet military police officer pose with a new sign marking the boundary between the British and Soviet zones in Germany.

YOU ARE NOW ENTERING THE RUSSIAN ZONE

MIL. POLICE SIGN

munism, they said, the Soviet Union needed to be protected from capitalism and imperialism. The best way to do this, they argued, would be to establish communist states in eastern Europe. They would act as a buffer between the Soviet Union and the West.

The iron curtain

In the West, meanwhile, Soviet intentions caused alarm. In a speech in March 1946, former prime minister Churchill referred to the division of Europe by an "iron curtain." Of the Soviets, he said, "There is nothing they admire so much as strength, and there is nothing for which they have less respect than weakness."

Many people were shocked by the attack on their wartime allies. Churchill's suspicions were shared by Truman, however. The president noted that "Unless Russia is faced with an iron fist and strong language, another war is in the making."

Fear of communism

Fear of communism hardened, both abroad and at home. In 1947, Truman initiated an investigation into the loyalty of U.S. civil servants. Of the three million workers involved, about 300 people were fired for their communist associations. Meanwhile, U.S. financier Bernard Baruch made a speech in which he gave a name to the intense mutual hostility between the United States and the Soviet Union. He said, "Let us not be deceived. Today we are in the midst of a cold war."

▲ The U.S. secretary of state, Edward R. Stettinius, signs the charter of the United Nations (UN) on June 26, 1945. Stalin agreed at Yalta to help establish the new organization. The UN became a location for much confrontation between the superpowers during the Cold War.

▲ Yugoslavs in Belgrade celebrate Red Army Day in February 1945. Despite such demonstrations, Yugoslavia and its leader, Tito, largely resisted Soviet influence.

Like Roosevelt, Truman came to accept that Soviet influence in eastern Europe was inevitable. He was concerned, however, about communist influence in states at the edges of the Soviets' sphere of influence, such as Greece and Turkey. Communists had played an important part in Greek resistance. After the end of the war, they staged a prolonged armed uprising against the Greek government.

In February 1947, the British government announced that it could no longer afford to provide military and economic aid to Greece and Turkey against communist rebels in both countries. The British appealed directly to the United States for help.

The Truman Doctrine

Truman and his foreign policy experts decided that the best way to prevent a further expansion of Soviet influence was a policy of "containment." In March 1947, Truman addressed both houses of Congress. He announced what became known as the "Truman Doctrine." The United States would support "free peoples" fighting to resist "aggressive movements that seek to impose on them totalitarian regimes."

The policy was directly aimed at the Soviet Union. It was also a clear signal that the United States had no intention of returning to isolation, as it had after World War I. It would be actively involved in European affairs to counter Soviet influence.

The United States immediately sent the Greek government arms and other support. By 1949, the Greeks had defeated the uprising. There was another $60 million of aid for Turkey, where it helped to stabilize the country.

Eastern Europe

In eastern Europe, meanwhile, the Soviets consolidated their influence. The coalition governments that emerged directly after the war soon became dominated by communists. The Allies had insisted that the liberated countries remove from political or public life anyone who had cooperated with the Axis during the war. In many countries, the communists were the strongest political group left. They were reinforced by the military strength of the Red Army, which also largely controlled the region's police forces.

The Soviets staged a series of elections in eastern Europe. They were not really "free." They mostly returned communist governments. When they did not,

Churchill's speech in Fulton, Missouri, 1946 _____

Churchill's speech in Fulton, Missouri, on March 5, 1946, introduced many people to the idea of the "iron curtain." Churchill had already used the phrase himself the previous year in a letter to Roosevelt. It had been coined by a British socialist named Ethel Snowden in 1919.

Churchill was no longer prime minister when he made the speech. He still had great prestige abroad, however. By March 1946, communist coalition governments had been established in Poland, Hungary, Romania, Bulgaria, and Albania. Churchill said: "From Stettin in the Baltic to Trieste in the Adriatic, an iron curtain has descended across the continent." The great capitals of central Europe—Berlin, Prague, Budapest, Belgrade, Bucharest, and Sofia—were all under the influence of Moscow.

Churchill acknowledged Russia's right to strengthen its western border. But he also warned of the dangers of the spread of Soviet influence, and called for a Western alliance to withstand the communist threat. Churchill's invitation to form an anti-Soviet alliance came only a year after the Allies' conference at Potsdam.

Stalin denounced the speech. He called Churchill a warmongerer. He accused the Allies of breaking faith over Potsdam. They had not, for example, shared the secrets of the atomic bomb. Allied leaders claimed that it was Stalin who had broken faith.

▲ Winston Churchill (left) stands in front of U.S. president Harry S. Truman at Westminster College, Fulton, Missouri, where Churchill gave his "Iron Curtain" speech.

Communism in Western Europe

Communist parties in western Europe were established between 1918 and 1923, following the Russian Revolution. They were influenced by Moscow, but their roots lay in European socialism that went back to the 19th century. Most became politically popular during the hard times of the 1920s and 1930s.

During World War II, communist parties gained further popularity for their role in resisting Nazi occupation. During and immediately after the conflict, the majority of European communist parties cooperated with other political groups in the war effort and postwar recovery. They became a part of the political system. There was a real possibility, for example, that communist parties would be elected in both France and Italy. In Greece, on the other hand, communists fought a full-scale guerrilla war against the royalist government from 1946 to 1949, which ultimately failed.

From 1948 to 1956, western European communists adopted a more confrontational approach. They incited strikes and mobilized peasants to seek land reform. They also organized mass demonstrations against the European Recovery Program (the Marshall Plan) and the North Atlantic Treaty Organization (NATO). The communists' tactics and opposition to programs that stimulated economic recovery greatly diminished their appeal. As the economies of western Europe improved, the popularity of communist parties declined.

◀ Troops of the Greek government fight off communists in March 1948, during the civil war. In most of Europe, communists avoided rebellion in favor of democratic politics.

the Red Army stepped in to seize power. By summer 1948, nearly the whole of eastern Europe was ruled by Soviet-controlled communist parties in a series of one-party states.

The Marshall plan

Containment had an economic parallel. U.S. secretary of state George C. Marshall announced in June 1947 the U.S. intention to aid economic recovery in Europe. A strong European economy would encourage political stability. That would help turn European nations away from communism.

The Economic Recovery Program was popularly named for its creator, the Marshall Plan. By September 1947, 16 nations from western Europe had drawn up a plan of what aid they required. Over the next four years, they received over $13 billion of U.S. aid among them. The plan was a major factor in the

The Truman Doctrine

On March 12, 1947, Harry S. Truman asked Congress to provide aid to Greece and Turkey. Both governments were resisting communist attempts to take power. The president laid out what became known as the Truman Doctrine. He said that the world faced a choice of two ways of life. One was marked by "by free institutions, representative government, free elections...." The other was "based upon the will of a minority forcibly imposed on the majority. It relies on terror and oppression."

Truman added: "I believe that it must be the policy of the United States to support free peoples who are resisting attempted subjugation by armed minorities or by outside pressures." The implication of the speech was that the United States was committed to resisting Soviet expansion and communist influence. Truman made the dispute between the United States and Russia into a choice

▲ Truman asks a joint session of Congress for aid for Greece and Turkey, March 12, 1947.

between "democracy" and "totalitarianism." Congress released the funds Truman wanted. In 1949, the civil war in Greece ended in defeat for the communists, and Turkey remained within the Western sphere of influence.

▼ Czech workers' militia march into Prague during the communist seizure of power in February 1948.

The Marshall Plan

Secretary of State George C. Marshall intended his plan to provide economic assistance wherever it was needed. He said, "Our policy is directed not against any country or doctrine but against hunger, poverty, desperation, and chaos." Marshall invited states under Soviet influence to take part. The Soviet Union soon withdrew, however. It was followed by the nations of eastern Europe.

The Marshall Plan was closely linked to the Truman Doctrine. They have been called "two halves of the same walnut." They both helped U.S. political and economic interests. They were not only intended to contain communism and to bring about economic recovery in Europe. In return, the recipient countries would be expected to purchase U.S. goods and provide investment opportunities for U.S capital. That would stimulate the U.S. economy.

▲ George C. Marshall said that without "normal political health" there could be "no stability and no assured peace."

reconstruction of western Europe. Marshall Aid helped foster the recovery of agriculture and industry, which in many countries had been devastated by the war.

The initial Soviet response to the Marshall Plan was positive, but it soon became more negative. The Soviets rejected the program. They pressed their eastern European neighbors to do the same. Andrei Vyshinsky, the deputy foreign minister, told the United Nations in September 1947 that the United States was "imposing its will on independent states." He said that the plan would place European countries under the "economic and political control of the United States."

Vyshinsky predicted that the plan would divide "Europe into two camps." By provoking Soviet fears of U.S. imperialist intentions, the Truman Doctrine did indeed lead to a further breakdown of trust and cooperation between the two superpowers.

Yugoslavia and Czechoslovakia

The Soviet response to the Truman Doctrine and the Marshall Plan was to

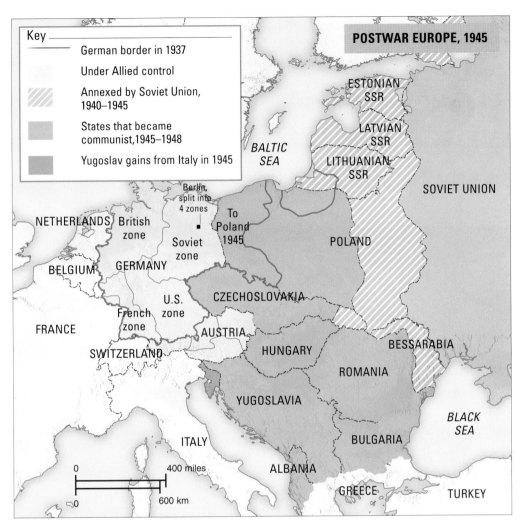

POSTWAR EUROPE, 1945

Key
— German border in 1937
  Under Allied control
  Annexed by Soviet Union, 1940–1945
  States that became communist, 1945–1948
  Yugoslav gains from Italy in 1945

◀ Map of postwar Europe showing the new national borders and Soviet and Western spheres of influence. The Baltic states became Soviet Socialist Republics (SSRs).

▼ European delegates meet in Paris to discuss their requirements from the Marshall Plan. The Soviet Union discouraged the eastern European states from attending.

establish the Cominform (Communist Information Bureau) in September 1947. The organization intended to bring eastern Europe more tightly under Soviet influence. Its nations were to trade only with other Cominform members; contact with noncommunist countries was discouraged.

Yugoslavia was in a different situation from other eastern European states. It had been liberated by Communist partisans led by Josip Broz (known as Tito) rather than by the Red Army. Tito was unwilling to follow Moscow's line if he thought it was against Yugoslav interests. In 1948, the Soviets accused him of being "unfriendly" toward the Soviet Union. Tito withdrew Yugoslavia from the Cominform.

Czechoslovakia, meanwhile, was the only democratic state left in eastern Europe. Since elections in 1946, it had been governed by a coalition of communists and left-wing socialists. Many

The Berlin Blockade and Airlift

The postwar peace settlements had divided Germany and its capital, Berlin, into four zones. Each zone was administered by one of the Allied powers: the United States, Britain, France, and the Soviet Union. Berlin lay deep inside the Soviet zone of Germany. The Western powers organized the economic and political recovery of their zones along democratic and capitalist lines. Stalin, however, was determined to keep Germany weak.

Early in 1948, the three Western zones formed a single economic unit. In June, they introduced a new currency (the Deutschmark). Stalin reacted by closing all road, rail, and canal links between West Berlin and West Germany. He aimed to force the Western allies to withdraw from Berlin.

The Western powers believed that a retreat would encourage a Soviet attack on West Germany. They set out to fly in food, coal, and other supplies to the city. Stalin did not dare risk shooting down Allied planes, because of U.S. atomic weapons.

The airlift lasted for 11 months, and included 277,000 flights. Airplanes took off every three minutes, around the clock. The remarkable operation kept 2.5 million West Berliners alive over the winter. In May 1949, the Soviets admitted failure by lifting the blockade.

◀ Troops unload a U.S. C-74 Globemaster in Berlin as part of the airlift. The flights brought in 15,000 tons of supplies every day.

people saw it as an important bridge between East and West. As elections approached in May 1948, however, critics blamed the communists for rejecting Marshall Aid, even though the Czechs were suffering from food shortages. The communists seized power in an armed uprising. They imposed all-communist lists of candidates in the elections. The Western powers objected but did not intervene.

In Berlin, meanwhile, the Soviets clearly demonstrated their intention to drive the Western powers from the city. Early in 1948 they blocked all land routes to the city through East Germany. The Allies organized a huge airlift to fly supplies into the western sector of the city. The Soviet blockade was lifted after 11 months. Soon afterward the Allies formed their zones of Germany into the Federal Republic of West Germany. The Soviet zone became the German Democratic Republic. The two nations were finally reunited in 1990.

New alliances

In 1948, the western European recipients of Marshall Aid established the Organization for European Economic Cooperation (OEEC) to administer the aid. The group became one of the first Western alliances of the Cold War.

The western Europeans also united in military alliances. In March 1948, Britain, France, and the Benelux countries (Belgium, the Netherlands, and Luxembourg) signed the Brussels Treaty. In April 1949, partly in response to the blockade of Berlin, the signatories of the Brussels Treaty joined the North Atlantic Treaty Organization (NATO). The other members were Canada, Denmark, Iceland, Italy, Norway, Portugal, and the United States. They all pledged to treat an attack on any one of them as an attack on them all.

Stalin responded by setting up the Council for Mutual Economic Assistance (Comecon) in January 1949. It coordinated socialist economic planning in eastern Europe. In May 1955, the Soviet Union formed the Warsaw Pact, its allies' version of NATO.

The Cold War resulted in a Europe divided into two hostile and irreconcilable ideological camps, sustained by different economic systems and protected by military pacts, which in turn led to an escalating arms race. The gulf of mistrust continued to separate East and West until the 1990s.

▲ Children are evacuated from Berlin at the start of winter in 1948. Many were sent to West Germany to avoid the hardships of winter under the Soviet blockade.

Eyewitness

66 It would not be fair to be over-critical, particularly when the Western Powers mounted such a fine rescue operation for Berlin. Maybe there were delays.... I would prefer to stress the positive aspects of the Blockade. First, it was a heroic episode in which the Allied pilots and the Berliners played the main roles. Then it brought about a feeling of real cooperation between the Berliners and the Allies. Those were grey, grim days; but our people showed their steadfastness, their courage, their dry humour and their basic decency. 99

Willy Brandt, mayor of West Berlin and later chancellor of West Germany, on the Berlin Airlift

THE WAR AND MEMORY

World War II was one of the defining events of the 20th century. Its legacy shaped the rest of the millennium on many levels

Politically, the war established the United States and the Soviet Union as the world's great superpowers. It set the scene for the ideological standoff between them known as the Cold War. It also left a lasting suspicion in the West of political extremism.

Culturally, the war inspired many writers, filmmakers, and composers. Economically, the war had an unexpected result. It laid the groundwork for the rapid recovery of the major defeated powers, West Germany and Japan. Their economic growth was encour-aged by the Allies. The Allies did not want to repeat the mistake of the World War I peace settlement. It had weakened Germany so much that it affected the whole world economy.

One of the most profound legacies of World War II was emotional and pyschological. Millions of people who lived through the war are still alive. For them, the war is not simply history. It is a part of their lives. Many have shared their

experiences. Young people today are familiar with many aspects of the war because of the stories of their families or other survivors.

The changing war

New sources of information about World War II are still becoming available to historians. The fall of the Soviet Union in 1991, for example, allowed the first access to its vast archives about the war on the Eastern Front. The archives continue to yield new information.

Other information is contained in official documents that remain secret. In Britain, for example, some war documents were classified as secret for 50 years. Documents declassified at the start of 2006 revealed for the first time that prime minister Winston Churchill wanted to see Adolf Hitler put to death by electric chair, if he were captured alive.

Continuing controversy

Most new information about the war adds details or clarifies a particular person's motives. The broad story is now well known. But many areas of controversy still spark intense debate.

Some questions relate to the conduct of the war. They include why Hitler decided to declare war on the United States on December 11, 1941. His decision, it is now clear, condemned Germany to eventual defeat in the face of the United States's huge economic and population resources.

Other questions reflect moral dilemmas: Did the United States need to drop the atomic bomb on the cities of

▼ A railroad track leads through the entrance of Birkenau, part of the Auschwitz concentration camp. Auschwitz is now a museum to the victims of the Holocaust.

The USS *Arizona* Memorial

One of the best known U.S. war memorials is the striking USS *Arizona* Memorial at Pearl Harbor, Hawaii. It commemorates the servicemen who died in the first attack on the United States of the war, the Japanese air raid on December 7, 1941. A long concrete building in the harbor covers the spot where the wreckage of the *Arizona* sank during the attack with the loss of about 1,000 men, whose bodies remain entombed on the seabed. Opened in 1961, 20 years after the attack, the monument was funded by private contributions of about $500,000. One donor was the rock and roll singer Elvis Presley. He organized a concert in Hawaii to raise money for the fund.

▲ Smoke billows from the USS *Arizona* soon after the start of the Japanese attack on Pearl Harbor. About 1,000 men died when the ship sank.

▼ The USS *Arizona* Memorial covers the spot where the wreck of the ship lies on the floor of the harbor.

Hiroshima and Nagasaki to end the war in Japan?

Other questions concern practical matters such as compensation. They are the basis for court cases. Should the Japanese compensate Allied prisoners of war who were used as slave labor in atrocious conditions, for example? Should the United States compensate Japanese citizens who were interned, often at the cost of their businesses and property? And should the Germans compensate Jewish families whose possessions were seized by the Nazis?

As the number of war survivors diminishes, such questions become less frequent. Nevertheless, the war remains unfinished business in many ways.

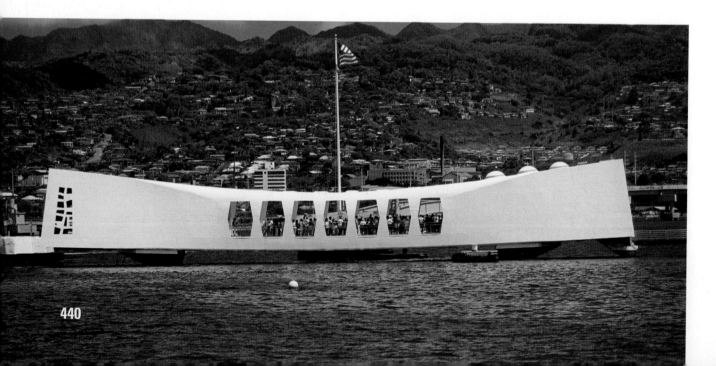

Unexploded bombs are sometimes discovered, or crashed aircraft. In 2005, a U.S. court sent John Demjanjuk to Ukraine, where he had previously lived. Ukraine wanted to put the 85-year-old man on trial for having been a guard in a concentration camp.

Memorials

The year 2005 marked the 60th anniversary of the last year of the war. Hundreds of thousands of people took part in ceremonies to mark the anniversary of Victory in Europe (VE) Day and Victory in Japan (VJ) Day. The anniversaries will probably not be marked in such a significant way again. Neither VE nor VJ days are significant celebrations in a usual year. By the time of the 70th anniversary in 2015, the youngest combat veteran of the war will likely be at least 85 years old.

The commemoration of those who died in the war continues. National war memorials are the sites of public mourning on occasions such as Memorial Day. In Britain, the names of the dead were often added to the memorials created to honor the dead of World War I. The annual Remembrance Day ceremonies also echo the earlier conflict. They take place on November 11, the date of the end of World War I in 1918.

U.S. memorials

The United States has many memorials of World War II. There are both national and local monuments. Some have been controversial. The National Memorial in Washington, D.C., for example, was not built until 2001. The monument features a memorial plaza and reflecting pool. It was built against the protests of veterans. They said that

▼ Granite pillars and memorial arches at the U.S. National Monument. Each pillar is inscribed with the name of one of the states.

War guilt in Germany

Since the war, many Germans have professed guilt about what their countrymen did in the name of Germany. Some have relatives who took part in atrocities. Other nations still blame the Germans for starting the war. English soccer fans, for example, taunt German fans at international matches between the countries.

Within Germany, many people have argued that the Nazis tricked the population. They say that the Nazis never revealed the true racism at the heart of their territorial ambitions. They say that people who ended up in the armed services had no choice; they were "only following orders." Historian Daniel Goldhagen created a storm in 1996 with his book *Hitler's Willing Executioners*. Goldhagen argued that most Germans must have known about at least some of the crimes committed by the Nazis.

the design was not uplifting. They were offended that 4,000 gold stars would mark the 400,000 U.S. dead. They argued powerfully that a single star for each hundred dead did not really mark the sacrifice of each individual.

The Tomb of the Unknown Soldier stands in the National Cemetery at Arlington, Virginia. It commemorates all U.S. war dead who have no marked burial place. It was not built until 1958, however. Because of the delay it also holds the remains of a serviceman from the Korean War (1950–1953). The USS *Arizona* Memorial in Hawaii, meanwhile, commemorates the dead in the attack on Pearl Harbor on December 7, 1941.

There are also international memorials to the victims of the Holocaust. They include the former concentration camps at Dachau and Auschwitz-Birkenau, and Yad Vashem, in Jerusalem, Israel. The United States

▶ U.S. citizen John Demjanjuk stands trial in Israel in 1987 for war crimes. He was released to return to the United States, but in 2005 was ordered to be deported to Ukraine for a further trial on suspicion of being a concentration camp guard.

◀ A Jewish visitor at the Holocaust memorial in Berlin. Visitors walk through deep ravines between the stone blocks.

▼ Soviet veterans parade in Moscow in May 2005 to celebrate the 60th anniversary of the end of the war.

Holocaust Memorial Museum opened in Washington, D.C., in 1993.

In 2005 German chancellor Gerhard Schroeder played a prominent role in commemorations of the 60th anniversary of the liberation of the concentration camps. The Germans also opened their own Holocaust monument in the capital, Berlin. Designed by U.S. architect Peter Eisenman, the monument is a field of huge concrete blocks. Visitors find themselves in deep ravines between plain concrete walls. The experience is profoundly moving.

The war and nationality

The war is not only remembered in physical memorials. Some wartime episodes have shaped how different nations see themselves and others. They are a little like national legends. Following the September 11, 2001, attacks on New York City and Washington, D.C., politicians tried to rally national morale. They reminded Americans of the "spirit of the Blitz," or the bravery of Londoners in the face of nightly raids by German bombers in 1940. For Americans, the courageous Marine is a lasting hero. So is the "Grunt," the affectionate nickname for an infantryman. They have taken a place alongside other symbols of self-reliance, such as the pioneers of the West.

In France and the Netherlands, the story of the Resistance is a

GI Bill of Rights

One of the most profound effects of the war on the United States was the result of the Serviceman's Readjustment Act of 1944, popularly known as the GI Bill, or GI Bill of Rights. The act provided a wide range of benefits to the millions of Americans who had served in the armed forces. With their families, those veterans made up about a third of the U.S. population. The act provided help to buy a home or a farm, for example. One of its most popular provisions gave veterans financial support to attend college. Millions of people took up the chance to gain an education that previously would have been denied them.

▲ The British liner *Queen Mary* arrives in New York on June 20, 1945, carrying thousands of U.S. troops home from the fighting in Europe. About 10.5 million service personnel were demobilized in only two years; many benefited from the GI Bill.

reminder of courage in the face of adversity. In Russia, the endurance of the citizens of Leningrad, who survived a siege that lasted 900 days, remains a great patriotic story.

The war also had an enormous pyschological effect on the defeated powers. Generations of Germans grew up under a burden of guilt for the crimes of the Nazis. Many Germans have had to face the fact that members of their own families or communities were involved in the atrocities.

Turning away from aggression

In both victorious and defeated nations, people thought that there should never again be such a conflict as World War II. For many Japanese, the experience of defeat was a great shock. Some observers believe that it forced the Japanese to turn their backs on militaristic aggression. Instead they focused on economic growth. Japan's economy became the second-largest in the world, after only the United States.

In Europe, meanwhile, West German politicians joined their French equivalents to promote the idea of creating a European union. Their plan led to the European Market and, later, a continent-wide European Union. The war's end also saw the creation of the United Nations. This international body was set up to replace the League of Nations. It aimed to avoid war by promoting international cooperation.

The survival of extremism

Despite such cooperation, the extremist political views that helped cause the war have not disappeared. Some extremists cling to a fanantical nationalism. They use violence to try to prove the superiority of their own nation. Soccer "thugs" in numerous European countries chant racist slogans similar to those of the Nazis. Groups both inside and outside Germany admire Adolf Hitler for his attempt to "purify" the Aryan race. Only a few small groups of young people adopt Nazi symbols, such

◀ Stereotypes of the war: The Allied leaders (left to right) Stalin, Roosevelt, and Churchill. Hailed for their part in victory, all three have since been criticized—particularly Stalin.

as the swastika or the straight-arm salute. The appeal of extreme right-wing ideas is wider, however. In the 1990s, Alessandra Mussolini, grand-daughter of Benito Mussolini, became a deputy in the Italian parliament as the leader of a nationalist political party. After the terrorist attacks of 9/11, right-wing parties took a leading role in many countries. They encouraged a backlash against Muslims in countries such as Great Britain and France.

Reinterpretation

Nations and their citizens have fixed ideas not only of their own role in the war, but also of those of their allies and enemies. Some national stereotypes still exist. The calm British reaction to the Blitz was a sign of their "stiff upper lip." U.S. troops gained a reputation as self-reliant, but also as brash and showy. The Japanese were "ruthless" and unfeeling, the Germans cold and efficient, and the Australians always cheerful. The Italians are mocked for

switching sides when it seemed as if they might lose the war.

Such stereotypes persist, even though the millions of men and women who served in the conflict were individuals, not national stereotypes. There were kind Germans as well as cruel ones, and

▼ Stereotypes of the war: Adolf Hitler in 1934. The German dictator has become a symbol of evil, mocked even for his physical appearance.

The new Nazism

In the 1980s and 1990s, small groups of young people in countries in central and eastern Europe were attracted to neo-Nazism, or "new Nazism." They were particularly prominent in Germany itself. They also emerged in Russia and the former territories of the Soviet Union.

The neo-Nazis were young and economically disadvantaged. They were almost always male. They adopted military dress and staged aggressive public demonstrations of their belief in the superiority of Aryan races and the glorification of violence.

Like Hitler, they blamed the problems in their own lives on immigrants and international conspiracies. They carried out racist attacks on ethnic minorities.

some Allied personnel who commited atrocities as well as those who played by the rules.

Role of individuals

Even the roles of individuals are not as clear as they first appeared. Roosevelt, for example, has been accused of having been in a position to avoid the Japanese attack on Pearl Harbor. His critics say that he did not because he wanted an excuse to bring the United States into the war. Joseph Stalin, meanwhile, was vital to the eventual Allied victory. However, the Soviet leader was arguably as immoral as Hitler. Conservative estimates reckon that Stalin was repsonsible for 30 million deaths in the Soviet Union. But during wartime, the Allies struck a deal with Stalin. He would help their war effort. In return, they would allow him control over eastern Europe. Despite Allied hopes, the result was decades of oppression in nations such as Czechoslovakia, Poland, and Romania.

Churchill accused

In 2002, Winston Churchill was voted the Greatest Briton in a popular TV poll. That same year, German historian Jorg Friedrich said that Churchill was a war criminal. Friedrich wrote a book about the Allied bombing campaign of Germany. He blamed Churchill for causing hundreds of thousand of unnecessary deaths in 1944 and 1945. By that time, Friedrich said, Germany was already defeated.

A few years earlier, a similar controversy was started by a book that described Germans as "Hitler's willing

The Holocaust on trial

In February 2006, British historian David Irving was sentenced to three years in jail in Austria. On an earlier visit to Austria, Irving had said that the Holocaust did not take place. Denying the Holocaust is a crime in Austria.

Irving had been in court before for his beliefs. In 1993 U.S. writer Deborah Lipstadt accused him of manipulating historical evidence in order to deny the Holocaust. In 2000 Irving took Lipstadt to court. He said that she had libeled his research. The judge disagreed. He found in favor of Lipstadt. He concluded that "[Irving] is an active Holocaust denier, anti-Semitic racist." Irving was left bankrupt. Any reputation he had as a reputable historian of Germany was in tatters.

▲ David Irving arrives at court for his libel action in 2000. He lost his action against the author Deborah Lipstadt.

executioners." It has become a popular theory that Germans took part in atrocities because they had no choice but to follow orders. Author Daniel Goldhagen said that was not true. He argued that many ordinary Germans actually shared the Nazis' views.

The Holocaust

One of the most controversial ways people "reinterpret" the war is to deny the Holocaust. A few historians say that the Nazis did not kill six million Jews and others. They say that the Allies and Jewish people made the story up to discredit the Nazis. The historians are often very right wing. They do not include any mainstream academics, and they have no evidence for their theories.

Many other people think that denying the Holocaust is dangerous. They say that it might lead to something similar happening again. In some countries, including Germany and Austria, denying that the Holocaust took place has been made a crime. Such laws show that the legacy of World War II remains important at the start of the 21st century.

▲ A large crowd marks Holocaust Remembrance Day on May 4, 2005, at the Yad Vashem Holocaust Museum in Jerusalem, Israel.